THE "GOOD SOLDIER" ON TRIAL

THE "GOOD SOLDIER" ON TRIAL

A SOCIOLOGICAL STUDY OF
MISCONDUCT BY THE US MILITARY
PERTAINING TO OPERATION IRON TRIANGLE, IRAQ

Stjepan G. Mestrovic

Algora Publishing
New York

Library of Congress Cataloging-in-Publication Data —

Mestrovic, Stjepan Gabriel.
The "Good Soldier" on Trial: A sociological study of misconduct by the US military
pertaining to Operation Iron Triangle, Iraq / Stjepan G. Mestrovic.
        p. cm.
        Sequel to: Rules of engagement?: a social anatomy of an American war crime in Iraq:
Operation Iron Triangle. c2008.
        Includes bibliographical references and index.
        ISBN 978-0-87586-741-0 (trade paper: alk. paper) — ISBN 978-0-87586-742-7 (hard
cover: alk. paper) 1. Operation Iron Triangle, Iraq, 2006. 2. Iraq War, 2003—Atrocities.
3. War crimes—Iraq—Tikrit Region. 4. Trials (Military offenses)—United States. 5.
Soldiers—United States—Biography. 6. Soldiers—Iraq—Social conditions. 7. Soldiers—
Iraq—Psychology. 8. United States. Army. Airborne Division, 101st. 9. Iraq War,
2003—Social aspects. 10. Iraq War, 2003—Psychological aspects. I. Mestrovic, Stjepan
Gabriel. Rules of engagement? II. Title.
        DS79.766.T54M46 2009
        364.1'38—dc22
                                2009028812

Front Cover: Photo showing two US soldiers and the unarmed Iraqi male who came
out of "House #2" holding up a baby in self-defense. The soldiers spared the lives of the
baby and the man in this instance.

Back Cover: Photo of the three co-accused soldiers in this case, (left to right) PFC
Corey Clagett, Specialist William Hunsaker, and SSG Raymond L. Girouard, in shackles,
minutes prior to their pre-trial (Article 32) hearing. At the moment this photo was taken,
they had still not had contact with their civilian defense attorneys who were stranded by
the Army in Kuwait.

Printed in the United States

To my father, Tvrtko Mestrovic

TABLE OF CONTENTS

TABLE OF DOCUMENTS

Preface

This book is an empirical, qualitative study of social issues as well as the personal troubles of various individuals who were caught up in the drama of Operation Iron Triangle and its aftermath. In some ways, it is a sequel to my previous book on this subject, *Rules of Engagement?* Nevertheless, it can be read independently of the first book. The main difference is that in the present book I resolve many of the questions and mysteries raised in the first book.

This study is inductive, which means that I confronted the data and facts first and developed afterwards the conceptual vocabulary to make sense of the data.

People are skeptical that a scientist can truly study a subject without pre-conceptions. But I state here honestly that I could not have imagined the chicanery and Machiavellian schemes that leap from the data.

As I became more immersed in the topic, I gradually detected a decisive shift in the perspective shown in books written during, about, and in America from the World War II era versus the present. I list below some of the books from a by-gone era that serve as sharp reference points for comparison and contrast with the present era and Operation Iron Triangle. These are considered classic, orthodox, widely-accepted books in academia. I have added the central or main points of each work, though I am fully aware that in the present era, postmodernism denies a center or main point to anything, and focuses instead on what is marginal and peripheral. Nevertheless, my intention is to use the following books as a framework to help the reader make sense of the patterns of empirical data that follows:

- Samuel Stouffer's *The American Soldier*[1] found that the World War II soldier was down-to-earth, reluctant to kill, harbored no hatred for the enemy, and above all, fought for his comrades rather than for democracy, mom, apple pie, or any

---

1 Samuel Stouffer, *The American Soldier (volumes 1-3)* (Princeton: Princeton University Press, 1949).

other idea. In this classic study, Stouffer popularized the concepts of "reference groups" (by which he meant that people in general and especially soldiers evaluate and judge everything based upon the particular peer-group they use as a standard or reference point) and "relative deprivation" (by which he meant that victory, defeat, health, illness etc. are all evaluated relative to the common or average perception in the peer group). Stouffer emphasized that high unit morale serves as protection from combat stress. His findings stand in sharp contrast to the facts uncovered about Charlie Company, which was involved in the Operation Iron Triangle massacres: These soldiers were socialized to behave like predators, to hate the enemy, and to fight to avenge 9/11 rather than for their comrades. Constant re-shuffling of troops prevented bonding and the formation of real "reference groups," and unit morale was poor. Numerous soldiers suffered from various forms of combat stress, including PTSD.

• S.L.A. Marshall's *Men Against Fire*[1] is another classic which is cited most often with regard to the finding that, in any given battle, no more than 25% of the soldiers will open fire. The remaining 75% freeze. His central point is that soldiers are reluctant to kill, and he proposes ways of working within the parameters of what he regards as an unchangeable fact of human nature. Contemporary authors who cite Marshall, such as Dave Grossman, are preoccupied with behaviorist methods and operant conditioning to raise the fire ratio and to make soldiers more willing to kill. I will show that the brigade commander for Charlie Company tried to condition the soldiers to kill, including the use of kill boards, the use of coins and knives as rewards for killing, and other methods of operant conditioning. In the end, the classical understanding of the American soldier in Marshall's study explains the tragedy of Operation Iron Triangle, because his teachings were not followed.

• In *The Chrysanthemum and the Sword*,[2] Ruth Benedict sought out "patterns of culture" between Japan and the United States during World War II. She sought to explain how and why Japanese culture regarded its own as well as American prisoners as "damaged goods" and abused them in general. By contrast, American culture saw no shame in being a prisoner and treated foreign as well as domestic prisoners with general compassion and mercy. I contrast Benedict's findings with the general trend of abusing prisoners in the current war on terror, from Abu Ghraib through Gitmo and other sites to military missions such as Operation Iron Triangle. What has changed and why?

• *Lone Star Stalag: German Prisoners of War at Camp Hearne* by Michael R. Waters[3] examines in great detail the deliberately kind treatment Americans gave to German and Nazi POWs during World War II at Camp Hearne, Texas. He cites empirical data, photographs, and other evidence to demonstrate that German POWs

---

1 S.L.A. Marshall, *Men Against Fire: The Problem of Battle Command* (Tulsa: University of Oklahoma Press [1947] 2000).

2 Ruth Benedict, *The Chrysanthemum and the Sword: Patterns of Japanese Culture* (Boston: Houghton Mifflin [1946] 1989).

3 Michael R. Waters, *Lone Star Stalag: German Prisoners of War at Camp Hearne* (College Station: Texas A&M University Press (2004).

---

were won over by their American captors and returned to Germany to spread the word about American generosity. POWs were allowed to drink beer, ate better food than most Americans (who were rationing food), had their own theater productions, and in general, seemed to enjoy their brief stay in America. Waters shows that this result was not an accident but the result of a deliberate policy by the US government to win the hearts and minds of its enemies. These findings stand in sharp contrast to the disturbing treatment documented in my study of US government mistreatment of its own soldier–prisoners as well as foreign "detainees."

● Gregory Bateson[1] was an anthropologist who introduced the powerful concept of the "double-bind" situation as an explanatory factor in understanding individual as well as social and cultural dysfunctions. A double-bind is basically an intolerable situation in which individuals or groups believe that they are damned if they do something and also damned if they don't do the very same thing. It is a lose–lose situation, found in dysfunctional families but, according to Bateson, also in dysfunctional cultures. I uncover hundreds of instances of double-bind situations in the present study, in the hope that once these situations are recognized, they will be corrected.

● I cite and quote from Joseph Heller's novel *Catch-22*[2] throughout my study because his fictional account sadly corresponds to numerous situations found in Charlie Company and the various investigations, court hearings, and proceedings. Catch-22 is a sort of double-bind situation, and the court transcripts are full of such situations. Real life in the US military should not resemble life in a scathing, satirical, and fictional novel.

● David Riesman's *The Lonely Crowd*[3], first published in 1950, remains the best-selling sociology text of all time, with more than 1.5 million copies sold. It is directly relevant to the present study because Riesman was studying the cultural transition from my generation's parents to my children's generation. He portrayed the World War II generation as "inner-directed," meaning that they had few choices in consumer goods or reference groups but were raised with firm and unchanging inner "gyroscopes." He was a veritable prophet in predicting that the current "other-directed" generation is so beset by a Milky Way Galaxy of choices in all areas of life that it tends toward isolation, apathy, and resignation. The lack of emotional involvement in the current war as well as the lives of the soldiers who are fighting in it illustrates his overall point. Can this generational issue be changed?

In addition, I will rely throughout this book on two sociological classics from the 1890s. The first is Thorstein Veblen's *Theory of the Leisure Class*,[4] which is directly rel-

---

1 Gregory Bateson, "Cultural Problems Posed by a Study of Schizophrenic Process," pp. 125-47 in Alfred Auerbach, *Schizophrenia: An Integrated Approach* (New York: Ronald Press, 1959).

2 Joseph Heller, *Catch-22* (New York: Simon & Schuster [1955] 1999).

3 David Riesman, *The Lonely Crowd: A Study of the Changing American Character* (New Haven: Yale University Press [1950] 2002).

4 Thorstein Veblen, *The Theory of the Leisure Class* (New York: Penguin [1899] 1965).

---

evant because of his focus on prestigious, "honorific," elitist, and barbaric tendencies in modern societies. In this, our new millennium, he is still correct that wars are instigated and led by the leisure class because it regards wars as "honorific." The second is Emile Durkheim's classic, *Suicide: A Study in Sociology*[1]. Durkheim was not writing about "suicide" strictly defined as the taking of one's life, but a continuum of aggressive behaviors aimed at the self or others. His overall finding still stands: A society that is integrated, unified, and bound together by common, average, sentiments is healthier and less destructive (even toward itself) than a society that is divided, scattered, and which isolates its individuals. His findings also pertain to military societies. Both thinkers admitted that wars are sometimes necessary. But both warned against the dangers of being seduced by the prestige of war and of the danger that social unity at home disintegrates during the course of war.

I am fully aware that some of my colleagues in academia will object to my choice or interpretation of these works. I am also aware that nowadays, according to some academics, no work is really considered "classic" and all works are subject to deconstruction. I prefer to think that readers have a right to their own interpretations and that genuine dialogue is constructive.

But let me be clear that my aim in this book is *not* to tear down or "deconstruct" the military. It is to offer constructive even if sharp criticism in the hope that the present situation may be improved. Even my method of criticism is orthodox and follows the American tradition of Mark Twain. And from start to finish, in this book, I stay with orthodox, average, standard, acceptable concepts, theories, and ideas. I disagree strongly with Jean Baudrillard and other post-modernists who claim that the present war is "simulacra," "hyper-real" and has no meaning. It seems obvious that real people died on the mission that is the subject of this study; real soldiers are currently in prison because of the way the army handled the case, and real and mostly negative consequences follow for the United States as a result of this and similar fiascos. Such grave issues will not be perceived or repaired by turning to marginal, post-structural, unorthodox ideas, concepts and theories.

It would be a mistake to read the present work as a narrow study of Operation Iron Triangle or of the main protagonist in this book, William Hunsaker, even if it is about him, his comrades, and the mission to some extent. I intend this book to be a study in sociology, which is to say, it is about "patterns of culture" that emerge from hundreds of facts, and ultimately, it is about American society. After all, I am a professor of sociology, and this is what I have been trained to do.

Regardless of the perspective that a reader uses to read this book, I hope that he or she will form conclusions based upon the hundreds of documented facts used in this study.

I wish to make it clear that in this book I do not make use of and do not arrive at any legal opinions of the guilt or innocence of any of the persons described, including the convicted soldiers. It is true that certain soldiers were convicted of a complex array of charges and specifications, but I approach their convictions, hearings, investigations, and all related events through the perspective of a social scientist. In other

---

1 Emile Durkheim, *Suicide: A Study in Sociology* (New York: Free Press [1897] 1967).

words, I am always analyzing the "social construction of reality" relative to groups. Similarly, when I use terms such as conspiracy and cover-up, I am not referring to the legal understanding of these and related terms, but to commonsense and sociological approaches. My overall point is that legal terms and processes have reached the point where they are comprehensible only to a small, elite, coterie of lawyers, judges, and legal experts, and are incomprehensible to the accused and to the average person. My "reference groups" as an author, throughout this study, are the average person and the trained sociologist. I analyze lawyers, judges, investigators, commanders, soldiers and others involved in this drama with the assumption that they belong to different reference groups.

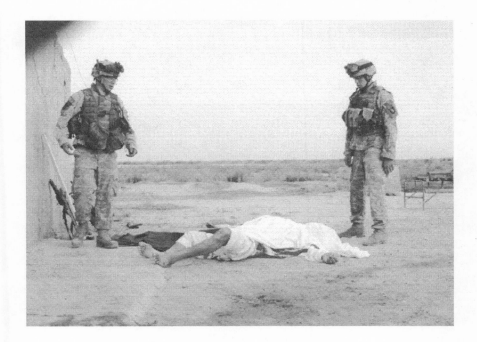

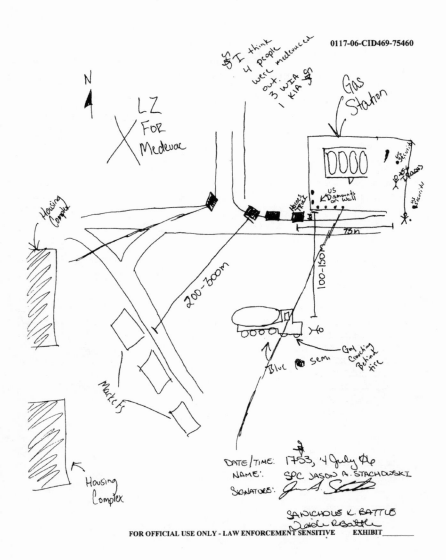

SS I think 4 people were medevacced out. 3 WIA 1 KIA SS

Gas Station

LZ FOR Medevac

Housing Complex

Hanes Tree
US KIA slumped on wall
US Security
US Security
US Security

75n

200-300m

100-150m

Match's

Blue Semi

Guy Crouching Behind Tire

Housing Complex

DATE/TIME: 1753, 4 July 06
NAME: SPC JASON A. STACHOWSKI
SIGNATURE:

SA NICHOLE K. BATTLE

SWORN STATEMENT

For use of this form, see AR 190-45; the proponent agency is Office of The Deputy Chief of Staff for Personnel.

LOCATION	DATE	TIME	FILE NUMBER
COB Speicher, Tikrit, Iraq APO AE 09393	4JUL06	1730	

LAST NAME, FIRST NAME, MIDDLE NAME	SOCIAL SECURITY NUMBER	GRADE/STATUS
Chavez, David (NMN)		E5/AD

ORGANIZATION OR ADDRESS
HHC 3/187 Inf, FOB Brassfield-Mora, Samara, Iraq APO AE 09349

I, __David Chavez Jr.__, WANT TO MAKE THE FOLLOWING STATEMENT UNDER OATH:

While attached to C co. we have had several issue about the way the company operated. We're Myself and the other snipers have felt unsafe about working with Cco. I feel that most of the company has been brainwashed throughout the deployment to kill more when ever possible. I feel that the problems are caused by the 1SGT and Co. Every meeting I've been to involving Cco their ROE has suggested killing locals who don't appear to be a real threat. Such as killing locals who are unarmed but might leave the general area. Cco's 1SGT has the mentality that all locals should be killed. He has said that all Iraqi's should be killed, to me several times while I have ridden with him in his HMMWV. I have felt usafe working with Cco because of the company killing innocent civilians and creating stories to cover them up. I have not personally witnessed any of these occasions but I hear Cco soldiers talking about them. One story was about Cco killing 3 locals in a tomato truck. What really happend was the gunner was nervous behind the .50 caliber machine gun and killed 3 civilians. After the 3 civilians were killed the LT of the platoon shot out both tires so it would appear that the vehicle wouldn't stop after having it's tires shot out and that it forced them to use lethal force. Then upon returning to the unit after Iron Triangle I heard stories of the executions. First I was told by platoon members that then we given orders to

EXHIBIT	INITIALS OF PERSON MAKING STATEMENT D.C	PAGE 1 OF 4 PAGES

ADDITIONAL PAGES MUST CONTAIN THE HEADING "STATEMENT OF ___ TAKEN AT ___ DATED ___ CONTINUED." THE BOTTOM OF EACH ADDITIONAL PAGE MUST BEAR THE INITIALS OF THE PERSON MAKING THE STATEMENT AND BE INITIALED AS "PAGE ___ OF ___ PAGES." WHEN ADDITIONAL PAGES ARE UTILIZED, THE BACK OF PAGE 1 WILL BE LINED OUT, AND THE STATEMENT WILL BE CONCLUDED ON THE REVERSE SIDE OF ANOTHER COPY OF THIS FORM.

DA FORM 2823, 1 JUL 72

FOR OFFICIAL USE ONLY LAW ENFORCEMENT SENSITIVE

SUPERSEDES DA FORM 2823, 1 JAN 68, WHICH WILL BE USED.

EXHIBIT ___

STATEMENT OF _Sgt David Chavez_____

TAKEN AT _COB Speicher, Iraq, APO AE 09393_ DATED ___4 Jul 06___   CONTINUED

STATEMENT (Continued)

"kill everyone on the objective. As for the executions
I overheard member of 3rd plt Cco. describe it.
That the team that entered the house detained 3 males
in the house. Radioed to Cco's 1SGT that they had
3 detainees. 1SGT responded with "Why do you have
3 detainees who are supposed to be dead". Then the
soldiers took the detainees outside and cut the
zip-cuffs off the detainees hands to make it appear
that they broke them off. Mean while the soldiers were
hitting each other and SPC Hunsacker cut himself in the face
to make it appear that the detainees put up a fight.
Then the detainees were told to run away. Then when
they were about 100 meters away they were shot by
the soldiers. After that they threatend another soldier
that they would kill him if he told what had happened.
Then they radioed to Cco command that they had
3 enemy KIA.
Q: SA McCormick,
A: Sgt Chavez
Q: Have ROE briefs you've attended with other companies been
   as loose as C Co's?
A: Cco's ROE has been the only company to authorize killing
   of civilians who are ~~not~~ unarmed or don't appear to be
   a threat but are leaving a general area or are of military
   age. As opposed to other companies where the local
   would have to pose a threat.
Q: Do you remember specific date's to when 1sg Geressy made those
   comments to you?
A: Those comments were made on different occassion from
   January 06 through May 06
Q: Do you remember any specifics as far as C Co. Covering
   things up; other than the Tomato Truck incident?
A: The tomato truck incident is the only one I've heard "

0117-06-CID469-74460

FILE NUMBER_____

STATEMENT OF Sgt David Chavez

TAKEN AT CoB Speicher, Iraq APO AE 09393 DATED 4 Jul 06   CONTINUED

STATEMENT (Continued)

DC details about.

Q: When have you overheard C Co talking about covering things up, and can you identify which soldiers stated what?

A: I overhear these things before missions and while riding with C Co but the conversations are between many different soldiers throughout the company.

Q: Who mentioned the tomato truck?

A: A soldier from 1st platoon C Co.

Q: When did you return from leave after Iron Triangle?

A: I returned from leave in late May.

Q: Do you remember which 3rd plt C Co members said what?

A: I do not remember which soldiers were talking about the incident.

Q: How well do you know members of C Co?

A: Not very well. They take my team to and from objectives then leave us alone to do our job.

Q: Are you sure it was 3rd platoon who was discussing the incident?

A: Yes 3 plt soldier wer discussing what happened on Iron Triangle as well as SGT Kugler, SPC Stachowski and PFC Fuson

Q: Was this information discussed after SSG Girourd, PFC Clagett & SPC Hunsaker were "taken away"?

A: Yes.

Q: Do you have anything else to add?

A: No. End of statement. DC

INITIALS OF PERSON MAKING STATEMENT: DC   PAGE 3 OF 4 PAGES
FOR OFFICIAL USE ONLY - LAW ENFORCEMENT SENSITIVE   EXHIBIT_____

SWORN STATEMENT

LOCATION: Tikrit CID Office
Contingency Operating Base (COB) Speicher
Tikrit, Iraq, APO AE 09393

DATE: 4 Jul 06   **TIME:** 1151 *CB*

NAME: Curtis S. Ballance   **SSN:** ███████   **GRADE/STATUS:** E7/AD

ORGANIZATION OR ADDRESS: Headquarters and Headquarters Company, 3/187th Infantry, FOB Brassfield-Mora, APO AE 09393

I SFC Curtis S. Ballance , **WANT TO MAKE THE FOLLOWING STATEMENT UNDER OATH:**

During Operation Triangle I was on mid tour leave. On arriving back to FOB Brassfield Mora on the 15th of May. I was approached by the acting Platoon Sergeant (PSG), SSG Cameron Armendariz, Headquarters and Headquarters Company (HHC) that something's that occurred on Operation Iron Triangle were wrong. Members of the Scout Platoon had provided sworn statements and that he thinks they were not handled properly. SSG Armendariz said he turned in the sworn statements to our Platoon Leader, 1LT Duggan now CPT. SSG Armendariz asked him who he turned the sworn statements into and DUGGAN said he had turned them into either the Charlie Company Commander or the 1SG. I am not sure who, but I don't think he would have turned them into anyone other than the CDR or 1SG. SSG Armendariz said no, I want them turned into Battalion (BN). Then 1LT Duggan said I turned them into Iron 5, Maj Delvaux. Armendariz said okay. Then I returned on the 15th of May he had told me the above story and I said ok we will wait for a couple of days to see if CID will interview the platoon soldiers that were involved. CID came to Brassfield and interviewed members of Charlie Company but not my soldiers. Then I went and told the CPT Brientbutcher, HHC, Executive Officer (XO) that I don't think the sworn statements were taken to BN. He said I will go ask Iron 5, Maj Delvaux. Brientbutcher said he asked MAJ Delvaux, Sir did you read the scouts sworn statements. MAJ Delvaux replied all those statements got pushed up to some field grade I think it was from FOB Wilson the investigating officer. Brientbutcher said, he asked MAJ Delvaux did he see the Scout's sworn statements and he said Delvaux did not answer yes or no. Then myself and Cpt Brientbutcher waited for few more weeks then sometime in late May or first of June we took 2 copies to the Bn Commander, LTC Johnson and he said that it was being looked into.

Q: SA BATTLE
A: SFC BALLANCE
Q: Who are the soldiers who wrote sworn statements in regards to Iron Triangle?
A: SPC STACHOWSKI and PFC FUSON. SGT KUGLAR was on Iron Triangle but I am not sure if he provided a statement? *CB*

INITIALS OF PERSON
MAKING STATEMENT _____
DA FORM 2823 (*Computer Generated*)

PAGE 1 OF 4 PAGES

EXHIBIT_____

CASE#

STATEMENT OF Curtis S. Ballance, TAKEN AT Tikrit CID Office,, COB SPEICHER, TIKRIT, IRAQ, DATED 4 July, 2006, CONTINUED.

Q: Did you soldiers tell you what happened on Iron Triangle?

A: They told me one story that during the operation that 1lt Horne said waste all of them on some objection that they were on. And members of 1Lt Horne platoon, along with my soldiers said there are women and children and 1Lt Horne said fuck them its collateral damage. But they did not take the order. This was the main thing I could remember but I vaguely remember one of my soldiers saying something about a local national already was dead and a C Company soldier came up to the dead Iraqi and shot him with the saw and practically cut him in half.

Q: Have your soldiers told you anything else about members of the 3/187th committing war crimes against the local community?

A: I was told that 1SG Geressey had taken a dead Iraqi male and placed him on the hood of the HMMWV and take him to the family members. He then removed the Iraqi hand from the body bag and slapped a local national with it and told them this was what was going to happen to you if you don't stop. I am not sure of this information but my soldiers can tell you more. Around Jan or Feb 06, KUGLAR came to me and said an Iraqi male was detained with zip ties and with his hands behind his back and 1LT HAWKINS pushed this guy down and I think he broke his jaw. Kuglar went on to say that he told Hawkins to leave the guy alone and Hawkins related he was resisting arrest. Kuglar said he was not and that the guy was detained and to leave him alone. Kuglar related there was a 15-6 and he did not tell what he knew because he was afraid. But that he did witness the guy get roughed up after he was detained.

Q: Why didn't you and your soldiers come forward with this information previously?

A: Because we sent the sworn statements up through the chain of command and we sat around and waited. Nothing happened. We continued to get someone to listen to us. We don't trust the battalion. We were glad when this office contacted us. The atmosphere in the battalion is bad. Charlie Company has done a lot of things and when they write sworn statements for 15-6 investigations they write them all together. We wanted from the beginning for our soldiers to tell their story. They provided sworn statements and I don't think CID or the battalion commander had seen them. When I provided the statements to the battalion commander he said the case was already being investigated. I know he was not on leave during the same time as I. I provided them to him on or about the beginning of June, after the press release. I know Armendariz did submit an anonymous tip through the CID website.

Q: Did any of your soldiers witness the deaths of the four detainees in which were killed on the island during Iron Triangle?

A: No.

Q: Do you know if they have any knowledge of the deaths?

A: Just by what they have heard from the rumors and what was released in the news.

INITIALS OF PERSON
MAKING STATEMENT ___

DA FORM 2823 (*Computer Generated*)

PAGE 2 OF _4_ PAGES

EXHIBIT_____

FOR OFFICIAL USE ONLY- LAW ENFORCEMENT SENSITIVE

FOR OFFICIAL USE ONLY - LAW ENFORCEMENT SENSITIVE   EXHIBIT_____

CASE#

STATEMENT OF CURTIS S. BALLANCE , TAKEN AT Tikrit CID Office,, COB SPEICHER, TIKRIT, IRAQ, DATED 4 July, 2006, CONTINUED.

Q: Do you think the command clement is a cause for Charlie having so many deaths or detainee abuse allegations?
A: I am not sure it's the battalion but I do think Geressey and Hart have created the climate.
Q: Why do you say this?
A: Geressey attitude is everyone is fucked up but him. He says things that are very negative. It is always about killing somebody or the company is getting picked on. He does not take responsibility for their actions and they can not do no wrong in MAJ Delvaux's eyes. Charlie Company has a kill chart in their Command Post. I heard Geressy asked one of the platoons what was up and why didn't they have as many kills as the other platoon.
Q: Do you think MAJ Delvaux withheld the sworn statements provided by your platoon members?
A: That is a tough question. I think if they did get passed up my platoon members would have been interviewed. He may have not received them. I don't know.
Q: Do you still have a copy of the statements?
A: No. Brientbutcher has a copy and the soldiers probably have copies.
Q: How many members of you platoon are attached to Charlie?
A: Seven and they rotate in and out: Stachowski, Chavez, Kuglar are here today. Merritt and Stayer are on leave. They just left on and they are due back around the 25th of Jul. Scott and Gitshlag are currently attached to Bravo Company but have been attached to Charlie.
Q: Do you have anything else to add to this statement?
A: My soldiers just want their stories told. They provided statements and no one has interviewed them. They did not see what happened to the 4 detainees but they can tell you that Charlie Company has done things that on this mission and others that are criminal. This investigation in just one of the many that I think they are covering up and not doing the right thing. I never worked with them. I think the use the ROE as a means to kill people. Everyone does not deserve to be killed because they breached a convoy or because they are not actively resisting. They also could not be doing anything and are killed because the ROE said shoot all military aged males. But that does not give anyone an excuse to do so.
Q: What happened to the original statements provided by your platoon members?
A: I think the originals were provided to CPT HART. Then Armendariz said he asked the Duggan about the statements and said he wanted them to go to the Battalion.
Q: Do you have anything else to add to this statement?
A: No. ///END OF STATEMENT///

INITIALS OF PERSON
MAKING STATEMENT
DA FORM 2823 (Computer Generated)

PAGE 3 OF 4 PAGES

EXHIBIT_____

CASE#

STATEMENT OF CURTIS S. BALLANCE , TAKEN AT Tikrit CID Office,, COB SPEICHER, TIKRIT, IRAQ, DATED 4 July, 2006, CONTINUED.

I, Curtis S. BALLANCE, READ OR HAVE HAD READ TO ME THIS STATEMENT WHICH BEGINS ON PAGE 1 AND ENDS ON PAGE 4. I FULLY UNDERSTAND THE CONTENTS OF THE ENTIRE STATEMENT MADE BY ME. THE STATEMENT IS TRUE. I HAVE INITIALED ALL CORRECTIONS AND HAVE INITIALED THE BOTTOM OF EACH PAGE CONTAINING THE STATEMENT. I HAVE MADE THIS STATEMENT FREELY WITHOUT HOPE OF BENEFIT OR REWARD, WITHOUT THREAT OF PUNISHMENT, AND WITHOUT COERCION, UNLAWFUL INFLUENCE, OR UNLAWFUL INDUCEMENT.

(Signature of Person Making Statement)

Subscribed and sworn to before me, a person authorized by law to administer oaths, this Tuesday, July 04, 2006, at Tikrit CID Office COB Speicher, Tikrit, Iraq, APO AE 09393

(Signature of Person Administering Oath)

SA NICHOLE R. BATTLE
Typed Name of Person Administering Oath)
Article 136 (b) UCMJ
(Authority to Administer Oath)

_____

_____

Witness

_____

_____

INITIALS OF PERSON
MAKING STATEMENT _____
DA FORM 2823 (*Computer Generated*)

PAGE 4 OF 4 PAGES

EXHIBIT_____

Chapter 1. Introduction

> "[He] was guilty, of course, or he would have not been accused, and since the only way to prove it was to find him guilty, it was their patriotic duty to do so."
> — Joseph Heller, *Catch-22*, p. 83

My purpose in this book is to try to prevent the tragic story of Operation Iron Triangle from being swallowed up by the black hole of history. It is also my hope that the US government will review the convictions related to this mission and reform the military justice system to secure authentic justice. My contemporaries have already overlooked, forgotten or characterized it in shallow terms as an ordinary murder case that was handled by the military justice system. In fact, this is an intricate story of conspiracy, cover-up and intrigue — on the part of the government, not the soldiers. The prosecutor in this case went out of his way to call the soldiers "war criminals." The open secret, the contradiction staring everyone in the face — yet largely unseen — is that a crime *becomes* a "war crime" when it involves the government, which is to say, when a crime is the result of unlawful social policies and plans. A soldier killing a prisoner or a fellow soldier for personal reasons would be committing a "garden-variety" crime. A soldier who kills while following a lawful rule of engagement (ROE) is merely doing his or her job in war. Society does not label as murder the killing performed in the name of a lawful ROE during warfare — such killings are called casualties of war and are considered justified. But a soldier who kills while following an unlawful ROE becomes involved in a war crime. Traditionally, responsibility for war crimes is attributed to governments and commanders. The founding father of sociology, Emile Durkheim, wrote: "The immorality of war depends entirely on the leaders who willed it — the soldier and even those government officials who had

15

no part in the decision remain innocent."[1] In other words, it is the civilian and military commanders who are usually labeled as war criminals when war crimes occur. Society has applied this traditional rule (labeled "the doctrine of command responsibility") from Nuremberg and the Yamashita case to the war crimes in Bosnia that were tried at the International Tribunal for the Former Yugoslavia. But in the current war on terror, the open secret is that responsibility for war crimes is attributed to low-ranking soldiers. How can this be? How has the US government managed to overturn traditional understandings of war crimes and command responsibility? Why have Americans accepted the government's position that leaders who set into motion unlawful policies that led to torture and abuse at Abu Ghraib, Guantanamo, and elsewhere are exempt from accountability? The American public seems to accept without protest the government's and the media's explanation that a handful of so-called "rotten apples" (lower-ranking soldiers) deserved to go to prison for the abuses that were committed at Abu Ghraib, Gitmo,[2] Iron Triangle, and other sites of war crimes even though those soldiers were not the authors of the abusive policies. Who are the real war criminals in the war crimes that were committed during Operation Iron Triangle on May 9, 2006?

In normal times, my goals in this book might be judged immediately as extremist and inflammatory. I present plenty of documented evidence, most of it sworn testimony and excerpts from court transcripts, to make even the most suspicious reader entertain the possibility of government cover-up in the Operation Iron Triangle case. The conspiracy, cover-up and intrigue are not a real surprise, because America has already gone through a similar story regarding the infamous abuse at Abu Ghraib. In the fall of 2008, the Levin–McCain report finally concluded, in no uncertain terms, that the few "rotten apples" were *not* the authors of the abuse and that White House officials and lawyers were responsible for issuing unlawful policies.[3] The abuse occurred in the year 2003. The so-called "rotten apples" were sent to prison in the year 2005. But even when the truth about government responsibility for the abuse was finally declared in the year 2008, the accused soldiers were not really vindicated No one bothered with an apology to them, releasing them from prison, or punishing the White House officials and lawyers who were truly responsible for the abuse. On the contrary, President Obama reversed himself on his campaign promises to hold Bush Administration officials accountable, and continued the previous administration's cover-up. Clearly, the story of abuse and war crimes in the current war on terror is not just about specific leaders and individuals, but about social policies and American attitudes. In a word, it is a sociological issue.

But to grasp the conspiracy and cover-up, one needs more than facts. One needs the "sociological imagination," which is to say, the ability to make connections between the event being analyzed here, other events, military society, and civilian society. One needs to be able to see "patterns of culture." I have already linked the war crimes committed at Operation Iron Triangle to Abu Ghraib, but there are scores of

---

1 Neil Gross and Robert Alun Jones (eds.) *Durkheim's Philosophy Lectures* (Cambridge: Cambridge University Press, 2004), p. 266.

2 See http://www.commondreams.org/headline/2009/07/03-0

3 http://levin.senate.gov/newsroom/supporting/2008/Detainees121108.pdf

---

other sites of abuse, including Gitmo. And there are connections and patterns between military abuses and abuses in the civilian world as well. For example, who has failed to notice that the new millennium is not a normal era? Wall Street and the entire capitalist system were strained to the breaking point at about the same time as this and other war crimes occurred in the war on terror. Who could have imagined or predicted such dramatic threats to the social system? It is important to note that in both grand fiascos, the war on terror and the collapse of Wall Street, the military commanders as well as the "captains of industry,"[1] respectively, escaped responsibility for the most part. In both cases, blame was shifted to the common soldier and the common citizen. The government bailed out Wall Street, but not ordⅡinary citizens who lost homes, retirements, and their financial well-being. Similarly, regarding war crimes, the government "bailed out" its commanders, but sent ordinary and good soldiers to prison, and destroyed their families, pensions, and lives. Commonsense and sociology hold that society is an interconnected system, such that a dysfunction in one part of society will be related to dysfunctions in other parts. There is no need here to analyze some of the other, major dysfunctions in public policy and social life in the new millennium, from health care and the banking industry to environmental policies and crises in the housing market. The important point is that this book is not just about Operation Iron Triangle, but about this tragic mission and its connections to American society in the new millennium.

I will focus on the "patterns of culture" — as they were called by towering figures in the social sciences in the 1950s such as David Riesman, Talcott Parsons, Ruth Benedict, C. Wright Mills and others — and the social issues embedded in the story of the personal troubles of the individuals involved in the tragic mission that was called Operation Iron Triangle. At the time of this mission, it was US policy in the war on terror to kill as many insurgents as possible, and this resulted in scores of unnecessary civilian deaths. In fact, it was never clear whether the alleged "insurgents" were enemy terrorists or innocent civilians. "Patterns of culture" sounds like an abstraction. I tell my students that this phrase means, "Everything in society is connected to everything else in society." How a given society treats its prisoners, children, and especially its less-fortunate citizens forms a pattern that is discernible if one uses the sociological imagination.

"Nowadays men [and women] often feel that their private lives are a series of traps." This is the sentence with which the renowned sociologist and former Aggie (student at Texas A&M University, historically the Agricultural and Mechanical College of Texas), C. Wright Mills, begins his classic book, *The Sociological Imagination*.[2] His assessment still stands. Mills argued that one's personal troubles such as divorce, suicide and bankruptcy are always related to social issues such as society's high divorce and suicide rates and failures of the economic system. Similarly, the personal troubles of the soldiers on the infamous mission of May 9, 2006 that was called Operation Iron

---

1 This is a term invented by Thorstein Veblen to refer to the predatory practices of corporations and the business enterprise in America.

2 C. Wright Mills, *The Sociological Imagination* (New York: Oxford University Press, 1959). See also the excellent analysis of Mills by Keith Kerr, *Postmodern Cowboy: C. Wright Mills and a New 21st-Century Sociology* (Boulder, CO: Paradigm, 2009).

Triangle are connected with systemic dysfunctions in the army as well as American society in this era. The brigade commander issued an unlawful ROE, to kill every military-aged Iraqi on sight. But similar unlawful ROE continue to be issued on missions in Iraq and Afghanistan[1]. Two soldiers were convicted of conspiracy and premeditated murder. But transcripts show that many similar killings of unarmed Iraqis occurred on this and other missions, and no one was prosecuted for these other, documented, similar killings. The seemingly obvious, commonsense, yet neglected point is that no person is an island, and every personal problem is related to social issues. Blaming or even trying to comprehend an individual for suicide, murder, divorce, bankruptcy, or any other trouble has to be tempered with responsibility by a social system for factors that lead to suicide, murder, divorce, bankruptcy or any other trouble. Mills labeled the ability to make the connection between personal *troubles* and social *issues* the "sociological imagination." This insight may seem so obvious that it hardly needs the fancy title, but apparently it is not as obvious as one might think. Journalists, lawyers, and even some academics tend to become so embedded in the narrow views of their reference groups[2] that they fail to grasp the commonsense point of view regarding any phenomenon under study. Mills did not mean that only sociologists are capable of exercising the sociological imagination — in fact, many sociologists fail grasp it, and reduce social issues to mathematical formulas. The significant points are: First, that when any person grasps the connection between personal troubles and social issues, he or she is using the sociological imagination. Second, the sociological imagination is ultimately the domain of the common person, the layperson, the average person, or what Durkheim called the "collective" or "common" conscience. All the classical sociologists address the "average" person or public opinion, not the elitists in their or any other professions. This, also, seems to be an obvious yet invisible and neglected insight: sociology could not possibly exist as the science of societies if it did not study what is average and common. By authentic sociology's standards, it follows that any study of elites (commanders, leaders, "captains of industry" etc.) is not sociological, even if such studies are interesting. And any elitist studies, namely, those which can be understood only by other experts, are not properly sociological even if they purport to study society. But I have no intention to rehash what C. Wright Mills and others have already argued.

What are the series of traps to which Mills refers in this case? They include, but are not limited to, the following:

• American soldiers are socialized to obey orders but are culpable if the orders are unlawful.

• The military justice system looks the other way when its law enforcement agents and prosecutors cross the line into unlawful behavior even though the gov-

---

1 David Kilcullen, "Death from above, outrage down below," *New York Times* 16 May 2009.

2 Sociologists define a reference group as "a social group that serves as a point of reference in making evaluations or decisions." Samuel Stouffer writes: "This idea is simple, almost obvious, but its utility comes in reconciling data ... The idea would seem to have a kinship to and, in part, include such well-known sociological concepts as 'social frames of reference,' 'patterns of expectation,' or 'definitions of the situation'" (p. 125 in Vol. 1 of *The American Soldier*).

ernment is supposed to have "clean hands" in prosecuting the accused.

• Soldiers are taught the values of honesty and integrity in relation to each other, but these virtues are used against them when investigators and commanders openly lie to them.

In this book, I shall document hundreds of instances of such deceit, chicanery, and dubious behavior on the part of the government. But the more important point is that the long list of chicanery amounts to creating situations and a command climate that Gregory Bateson called "the double-bind," a "series of traps" described by Mills, and that resembles real life in the fictional account by Joseph Heller in *Catch-22*.

Authors who chronicle significant events in the new millennium, pertaining to the war on terror or in general, seem to fail to display even a minimal amount of sociological imagination. For example, consider the brief account by Thomas Ricks in his best-selling book, *The Gamble*[1], of the event that is the central focus in this book, the killing of Iraqi prisoners by US Army soldiers on May 9, 2006 near Samarra, Iraq. To be sure, Ricks frames the event in terms of the overall issues that made the current war on terror a "fiasco," namely, "the shortsighted and misguided approach the US military took in invading and occupying Iraq from 2003 to 2006: Protect yourself at all costs, focus on attacking the enemy, and treat the Iraqi civilians as the playing field on which the contest occurs" (p. 5).Ricks is also correct that the "Bush administration really hadn't carried out a serious strategic review that asked the basic questions: What are we trying to do — that is, what are our key goals?" (p.14). But Ricks, like so many other contemporary authors, turns his attention primarily to General Petraeus and other elite military leaders. He fails to connect the tragic events of Operation Iron Triangle to the public issue of how the US military was conducting the war in Iraq in the name of the American people. For example, he writes:

> The court-martial took an illuminating turn: The accused cited the aggressive tone set by their brigade commander, Col. Michael Steele, whose ham-fisted approached long had raised eyebrows in the Army. Retired Army Col. James Hallums, one of his predecessors in commanding the same unit, and himself a veteran of much combat, commented, "The supermacho image that Steele projected permeated his unit, and in my opinion, led directly to atrocities." When the brigade deployed, Steele, whose role in the fighting in Somalia in 1993 was captured in the book and film *Black Hawk Down*, had given a speech that was captured on videotape by documentarians following the unit, "Anytime you fight, you always kill the other sonofabitch," he had told his soldiers. "Do not let him live today so he will fight you tomorrow. Kill him today."... The documentary, made by John Laurence, a veteran war correspondent, captured how one of Steele's sergeants interpreted that approach. Speaking to his soldiers before a raid, the sergeant instructed them, "We are not bringing anyone back alive." (p. 35)

Ricks does not analyze or discuss the meaning of his one-page account of this incident other than to argue that General David Petraeus sought to reverse this "ham-fisted" approach to warfare with the change of strategy that was labeled as "the surge."

---

1   Thomas Ricks, *The Gamble: General David Petraeus and the American Military Adventure in Iraq 2006-2008* (New York: Penguin, 2009).

But did Petraeus really reverse it? The point is that the brigade commander issued an unlawful ROE, which was authorized by his superiors, which is linked through the chain of command to the Pentagon and beyond, and which is still used in the war on terror.

It is not a question of "fiasco" versus "the surge," or General Petraeus versus his predecessors, but of common, average, American cultural attitudes toward the enemy and of treating prisoners. Perhaps one should be grateful that Ricks mentions the incident at all. But he does not even mention the name of the mission in question, Operation Iron Triangle. In other words, this tragedy was not a solitary event which involved four soldiers deciding on their own to kill prisoners, but of a mission approved by the entire chain of command to kill any military-aged Iraqi male. It is the latter point, the involvement of the chain of command, which makes the event a war crime. And the tragedy was not the result of one colonel's personal views or troubles, because — obviously — the colonel was part of a chain of command. Strictly speaking, the soldiers carried out their orders.

Ricks refers to the incident in question with the overly-simplistic description that "soldiers killed three detainees they had captured and hand-cuffed" and that "ultimately, four of them would be charged." Charged with what? Ricks does not clarify. The correct answer is that they were charged with war crimes, which automatically presume government responsibility, a connection between the White House and the soldier who pulled the trigger at the very tip of the other end of the chain of command. Furthermore, it is *not* true that the descriptions of Col. Steele's orders took place in "the court-martial." These descriptions took place solely in the pre-trial or Article 32 hearing. The courts-martial for two of the accused soldiers were canceled!

Col. Steele refused to testify at the pre-trial hearing. He and his unlawful orders were not even mentioned at the plea-bargains or the one court-martial, under threat from the prosecutor that if he and the unlawful ROE were mentioned, the soldiers would get life sentences or the deals would be revoked. Later in this book, the reader will have the opportunity to examine the coercive, unlawful, and deceptive tactics used by investigators and prosecutors to obtain contradictory confessions and desperate plea-bargains.

ANALYZING COLONEL STEELE'S SPEECH

COL Steele actually made several speeches related to the unlawful ROE, and it is not clear which one Ricks is citing. One of these speeches may be found on You Tube[1] and is worth quoting in full. COL Steele said:

> Over the next ten days, everyone in this room will get on a plane and we will fly to Southwest Asia. Man, this is what we have been talking about for the last year. All this training, this is it; we're here. And now it's time to go. We are going into the worst part of Iraq. That's not something you droop your head down and say woe is me; that's something you stick your chest out and you say Damn Right we're going there. Because where we're going they could not send a bunch of Girl Scouts and left-handed midgets to do what needs to be done. He didn't have a choice, who else is he going

---

1 http://www.youtube.com/watch?v=fxy-Rsd2wsm

to send? This is real, and the guy who is going to win on the battlefield is the one who gets violent the fastest. So that's the context. Here are the things I want you to know. Number One, anytime you fight, *anytime you fight,* you always kill the other son-of-a-bitch. Always. *Do not let him live today, so he will fight you tomorrow.* Kill him today. They'll make more of them, they're out there damn everywhere, there's plenty of them. Kill him today. Don't let him live. I spent much of our time, unfortunately, in meetings. And I listen to guys talk, and I have to just kind of take it in [and phase out] before I start hyperventilating. Well what's my problem if I hear this stuff; and they say well you know when they're shootin' at you, what we need to do is, we need to go over and we need to kick their feet out from under them, flex cuff them, put them in a room and get them some water because they are probably dehydrated and not thinking well, get them some food because they have not eaten well, put your arm around them and give them an open mouthed kiss, tell them you love them, and after we've befriended them they are going to tell us all this intelligence. Man that is bullshit! That is bullshit. So, I want to be very clear. If you go out and somebody presents a lethal threat to you, then you shoot him. Do not feel bad and think *that you should have brought him back* because I didn't want to talk to him. Then when you walk out that gate, fly out that gate, drive out that gate, I expect you to look like a killer. I have been in more third world countries than anybody in this room, and I tell you most of them do not speak English. They all speak food chain. And from the time you set foot in their country, they're checking you out, from top to bottom. They've figured out where you are on the food chain. Because if you look like prey, what happens? You get eaten. If you stand there and look people dead in the eye, you have your weapon at ready, and don't you flinch. You look like you're not scared. Even if you are scared, you look like you're not scared. You send the message that *I am the dominant predator on this street, and if you mess with me I will eat you.* We are not going to be driving around Iraq raping, bartering, pillaging, being undisciplined. That's not what I'm talking about. I'm talking about the moment of truth, when you're about to kill the other son of-a-bitch; I do not want you to choke down that pipe when thinking, man that's a pretty nice looking car he's driving, just shoot the damn car. Four years and two days ago, this flag was hanging over building number 7 World Trade Center, and a police officer, a good friend of mine, after they got everybody out of the building, went back to check one more time as he was leaving, just then, he saw the flag, went back and recovered the flag, got out, 10-15 minutes later what was left of the tower came down. This flag was where the fight started. I think it is very appropriate to take a piece of the World Trade Center back where they started it, and we're going to finish it. Our history's in this flag. And I wanted you to know what this flag means if you come to the headquarters and you see it down there. *Man, it's time to go hunting. And that's exactly the attitude I expect you to have. Every time you walk out that gate, you are hunting. You are the hunter, you are the predator, you are looking for the prey, and that's all* [emphasis added].

In analyzing this speech, I will follow the lead of Stouffer's classic *The American Soldier*, in which Stouffer states repeatedly that he is interested in the *average* understanding of orders by US soldiers. Various professionals, non-average soldiers, elitists, and even misfits will have their own interpretation of what Steele said and might have meant. But the sociological imagination demands that one examines this speech from the point of view of the average soldier. The average person and the average soldier will no doubt conclude that Steele was saying that he did not want them to take prisoners but to kill without hesitation. Later in this book, I will quote soldiers during the Article 32 hearing who swore under oath that this is precisely what they understood their orders to be: Taking prisoners was understood by them as disobedience to their orders.

But Steele's admonitions are the complete opposite of the average American soldier's as depicted in the classic book by Stouffer. Stouffer demonstrated convincingly that the average World War II American soldier did *not* want to kill except in self-defense and *did* want to take prisoners and treat prisoners with dignity and respect. What has changed since Stouffer's study? The sociological imagination compels one to make the connection to similar phrases used by the Bush Administration. In telling his soldiers to take the fight to an unknown enemy who does not wear a uniform, be a predator, and kill the enemy today so that he will not be a threat tomorrow, Steele was merely echoing the national line. Has the average American soldier changed since World War II, or was the Bush Administration out of sync with the average American's attitudes toward war? What makes the Operation Iron Triangle mission intriguing is that initially, the soldiers disobeyed the brigade commander's order to kill every male on sight and take no prisoners! The soldiers in Operation Iron Triangle behaved more like Stouffer portrays them than what Steele wanted out of them — but they were caught in a double-bind, as I will demonstrate in great detail later in the book. They were damned if they killed the prisoners and damned if they did not kill the prisoners. When the soldiers arrived at the site, they encountered no resistance, and instead of finding terrorists, they found farmers, women, children, and sheep. They followed their orders and killed one unarmed man, but hesitated in killing the other men and took four prisoners. Had they killed immediately all the Iraqi males they encountered, all the killings would have been considered lawful in relation to the unlawful ROE which had been operating for quite some time, and the mission would never have become an issue. Similar killings were conducted by Charlie Company on other missions and posed no problems for the command. When the first sergeant heard that they took prisoners, he cursed and yelled loudly on the radio that they should not have taken prisoners. Three of the soldiers then killed three of the prisoners.

Commonsense or the average understanding of the situation suggests that all the commissioned officers in the chain of command share some of the responsibility for the killings. Indeed, in every court-martial that I have observed, I have heard colonels and other commissioned officers state during jury selection that incidents of this sort are due to "failure in leadership." I take this to mean that the average commissioned officer is trained to believe that he or she is ultimately responsible for the behavior of subordinates. Why wasn't this common or average understanding of command responsibility followed in responding to the tragedy of Operation Iron Triangle? It was precisely when the brigade commander's leadership was eventually called into question in this case that the machinery of the military justice system turned against the enlisted soldiers. We shall explore the reasons for this dynamic later.

To repeat: the sociological imagination avoids focusing on any one individual or social issue alone, at the exclusion of the individual or the social issue. The personal issue must be conjoined to a cultural pattern. This rule applies to the brigade commander's speech and order. In no way was his order atypical, given that in the current war on terror, the United States established the pre-emptive strike as public policy. This policy came to be known as the Bush Doctrine[1] and the US attacked Iraq even though Iraq showed no hostile intent and posed no danger toward the US. The brigade commander's speech and order are a microcosm of the pre-emptive strike doctrine: the ROE for Operation Iron Triangle basically involved a pre-emptive strike on unsuspecting, unarmed, and non-hostile Iraqis. This is an unmistakable cultural pattern. Again, the haunting question is whether this particular cultural pattern is in line or out of sync with long-standing, average, American values.

The Bush Doctrine is a radical departure from Stouffer's description of the US soldier and US policy during World War II. Other studies of the World War II era document that in newspapers, literature, films, and cultural products in general, Americans held the widespread, average belief that they were engaged in self-defense.[2] Japan's attack on Pearl Harbor galvanized this deeply-engrained American pattern of values concerning justifiable self-defense. This cannot be said about average American beliefs about the war in Iraq without some equivocation. To be sure, the catastrophic event of 9/11 was an act of aggression against the US — but Iraq had no connection to it whatsoever. For most of his eight years in office, President Bush tried to connect Iraq with 9/11, to make the attack on the World Trade center the equivalent of the attack on Pearl Harbor — but the final verdict is that the average American is not convinced of this connection. President Bush's approval ratings kept sinking as the war dragged on and when he left office, most Americans had concluded that the war in Iraq was a mistake. However, note that like President Bush, the brigade commander incorrectly connected 9/11 to the alleged terrorists that were supposed to be killed during Operation Iron Triangle in Iraq. This mistake in sociological imagination is on the hypothetical order of the US attacking China as retaliation for the Japanese attack on Pearl Harbor. This story is not about the brigade commander's personal troubles, foibles, judgment, or misjudgment, but about the connection between his pep talk and the general policies of the US toward Iraq. The tragedy of Operation Iron Triangle is a microcosm of the larger tragedy and fiasco[3] of the war against Iraq.

Nowhere in Stouffer's study can one find language similar to the brigade commander's advice that the US soldier is the "predator" and the Iraqis are the "prey." The closest reference point that one can find in literature regarding such descriptions of American institutional predators is Thorstein Veblen's description of American corporate leaders and "robber barons" — but even Veblen does not refer to the army as predatory. On the contrary, Veblen describes the US army in terms of "honorific" values. Based upon existing literature, it seems unthinkable that a World War II soldier would have thought about a battle in terms of "going hunting." Stouffer empha-

---

1 National Security Strategy of the US, White House, September 17, 2002.

2 See Benjamin L. Alpers (1998), "This is the Army: Imagining a Democratic Military in World War II," *Journal of American History*, pp. 129-63.

3 Thomas Ricks, *Fiasco: The American Military Adventure in Iraq* (New York: Penguin, 2007).

sizes the following generalizations about the army experience for US soldiers during World War II:

> The Army was a new world for most civilian soldiers. Of its many contrasts with civilian institutions, three may be cited:
>
> • Its authoritarian organization, demanding rigid obedience.
>
> • Its highly stratified social system, in which hierarchies of deference were formally and minutely established by official regulation subject to penalties for infraction, on and off duty.
>
> • Its emphasis on traditional ways of doing things and its disencouragement of initiative. (Vol 1., p. 55.)

It seems that the first two points, authoritarianism and stratification, are still true regarding today's army. But the last point about tradition seems to have changed, in Steele's brigade and the military in general. Stouffer and scores of other authors emphasize that traditionally, the US army is not militant or militaristic because it fights battles and wars primarily on the basis of self-defense.[1] In other words, the traditional American soldier did not have the concept of "predator" in his vocabulary as a self-descriptor. The new factor in the current war is the introduction of the non-traditional, predatory idea of the pre-emptive strike, at all levels, in conjunction with demands for rigid obedience and a highly stratified social system. This formula helps to explain the tragedy of Operation Iron Triangle, the abuse at Abu Ghraib, torture at Guantanamo, and scores of other events that have damaged the reputation of the United States in the current war.

The common strand is that soldiers go "hot" on missions that involve knocking on doors or engaging the enemy, when it might be more prudent to go "cold." The authoritarianism and rigid hierarchy make it difficult if not impossible for any individual or reference group to question or disobey the predatory policies and orders. This is especially true for enlisted soldiers for both psychological and legal reasons. Officers have much more latitude in refusing to follow an unlawful or immoral order than do enlisted personnel.

FINDING PATTERNS IN HUNDREDS OF FACTS

The anthropologist Ruth Benedict was interested in the questions why Japanese soldiers in World War II kept fighting even though they knew they had lost the war, and why they abused their own as well as American prisoners of war. She answered these questions by analyzing "hundreds of facts [that] fall into over-all patterns" (p. 12). The patterns she found include that Japanese World War II society as a whole was focused on the emotion of "shame" and believed that prisoners were "damaged goods" that should be mistreated. By contrast, Americans from that era saw no shame

---

1   See T.P. Schwartz and Robert M. Marsh (1999), "The American soldiers studies of WWII: A 50th anniversary commemorative," *Journal of Political and Military Sociology* 27(1):21-37. Among their many summaries of findings, the authors conclude that there was a "low prevalence among combat troops of strong expressions of hostility toward enemy soldiers," that US soldiers had a "sense of fairness," that combat effectiveness of soldiers peaked after three months, that 72% cited "battle fatigue" as the worst effect of war on them, and that combat veterans hated war.

in being a prisoner, foreign or domestic, and generally treated Japanese and German prisoners with mercy and kindness. An illustration of this pattern is found in *Lone Star Stalag*, which describes the favorable treatment German POWs received from their American guards at a POW camp in Hearne, Texas. I shall refer to both works and patterns throughout this book. I mention both at this juncture to highlight that I will be following the method of seeking out patterns in hundreds of details. In the remainder of this book, I shall cite hundreds if not thousands of details as they emerge from sworn statements and court transcripts. In the conclusion, I shall identify patterns.

At this point in the discussion, I shall tip my hand and note the major discrepancy in patterns uncovered during World War II versus today. Specifically, there seems to be consensus that American soldiers treated prisoners, foreign and domestic, humanely for the most part. But the last eight years of the war on terror have produced a relentless stream of reports of abuse of prisoners from Abu Ghraib to Gitmo and beyond. This seems to be a striking departure from the traditional American manner of treating prisoners.

Additionally, as I will demonstrate in the rest of this book, the US army mistreated and abused its own soldier–prisoners. As illustration, consider the following portion of testimony by Specialist William Hunsaker, one of the accused soldiers in Operation Iron Triangle, during a pre-trial hearing. It is important to keep in mind that his account was given while he formally held the status of being innocent until proven guilty by American cultural norms and the US Constitution. He was questioned by defense attorney Michael Waddington:

> Q: And during the period prior to the Article 32 Investigation, what were the conditions of your confinement? Can you describe what the living circumstances were like?
>
> A: I spent the first 5 weeks in a 7 by 7 steel cage.
>
> Q: And how was the cage itself set up? What was your living space like in that space?
>
> A: The cage in itself was probably 7 feet by 7 feet, and when you include the metal bench, I guess you could say, that holds your sleeping mat on there, and the toilet, you had approximately maybe 3 by 5 feet worth of, if not less, of moving room.
>
> Q: How many hours a day did you spend in this 7 foot by 7 foot cage?
>
> A: About 23 hours a day.

It is difficult to read the word "cage" and fail to think of prisoners at Guantanamo Bay locked in cages, or even of animals confined to cages. Incredibly, the prosecutor did not object to the use of the word "cage." I confirmed later with Hunsaker that he was truly confined in a metal cage; that the lights were on 24 hours a day, 7 days per week; and that he was forbidden to put a blanket over his head in order to block out the light and fall asleep. The small size of the cage borders on human rights violations of standards for confinement. In commonsense terms, Hunsaker was in solitary confinement while awaiting trial. And this, despite the fact that according to the tenets of American culture as well as law, Hunsaker was presumed to be innocent until proven guilty during this "pre-trial confinement."

Q: And during the other hour within the 24-hour period, how was that spent?

A: Depending who was on guard, I would either spend the whole hour in the gym or on the phone, which included my shower time and there were some guards that, you know, "I have got to have you back in there early." So sometimes I would spend about 40 minutes outside.

It is important to note that both the guards and the accused are US Army soldiers, and as such, presumably share values that are common to low-ranking soldiers. He and his guards were in the same reference group even if though he was inside the cage and they were outside. In other words, one might assume that the guards would be inclined to be sympathetic to the accused and to chafe at the idea of treating him as if he were a terrorist or an animal. During World War II, on average, it seems that both US and enemy soldiers were treated relatively well by their American captors. This is in stark contrast to the fact that in the current war on terror, the cultural pattern seems to be that both US and enemy prisoners are mistreated by their American captors. What changed?

Later in this book, I will demonstrate that Hunsaker's comrade, Corey Clagett, was similarly isolated and mistreated by his US military guards. In addition to punishing a person who has not been convicted of any crime, this solitary confinement serves a dual function: It sends a message to the accused that he is guilty (even if the law presumes that he is innocent) at the same time that it begins to create a wider gulf of social distance between the guards and the accused. Over time, dehumanizing treatment of this sort dehumanizes *both* the guard and the accused: Both come to believe that the accused is guilty (even though he has not been convicted of anything at this point) and deserves the treatment he receives and will receive. This is a classic Catch-22 or double-bind situation: The accused is innocent until proven guilty, and should not be treated as if he were guilty, so he comes to feel guilty and is treated as guilty to justify the discrepancy in how he is treated.

Q: At the time that you were returned to COB Speicher for the Article 32 Investigation, how were you confined while you were at COB Speicher?

A: We were all segregated into separate tents at Tent City, just down the street ... and we had to spend most of the entire time, unless we were with our lawyers or at the 32 hearing, in shackles, which includes the leg chains, the handcuffs, and the blue box with the belly chain attached to it, which included also sleeping in them when we were in the tent.

Q: Just to be clear, you said that you were required to sleep in these restraints as well?

A: Yes.

Q: After the Article 32 Investigation was complete, where were you — were you returned to Kuwait for confinement there?

A: Yes.

Q: And what were your conditions like at that time?

A: I spent about another day in the cage and then they moved me to a tent that was blocked within a chain link fence with concertina wire around the top of it, and I stayed in that tent by myself, isolated. I spent 23 hours a day in there also. I was let out for 1 hour to eat and for recreation.

Commonsense leads one to wonder: Why would the army go to such great lengths to confine one of its soldiers on a military base that is already a confined and controlled area? Where could a soldier in uniform possibly flee on a US military base in a foreign country? Given that Hunsaker's alleged crime took place during battle, not against comrades or in a civilian context, what possible justification could there be for confinement, and especially under these abusive conditions? After all, the accused had no prior criminal record and was not a danger to his comrades. In effect, the accused had been sentenced to solitary confinement prior to his trial.

In the everyday language of American popular culture, the accused US soldier was treated as if he were a "crazy, psycho, dangerous killer" or terrorist. More precisely, he was being treated worse than alleged terrorists in custody, because the Army, after the Abu Ghraib fiasco, went out of its way to claim that it treats its Arab prisoners humanely. The unspoken message to everyone on the military base was that the accused US soldier is as bad a person as the enemy they were fighting in Iraq. He was presumed to be the enemy within.

Q: At some point, you were moved from Kuwait back to the United States?

A: Yes.

Q: Where were you confined upon your return to the United States?

A: We were confined at the Navy Brig in Charleston, North Carolina and, I don't really remember the name of the brig right now. They never really told me. But they put me in a max right away, as soon as I got there. I spent about 3 weeks in max, which is a cell, just a little bitty ole concrete cell. I wasn't allowed to come out, except for 1 hour of the day, which included my shower and I am supposed to get rec but that just included walking around in a grassy knoll area, still in shackles. If I had to come out and take a shower and go back in, I had to be in shackles, even if I was moving 2 feet.

For the record, Charleston is in South Carolina, not North Carolina. But in any event, it seems that the accused was not aware of the name or geographical location of his "little bitty ole concrete cell." It is ironic that at the same time that Hunsaker was confined at the Naval Brig in Charleston, three notorious, suspected terrorists were confined at this same prison.[1] It seems that the accused was literally treated like an animal, down to being walked like a dog in a grassy knoll area.

---

1   These suspected terrorists included Yasser Hamdi, Jose Padilla, and Ali Saleh Kahlah al-Marri. Hamdi and Padilla were the subjects of two famous US Supreme Court decisions which ruled against the government.

Q: What were the approximate dimensions of this cell that you were in during this period that you were in max confinement?

A: Just a little bit bigger than the one in Kuwait ... maybe 10 by 5.

Q: How long did that situation continue?

A: That continued for about 2 and a half weeks and then they took me off max and I was allowed to come out of the cell. I still stayed in the same cell. I come out — I can come out of the cell now, but I am only allowed in the dayroom area, which is just right outside of the door. It is an area not much bigger than this courtroom.

Q: Are you permitted to interact with or do you interact with other prisoners at Charleston?

A: No. They have me in special quarters, which is a segregated area, where they put usually people that act up or the worse criminals sometimes, and they have to stay in max because of whatever they are confined for, and I am not allowed to talk to them because they are prisoners and plus, they are being punished, and so I don't have anyone to talk to.

The situation described by the accused may be re-described in commonsense terms as follows: The accused US soldier, Hunsaker, who was presumed to be innocent until proven guilty, was segregated even from other US soldiers who were being punished and who were presumably convicted of being guilty of something. One can predict, based upon numerous studies on the effects of solitary confinement, that the mental health of all the prisoners in these circumstances would deteriorate over time. It is an open question whether these are unintended or intentional consequences.

Q: During the period that you were being transported from Kuwait to the United States, were you in a position to make contact with your defense counsel, either Mr. Waddington or Captain Hynes?

A: No, sir. We weren't allowed to make contact with anybody, not even our families, because we were issued a Gag Order. We were not allowed to talk to no one.

Q: What did you understand this Gag Order to mean or to entail?

A: Talk to nobody, whatsoever.

Q: And that included defense counsel?

A: That included everybody, sir, is what we were told.

During all these disclosures, the prosecution did not voice any objections, so that one may presume that all this sworn testimony is true, or at least that the prosecution had no rebuttal. Again, it is helpful to compare the accused's descriptions of his treatment with the well-known and documented treatment of foreign prisoners at Gitmo, who were similarly isolated and not allowed to speak with each other. The important point is that the accused US soldier is being treated as if he were a foreign enemy, even to the extreme length of not allowing him to consult with his attorneys, which is his Constitutional right.

Q: Since you have been at the Charleston Naval Brig, what kind of access or what kind of ease of access have you had with respect to contacting detailed military counsel or your civilian defense counsel?

A: I have to put in a request chit and everything goes through paperwork. If I want to make a phone call to any lawyer, it has to be, put in a request and sometimes they will request it that same day and some days it may take 3 or 4 days, and in the beginning, I kind of had problems trying to contact my previous lawyer and in that aspect, he wasn't getting my messages and apparently, from what I heard, he was trying to contact the brig, but they weren't giving me any of his so, we had no contact.

Q: Would it be fair to say that you have had difficulty in making contact?

A: Extreme difficulty.

Chapter 2. The Hidden Patterns of Violence in War Crimes

> "Those philosophies which are stable only in the presence of their own confutation are in fact systems which promote paranoid symptoms among their members."
> — Gregory Bateson, p. 131

Translated into everyday English, Bateson found that any and all social systems which silence (confute) opposition, questions, and dialogue in their ranks will create an unhealthy social climate.

In March of 2009, I flew to Boston to see and engage in dialogue with an attorney named Geoffrey Nathan. He was representing William Hunsaker in clemency proceedings and had e-mailed me to see whether I was willing to help him with the case. It was a bitterly cold yet sunny day as I made my way across Boston Common to his office on 132 Boylston Street. His office was on the fifth floor, and offered a grand view of the state capitol. In his demeanor, dress, appearance, and language, Mr. Nathan came across as extraordinarily professional, and also as someone who wasted nothing, including ideas and time. Although he seemed approachable, he spoke in rapid-fire style, as if he were laying out bullet-points in a presentation.

He said that he didn't expect me to fly all the way from Texas to Boston to see him, and I replied that I always prefer face-to-face contact in making decisions. I knew nothing about the Hunsaker case other than what I had read about him in legal statements pertaining to Corey Clagett's case. The obvious and important point is that Clagett and Hunsaker were among the co-accused in the Operation Iron Triangle mission, so that their cases are related to each other, and to other "cases" on the mission that never went to trial. Somehow this obvious point gets lost in the government's depiction of these and other soldiers as isolated individuals.

According to Mr. Nathan, Mr. Hunsaker had told him that one of his duties in Iraq was to routinely pick up the severed heads left by insurgents, tag and bag the body parts, and put them in a freezer. Mr. Nathan said that it was proving difficult to confirm this claim because the army would not confirm such duties for any of its soldiers. As Mr. Nathan spoke, two thoughts ran through my mind. The first was that such gruesome tasks would be an obvious source of PTSD on a widespread scale for US soldiers and for Mr. Hunsaker in particular. The second was that it reminded me of testimony by an army intelligence officer in the court-martial of Sergeant Michael Leahy that took place in February of 2009 at the army base in Vilseck, Germany. I served as an expert witness in sociology at that trial, and listened carefully to the intelligence officer's testimony. He testified that in the years 2006 and 2007, Iraqi-on-Iraqi ethnic cleansing was so extensive that up to 200 Iraqi bodies per day were found by the US soldiers while they were on their daily patrols.

After speaking with Mr. Nathan, I e-mailed that particular intelligence officer and asked him for more information on this topic, particularly on the issue of who disposed of the bodies and body parts. Were US soldiers or Iraqis or both involved in removing the bodies? It was no surprise to me that the intelligence officer never replied. My point is that Mr. Hunsaker's claim echoes the intelligence officer's testimony about the widespread nature of Iraqi-on-Iraqi ethnic cleansing. These two claims are two parts of the sociological imagination concerning the reality of ethnic cleansing that have yet to be connected. After eight years of war, next to nothing is publicly documented about Iraqi-on-Iraqi violence and its impact on Iraqis or US soldiers. Nobody seems to be interested in the issue of the dead bodies that are the result of ethnic cleansing. Based on the mountains of research on stress, one would expect that both Iraqis and US soldiers exposed to such violence and its aftermath — namely, dead bodies and body parts — will suffer widespread PTSD. The widespread PTSD, in turn, will demolish unit morale and cause further violence toward self or others. I told Mr. Nathan what I had learned in the Leahy trial, and we connected the dots to the Hunsaker case. I also told him about my previous research on ethnic cleansing in Bosnia, where I had had the opportunity to travel to actual sites of battles and ethnic cleansing.

It would consume too much space to repeat here what I told him and what I have learned about ethnic cleansing from research in Bosnia and my experience as an expert witness at The Hague. I will just summarize my findings briefly. Ethnic cleansing is not an abstraction. It is not "clean" but dirty. It is not organized — as too many social theorists and journalist assume — but extremely chaotic. Allied armies turn on each other. Like cancer, an army unit turns against itself. Families that used to drink coffee together every day suddenly change and rape or kill a neighbor's children. Civilians as well as soldiers — regular as well as irregular soldiers — are deprived of food, water, sleep, and any sense of normalcy. Human empathy vanishes. People who were once considered normal, average, and decent suddenly commit the most heinous crimes. If I had to summarize with one word the reality of the new element that ethnic cleansing introduces into so-called laws of organized warfare, it would be: chaos.

Mr. Nathan lamented that he was the busiest attorney before the United States Army clemency and parole board. He asked rhetorically, "Why is it that corporate America's law firms will not provide me with assistance despite my requests, even though they seem to be extremely busy representing Gitmo detainees?" This is a good question. One of several possible answers is that there is more publicity to be had defending detainees than US soldiers, due in part to the known proclivities of the information media. He added that the chairman of the clemency and parole board confirmed that he was the only lawyer who volunteered his services to represent combat duty soldiers seeking clemency and parole. "Why is it that I am the only lawyer in the United States who volunteered my services to represent our soldiers?" he asked out loud and looked at me. Indeed, in my work with courts-martial, I have never come across a corporate law firm representing a US soldier before, during, or after a court-martial. All of the civilian lawyers with whom I had worked for the defense of US soldiers were solo practitioners, most are former JAG officers, and all of them did the work either pro bono or, as Mr. Nathan put it, "quasi-pro-bono." There was no profit for them in such cases, because families of enlisted soldiers are typically not wealthy.

Mr. Nathan's questions prompted me to think about my own profession of sociology and my role in these cases. I could lament that the American Sociological Association and my colleagues in general advocate on behalf of many reference groups such as women, gays and lesbians, and various minorities, but never on behalf of US soldiers. Feminists are interested in studying the oppression of women relative to career advancement but not interested in the plight of female US soldiers or Iraqi women at Abu Ghraib, for example. Most people hate Lynndie England because of government and media depictions of her, but they do not know that she suffered from PTSD, depression, and extreme anxiety while the army used her gender as a weapon against Iraqis to cause them humiliation.[1] Race and ethnic relations is a popular field in sociology, but primarily in relation to American culture — I have never come across a study of racism and ethnic relations or ethnic cleansing in Iraq, with regard to Iraqi-on-Iraqi violence or US–Iraqi violence. My published work on war crime trials in Iraq has been politely ignored by my colleagues. I felt and continue to feel as lonely as Mr. Nathan since I am the only sociologist in America who serves as an expert witness in defense of US soldiers. Perhaps Mr. Nathan is correct that one should ask the question, "Why is that the case?" I did my work pro bono in half the cases, and the rest were paid for by the army — and the pay is paltry. On the other hand, social scientists are involved in droves helping the government devise and implement torture techniques.[2] But these self-disclosures about feeling disconnected from the rest of American culture on the topic of US soldiers and war crimes made me feel connected to Mr. Nathan. Returning Iraq War veterans almost universally report feeling similarly disconnected or alienated from American culture. Stouffer also found that World War II "returnees were a disgruntled group" and that one third "expressed feeling estranged from civilian life" (volume 2, p. 643).

During the conversation with Mr. Nathan, I realized that he and I seemed to be on the lonely edge of the sociological imagination. The average lawyer and social scientist simply do not seem to be interested in the US soldier who is accused of war crimes. I said to him that the average American would be interested and would care

---

1 Stjepan G. Mestrovic, *The Trials of Abu Ghraib: An Expert Witness Account of Shame and Honor* (Boulder, CO: Paradigm, 2007).

2 Jane Mayer, *The Dark Side: The Inside Story of How the War on Terror Turned Into a War on American Ideals* (New York: Anchor, 2009).

if they knew what he and I knew about these cases. But American journalists generally take the government position, and do not report the many intricate details of the cases that form a discernable pattern. He agreed, and lamented on the many news outlets that he had tried to approach and who had rebuffed him. I voiced similar laments. We talked about Raffi Khatchadourian, a journalist from *The New Yorker* who had approached both of us for information on the Operation Iron Triangle cases. He and I both gave this journalist all the information that we could, but he had not published his story as of our conversation, and he stopped returning our phone calls and e-mails.

Undaunted, Mr. Nathan said he was seeking Congressional involvement and eventually, Congressional hearings on the Iron Triangle cases. He felt that the clemency and parole board would not act favorably toward his clients unless Congress got involved. I said that I saw no hope for Congress getting involved, because any such investigations would point an accusatory finger back at Congress for authorizing the techniques, policies, and orders that got our soldiers into trouble. "Then what are you going to do?" he asked me. "I feel like you're cross-examining me, Mr. Nathan, and I'm in your office, not the witness stand," I replied. He laughed. I told him that I would keep writing my books even if few people read them, because I'm a professor, and that's what professors do. "Besides," I added, "my university and department support what I'm doing." This prompted him to ask me whether I had read *The Gamble* by Thomas Ricks. I said that I had not. He said that Ricks devotes two pages to Operation Iron Triangle, and that is better than nothing. This time I laughed, and said that I would read it. He asked me to send him an autographed copy of my book, *Rules of Engagement?* I did.

Mr. Nathan was relentless in his criticisms of the government in the Iron Triangle cases. "There were no bodies found, no forensic tests were made, there was no physical evidence, there were no visits to the crime scene, no interviews with the families," he said. He added: "This case never would have gone to trial in the civilian world." I said that the law was Greek to me, and I was not qualified to comment on it. I added: "I have no idea what you guys are saying and doing as lawyers in the courtroom, but I have plenty to say about what you are saying and doing from my vantage point as a sociologist." He suggested that we both buy tickets to Baghdad and visit the crime scene and interview the families of the Iraqi victims. "Were they terrorists or farmers?" he asked. I replied: "I don't want to get killed." But he said we could get bodyguards. I asked how much that would cost. He said it would be in the tens of thousands. I finally convinced him that getting such funding was unlikely.

We spoke about the civilian lawyers with whom I had worked thus far: Frank Spinner and Paul Bergrin. "Spinner is a fine man and a fine lawyer," he said, and I agreed. "What's Bergrin like?" he asked. "He's larger-than-life, looks like he stepped out of a movie set with his immaculate and expensive suits, and he gives the government lawyers hell," I said. We spoke about the charges of money-laundering and prostitution that were leveled at Mr. Bergrin exactly one week before Corey Clagett's court-martial was supposed to begin. I told Mr. Nathan that to this day I feel that there was some sort of government collusion in the timing of those charges, because the end result was that Clagett's trial was cancelled, I could not testify on his behalf, and Clagett felt forced to plead guilty. Most of the charges against Mr. Bergrin were eventually dropped, and he also agreed to a plea-bargain for lesser charges in order to avoid going to prison. A few months after he was mostly cleared of all charges, new charges — this time involving conspiracy to commit murder — were leveled at him.[1] Later in this book, I shall discuss the unanimous opinion of all the attorneys with whom I have interacted: that conspiracy laws in the US are so "loose" that they can mean whatever the government wants them to mean. "There is just too much intrigue in these Operation Iron Triangle cases," I said. "There is another lawyer you need to speak with," Mr. Nathan said. It was Michael Waddington, who represented Hunsaker while Bergrin represented Clagett. Eventually I did speak with Mr. Waddington.

"What school did you go to?" he asked. "Harvard," I said. "Was that the big degree or the small degree?" I explained that it was one small degree (undergraduate) and two medium degrees (master's degrees), one in theology and the other in clinical psychology, and that they had an "inbreeding rule" that after three degrees, you have to go somewhere else, so that I got my PhD at Syracuse University. "Stop cross-examining me," I said to him again. It was painful for a moment to think back on how Harvard had changed since I studied there. I was there during the seventies, when professors such as David Riesman, Talcott Parsons, and other "grand theorists" inspired me and other students with lofty visions of curiosity, improving society, and seeking out patterns and connections in culture. Carry-overs from the 1960s such as George Wald in biology criticized loudly colleagues in "the establishment" who were "just polishing their buttons" instead of trying to solve America's problems. In this new millennium, I read in the newspapers that Harvard law professors are among those who advised or signed off on the brutal "interrogation techniques" at Abu Ghraib and Guantanamo.[2] And the current Harvard sociology department has no one with the stature or charisma of David Riesman, who steadfastly criticized US foreign policy when he thought it was unjust or mistaken.

Finally, I agreed to help Mr. Nathan with Mr. Hunsaker's clemency and asked to see his entire file. We spoke about issues of confidentiality and Mr. Nathan handed me a letter signed by Mr. Hunsaker in which he waived his attorney–client privilege. He said that he would put me in touch with the soldier's mother, Fran Hunsaker. He said that her finances had been nearly wiped out by legal expenses in trying to help her son, and I said I would do the work pro bono. We discussed a joint visit to Mr. Hunsaker at Ft. Leavenworth Disciplinary Barracks (DB) sometime in the summer of 2009. Mr. Nathan handed the Hunsaker file to me and I took it back with me to study in Texas.

CONNECTIONS MADE BY MR. NATHAN

The Operation Iron Triangle cases, like the war on terror as a whole, seems disconnected and disjointed to the average person. The government and the media pres-

1   Joe Ryan, "Paul Bergrin, former federal prosecutor, is indicted for alleged role in killing of informant," *The New Jersey Star-Ledger* May 20, 2009.
2   Scott Shane, "US lawyers agreed on the legality of brutal tactics," *New York Times*, 6 June 2009.

ent seemingly isolated incidents, events, battles, scandals, victories, and crimes that make it nearly impossible for the average person to "connect the dots" and see any pattern. Like all the other defense attorneys, Mr. Nathan found and pointed out patterns and connections. In one of his letters to Congresswoman Tsongas in Boston, Mr. Nathan wrote the following:

> The United States Congress needs to have hearings concerning parity of sentences for soldiers convicted of premeditated murder of Iraqi insurgents. Some of my clients received sentences of life without parole, some received 8 years, same facts. All of them lost their benefits, rank, pay and pension. Families were kicked off the base where they had lived forever ... children lost medical care ... grandparents were caused to be homeless .... [G]ood soldiers who freaked out in the field of battle largely as a result of sleep deprivation and lack of battlefield backup are spending a lot of time in jail [emphasis added].

Apparently nothing came of this letter to the Congresswoman. I agree with Mr. Nathan's assessment of the effects of sleep deprivation, not only because of the research that I have read, but because I sat in a courtroom and listened to the army's expert on sleep deprivation, Colonel Charles Hoge, testify to the truth of what Mr. Nathan was asserting. Chronic sleep deprivation is part of the hidden pattern of war, and it leads directly to violence, accidents, and impaired performance among soldiers. Colonel Edward Horvath told me that the issue of chronic sleep deprivation played a major role in revamping and humanizing physician residency two decades ago. Stouffer focused on sleep deprivation as a major factor in explaining high casualty rates in dysfunctional military units during World War II. Why have these historical insights into the importance of sleep for the soldier been overlooked in the current war? Media depictions of soldiers and war simply fail to address the issue of sleep as a basic biological for every human being as well as a fundamental logistical need for the army, on par with food and water.[1]

Mr. Nathan made a presentation to the army's clemency and parole board in Alexandria, Virginia on December 6, 2007. He was speaking on behalf of William Hunsaker. Some of the points he raised are confirmed by testimony in the Article 32 hearing, which will be analyzed in great detail later in this book. But other points are part the hidden pattern that was kept out of testimony, even though every claim he makes is documented in written, sworn statements.

Mr. Nathan told the board: The ROE for Operation Iron Triangle, issued by COL Steele, were to kill all military age males on the island. There was a systematic effort made by the brigade to desensitize the troops about killing: There was a kill board in the command center to track how well the soldiers were doing. When soldiers in Steele's command scored a kill, he rewarded them with a "kill coin." "COL Steele's policy on firing warning shots was shooting the person next to the one you want to warn." During Operation Iron Triangle, First Sergeant Geressy said on the radio, "Why do we have three f____ detainees? Why aren't they dead?" To repeat: all these facts are documented in sworn testimony from the Article 32 hearing. The reader must ask the question: how did the government manage to disconnect all these facts to make it

---

1 Seth Robson, "Report: troops need more sleep," *Stars and Stripes*, 17 March 2009.

seem that Clagett and Hunsaker were lonely criminals? And how did the information media manage to go along with the government's false version of events?

There are many other facts that never made it into the court record, and they all point to a pattern. One set of facts concerns the First Sergeant, Eric Geressy. CPT Breitenbucher wrote that on one occasion, the First Sergeant told him to get out of his sight because he was getting soft. By this the First Sergeant meant that the captain would not kill an enemy without positive identification. In another instance, and after killing an insurgent, Sergeant Geressy put the dead body on the hood of a HMMMV (Humvee) and paraded it around the Thar Thar market in Iraq. Sergeant David Chavez wrote that he felt unsafe working with Charlie Company (which was implicated in the Iron Triangle killings) and that most of the company had been brainwashed by the commanding officer and the First Sergeant to kill whenever possible. PFC Joshua Fuson stated that the commander and first sergeant of Charlie Company have an attitude toward Iraqis that all of them are the enemy and the more kills the better. "Specialist Jason Stachowski states, 1ˢᵗ Sgt Geressy's tone in the majority of the missions is to kill." Clearly, this pattern of attitudes in Charlie Company is related to US policy in general toward Iraqis that is depicted by Ricks in his books *Fiasco* and *The Gamble*.

Mr. Nathan told the board: "When you have bad leadership at the top it not only affects the enlisted, it also seriously affects the junior officers, who are on the front line who are leading our men." One of Mr. Nathan's strategies was to focus on what all the junior officers were saying and doing on that fateful day: LT Horne, LT Hawkins, and LT Wehrheim. He is correct that the investigation and trial process focused only on LT Wehrheim, who testified at the Article 32 hearing, and his statements will be analyzed later. But two other platoon leaders, Lieutenant Horne and Lieutenant Hawkins did not testify. While four soldiers in Wehrheim's platoon were convicted, soldiers in the other platoons engaged in similar killings but no one in those units was charged with wrongdoing. It is commonsense that when an atrocity occurs, there will be a pattern of violence, so that one needs to examine all the units. The fact that only Wehrheim's soldiers were investigated and convicted gives one pause, but we will turn to that issue in the next chapter.

LT Horne was ordering his soldiers to kill unarmed Iraqis, "kill them all," even if they were posing no threat. When he was told women and children were present, he stated, "F___ that, it is all collateral damage." LT Hawkins roughed up prisoners to the point that he broke one's jaw and had to be told by a sergeant to back off. Mr. Nathan also posed the thought-provoking questions: Why did LT Wehrheim break with army procedure and take the dead Iraqi's body with him on the helicopter instead of the live prisoners? Why did he leave his radio man who was supposed to be with him at all times? Mr. Nathan added: "It makes me wonder if he [Wehrheim] wasn't in on the plan." Mr. Nathan's suspicions about a Machiavellian conspiracy by the platoon leader and his commanders are echoed in comments by military defense attorney CPT Sasha Rutizer in the closing moments of the Article 32 hearing.

Mr. Nathan did what lawyers do. He pointed to suppressed evidence of widespread killing and poisoned command climate on the mission as a mitigating factor for his client. The clemency and parole board did what it mostly does, which is that

it rejected his appeal for clemency on Hunsaker's behalf. The board offered no explanation for its decision. Another connection is that I would appear before this same
board as part of a three-person panel on behalf of Corey Clagett on April 1, 2009. The
same board rejected our appeal for clemency and again, offered no explanation at all.

All this new information begs many questions: Who were these soldiers uncovered by Mr. Nathan who dared to criticize the unlawful ROE and their commanding
officers? What happened to their sworn statements? Why was their testimony not
included in the long investigation and trial process? It appears that most of them
were snipers under the command of CPT Duggan, affiliated with Charlie Company,
but not directly under its command. As such, they had an outsider's perspective to
some extent. Apparently, they made two sets of sworn statements. The first set was
made around May 11th, but they wrote their complaints separately from the group
session for writing sworn statements in Charlie Company. The sworn statements by
the snipers were "lost" and never passed up the chain of command. When their commander inquired into why his snipers were being ignored, and ultimately informed
CID, a second set of statements were taken on or about July 4, 2006. That late date
still would have allowed for their statements and testimony to be included in the Article 32 hearing that began on August 1st, but the second set of statements, though not
lost, was never used. I shall explore in the next chapter the layers of cover up pertaining to their statements. In this chapter, I will analyze the gist of their criticisms of 2nd
platoon in Charlie Company, and its significance for understanding what happened
at Operation Iron Triangle.

Sworn Statement by David Chavez

Sergeant Chavez was a sniper assigned to Charlie Company and was on Operation Iron Triangle. His social role as a sniper is that he was "in" the reference group of
Charlie Company at the same time that he was partly "outside" it. This in-yet-out of
the group reference point[1] may explain why he was critical of his superiors and comrades. He explains a climate of fear and lawlessness in his sworn statement:

> Myself and the other snipers have felt unsafe about working with
> Charlie Company. I feel that most of the company has been brainwashed
> throughout the deployment to kill more whenever possible. I feel that
> the problems are caused by the 1SGT and CO. Every meeting I've been to
> involving Charlie Company their ROE has suggested killing locals who
> don't appear to be a real threat. Such as killing locals who are unarmed
> but might leave the general area. Charlie Company's 1SgT has the mental-
> ity that all locals should be killed. He has said that all Iraqis should be
> killed to me several times while I have ridden with him in his HMMWV.
> I have felt unsafe working with Charlie Company because of the company
> killing innocent civilians and creating stories to cover them up.... One
> story was about Charlie Company killing three locals in a tomato truck.
> What really happened was the gunner was nervous behind the .50 caliber
> machine gun and killed 3 civilians. After the 3 civilians were killed the
> LT of the platoon shot out both tires so it would appear that the vehicle

---

1 The sociologist Georg Simmel referred to this phenomenon as being "near and far at the
same time" in "The Stranger," in Donald N. Levine (ed.), *Georg Simmel on Individuality and
Social Forms* (Chicago: University of Chicago Press, 1971, pp. 143-49).

wouldn't stop after having its tires shot out and that it forced them to use lethal force....

Q: Have ROE briefs you've attended with other companies been as loose as Charlie Company's?

A: CCO's ROE has been the only company to authorize killing of civilians who are unarmed or don't appear to be a threat but are leaving a general area or are of military age. As opposed to other companies where the local would have to pose a threat.

SWORN STATEMENT BY CURTIS S. BALLANCE

Sergeant First Class Ballance reported another piece of the puzzle to CID regarding Charlie Company's overall behavior on Operation Iron Triangle. He also introduces the element of cover-up by his superiors: numerous sworn statements such as his apparently never made it up the chain of command. More significantly, the special agent who interviewed him on July 4th, Nichole Battle, would testify at the subsequent Article 32 hearing. But she never mentioned interviews with Balance or other soldiers who reported widespread killings such as the ones for which Clagett and Hunsaker were prosecuted. The point is that CID was also in on the cover-up:

Q: Did your soldiers tell you what happened on Iron Triangle?

A: They told me one story that during the operation that 1LT Horne said waste all of them on some objective they were on. And members of 1LT Horne's platoon, along with my soldiers said there are women and children and 1LT Horne said f___ them it's collateral damage. But they did not take the order.....

Q: Have your soldiers told you anything else about members of the 3/187th committing war crimes against the local community?

A: I was told that 1SG Geressy had taken a dead Iraqi male and placed him on the hood of the HMMWV and take him to the family members. He then removed the Iraqi hand from the body bag and slapped a local national with it and told them this was what going to happen to you....

Q: Why didn't you and your soldiers come forward with this information previously?

A: Because we sent the sworn statements up through the chain of command and we sat around and waited. Nothing happened. We continued to try to get someone to listen to us. We don't trust the battalion. We were glad when this office contacted us. The atmosphere in the battalion is bad. Charlie Company has done a lot of things and *when they write sworn statements for 15-6 investigations they write them all together.* We wanted from the beginning for our soldiers to tell their story.....

Q: Do you have anything else to add to this statement?

A: My soldiers just want their stories told. They provided statements and no one has interviewed them. They did not see what happened to the 4 detainees but they can tell you that *Charlie Company has done things that on this mission and others that are criminal.* This investigation is just one of the many that I think they are covering up and not doing the right thing. I never worked with them. I think they *use the ROE as a means to kill people.* Everyone does not deserve to be killed because they breached a convoy or because they are not actively resisting. They also could not be doing anything and *are killed because the ROE said shoot all military aged males.* But that does not give anyone an excuse to do so [emphasis added].

Sworn Statement by Jason Alan Stachowski

Specialist Stachowski gave a chilling sworn statement of unlawful killings that were occurring at roughly the same time and on the same mission that involved Claggett and Hunsaker, but in a different platoon on the other end of the island. A clearly discernible pattern begins to emerge:

Upon arrival at the gas station during Operation Iron Triangle, I was riding in the second vehicle in the order of movement.... After dismounting, 7–8 soldiers, including myself, were headed into the actual gas station to clear it. I noticed a man in a white man dress sitting on the curb. This man clearly posed no threat to Coalition forces. From behind me, I heard 1LT Horne's voice and he said, "That guy, kill that guy right there!" Since this man was not a threat, he was not engaged. SGT Beal had said something to the effect of "We're not going to kill a guy for just sitting there." This man was then instructed to raise his hands, lie face down, and stay still. At this time, we [dismounted soldiers] entered the gas station. Upon entering, we saw 5-6 male local nationals who were standing around talking. These individuals were clearly posing no threat to Coalition Forces. To the best of my knowledge, it was at or about this time when I had heard 1LT Horne say "Kill them, kill them all" or "Kill them, kill everyone in there." The men were also instructed to raise their hands, and to lie face down. All of these men willingly complied. At this time ... Coalition Forces were firing at buildings, a small market, and any vehicles that were on the objective. I was firing in the general direction, but don't remember firing at any specific target. I fired approximately 12–15 rounds. There was a heavy volume of fire that was fired off from Coalition Forces, and this volume had raised an enormous dust cloud..... I then witnessed a local national getting out of the truck, wearing a black man dress, and running in front of his vehicle ... This man, as it had appeared to me, lay down in front of his vehicle, to show as clearly as possible, that he was not a threat..... This man was then flipped over and it was obvious to me, that this man was dead.... I felt that we had initiated fire and that the man in front of the vehicle was murdered. I saw him get out of the vehicle and hustle toward the front. I do know he was on the ground face down and members of C 3/187th shot him after he was down.... But why shoot when he was face down? I agreed with Fuson that this was not the time to stop doing our job.... At this point, I had looked around for any enemy weapons and found nothing....

Q: Have you ever witnessed anything else you thought was wrong committed by members of the 3/187th?

A: Just what I have written about LT Horne. Charlie Company has a kill board and they keep track of how many kills they have within the company.... 1SG Geressy's tone in the majority of the missions is to kill....

Q: Was there any way that members of Charlie Company would think this vehicle was a threat?

A: This objective was supposed to be hostile and the ROE that was given by Horne or Hart was all military aged males were to be killed. This guy did not have a weapon and he was not posing a threat. He was getting out of a vehicle that had been shot up and in doing so he was shot while lying on the ground. I am not sure if he was shot prior to but he was shot after he was face down on the ground. *Based on the ROE they could have killed him. But morally it was wrong* [emphasis added].

Q: Who did you provide your original statements to in regards to this incident.

A: When we got back from the objective and Iron Triangle was done ... and gave them to CPT Duggan. He said he was going to give a copy to Charlie Company and the battalion Executive Officer (XO).... However, I was approached about three weeks ago by CPT Brientbutcher [sic] and he said that he had never received a copy of our sworn statements. I gave him a copy of both our statements. We signed them and took a picture of them front and back of each.

The reader should note that Special Agent Battle took this sworn statement as well and should keep this in mind when analyzing her testimony at the Article 32 hearing in subsequent chapters. A clear pattern and connection has emerged. In both LT Horne's and LT Wehrheim's platoons, the platoon sergeants refused to obey their commanding officer's unlawful orders to kill unarmed Iraqis. Prisoners were taken and lives were spared. This observation again validates Marshall's classic study which found that American soldiers are reluctant to kill except in self-defense. On the other hand, the equally clear pattern is that in both platoons, some soldiers did open fire in compliance with the unlawful orders, and no one was certain who actually killed any of the Iraqis that died. In both platoons, soldiers fired upon homes and vehicles despite their stated objections to these orders. For example, Stachowski, above, criticizes what he regards as the immoral ROE of his unit, but admits that he fired off some rounds in the "general direction" of the outgoing fire. This observation validates Stouffer's finding that soldiers feel overwhelming pressure to do what their reference group is doing, even if they sometimes resent and disobey their commanding officers.

SWORN STATEMENT BY JOSHUA D. FUSON

Fuson was also a sniper assigned to Charlie Company and "was assigned to Charlie Co. during operation Iron Triangle as a part of a 3-man sniper team." His sworn statement corroborates Stachowski and other soldiers:

When we got to about 15 meters away from the local, Lt. Horn [*sic*] (still back at the trucks on the headset radio) yells at us to kill the local sitting there. There were several other locals in the gas station who appeared to be working and talking. They saw us and did not resist or flee but began to come towards us and were following our directions. About the same time all the vehicles behind us began to engage a building complex roughly around 700 meters away and they engaged vehicles between them and the building's gas station.... Again we did not follow Lt. Horn's orders as the locals were not posing a threat.... I can remember Sgt Beal asking Lt. Horn what the hell we were shooting at and saying that if there were kids over there that he was gonna kick someone's ass. Lt. Horn's response to that was "f___ that — it's all collateral damage." I found out later that the reason we engaged those buildings was because it had been identified as an insurgent safe house. I do not know why the vehicles were engaged.... I believe it was two women and four men that we med-evaced....

Q: How did these ROE vary from previous ROE you had received on other missions?

A: On previous missions we had to feel or be threatened before we could engage anyone or anything.

Q: Further describe the actions of "the local" at the gas station prior to the order to kill him.

A: He was just sitting there on the sidewalk — not doing anything — he saw approach and did not flee and complied with our orders. The only thing he had in his hands were some papers.

Q: Why do you believe 1LT HORNE gave the order to kill him if he was not posing a threat?

A: He may have been informed by the "informant" and the interpreter in his truck that the man was an insurgent.

Q: Who was the informant?

A: A local who we took off the first objective.

Q: Is it SOP to kill someone who is not posing a threat if they are identified as an insurgent by an informant? Explain in further details what typically happens in those situations.

A: No — it is not SOP to kill someone who is identified as an insurgent. If we have a local being identified as an insurgent we would move to detain him — only if he resisted or fled would he then possibly be engaged. Just because a local identifies someone as an insurgent does not mean he is telling the truth or that the accused really is an insurgent. There could be any number of reasons why a local would lie about another — different tribes, family feuds, just an enemy. If the person is not a threat there is hardly ever a reason to engage them.

Q: Did 1LT HORNE say or do anything when his orders were not followed?

A: No.

Q: Why did you not follow his orders?

A: *I felt his orders to kill the man were morally wrong and against a US Soldier's values.....*

Q: When were the statements handed to MAJ DEVOUX?

A: Around the 16th of May or so.

Q: Which person handed the statements to LTC JOHNSON? How do you know they were handed to him?

A: SFC Balance and CPT Britenbugher [*sic*] handed it to him together. I know because SFC Balance [*sic*] told me they did it.....

Q: How do you think the 1SG and Commander of C Co. encourage hostility?

A: Their attitude toward Iraqis — they view everyone as an enemy and think the more kills their soldiers have the better they are....

Q: To your knowledge, was 1LT HORNE ever questioned or an inquiry done into his actions on Iron Triangle?

A: I do not know.

Q: With your grasp of the mission, the ROE, and the situation; do you believe the orders given by 1LT HORNE were sufficient to have him re-lieved of command?

A: Yes. I do not believe he should be in charge of troops in combat be-cause of the decisions he made that day....

Q: Why do you think others in C Company have not come forward?

A: *I think most are scared of their chain of command and are not sure what to do. Others may just not care* [emphasis added].

This statement provides more confirmation for the pattern that the sworn state-ments taken from soldiers in LT Horne's platoon, which were clearly critical of the unlawful ROE and the chain of command, were ignored. On the other hand, the initial sworn statements taken from LT Wehrheim's platoon, which were clearly a cover-up and not critical of the ROE or the chain of command, were the ones initially accepted and validated by the battalion commanders. CID had at least two sets of diametrically opposed statements from LT Horne's and LT Wehrheim's platoons. Murder occurred in both platoons. Soldiers tried to disobey the unlawful ROE in both platoons. But LT Horne's soldiers were willing to expose him while LT Wehrheim's soldiers were not. Why did CID choose to prosecute some of LT Wehrheim's soldiers based upon perjury? It would have been more logical and efficient to prosecute LT Horne or some of his soldiers based upon honest statements. The obvious answer is that it was easier to throw the low-ranking soldiers, Clagett and Hunsaker, "under the bus," as the saying goes. It would have been much more difficult to prosecute LT Horne or any of the junior officers because they were privy to months of briefings on the unlawful ROE, and would have brought down their commanders with them. Here we encounter the specter of conspiracy and Machiavellian schemes. Commonsense dictates that the army reasoned, in a cost-benefit analysis, that it was in its interest to prosecute soldiers in LT Wehrheim's platoon, because they could depict them as perjurers and thereby not risk exposing the commanders. But it was not in the army's short-term interest to rely upon honest statements by soldiers in LT Horne's platoon who were clearly willing to testify under oath that their commanding officers were immoral, unprofessional, violated laws, and violated US Army values.

Sworn Statement by Jonathon P. Breitenbucher

In his sworn statement, Captain Breitenbucher cited a rather long list of superior officers to whom he and other soldiers had complained about the outcome of Operation Iron Triangle. The battalion commander, LTC Nathaniel Johnson, told him that he had never seen any of the sworn statements. But this is the same LTC Johnson who approved the unlawful ROE, initiated proceedings against Clagett, Hunsaker, Graber, and Girouard, and above all, who requested the death penalty for these soldiers. "The next morning SFC Curtis Ballance and myself took the documents to the Battalion Commander. SFC Curtis Balance, a day later, told me that the Battalion Commander had informed him that the situation had already been investigated." But, Captain Breitenbucher observes in his statement, LTC Johnson "is the approving authority for kill-kill orders." The CID agent asked him to explain a kill-kill order, and the Captain answered that the target is not given a chance to surrender; rather, "my understanding is the authority is there to kill the individual after positive identification." The Captain described a situation in which the battalion commander would have to investigate himself and his superiors if he were to take seriously the sworn statements that documented the unlawful killings in LT Horne's platoon. It is highly significant that the meaning of the unlawful ROE or "kill-kill" orders was that no prisoners were to be taken, because Clagett, Hunsaker, Graber, and Girouard were prosecuted for killing prisoners. Captain Breitenbucher was never asked to testify at the Article 32 hearing or any of the subsequent courts-martial proceedings.

Q: What is the command climate like at FOB Brassfield-Mora?

A: Everybody is wondering what is going on.

Q: In regard to?

A: Everything.

Q: Do you know what LTC JOHNSON did with the statements you gave him?

A: No....

Q: How do you know who the approving authority for a "kill-kill" order is?

A: Cause LTC JOHNSON said it.....

Q: Why are you coming forward with this information?

A: Cause I don't believe the information was passed to the proper personnel.

Q: What do you know about an incident on 17 Jan 06, during which members of 3rd Platoon, C CO, 3-187 shot and killed two men in a semi-truck (possibly hauling a load of tomatoes) on MSR Tampa on the Tigris River Bridge?

A: I know what the question just stated.

Q: What do you know about ILT HAWKINS pushing or throwing an Iraqi male to the ground, resulting in the man sustaining a broken jaw or any other injury?

A: I have heard of it....

Q: What do you know about an operation in which members of 3-17 INF killed a 7-year-old girl during an operation on 22 May targeting a HVT [high value target]?

A: I know that it happened, that's all...

Q: What are your feelings about "kill-kill" orders?

A: I think it is a gross misinterpretation of the ROE. The ROE states that in order to engage the enemy they must have hostile intent.

Q: What is your feeling on the statements from the scouts?

A: ... the biggest thing I recall is the order given by ILT HORNE to "kill them, kill all of them."

The euphemism "high value target" has been in circulation for about eight years now. The "kill-kill" orders to liquidate a HVT without giving the "target" a chance to surrender amount to authorized assassinations. Several other incidents involving unlawful killing of civilians emerge in this statement, including the frequently cited "tomato truck" incident. None of these incidents were ever prosecuted. All of them form a pattern in sync with the Iron Triangle killings. Only the killing of the 7-year-old girl would be mentioned in the subsequent Article 32 hearing, and then in the context of collateral damage. One is left wondering why this captain was willing to criticize his reference group, namely, fellow commissioned officers as well as commanders.

Sworn Testimony of John P. Duggan

CPT Duggan was the commander of the snipers who were attached to Charlie Company. He stated that his snipers "wanted to make sworn statements regarding the actions of 1LT Horne" during Operation Iron Triangle. Most of the time, soldiers are compelled to make sworn statements, but Duggan's soldiers wanted to make them.

Q: Did 1LT HORNE's actions appear to violate the Laws of Armed Conflict?

A: I believe there possibly were violations in there. Some of his decisions were questionable.

Q: Can you provide examples?

A: His instructions to kill a guy sitting on the curb and his instructions later to kill the men inside the gas station.

Q: Have you heard of an incident involving the death of a pregnant woman near the Samara Hospital?

A: Yes, I was not present but I remember reading about it on the news and hearing about it from individuals from B Co....

Q: Do you have anything else to add?

A: The only gap that I can see in the history of the three sworn statements is why they did not end up in the commander's inquiry made after the operation took place.

Perhaps no one will ever discover why the statements by the snipers were squelched. But several immediate consequences followed from the fact that their statements were not included in the inquiry following Operation Iron Triangle. None of them would be called to testify in the Article 32 hearing. Their statements were never part of the official investigation of the mission. The gas station incident would never come up in the court-martial process. The pattern of killings in Charlie Company would remain hidden and could not be used by the defense in the courts-martial. It is an open question whether these were intentional consequences due to conspiracy on the part of the government or unintended consequences. But one thing is certain: the gas station and other incidents of using the unlawful ROE point to an unmistakable pattern. And the cover-up — if there was one — of this pattern would be consistent with the pattern of covering up abuses at Abu Ghraib and Guantanamo, and laying all the blame for an unlawful policy onto a handful of so-called "rotten apples."

Sworn Testimony of First Sergeant Eric Geressy

In a long, 10-page, single-spaced, typed, sworn statement, First Sergeant Geressy was asked about some of the charges that had been made by the snipers and other soldiers. Regarding the tomato truck incident, he said that his soldiers "said the vehicle started to drive quickly at them and they fired a disabling shot at the grill when they fired the men in the tomato truck opened fire." This interpretation contradicts soldiers who said that the drivers in the "tomato truck" were unarmed and showed no hostile intent. Regarding the kill board, he said: "It was a tool to try and help the Soldiers get over the guilty feeling that some Soldiers might have after killing the enemy." Geressy closed his statement with the claim: "In Charlie Company we try our best to take care of the Soldiers, make sure they do the right thing, and to get them back home. We have been very aggressive in taking the fight to the enemy and not letting the enemy take the fight to us." The CID agent had many questions:

Q: What was lLT HORNE's ROE on that part of the mission?

A: The only declared hostile force was on Objective Murray [the island]. The ROE that should have been used was any hostile act or hostile intent could you then engage the enemy....

Q: At any time was there a kill or capture order for all military age males at the gas station area?

A: No....

Q: Had you previously heard of any conspiracy to cover up any other actions on that incident?

A: No....

Q: Why was action not taken against lLT HORNE for the decisions he made and the unlawful orders given?

A: In my opinion, based upon the information he had and his prior knowledge of the area....

Q: Were the statements given by the snipers/scouts added to the commander's inquiry that had previously been given to 3/320th?

A: I have no idea....

Q: Whose idea was the "kill board?"

A: Mine. I got the idea from the one hanging at Battalion. I just kept it running, *the intent was to desensitize the soldier for when they have to kill the enemy and drive on to what they have to do every day* [emphasis added].

If Geressy's remarks are treated as truthful and consistent, namely, that lLT Horne was *not* authorized to use the unlawful ROE but lLT Wehrheim was authorized to kill every male on the island — whether or not he was taken prisoner — then certain logical conclusions should have followed. First, lLT Horne should have been prosecuted for using an unlawful ROE. But he was not, and the reports of his behavior were squelched from going up the chain of command. Second, lLT Wehrheim's soldiers should not have been prosecuted for following the unlawful ROE — they killed every male Iraqi they could, including the ones they took prisoners. But Wehrheim's soldiers were the ones who were prosecuted. Geressy's explanations are not logical, but they are consistent with the pattern described by the snipers: that Charlie Company rationalizes its kills in any way that is expedient. First Sergeant Geressy invoked his rights and refused to testify at the Article 32 hearing.

There is something odd in Geressy's admission that the kill board was used intentionally by the command to "desensitize" soldier toward killing. Lawyers generally use such intentional efforts to desensitize and dehumanize soldiers as evidence of corrupt command climates, but Geressy did not seem to see any reason to feel ashamed for the remark. Later in this book, I shall connect Geressy's remarks with other, documented, systemic efforts to desensitize soldiers toward killing.

A Compilation of Other Sworn Testimony

Many other sworn statements were given concerning other massacres committed by Charlie Company during Operation Iron Triangle as well as other missions. Since space does not permit a more complete analysis, in the remainder of this section I will compile comments concerning other killings; the testimony came from many soldiers in addition to the sniper unit and its commanders.

Sergeant Armando L. Acevedo was asked by a CID agent: "Have you ever been authorized to kill High Value Targets (HVT) immediately upon positive identification (PID) without allowing them a chance to surrender? If so when, where and by whom?" He replied: "Yes, I have. On the 22nd of May we had an operation to destroy an IED cell in our sector. Our HVT was named Adnon, and our objective was on the south side of the bypass bridge. The order to kill upon PID was given from 1SG Geressy and CPT Hart and that the guidance came from the Battalion level."

Note that this mission was carried out after Operation Iron Triangle. Clearly, no lessons were learned. Hunting down and killing HVTs was frequently reported by journalists during the war in Iraq — and reported with considerable enthusiasm — with no protests from jurists, human rights organizations, journalists, or other elite professionals. In other words, there is a connection, a pattern, in the actions of Charlie Company and numerous other similar killings.

Sergeant Paul Daily Terrell told special agent Nicole Battle: "I heard 1SG Geressy talking to someone from SSG Girouard's squad on the situation back at the objective ... 1SG said something about the detainees still being alive or why does SSG Girouard's squad have three detainees." Terrell gave a more detailed account of why SSG Girouard did *not* follow the unlawful ROE on the mission, and disclosed the new piece of information that COL Steele personally rewarded Girouard for the kills prior to Girouard and three of his soldiers being prosecuted:

> We were to kill every military age male. I was surprised the guy with the baby was not killed. Girouard's squad would have killed the guy if he did not have the baby. Girouard was screaming God Damn punk want put down the baby and the guy would move the baby and Girouard would move the weapon. I know when we were coming over here people would say I can't wait to kill one of those "Bibbs." I would say you don't want that because it would be something you would have to live with for the rest of your life. *COL Steele came out on the objective and gave members of Girouard's squad a knife for the kills, the knife was about 12 inches long. I have never seen*

him give out anything before. The ROE changed and he also gave out that knife like it was a good thing [emphasis added].

The medic, Micah Brandon Bivens, also described to special agent Battle other, similar incidents:

> Q: Do you think there have been some times when Iraqi people have been shot without cause?
>
> A: Yes, there was an IED that happened in our sector and a cordon was emplaced. There were two cars were fleeing the area and, 1SG Geressy said over the radio to kill the people that were running.... They fired at the cars and killed the driver of the first car, there was a little boy about 4 years old with a bullet wound to his leg, a little girls about 6 years old that had shrapnel in her chin and wrist, an adult woman with two gunshot wounds to the legs and an adult male with a gunshot wound to the head. In the second car the driver had a deep grazing wound to his leg....
>
> Q: Do you think the ROE has anything to do with the large amount of kills Charlie Company has?
>
> A: Yes, because there is a list. The high value target (HVT) list has persons on it who are confirmed bad guys and they are to be killed on sight after confirmation that it is actually them. Operation Iron Triangle ROE was to kill all military age males on the island.
>
> Q: Are there other incidents in which you believe innocent people were killed?
>
> A: Yes. On an operation before I left for leave there was a little girl who got shot. She was in the house and she and her father were shot and killed. He was on the list. I did not see this first hand *but it's like shoot first and ask questions later* [emphasis added].

The third sniper, Geoffrey Daniel Kugler described how when he heard the order from LT Horne to kill the Iraqis at the gas station, he looked to his friend and said, "Hey, this is f___ed up." "I told him, shoot and miss, scare them."

> Q: What was your opinion of the mission?
>
> A: That it got out of control. Part of it was the ROE.

Special Agent Nicole Battle interviewed SSG Cameron Ronald Armendariz, who added yet another incident from Operation Iron Triangle:

> The second incident was Keugler in an over watch position and radioed that he noticed two men digging in a field. He received confirmation via radio and he was told to engage. He stated he fired over their heads. Purposely missing and radioed back that he was unable to get a clear shot. He was told to go intercept the two individuals, which he did. They turned out to be an elderly farmer and his mentally challenged son, planting in the field.

Q: Have they told you any other incidents that may have taken place while attached to Charlie Company that they felt was wrong or criminal?

A: They say they were excluded from giving sworn statements during the time Charlie was giving their sworn statements....

Q: Did they write sworn statements?

A: Yes they did and they provided them to me and CPT DUGGAN, Platoon Leader. DUGGAN told me he provided them to CPT Hart and MAJ Delvaux....

Q: Why didn't they contact this [CID] office sooner?

A: We thought CID was going to come down and contact us because they had provided sworn statements to the chain of command.

Q: Do you have anything else to add to this statement?

A: Yes. I am disgusted with the battalion. The lack of integrity of the senior command group. PFC's in the battalion would make jokes about Charlie Company is the kill company and the senior officers pretend to have no idea about what is going on.

CONCLUSIONS

One of many ironies in assessing the hidden background of this case is that on 8 September 2008, First Sergeant Eric Geressy was awarded a Silver Star for his gallantry in Iraq. By this time, Clagett, Hunsaker, Graber, and Girouard were all in prison. COL Steele was present and spoke at the ceremony. Geressy's mother was also present, and made an intriguing comment about her son: "When he was a teenager he was a handful and I figured Oh my God, he's going to come back in chains, but he surprised us all and no one more than me."[1] Why would a mother make such a comment at her son's award ceremony? This is a classic example of Bateson's double-bind, whereby a mother simultaneously praises and criticizes her child. The irony is that Geressy came back with a medal while several of his soldiers came back in chains for following policies established by him and other commanders.

The evidence presented in this chapter leads to several conclusions. In all cases involving abuse or war crimes, the government goes out of its way to depict the accused as lone wolves, "rotten apples," and in general, as isolated "bad guys" who have dishonored the army. This is a myth, unsupported by facts in any of the war crimes cases, from Abu Ghraib to Operation Iron Triangle. The facts in this case, as in all others, are in line with the classic studies in the social sciences: American soldiers are extremely reluctant to kill or abuse the enemy. When they do commit war crimes, they always act in the context of reference groups that exhibit poisoned command and social climates. The soldiers who are able to notice and criticize the war crimes are typically affiliated with different reference groups with a healthier command and

---

1 http://www.army.mil/-news/2008/09/08/12211-geressy-earns-silver-star/

social climate — this is clearly the case with the snipers who worked with but did not belong to Charlie Company. Similarly, the whistleblowers at Abu Ghraib were not locked into the daily misery of working in the poisoned social climate in Tier 1A.

But additional conclusions may be drawn from the conclusions above. Once war crimes have been committed because of a poisoned reference group which normalizes unlawful ROE, those crimes cannot be effectively investigated or prosecuted by the very poisoned reference group that caused the war crimes. Genuine justice, investigation, and remedy must come from another, healthier and independent reference group. Instead of following this commonsense conclusion, the army compounded the atrocities at Operation Iron Triangle. The very commanding officers who issued, reinforced, and perpetuated the unlawful ROE investigated and prosecuted the crimes committed as the result of the bad ROE. Commonsense dictates that commanders will not indict or prosecute themselves. The commanders had to find scapegoats. LT Horne was an unlikely candidate for prosecution because he could indict his fellow officers. Clagett, Hunsaker, Graber, and Girouard were perfect for the role of scapegoats because of their low rank and because they were already trapped by going along with the cover-up orchestrated by their platoon leader.

This state of affairs leads to the intricate conspiracy that followed. Obviously, no one had to be prosecuted, given that the initial investigations cleared everyone in the brigade, from the commanders to the soldiers, of any and all wrongdoing. Evidence suggests that this military unit had routinely covered up previous crimes. Why would this mission be any different? There may be several unknown factors, but at least two are obvious. First, no one predicted the tenacity of the snipers and their junior officers in insisting that their criticisms be heard by CID and the chain of command. Second, Major Sullivan's investigative report — which will be analyzed in the next chapter — included a loose end that was not noticed in the initial cover-up. He reported officially and formally that the blind folds were still on the bodies of the dead Iraqis at the make-shift morgue, and somebody had cut them at the morgue. The obvious, commonsense question raised by this fact is: "Why would American soldiers kill blindfolded enemy combatants?" Now the brigade had a problem. The original story by LT Wehrheim's soldiers that the Iraqi prisoners had cut themselves free would not stand. At this point, somebody had to be "thrown under the bus." It seems to be a universal principle that in such situations, the scapegoats are always the weakest and most vulnerable members of the reference group. Suddenly, the group turns on them, and transforms them into the enemy within. I leave it up to the reader to verify this principle from numerous historical examples, such as the Salem witch trials, to everyday agonies of the scapegoat in dysfunctional families. A healthy, functional social group will produce wonders. But a dysfunctional, poisoned, threatened reference group will inexorably destroy its weakest members for its apparent survival.

Chapter 3. Covering Up Major Sullivan's Cover-Up Report

> "They can prepare as many official reports as they want and choose whichever ones they need on any given occasion. Didn't you know that?"
> — Joseph Heller, *Catch-22*, p. 406

Recall that Lieutenant Colonel Nathaniel Johnson was the battalion commander who authorized the "kill-kill" orders. Yet he was also the commander who initiated the proceedings against the accused soldiers in this story, and appointed the investigative officer for the Article 32 hearing on 21 June 2006. In addition, on 11 July 2006, he officially requested that the charges against the soldiers be punished with the death penalty. In a memorandum to the investigative officer appointed by him, he wrote: "Additionally, you are to enumerate and explain in detail which, if any, of the aggravating factors listed in RCM 1004(c)(1) exist in this case which could potentially warrant a sentence of death for any of the above listed individuals."

The death penalty is extremely rare in military courts-martial. One of the most infamous cases of the death penalty in the army was immortalized in the book and film titled *The Execution of Private Slovik*.[1] Slovik was the only soldier executed during World War II for desertion, and his crime was brought on by combat stress. Stouffer reports that the army executed one hundred and two soldiers during World War II for murder and rape, but only one (Slovik) for desertion. The context for Stouffer's observations on the death penalty is the following: First, the army uses punishment, including the threat of the death penalty, as a technique to close the door to the tempting option for the soldier to disobey orders or exit the combat situation. Second, he devotes many pages to the issue of the army's "code of masculinity" (volume 2, p. 131), which leads to a complex view of comrades who go AWOL, disobey orders,

---

1 William B. Huie, *The Execution of Private Slovik* (New York: Westholme, 2004). Slovik was also from the 101st Airborne Division, which was involved in the Operation Iron Triangle killings.

or otherwise depart from expectations. The important point is that the very thought of soldiers killing (executing) other soldiers offends the moral code of army soldiers who regard each other as a surrogate family. He found that World War II soldiers were overwhelmingly sympathetic to their comrades for experiencing "shell shock," which they distinguished sharply from "cowardice" (volume 2, p. 178). In every single case in which I participated pertaining to the current war, enlisted soldiers exhibited a similar sympathy for comrades who were accused of "war crimes" and expressed bitterness at the army for prosecuting them. The "code of masculinity" uncovered by Stouffer seems to have survived intact in the current war. The problem is that prosecutors, defense attorneys, soldiers, and the public hold different understandings of what it means to "be a man" (volume 2, p. 131) versus a "coward" in combat. The Operation Iron Triangle defense attorneys were extremely upset at the possibility that the soldiers they were defending were facing the death penalty under the circumstances already examined, namely, a combat situation in a unit with many command climate problems. They reasoned that committing a murder in combat during a state of war is vastly different from civilian murders performed in the context of "aggravating factors" such as kidnapping or some other felony, which typically do qualify as death penalty cases. Soldiers have said to me: "It's not like we went into a school in the US and opened fire on school children. We were on a combat mission."

Ironically, the presiding officer of the Article 32 cited precisely the context of war as the "aggravating factor" that justified the death penalty. This is yet another example of a double-bind trap. Being in combat can be interpreted as an aggravating or a mitigating factor, depending upon one's reference point. On August 31, 2006, Lieutenant Colonel James P. Daniel wrote a memorandum to Lieutenant Colonel Nathan Johnson in which he stated:

> In accordance with the 11 July 2006 amendment to my appointment orders, I find the following aggravating factor listed in RCM 1004(c)(6) exists and warrants a sentence of death: that the offenses were committed in time of war and in territory in which the United States or an ally of the United States was then an occupying power or in which the armed forced of the United States were engaged in active hostilities.

All four of the accused were thereafter subjected to the possibility of the death penalty: SSG Raymond L. Girouard, Specialist William Hunsaker, PFC Corey Claggett, and Specialist Juston Graber. Why did the army turn so suddenly and viciously on four soldiers who had been exonerated in initial investigative reports? Answers to this question will emerge from a careful examination of events between May 11, 2006, the date of the first sworn statements, and August 1, 2006, when the Article 32 hearing was convened.

Mr. Waddington filed several motions, including a request for a speedy trial based upon the 6th Amendment of the United States Constitution, which was denied. He also requested testimony from the following individuals: COL Michael Steele, CPT Daniel Hart, CPT Jason Sienko, 1LT Justin Wehrheim, and 1SG Eric Geressy. Clearly, these are all the crucial actors in the drama under study here, and they could all illuminate details pertaining to Operation Iron Triangle and the ROE. Out of this list, only 1LT Wehrheim testified at the Article 32 hearing, and none of these individuals were compelled to testify at the subsequent court hearings.

Mr. Waddington also filed a reply to the government's request to delay Hunsaker's trial (formally known as a "motion for continuance"). Mr. Waddington argued in the reply that

> While in confinement in Kuwait, SPC Hunsaker was held in solitary confinement, [and] while in confinement in Kuwait, SPC Hunsaker had minimal access to legal counsel.... [He] was often required to sleep with hand irons on. At times, the hand irons were attached to his waist, severely restricting his movement.... [He] was ordinarily forced to keep the lights on inside of his confinement tent, even while he tried to sleep."

Hunsaker's motions for a speedy trial were denied. He was kept in solitary confinement throughout the pre-trial period in Kuwait or the Naval Brig in Charleston, South Carolina.

On 24 July 2006, the government issued a protective order. It read that any material marked as "classified" or "classifiable" could not be used as evidence. Mr. Waddington told me that there is no such thing as a category of "classifiable" evidence, and in practice, this turned out to be a catch-all to keep out of testimony anything the government did not want to be considered. Several documents were specifically mentioned as being off limits for the court-martial proceedings:

- the "investigation by Brigadier General Maffey,"
- the "14 March 06 Operation Iron Triangle Commander's Black Brief,"
- "the 4 May 06 OPORDER briefs to Operation Iron Triangle," and
- "the classified ... ROE annexes."

It is odd that the government would label as secret documents that could have helped in the defense of its own soldiers.

The protective order also listed specific information that could be used, including:

- "What an accused Soldier was subjectively told the ROE for Operation Iron Triangle was,"
- "actions and activities that took place ... on 9 May 2006 or 21 July 2006,"
- "unclassified substitutes" and "any relevant DA Form 2823 (Sworn Statement),"

The protective order was signed by Lieutenant Nathaniel Johnson, "Convening Authority."

A CLIMATE OF FEAR AND BETRAYAL DESCENDS UPON THE UNIT

Prior to any court proceedings, all soldiers had their cameras, film, videotapes, and VCRs confiscated by the government. Soldiers became very scared, as suggested by this e-mail exchange between a soldier named Jonathan Porter and the sergeant who recruited him. On Monday, May 15, 2006, Porter wrote to his mentor:

> Hey I'm doing fine over here until a couple of days ago. We went on a 3 day mission into the desert to fight some insurgents camped along the border. Well we ended up taking like 300 detainees. There were only like 50 of us so it was a pain in the ass screening them and feeding them and

shit. Well a couple of guys told me to cut the zip ties and shit off and say they tried to fight them and escape. CID is coming to investigate and this isn't sitting well on my conscience. This is the second time something like this happened with this same Infantry company. After I said that this was unacceptable to the one sergeant he told me later on that day to take the garbage from our camp out to a burn pit 1 mile out into the desert with all Iraqis. He told me to leave my weapon I wouldn't need it. Then when we got there the Iraqis drove me right into the fire pit. *I don't know if he's trying to scare me or kill me.* I'm stuck with these knuckle heads for about another month so I don't know what to do.

His sergeant replied to him:

This is beyond serious business. I am telling you as a leader and a friend, you need to keep this under wraps until the investigation is in full swing. What I am telling you is keep your mouth shut and be very careful who you talk to. When CID does come around make sure you use your right to remain silent until you see an attorney. See an attorney first. In the mean time remain safe, don't do anything that puts you or others in un-needed harms way.

The soldier wrote back:

Yeah the Battalion XO and CID came by and did their investigation but they didn't even ask me any questions. They only confiscated pictures from everyone. I find it funny cause one picture is of our brigade commander, Col. Steele with his foot on one of the detainee's heads. *Anyway he's the one that cut the zip ties off and blind folds* I'm gonna take your advice and just shut up and not say anything. I was just overwhelmed from what I saw when it first happened I guess. If they do ask me questions I will get an attorney like you said. Thank you if anything else comes up I'll let you know [emphasis added].

This soldier's former recruiter was investigated by CID and betrayed his recruit. He submitted the e-mail exchange and in his sworn statement (which is not classified) seized upon the key phrase from the soldier: "He also made a statement that put the BDE CDR COL Steele at the scene of the alleged shooting." At this point, the soldier, Jonathan Porter, was immediately investigated by CID and made an official sworn statement on May 22, 2006. Porter wrote, in part:

Colonel Steele came over to the bodies and picked one up by the head and then dropped it. Then that one of his PSD soldier took with a digital camera. Col. Steele then got out a Gerber [knife] and cut off one of the blind folds around the dead man's head and he cut off the zip ties too. 2 direct quotes I do remember Colonel Steele saying at about that very moment where Colonel Steele put his boot on one of the dead Iraqi's head and posed for a picture. "I guess we'll have to say these guys tried to escape," in a sarcastic tone. He also went on to say, "Good job but we need more bodies.".... The new bodies were also brought in the same way also blind folded and zip tied. Colonel Steele had left by this point.

Is it true that the brigade commander was present during the shooting and later participated in the cover-up by cutting the zip ties and blind folds? Porter's testimony was never invoked for testimony and cross-examination. The CID agent who took the recruiter's as well as Porter's sworn statements did not ask many questions. However, approximately one month later, Porter was reduced to the rank of a private as punishment under Article 15 for allegedly using cocaine (based upon urine tests). Porter simply disappeared from this story. Was he silenced by the government for knowing too much and, what's more important, daring to disclose it to a trusted mentor?

How Far Does the Cover-Up Extend and When Did It Begin?

Let us return to the strand of suppressed evidence from the discussion above, Porter's e-mail dated May 15th in which he claimed that he saw the brigade commander cut the "blind folds." The killings occurred on May 9th. The first set of sworn statements were written on May 11th, and an investigative report cleared all the soldiers of any wrongdoing on May 21st. Porter's sworn statement was taken on May 22nd, one day after the brigade cleared itself of any wrongdoing, and his claims threw a monkey wrench into the army's initial story and investigation. Why would anyone be inclined to cut the "blind folds" on dead bodies? The obvious answer is that in the initial reports issued by high-ranking officers in this military unit, the story was that the Iraqi prisoners had somehow cut their zip ties, loosened their "blind folds," and attempted to escape. One should note carefully that these reports and cover-stories were written by Captain Daniel Hart, the West Point graduate and company commander, and Major Timothy Sullivan, the investigating officer for what is known as an AR 15-6 investigation. An AR 15-6 investigation is a serious matter. For example, the famous Taguba report was an AR 15-6 investigation. I have already documented CPT Hart's report — which cleared Charlie Company of any wrongdoing — in *Rules of Engagement?*[1] The important point is that it was *not* the accused soldiers who invented the stories of the prisoners escaping as justification for killing them, along with the necessary fictions that their zip-ties were cut and blind folds removed. Rather, the commissioned officers invented these stories, and as noted previously, made sure that the entire 3rd squad stuck to this story. To repeat: the entire squad wrote out their sworn statements in a group setting while copying information from a blackboard.

Major Sullivan's detailed report inadvertently ruined the cover-up by making an important allusion to the dead bodies, the "blind folds," and other details that are out of sync with the cover story. He wrote in his official report, dated May 21, 2006:

> The bodies were evacuated from OBJ Murray and brought to the vicinity of the RED KNIGHT TAC/Field Trains area by helicopter. Upon their arrival at the Field Trains area ... the remains were viewed and photographed by members of the 3BCT Staff (MAJ Frank Jenio, Cecil Clark and Stephen Treanor, *and COL Michael Steele*). The photographs were taken for intelligence collection purposes (Exhibits 6–8). At this point the members of the BCT staff noticed that the EKIA *had Engineer tape around various parts of their head region*. The remains were further viewed by members of the TF 3-320 FA S2 section for documentation into the Biometric Analysis Tool set. *The evidence from that OBJ area, to include the knife that cut Hunsaker, was lost*

---

1 Stjepan G. Mestrovic, *Rules of Engagement? A Social Anatomy of an American War Crime — Operation Iron Triangle, Iraq* (New York: Algora, 2008).

> *somewhere during the transport of the prisoners and the turnover of the remains to TF 3-320 FA personnel. The remains were then transported to FOB Brassfield-Mora by the members of G/626 Forward Support Company* [emphasis added].

The reader should note carefully: the "blind folds" were actually engineer tape. In line with Porter's e-mails and sworn statement, Major Sullivan also placed Colonel Steele at the scene of the viewing of the bodies, and wrote that the bodies had engineer tape on their heads. Scores of witnesses are cited by Major Sullivan. The gruesome photographs of the bodies do *not* show any tape or any sort of "blind folds" on the heads of the victims. The obvious, commonsense conclusion is that someone cut the engineer tape prior to photographing the dead bodies at the army base — presumably to make it seem as if the Iraqi victims had loosened their "blind folds" prior to having been shot. But the photographs taken at the make-shift morgue were completely different from the photographs taken at the killing site, which showed the tape or "blind folds." It no longer seems a mystery that the government confiscated all the photographs. The knife that allegedly cut Hunsaker also disappeared mysteriously, and thereby prevented DNA evidence testing that would confirm or disprove the false version of events. Finally, the bodies were not autopsied, as required by directives, and the bodies simply disappeared.

Mr. Waddington showed me Department of Defense directives which require autopsies in cases that involve deaths of prisoners in the custody of the armed forces of the United States. Furthermore, the directives order that "the body will not be released from United States custody without written authorization from the investigative agency concerned." In the Iron Triangle killings, the three bodies of the dead Iraqis vanished from the hangar in which they were temporarily stored on the US Army base. Clearly, the directives were not followed, and one has a right to wonder which American military commander authorized the "release" of the dead bodies prior to autopsy or investigation. In the following chapter, I will refer to testimony from the Article 32 hearing which shows that the army made no effort to find or exhume the bodies. One should note carefully that in all the subsequent charge sheets, the soldiers were prosecuted for shooting "three male detainees of apparent Middle-Eastern descent whose names are unknown."

But there is more to this mystery. Mr. Waddington told me that at some point in the Article 32 investigation the prosecutor tried to enter into the court record three Iraqi death certificates that purportedly corresponded to the three dead bodies. Mr. Waddington found that one of the death certificates was for a 13-year-old boy, among other discrepancies. In a huff, the prosecutor withdrew the death certificates, and the death of the victims was never formally established. I said to Mr. Waddington that none of this exchange shows up in the trial transcript. He replied that this exchange, along with many other exchanges, was deliberately not put on the record.

Major Sullivan's report was a huge obstacle to the government's case because — especially in the hands of defense attorneys — it is the smoking gun that suggests a government cover-up, tampering with evidence, prosecutorial misconduct, obstruction of justice, conspiracy and a host of other grievances.

It is no surprise that Major Sullivan's report never made it into any court proceeding transcript. It would be treated by the government as if it did not exist. In a phrase, the cover-up had to be covered up, because it was flawed.

In fact, the defense attorneys did not know that it existed and did not have a copy of Major Sullivan's investigative report until February of 2007. Let us recall the time line: Major Sullivan's report was issued on May 21, 2006, the Article 32 was held on August 1, 2006, and the plea-bargains were held in the Spring of 2007. Thus, the defense attorneys went through the motions of the entire pre-trial hearing and preparations for trial without access to this crucial document authored by Major Sullivan, as well as its connection to Porter's statement. I asked Mr. Waddington whether the government was obligated to show them this document through rules of discovery, and he said that technically they were not, except at the actual trial. But of course, there were no actual trials for Hunsaker and Clagett (only plea-bargains), so that Major Sullivan's report was effectively covered up in this entire case.

THE SMOKING GUN: MAJOR SULLIVAN'S REPORT

Major Sullivan's report reaches the following overall conclusion:

> Given the circumstances of the assault and the briefed ROE, I find that the actions of SSG Girouard, Lemus, and SPC Hunsaker in engaging the male in the window of the house was justified, and that no adverse action be taken on these Soldiers for the initial engagement. In the case of the three detainees shot and killed by SPC Hunsaker and PFC Clagett, I find that the Soldiers clearly acted in self-defense fearing for their safety as they were physically assaulted by the detainees. As such, I find there was not a violation of the ROE or the Law of Armed Conflict (LOAC). *I recommend no action be taken against SPC Hunsaker or PFC Clagett for their actions with regards to the shooting of the three men* [emphasis added].

Typically, a recommendation in an official investigative report that no action be taken against soldiers is followed. The report is dated 21 May 2006, and as of that date, the case was closed. Ten days later, on 31 May 2006, CID was taking sworn statements from about seventy soldiers. What happened in that 10-day time frame to make the army not only disregard Major Sullivan's findings and recommendations, but cover-up his report, and turn its energy toward prosecuting four particular low-ranking soldiers? We will never know the answer, but several clues emerge from Major Sullivan's report.

He writes in the background section that he was appointed to serve as investigating officer on 11 May 2009. But that is the same day that LT Wehrheim's platoon made their sworn statements *in a group setting*. All the statements were basically identical, and the soldiers were putting into their own words information that was on a chalk board in front of them. The snipers whose statements were analyzed in the previous chapter were excluded from this group meeting, and their statements — which differed from this platoon — were initially lost, and, were *never included in Major Sullivan's report*. Major Sullivan dutifully lists the soldiers and officers whose sworn statements he had read and attached to his report: Clagett, Hunsaker, Mason, Kemp, Ryan, Girouard, Lemus, Helton, Graber, Bivens, and Wehrheim. There were scores of other reports with a different perspective that he did not list. Did Major Sullivan not see the other sniper statements which implicated LT Horne and the entire brigade, or did he choose not to include the sniper statements? If there was a conspiracy, as the army alleged later, clearly it started from the commissioned officers who instructed the soldiers, not spontaneously from the soldiers themselves. It was a top-down conspiracy, not a bottom-up conspiracy. To put it bluntly, certain commissioned officers decided which information would be included as well as excluded in the social construction of reality of what happened.

Major Sullivan states that on the entire mission, US soldiers "engaged and killed 15 Al Qaida in Iraq." His rationale was that intelligence pre-designated the dead men as Al Qaida terrorists, not that he had any objective proof: "This intelligence estimate included the positive identification of the OBJ MURRAY [subsequent phrase blacked out] thus reaffirming that the objective contained AQIZ terrorists." He also refers to another incident which managed to disappear from the larger story: "During the initial assault attack aviation assets did engage and kill three suspected AIF [anti-Iraqi forces] members attempting to flee the OBJ area in a boat." These could have been terrorists, and they could have been ordinary Iraqis trying to flee a battle. Under the section marked "findings," the written ROE are blacked out, along with the "Annex E (Rules of Engagement) to Operations Order 05-06 (Shareka) 3rd BCT, 101st ABN DIV (AASLT)." Nevertheless, he concluded that there were no violations of these ROE by any of the soldiers in any of the 15 killings.

Let us pause and analyze this situation from a commonsense perspective. A formal investigative report quotes the ROE verbatim, but the government blacks out the ROE when the document finally reaches the hands of the defense attorneys. The same report exonerates the soldiers from any crime in relation to this secret ROE. But later, the government prosecutes certain low-ranking soldiers for violations of this secret ROE. Any reasonable reader will question the government's motives in these regards.

Regarding the Laws of Armed Conflict (LOAC), the major concluded: "It is my assessment that the Soldiers of 2nd and 3rd squads, 2/C/3-187 IN displayed good judgment with regards to the application of Deadly Force on OBJ MURRAY on the morning of 9 MAY 06 and throughout the duration of OPERATION IRON TRIANGLE. If the Soldiers had wanted to abuse their power they had several opportunities to do so, but in every case demonstrated professional restraint." This is an odd conclusion, given what we already know about the conduct of LT Horne and 2nd squad — the gas station incidents. But again, the sworn statements concerning 2nd squad and the gas station incident were excluded from the report. Under the recommendations section, the major concludes:

> That no further administrative or UCMJ action be taken against any member of the platoon or chain of command for either the initial engagement of the military age male, or against SPC Hunsaker and PFC Clagett for the deaths of the detainees. In both cases, the use of force was consistent with the ROE.

Why, then, were Hunsaker and Clagett prosecuted, along with Girouard and Graber? The inconsistency between Major Sullivan's report and subsequent charges,

DEPARTMENT OF THE ARMY
Headquarters, 3rd Battalion, 320th Field Artillery
Forward Operating Base Remagen
Tikrit, Iraq 09393

AFZB-KD-K-XO   21 MAY 2006

MEMORANDUM THRU: Commander, 3RD Battalion, 320TH Field Artillery Regiment, FOB REMAGEN APO AE 09393

MEMORANDUM FOR: Commander, 3RD Brigade Combat Team, 101st Airborne Division (Air Assault), COB SPEICHER, APO AE 09394

SUBJECT: Addendum to DA FORM 1574 *Report of Proceedings by an Investigating Officer,* Section IV (Findings) and Section V (Recommendations); Shooting of four Iraqi Nationals on OBJ MURRAY 9 May 06

1. Background. On 11 May 06 I was appointed to serve as an Investigating Officer IAW AR 15-6 in order to determine the facts leading to the shooting deaths of three Iraqi nationals that were detainees of US forces (2/C/1-187 IN) and the shooting of one military aged male engaged during the initial assault.

    a. At 120900 MAY 06 I gathered the following members of 2nd and 3rd squads together in the 3-320 FA Conference room to discuss the events that led to the shooting of 4 Iraqi men on OBJ MURRAY vic ▇▇▇▇▇▇: PFC Corey Clagett, SPC William Hunsaker, PFC Bradley Mason, PFC Thomas Kemp, SGT Kevin Ryan, SSG Raymond Girouard, SGT Leonel Lemus, CPL Brandon Helton, SPC Juston Graber, SPC Micah Bivins, and 1LT Justin Wehreim.

    b. I traveled to COB SPEICHER o/a 16 May to brief MAJ Harms, 3BCT CJA, on my initial findings and seek any additional legal guidance. He recommended re-questioning SPC Hunsaker and PFC Clagett to get further details on the events at the time of the shooting of the three detainees.

    c. On 21 May 06, I briefed and questioned the same members of C/3-187 IN mentioned above. During this point I updated my sketch of OBJ MURRAY found in Exhibit 1. I questioned SPC Hunsaker and PFC Clagett to obtain further details of the events leading to the shooting of the three detainees left in their custody.

    d. On 28 May 06, I turned over the sworn statements from the members of C/3-187 IN over to LTC Bradley Huestis, MNC-I OSJA, who was part of BG Maffey's investigating team. The scanned copies of these statements are not legible. The statements were from the following soldiers: PFC Corey Clagett, SPC William Hunsaker, PFC Bradley Mason, PFC Thomas Kemp, SGT Kevin Ryan, SSG Raymond Girouard, SGT Leonel Lemus, CPL Brandon Helton, SPC Juston Graber, SPC Micah Bivins, and 1LT Justin Wehreim.

1

as well as the many internal inconsistencies within the report, will not disappear as if by magic. If there were 15 deaths, why were three deaths considered problematic after the report? Why were LT Horne's actions not considered problematic? How were the sworn statements by the snipers lost and why were they never included in any subsequent proceedings? How can one explain that the "blind folds" on the three dead bodies were cut after being examined on an army base? How did the dead bodies disappear? How did the knife disappear? What happened to all those photographs confiscated by the army? One will never be able to answer these and other questions fully. But commonsense dictates that based on all the facts and inconsistencies uncovered thus fair, the following is true: if there was a conspiracy, it was a conspiracy that involved the entire brigade, from top to bottom, including numerous

2. **Facts.** On the morning of 9 May 06, members of 2nd and 3rd squads 2/C/3-187 IN took part in Operation IRON TRIANGLE. The specific target of these squads was labeled as OBJ MURRAY. The men were briefed that the objective area had been the target of previous coalition force (CF) raids and that on the preceding raid, CF engaged and killed 15 Al Qaida in Iraq (AQIZ). Based on both Human and Signal Intelligence it appeared that AQIZF reoccupied the objective area since the previous raids thus precipitating Operation IRON TRIANGLE. This intelligence estimate included the positive identification of the OBJ MURRAY ████████████████████████████████████ thus reaffirming that the objective contained AQIZ terrorists.

a. At 090500 MAY 06, OBJ IRON TRIANGLE began with simultaneous air assaults by C/3-187 IN, A/2-9 ARS, A/3-187 IN, and B/3-320 FA. The southern part of OBJ MURRAY was the initial LZ for C/3-187 IN. During the initial assault attack aviation assets did engage and kill three suspected AIF members attempting to flee the OBJ area in a boat ████████████ After clearing the initial target house C/3-187 IN received instructions to continue to clear structures throughout the island (OBJ Murray). 2/C/3-187 IN was instructed to board aircraft and move to vic ████ It was at this time that the sequence of events unfolded leading to the shooting of four Iraqi military aged males.

b. As the members of 2nd and 3rd squads 2/C/3-187 exited the aircraft at this follow on OBJ they began moving towards a house. SSG Giroaud, SPC Hunsaker, and SGT Lemus observed a military aged male in a window and engaged the man (Slide 2, Exhibit 1). The 2nd squad and attached Iraqi Army (IA) soldiers maneuvered west to a berm and assumed an over watch position. SSG Girouard maneuvered his squad around to the front of the house and entered the building. SSG Girouard noticed three military aged males shielded behind two women. He and his men escorted the males out and detained them. The men were blindfolded with engineer tape and restrained with flex cuffs. Simultaneously SSG Girouard and two of his men went into the home, removed the wounded Iraqi male and their medic SPC Bivins attempted to treat his wounds. However, the man died minutes later. As the detainees were being searched, the IA Soldiers began to complain about the initial shooting and essentially became combat ineffective. The members of the two US squads then began to maneuver on a second house just to their north. SSG Girouard and LT Wehrheim established a support by fire position consisting of CPL Helton and SGT Ryan (Slide 5, Exhibit 1). LT Wehrheim and SSG Girouard, recognizing that there had been women in the first house, instructed CPL Helton to place fire over the house, but not to engage it unless the men were fired upon. After initiating fire and beginning to maneuver, a man exited the second house holding a young child in the air and out in front of him (Slide 12, Exhibit 1). The men held their fire and detained the man.

c. The members of the squads returned to the first house and continued processing their detainees. During this time, the US Soldiers had to order one of the IA soldiers away from the detainees at least twice. On at least one of the occasions the IA soldier was observed kneeling next to a detainee and had made physical contact while speaking to him. As the processing continued, LT Wehrheim received orders to assume PZ posture and move to a follow on OBJ. He took members of 2nd squad, the attached IA soldiers, and the EKIA and extracted by aircraft leaving only 3rd squad on the OBJ. SSG Girouard, squad leader 3/2/C/3-187 IN, then led 5 members of his squad (Slide 6, Exhibit 1) to take one of the detainees to the PZ and assume PZ posture. Prior to leading the group back to the PZ, SSG Girouard noticed that the flex cuffs used on the original three detainees were the "thin zip tie" type cuffs that he considered unsuitable. The task to re-cuff the detainees with stronger ties was given to PFC Clagget and SPC Hunsaker. PFC Mason was left on the west side of the house guarding the two detainees.

2

commissioned officers, CID agents, and low-ranking soldiers; and it was a conspiracy orchestrated from the top of the chain of command that flowed to the bottom. Clagett and Hunsaker were chosen to be the scapegoats for this conspiracy and cover-up. This unwelcome conclusion is not startling given that the Levin–McCain report uncovered a similar conspiracy and cover-up in the Abu Ghraib cases: the seven "rotten apples" were falsely depicted as dreaming up the torture by themselves, when, in fact, the "interrogation techniques" emanated from the White House, and those seven soldiers were chosen by their commanders, prosecutors, and CID agents to serve as scapegoats. The pattern and connection between these two separate sites of abuse is unmistakable to the average person.

d. As recounted in the sworn statements, the events depicted on slides 7 through 9 unfolded in the following manner. While bringing the detainees to their feet SPC Hunsaker noticed that the restraints of detainee #1 (Slide 7, Exhibit 1), were broken. PFC Clagget lifted detainees #2 and #3 to their feet by their cuffs. In the process, the cuffs of detainee #3 broke. With all three detainees on their feet and the blindfolds of #2 and #3 in slight disarray, PFC Clagett took out his Gerber and cut the cuffs of detainee #2. At this point all three detainees were standing, uncuffed and the blind folds of at least two of the detainees (#1 and #3) were in disarray, offering the men some limited vision. PFC Clagget went to re-cuff detainee #2 with the stronger cuffs that SSG Girourd gave them just a few minutes prior. At that point detainees #1 and #3 attacked SPC Hunsaker and PFC Clagget respectively. SPC Hunsaker described being cut with a knife on both sides of his face and throwing up his arm in a defensive manner and receiving a cut on his left arm (see Slide 10, Exhibit 1 to see the wounds). Simultaneously, PFC Mason was struck in the face by detainee #3. Clagget turned around and saw Hunsaker bleeding and heard him yell. Both Soldiers turned and saw the three men attempting to flee and engaged them with their weapons. The three detainees fell dead approximately 10-15 feet from the Soldiers in the postures depicted in the center 2 photos on slide 11.

e. The attached briefing sequence (Exhibit 1) ends with the events on OBJ MURRAY. I believe it is important to address the evacuation of the EKIA remains through the handover at FOB Brassfield-Mora for eventual turnover to the Iraqi authorities in the Samarra area. The bodies were evacuated from OBJ MURRAY and brought to the vicinity of the RED KNIGHT TAC / Field Trains area by helicopter. Upon their arrival at the Field Trains area, the bodies were unloaded by several members of TF 3-320 FA. The remains were viewed and photographed by members of the 3BCT Staff (MAJs Frank Jenio, Cecil Clark and Stephen Treanor, and COL Michael Steele). The photographs were taken for intelligence collection purposes (Exhibits 6-8). At this point the members of the BCT staff noticed that the EKIA had Engineer tape around various parts of their head region. The remains were further viewed by members of the TF 3-320 FA S2 section for documentation into the Biometric Analysis Tool Set. The evidence from that OBJ area, to include the knife that cut Hunsaker, was lost somewhere during the transport of the prisoners and the turnover of the remains to TF 3-320 FA personnel. The remains were then transported to FOB Brassfield-Mora by the members of G/626 Forward Support Company.

3. Findings.

a. **Rules of Engagement (ROE).**

ANNEX E (RULES OF ENGAGEMENT) TO OPERATIONS ORDER 05-06 (SHAREKA), 3rd BCT, 101st ABN DIV (AASLT)

The final piece of damning evidence that suggests a widespread conspiracy is that the defense attorneys were not shown Major Sullivan's report prior to or during the Article 32 hearing. The defense attorneys went through the gauntlet of the Article 32 hearing as if they were blindfolded, metaphorically speaking. Mr. Waddington makes this clear in his objections to the conclusions of the Article 32 hearing in early August 2006:

> At this point, neither Mr. Waddington nor Mr. Bergrin has seen ... the Rules of Engagement (ROE) and the AR 15-6 Investigation into the mission. The Rules of Engagement, mission objectives, the identity of the inhabitants of the island, and the type of enemy expected on the objective are highly relevant, exculpatory, mitigating, and extenuating for the Defense. Without having the opportunity to review and present evidence

Given the circumstances of the assault and the briefed ROE, I find that the actions of SSG Girouard, SGT Lemus, and SPC Hunsaker in engaging the male in the window of the house was justified, and that no adverse action be taken on these Soldiers for the initial engagement.

    (2) In the case of the three detainees shot and killed by SPC Hunsaker and PFC Clagget, I find that the Soldiers clearly acted in self defense fearing for their safety as they were physically assaulted by the detainees. As such, I find that there was not a violation of the ROE or the Law of Armed Conflict (LOAC). I recommend no action be taken against SPC Hunsaker or PFC Clagget for their actions with regards to the shooting of the three men.

    b. **Detainee Procedures.** Clearly there were several points of failure that set the conditions for the detainees to attack and then attempt to flee. However these errors are reflective of procedural mistakes and are not violations of any principle of the LOAC. The Soldiers present on the OBJ area did not adhere to the fundamental "Five Ss" (search, silence, segregate, secure and speed to the rear). After being detained, the one Iraqi either had possession of a the knife that he used to attack SPC Hunsaker, which would indicate a poor search was conducted, or the IA soldier that made contact with that detainee was able to hand the knife off, showing that the detainees were not segregated properly. The poor segregation also permitted two of the detainees to act simultaneously, which also demonstrates that SSG Girouard exercised poor judgment in leaving two soldiers to guard and handle three prisoners. The assumption can be made that at least two of the prisoners, due to the condition of their blind folds, realized that they had an opportunity to escape as they outnumbered their captors at that time. The flex cuffs and blind fold materials were inadequate to serve their purposes, and unit SOPs should be adjusted to ensure that the proper materials are provided to Soldiers to properly restrain individuals. The unit needs to retrain Soldiers in the handling of detainees. SPC Hunsaker and PFC Clagget allowed the detainees to all stand at once while being un-cuffed. This allowed the detainees to be put in a position that they could make a coordinated escape effort.

    c. **LOAC.** It is my assessment that the Soldiers of 2nd and 3rd squads, 2/C/3-187 IN, displayed good judgment with regards to the application of Deadly Force on OBJ MURRAY on the morning of 9 MAY 06 and throughout the duration of OPERATION IRON TRAINGLE. If the Soldiers had wanted to abuse their power they had several opportunities to do so, but in every case demonstrated professional restraint. When entering the first house, SSG Girouard and his clearing team showed discipline in restraining from entering with undo force and taking the time to positively identify the occupants and realize that they posed no immediate danger. Next, while maneuvering on the second house, SSG Girouard and 1LT Wehrheim demonstrated good judgment when instructing the machine gunner to fire over the house for fear of wounding or killing possible non-combatants. Without positive identification they employed their fire power judiciously and with discipline. At that same house, the maneuver element led by SSG Girouard showed restraint by not engaging the man that came out of the house using the child as a shield.

4. **Recommendations.**

    a. That no further administrative or UCMJ action be taken against any member of the platoon or chain of command for either the initial engagement of the military age male, or, against SPC Hunsaker and PFC Clagget the deaths of the detainees. In both cases, the use of force was consistent with the ROE.

4

covered by the protective order, the Defense has been denied a fair, thorough, and impartial Article 32 investigation.

    Mr. Waddington cannot help it that he sounds like a lawyer. In plain, everyday language, he is saying that he was forced to defend a client without having seen the investigative report which concluded that his client was not guilty of anything. It is certainly true that this situation is not fair. But the entire of purpose of any conspiracy is to create an unfair advantage for the conspirators.

b. The poor detainee handling and security issues, however, require immediate correction. SSG Girouard demonstrated a lapse in judgment during actions on the objective was limited to his supervision and the assignment of responsibilities of his soldiers, specifically for leaving two junior enlisted personnel to handle three prisoners. At the time of moving to PZ posture, the handling of the three detainees was arguably the most critical action at that point. He had two other NCOs (SGTs Ryan and Lemus) that he should have employed to assist in controlling the closing actions on the objective area supervision and movement of the detainees and movement of the Soldiers to the PZ. Given the intensity of the combat actions of that morning, I would recommend that SSG Girouard receive a written reprimand, to be filed locally, by his Battalion chain of command for his poor supervision of his men during that short period of time. Additionally, the unit should undergo retraining in the procedures for handling detainees so as to avoid mistakes that I would attribute to fatigue at the time of action and complacency.

5. POC for this action is MAJ Timothy Sullivan, VOIP 672-9605.

TIMOTHY P. SULLIVAN
MAJ, FA
AR 15-6 Investigating Officer

Contrast with the "New Yorker" Version of this Case

Raffi Khatchadourian's article on Operation Iron Triangle, published in the July 6, 2009, issue of *The New Yorker*,[1] surprised me. It is instructive to compare and contrast some of my key interpretations with his. In the big picture, the information and entertainment media (these two reference groups have become blurred, as evidenced by the fact that "fake news" programs such as "The Daily Show" and "The Colbert Report" are trusted by the public more than some official news outlets, according to numerous polls) have consistently failed to question or challenge government policies with regard to key issues on the war on terror. As a whole, they failed to challenge the mythology of the alleged weapons of mass destruction that the government used to justify invading Iraq in the first place. In general, they went along with the government's false depiction of the Abu Ghraib scandal as the result of a handful of rogue soldiers. More recently, they have failed to connect the important issues of PTSD, sleep deprivation, and failures in leadership to atrocities and the killings of civilians in Iraq and Afghanistan. In general, journalists have acted as cheerleaders for the government's policies in the current war, despite the fact that most of the American public has turned sour on the war. My intent in this section is to focus on the lack of sociological imagination shown by the information media regarding the subject of this book, and to use the recent article from *The New Yorker* as illustration of this problem. It should be clear from preceding statements and the overall theme of this book that my criticisms of this particular article in *The New Yorker* are not a personal attack but are part of my effort to use the sociological imagination. In other words, the drama of Operation Iron Triangle is not about any individuals, but concerns the interplay of personal troubles and public issues.

Khatchadourian completely omits any mention at all of Major Sullivan's and Captain Hart's reports (a formal report is a public document), which both concluded that no crimes had been committed during Operation Iron Triangle. These reports are

1 Raffi Khatchadourian, "The Kill Company," *The New Yorker* July 6, 2009, pp. 41-59.

From "Whitaker, Spencer A USA SSG USA 101st SSB"
        <spencer.whitaker@kuwait.swa.army.mil>

Sent Tuesday, August 1, 2006 0:39 am

To Jerome Duggan <jerome.duggan@us.army.mil> , waddingtonweb@hotmail.com

Cc William Fischbach <william.fischbach@us.army.mil> , kevin.m.hynes@us.army.mil

Bcc

Subject Hunsaker and Clagett 32

Gentlemen,

We have been in Kuwait since 30 July 2006. We are at Ali al-Salem. There have been several flights available to bring us to Camp Speicher before the Article 32. We just missed another flight on which we had guaranteed seats. However, for the following reasons, we have been denied access to any military aircraft or flights. Therefore, through no fault of our own we are unable to arrive at the 32 before its scheduled start time. We are literally stranded at Ali al Salem.

1) We do not have a letter of intent;
2) We do not have any paperwork or orders authorizing us to fly; and
3) We do not have a fund cite.

The itineraries were sent to you in ample time for the preparation of documents and logistics. Due to your lack of diligence, we were MADE unavailable and we demand that the Article 32 be continued and our clients not be prejudiced because of your failure to do you job.

Our clients will not go forward with the Article 32 without their counsel present.

Please file this e-mail as the first exhibit at the 32 should you attempt to proceed without us.

Paul Bergrin and Michael Waddington

important because both appear to be routine attempts to cover up the crimes during this mission. Readers who are not exposed to the existence or contents of these reports will resist the logical conclusion of government cover-up. Khatchadourian gives a terse summary t these reports without citing them or their detailed contents: "[D]espite numerous investigations the Army had never judged any of Charlie Company's operations to be criminal" (p. 48). This out-of-context conclusion begs the question: "Why, then, did the Army prosecute specific soldiers?" Obviously, the missing link in the explanation is that the investigations were attempts at cover up that went sour.

Khatchadourian states flatly that Steele refused to speak with him,[1] yet he freely writes of Steele's alleged intentions, beliefs, and even his dreams ("Steele was so haunted by Zarqawi that he dreamed about him"). The most important instance of this seemingly magical knowledge of Steele's intentions is illustrated by Khatchadourian's sentence: "Using a pocketknife, Steele removed the tape from the face of a corpse, so that it could be properly photographed." How does he know that this was Steele's reason for cutting the engineer tape? Steele refused to testify at any of the court proceedings, so no trial attorney had the opportunity to ask him or cross-examine him. Again, cross-examination is a public issue, so that Steele's alleged private motives should not be the primary focus. The more important point is that, as several defense attorneys told me, Steele's alleged *actions* may be construed as obstruction of justice and tampering with evidence, regardless of what his alleged intentions were. The other important question is why Khatchadourian would offer the rationalization

---

1 Khatchadourian writes: "The relationship between Chiarelli and Steele quickly developed into a feud (both men declined to talk about the deployment for this article)" (p. 48).

that Steele just wanted to get a good photo, if it is true that Steele would not speak to him.

Khatchadourian moves into the realm or reference group of academic, intellectual explanations for the events under discussion here, but again, he does not cite any sources other than Steele's alleged friend, David Grossman:

> It is the collective nature of violence in war, the shared culpability, that partly allows soldiers to find it within themselves to kill. Colonel Steele understood this. Part of "Psychological Inoculation of Combat" — his addendum to the Fort Campbell training program — was based on a book by retired Lieutenant Colonel David Grossman, "On Killing," copies of which he bought and distributed to his brigade. Grossman observes that most soldiers, even when confronted with mortal danger, hesitate before pulling the trigger; but his wariness, he argues, can be greatly overcome with conditioning (p. 54).

Let us dissect this incredible passage. Khatchadourian seems to be butchering Marshall's classic finding that soldiers are reluctant to kill, but does not cite Marshall. Marshall and other classic, intellectual works on this subject (especially Stouffer) do *not* discuss shared responsibility as a factor in making soldiers kill. They discuss unit morale and cohesion as a factor in ameliorating combat stress precisely because war and killing go against human nature. So what part of "this" did Steele understand or misunderstand? It is impossible to tell from Khatchadourian's account. It is highly significant that David Grossman's book was made a part of Steele's program to desensitize soldiers to killing. Hunsaker confirmed this for me, and physically showed me his copy of Grossman's book. If it is true that Grossman advocated operant conditioning for turning soldiers (who are reluctant to kill) into killers, then that would explain the pattern that we have already uncovered: the kill board, kill coins, kill knives, and now, free copies of Grossman's book. Operant conditioning is a method derived from B.F. Skinner's theory called behaviorism. Skinner showed that he could make rats and pigeons perform many unnatural behaviors by a strict regime of rewards and punishments. It seems that the soldiers in Charlie Company were treated as if they were rats and pigeons in an experiment by Skinner. However, Khatchadourian omits the important point that the alleged Grossman–Steele program, even if it was orthodox in this brigade, is highly unorthodox in the reference group of academia. It is a safe assertion that in most university courses in psychology and sociology, the Grossman–Steele program would be considered dehumanizing and wrong. There is something unorthodox about a journalist endorsing an unorthodox theory: "Colonel Steele understood this." First, Khatchadourian lapses into his omniscient narrator style, because no one can be certain what Steele understood without talking with him. Second, the phrasing suggests that Steele's alleged understanding is the orthodox, average, or common understanding of the sociology and psychology of killing in war. I believe that the alleged Grossman–Steele misunderstanding is highly unorthodox.

The difference in the consequences of the unorthodox, Grossman–Steele approach versus the orthodox, classical perspectives is enormous. The classical, orthodox perspective predicts correctly that conditioning soldiers to become killers will lead to combat stress, PTSD, higher suicide rates, alcoholism, and a host of other symptoms indicative of a dysfunctional society. The orthodox approach respects the limits of "human nature," which is just another name for average consensus. These problems have all been documented as having increased in the army as a whole during the current war. Suicides at Ft. Campbell in particular, the home base of the 101st Airborne Division, rose so dramatically in the year 2009 that the base was shut down for three days! Furthermore, the classical, orthodox perspective of Stouffer and Marshall correctly explains why the United States won World War II: In addition to the military strategies of America's commanders, the US army apparently exhibited the social integration and unit morale that are the central object of study in sociology.

Khatchadourian uses extremely positive words and phrases to describe Steele, his commissioned officers, and his policies: "cultivated pugnacity," "most daring unit," "Black Hawk Down," "daunting physical stature and reputation," "West Point," "award for perfect attendance," "football," and so on. On the other extreme, he uses extremely negative words and phrases in conjunction with his discussions of the convicted soldiers: "lack of discipline," "bragging," "monsters," "refuse to accept full culpability," and so on. Khatchadourian seems to go out of his way to write that Hunsaker, Clagett, and Girouard were from the states of Missouri, South Carolina, and Tennessee, respectively. Clearly, his tone toward citizens of these Southern states indicates that he regards them as backward. One cannot avoid noticing that Khatchadourian portrays Steele in "honorific," prestigious, and elitist language whereas he portrays the convicted soldiers as vulgar, common, and as nobodies. This approach may or may not appeal to readers of *The New Yorker*. The more important sociological points are these: First, most academics agree with Tocqueville's discovery in *Democracy in America* that Americans of all social classes tend to regard each other as equals. In a word, to be American is to be common and equal, and to strive to be in the middle class and the middle of everything, in the grand cultural pattern that constitutes American society. Second, Khatchadourian's elitist approach to Operation Iron Triangle, his homage to Colonel Steele, and his contempt for the ordinary soldier are captured by C. Wright Mills in *The Power Elite*[1] and *White Collar*[2] with the important caveat that Mills regards these elitist attitudes as un-American. Mills, who was born in Texas and was an Aggie, eventually ended up at Columbia University, but he always criticized European-style elitism in America. I stated from the outset of this study that sociology is fundamentally the study of the average and common person and collective values. Khatchadourian and Ricks, as the only two journalists who wrote anything about Operation Iron Triangle, seem to be fascinated by the colonels, generals, and others in the power elite. I will continue in the rest of this study to focus on the enlisted soldier's personal troubles in relation to social issues. Moreover, the power elite in the army is linked in a chain of command, so that this saga should not be understood solely in terms of the alleged motives of high-ranking officers. Clearly, the social issues that are central to this drama are the unlawful ROE which were dreamed up by the power elite in the name of the American people who seem to be unaware of them. Hunsaker, Clagett, and Girouard became trapped in the double bind caused by these social issues, which they did not create or even fully comprehend.

1 C. Wright Mills, *The Power Elite* (New York: Oxford University Press, 1956).
2 C. Wright Mills, *White Collar* (New York: Oxford University Press, 1951).

THE GOVERNMENT PLAYS HARDBALL WITH THE DEFENSE ATTORNEYS

In everyday American culture, one uses the phrase "playing hardball" to refer to the government, big corporations, or other powerful institutions putting their adversaries into disadvantageous positions. This is precisely what the government did to the two civilian attorneys, Michael Waddington and Paul Bergrin, throughout the court proceedings and especially as they prepared to fly to Iraq to defend their clients at the Article 32 hearing scheduled for 8 a.m. on August 1, 2006. In fact, the two civilian attorneys were not able to arrive at the hearing until late in the day on August 1st. The prosecutor promised that they would be met at the military airfield — but they were not. The two civilians were stranded in Kuwait for two days because the government did not follow through on its obligations to fill out the necessary paperwork to get them to the courthouse and to see their clients. Mr. Waddington (defense attorney for Hunsaker during the trial phase) told me that he believes the prosecutor "intentionally and deliberately" wanted to give him and Mr. Bergrin "a hard time" defending their clients. Several documents support Mr. Waddington's interpretation. The first is the official letter from the prosecutor to Mr. Waddington regarding his trip to Iraq for the Article 32 hearing:

> You will be traveling into a combat zone in a dangerous part of the world. By agreeing to come to Iraq, you assume several risks including, but not limited to, serious injury or death. First, by flying on a Government aircraft, you will be a potential target of enemy insurgents. Enemy forces have been known to fire missiles or rocket-propelled grenades (RPGs) at aircraft, which can cause substantial injuries or death. Second, if you travel by ground, you will again be a potential target of enemy insurgents who have been known to fire weapons (rifles and RPGs) and to plant improvised devices (IEDs) alongside roads traveled by Coalition Forces. Third, by staying on FOB Brassfield-Mora, you assume the risks of being hit by mortar, rocket, or other attacks.

This is a fairly fear-inducing letter. Army officers have told me that they were never provided such complete and scary risk disclosures when they were ordered to fly to Iraq. Obviously, the government had the option to hold the Article 32 hearing at an army base in the US, Germany, or other safe location. There is a pattern here: The first three of the seven Abu Ghraib courts-martial were also held in Iraq. The civilian lawyers had to risk their lives to defend their clients. Regarding the Abu Ghraib trials, the army finally relented and moved the trials to Ft. Hood, Texas. I should add that when I agreed to serve as expert witness in the Javal Davis court-martial, I, too, was told that I was "agreeing" to possible death or injury. Similarly, in the Operation Iron Triangle cases, the government finally agreed to hold the trials at Ft. Campbell, Kentucky — but only after the government made sure that there would be no trials, only plea bargains. By moving the trials and proceedings to Ft. Hood and Ft. Campbell, the government demonstrated that it could have held all the proceedings in the United States from the start. A reasonable person will most likely conclude that holding hearings in Iraq is part of the government's game of hardball.

Mr. Waddington agreed to proceed with the dangerous case and to go on the dangerous trip. On July 18, 2006, Mr. Waddington sent the prosecutor his travel itinerary.

On July 29th, he would fly from Atlanta to Amsterdam on KLM flight 662. He would then proceed on KLM 457 to Kuwait on a flight that lasted five hours and forty minutes. He would arrive into Kuwait at 10:20 p.m. on July 30th, and the Article 32 hearing was supposed to begin at 8 a.m. on the 1st of August — in Iraq. The prosecutor assured Mr. Waddington that he and Mr. Bergrin would be met and whisked out of Kuwait to Iraq by military transport. Behind the scenes, the prosecutor apparently had other designs, as I will demonstrate.

In Kuwait, Mr. Waddington met with Mr. Bergrin, who was also on his way to the hearing and was in the same predicament, and. The two civilian lawyers were stranded in Kuwait. At thirty-nine minutes past midnight on the 1st of August, Mr. Waddington sent the following e-mail to the prosecutor and copied it to his staff:

> We have been in Kuwait since 30 July 2006. We are at Ali al-Salem. There have been several flights available to bring us to Camp Speicher before the Article 32. We just missed another flight on which we had guaranteed seats. However, for the following reasons, we have been denied access to any military aircraft or flights. Therefore, through no fault of our own we are unable to arrive at the 32 before its scheduled start time. We are literally stranded at Ali al-Salem. We do not have a letter of intent. We do not have any paperwork or orders authorizing us to fly. And, we do not have a fund cite. The itineraries were sent to you in ample time for the preparation of documents and logistics. Due to your lack of diligence, we were MADE unavailable and we demand that the Article 32 be continued and our clients not be prejudiced because of your failure to do your job. Our clients will not go forward with the Article 32 without their counsel present. Please file this e-mail as the first exhibit at the 32 should you attempt to proceed without us.

This e-mail was signed, "Paul Bergrin and Michael Waddington."

What went wrong? As I know from similar experience, the army was supposed to give the lawyers letters authorizing them to enter a military base and to give them "fund cites," meaning special codes that would authorize the government to spend money to transport them. This is a technicality, because military transport flies constantly between bases at taxpayer expense, but a civilian must be formally authorized to make use of this transportation. I was put in a somewhat similar predicament when I was promised a smooth entry to the army base in Vilseck, Germany, where I would testify on behalf of another soldier, Sergeant Michael Leahy. The army promised that a soldier would meet me at the airport in Nuremberg, Germany, and drive me to Vilseck. Of course, nobody was there to meet me. I went to the information desk at the airport and asked the staff to call the army base, and they did. I spoke with a military policeman and explained my predicament. He promised to send someone to pick me up, and again, nobody came. I lost most of a working day at the airport waiting for the army to fulfill its promises. The staff at the information desk told me that the army disappoints incoming guests like this "all the time." They suggested that I take the train, so I finally took a German train to Vilseck and hitched a ride with some soldiers to the base. When I arrived, the guards would not let me on base despite my letter of intent signed by an appropriate official from the army. It took several more hours to finally get the army to fulfill its obligations.

Of course, some readers will be tempted to conclude that glitches do happen, and one should not generalize about the army's attitude toward civilians who want to defend its soldiers. But in Mr. Waddington's case, there is additional evidence of intent to obstruct him. Sergeant Spencer Whitaker e-mailed the prosecutor on July 31, 2006 at 4:25 am:

> Sir, Mr. Bergrin and Mr. Waddington have arrived here in Kuwait tonight. I have gotten them billeting and will work their IBA/ACH issue in the morning. I have them scheduled to fly out on Crome 34 on 31 Jul and arriving in Speicher around 0345 on 1 Aug. If I can be of any more assistance please let me know.

Arriving at 3:45 a.m. on the day of the hearing would be inconvenient, but would allow the lawyers time for a nap before 8 a.m. But the prosecutor did not respond, and the lawyers remained stranded. On July 24, 2006, the prosecutor e-mailed Sergeant Whitaker:

> I am attaching the itineraries for all civilian defense counsel in these upcoming cases. We are going to need to get Messrs. Bergrin and Waddington on a bird to Tikrit (Speicher) ASAP once they hit the ground. They need to be up here NLT the evening of 31 July.

Despite this seeming concern for the civilian lawyers on the part of the prosecutor, he makes no mention of the paperwork necessary to transport and admit the lawyers to the base. Yet Sergeant Whitaker informed the prosecutor of these issues in an e-mail dated July 19, 2006:

> Sir, I just spoke with the Civilian lady that works down the hall from me. Montrnesse told me that the gentlemen will need a LOI [letter of intent] just like the one you just sent.... She also informed me they should expect to be here [in Kuwait] for up to 48 hours before they fly up into Iraq for processing into theater. They will also need $7.00 or 2KD to pay to get their passports stamped at the airport upon their arrival. If I can get the gentlemen's standard name line and SSN I can see if they can be spaced blocked on a flight to BIAP but that takes about 24 to 48 hours to do.

Clearly, the prosecutor was informed well in advance of the bureaucracy that would be involved in getting the lawyers to the hearing. He was also told that the lawyers could arrive in Iraq 24 hours after arriving in Kuwait, at best, and 48 hours later at worst. One will never know the real reasons for the prosecutor's lack of diligence. However, one may conclude that lack of diligence in a death penalty case involving US soldiers shows an egregious lack of respect for the gravity of the situation, at best, and perhaps Machiavellian motives at worst. There can be no doubt that the lawyers and the accused soldiers they were trying to defend were at a huge disadvantage with regard to legal procedures due to actions and inaction by the government.

Chapter 4. The Article 32 Hearing, Or Perjuryfest, Begins

> " 'That's a very serious crime you've committed' ... 'What crime?' 'We don't
> know yet,' said the colonel. 'But we're going to find out. And we sure
> know it's very serious'."
> — Joseph Heller, *Catch-22, p. 350*

In military-law-speak, an Article 32 is the rough equivalent of a civilian pre-trial hearing. Its manifest purpose is to determine whether and which charges shall stick and be prosecuted versus charges that shall be dropped. The usual rules of evidence apply and testimony is offered under oath. It is a solemn American social institution. But like all other social events and institutions, it has a *latent* or hidden purpose. Both the prosecution and the defense work behind the scenes to gain advantage, avoid embarrassment, and position themselves for the legal fights that will follow. To a certain extent, the manifest-latent mix is normal, along the lines of schools fulfilling the manifest functions of socialization and opening minds to discovery versus the latent (and darker) functions of keeping young people out of the job market and stifling curiosity through the emphasis on credentialing.[1] Every professor knows that today's students are mostly interested in getting high grades (latent function), not in expanding their knowledge (manifest function). Similarly, one of the manifest cultural functions of the Article 32 is to demonstrate that the accused is "innocent until proven guilty" and thereby repeatedly revive the American cultural tradition and reputation of its legal process as the best in the world. But there is no doubt that many prosecutors and investigators are convinced that the accused should be treated as guilty until proven innocent, or see certain cases as a stepping-stone in their careers. Prosecutors and investigators otherwise engage in numerous, latent, even sinister functions of the law.

---

1   See Robert K. Merton, "Manifest and Latent Functions" in *Social Theory and Social Structure* (New York: Simon & Schuster, [1949] 1967).

Again, one should wonder how much of this manifest-latent tension is normal, versus when it crosses "the line" (whatever and wherever that cultural boundary lies) into conspiracy and misconduct. Of course, I am referring to the average person's understanding of "conspiracy," not legal definitions of conspiracy, for the obvious reason that the legal profession has vested interests in not regarding its actions in terms of conspiracy and in attaching this label to the actions of the accused. But we need not be constrained by the language games of the legal profession in this analysis. One of my goals is to pose the question: Who really engaged in conspiracy in commonsense terms, the government or the accused?

This particular Article 32 hearing seems especially tainted by latent functions that are at odds with American cultural ideals. We have seen that the prosecutor went out of his way to make sure that it would be held at Forward Operating Base Brassfield-Mora, Iraq, which made it a dangerous place due to mortar attacks and IEDs. At one point in the hearing, the prosecutor announced to the defense attorneys, for the record: "We are in a combat zone and while I would hate to see anything happen to a particular witness in this case it is not inconceivable that a witness that testified before this Article 32 hearing could be severely hurt or even killed in combat, so once again I would ask that you all make full use of your ability to cross-examine witnesses at this hearing."

The most important latent or hidden goal of this particular Article 32 appears to have been to keep Colonel Steele, documents pertaining to his unlawful ROE, Major Sullivan's report, and other "classifiable" reports out of the hearing and subsequent proceedings. This is evident from the fact that in the 954 pages of transcript for the Article 32, any and all testimony pertaining to the *written* ROE never appeared and any and all testimony pertaining to the *verbal* ROE was never mentioned in the subsequent proceedings. Can all this be a coincidence? In fact, the prosecutor expressly forbade any mention of such "classified" evidence in the court record. Defense attorneys told me that they were warned by the prosecutor that if they embarrassed the government, there would be no plea bargains and the government would continue to seek the death penalty.

The Article 32 convened at 6:50 p.m. on August 1, 2006 in Iraq. Mr. Waddington told me that he and Mr. Bergrin landed on the tarmac at the army base five to ten minutes prior to the start of the hearing. The civilian attorneys literally had no time to speak to their clients in person. The investigative officer in charge, hereafter referred to as the IO, was Lieutenant Colonel Daniel. The IO is not a judge. Investigative officers are not required to be military judges, but given the sensitivity and complexity of this case, one has to wonder why the Army chose to appoint an inexperienced IO to this hearing. This Article 32 hearing was this particular IO's first experience with such hearings. Surely the Army could have found an experienced IO, and especially one experienced with charges of murder. His first words were:

> Good evening. I've been appointed investigating officer to conduct a formal investigation to certain charges against Specialist Juston R. Graber, Private First Class Corey R. Clagett, Staff Sergeant Raymond L. Girouard, and Specialist William B. Hunsaker, ordered pursuant to Article 32(b) of

the Uniform Code of Military Justice, by Lieutenant Colonel Nathaniel Johnson Jr.

The IO went on to note that each of the accused was represented by civilian or military attorneys, or in some cases both. Thus, Graber was represented by Army captain William Suddeth; Clagett by Mr. Paul Bergrin and Captain Sasha Rutizer; Girouard by Captain Theodore Miller; and Hunsaker by Mr. Michael Waddington and Captain Kevin Hynes. The prosecutors were captains William Fishbach, Jerome Duggan, and Joseph Mackey. As is typical in military trial proceedings that I have witnessed, the civilian defense attorneys were more vocal and vigorous in their defense than the military defense attorneys for the obvious reasons that the military attorneys were in the army and therefore constrained by norms of respect and deference to military superiors. The prosecution had the option of holding a separate Article 32 for each of the co-accused, but chose to hold one hearing for all of them simultaneously. The civilian attorneys objected to this move, but were overruled.

The IO read off a long list of potential witnesses who could have been called to testify at the Article 32. What is noteworthy is that Colonel Steele was not on the list.

The defense attorney, Mr. Bergrin, launched into an aggressive *voir dire* of the IO's background and qualifications to supervise this hearing:

MR. BERGRIN: What materials have you read in preparation for this 32 Investigation?

IO: Evidence packet...

MR. BERGRIN: After you read the packet, reviewed the discs, did you have any further discussions with anybody about the case?

IO: Just my legal advisor.

MR. BERGRIN: Can you tell us the nature of the discussions with your legal advisor?

IO: Really it was helping informing — understanding the specifications of each charge, what the process was for this hearing, what my responsibilities were as far as the investigating officer. I have it all logged on my time record.

MR. BERGRIN: Have you ever acted as a 32 investigating officer in a prior case?

IO: No.

MR. BERGRIN: Have you ever sat on a court-martial?

IO: No.

It seems that this important Article 32 was on-the job-training for the IO. This IO had not even served as a military juror. Mr. Waddington followed-up with more questions, and focused on the prosecutor's move to make these offenses punishable by the death penalty. This is a significant and unusual move by the prosecutor, and of course, it was opposed by all of the defense attorneys.

MR. WADDINGTON: Sir, after this case was given to you, you received an additional memorandum asking you to look into factors to consider whether or not to make this a death penalty case. Did you discuss that memorandum and the standards that you were to apply here with your legal advisor?

IO: Yes.

MR. WADDINGTON: What did he tell you about the standards?

IO: He referred me to the *Manual for Courts-Martial*, and where to find this.

MR. WADDINGTON: Did he hint to you either way what the command is looking to do here?

IO: No.

MR. WADDINGTON: Based on your initial reading of the packet, what were your impressions of the case?

IO: It's surprising, shocking. *I think I found it interesting that there weren't as many witnesses that I thought there might be.* It's certainly a serious situation, and a lot of work [emphasis added].

MR. WADDINGTON: Do you know Colonel Steele?

IO: I've met him. I don't know him. We're —

MR. WADDINGTON: Have you ever worked —

IO: — not friends. I've never worked with him.

The IO is correct that the dearth of witnesses is surprising, even "shocking," at least with regard to the specific charges leveled at the accused. But did the IO know about killings that occurred on this mission (especially in LT Horne's platoon), which did not result in any charges? Did he have knowledge of Major Sullivan's report? It is certain that the defense attorneys did not have knowledge of Major Sullivan's report, and therefore could not ask the IO about it. As we have seen, there were scores of witnesses as well as about seventy sworn statements to other killings on the mission. Other defense attorneys also asked questions:

CPT SUDDETH: And earlier you indicated that you had an operational knowledge. What knowledge did you have?

IO: Well, being part of the division — division plans process and being aware — everyday I come in and review the operations that are upcoming and those that have occurred and see story boards. That's how I knew about Iron Triangle at the large brigade level. I mean, I knew what the operation was. I did not know about this specific incident.

CPT SUDDETH: Now what is your current position within the division?

IO: I am the Deputy Effects Coordinator for targeting effects.

It seems clear that the IO was directly involved in the mission at issue. As such, he obviously had vested interests in the success of the mission as well as the disposition of these cases. He was an insider to the operational planning for Operation Iron Triangle! As such, his role in the proceedings cannot be regarded as objective or neutral in commonsense terms. On the contrary, his role illustrates a conflict of interests regarding loyalty to his superiors and ensuring justice for the enlisted soldiers. Why didn't the Army appoint an IO who was completely removed from any involvement in this mission and thereby be more neutral? Mr. Bergrin followed up with more questions:

MR. BERGRIN: Sir, I just have one follow up question. Did you know what the rules of engagement were for Operation Iron Triangle?

IO: I know what the division rules of engagement are.

MR. BERGRIN: What did you understand to be the division rules of engagement?

IO: It's quite lengthy.

MR. BERGRIN: I'm talking about the rules of engagement for the operation.

IO: Specifically briefed by the 3rd Brigade chain of command for Iron Triangle?

MR. BERGRIN: Yes.

IO: No, I was not aware of that.

MR. BERGRIN: I have no further questions.

This is more evidence that the IO was an insider to the very command that was supposed to be meting out impartial justice to the soldiers. What exactly did the IO know about the ROE and for which level of command? It is extremely important to note that the army consists of strata or layers of command (division, brigade, battalion, company, and platoon) which are all linked in a "chain of command." The IO admitted that he was privy to one of the highest levels (division) of knowledge regarding the secret ROE. Defense attorneys informed me that they were warned beforehand to avoid referring to or divulging the exact wording of the written ROE, because it and related statements were classified or "classifiable." This was made clear to the defense attorneys during closed-door hearings referred to as "802's." In the Article 32, an oblique reference is made to this fact by the prosecutor, who states on page 29 of the transcript: "I just wanted to make sure that all parties were in receipt of the 24 July 2006 protective order signed by Lieutenant Colonel Johnson." The only way the defense attorneys could approach the topic of the ROE was through asking specific witnesses what they heard or thought that it was. But they were never allowed to broach what it actually was in writing. The opening minutes of the Article 32 placed the defense attorneys in a double-bind or lose–lose situation. They were not allowed to disclose or question the written ROE because it was classified, but that meant that they could not link the behavior of the soldiers to the written ROE. On the other hand, they could ask soldiers what they heard or understood the ROE to be, but they could not prove conclusively that what the soldiers heard was the real, written, classified ROE. This frustrating situation is similar to the double-bind established at the Abu Ghraib trials: the White House orders and techniques for inflicting torture were not released until the year 2008, but soldiers were convicted for using these techniques — which were classified at the time of the trials, in 2005 — as if they dreamed up the abuse and torture by themselves in the year 2003. These secretive dimensions of courts-martial obviously call into question whether the pre-trial and trial hearings were truly "open" by American cultural standards. Clearly, classified information that could have been helpful to the accused was deliberately withheld by the government in the Abu Ghraib, Iron Triangle, and other courts-martial.

The IO asked whether additional witnesses should be added to the witness list. Mr. Bergrin spoke up immediately:

> Yes. We would respectfully request Colonel Michael Steele, sir. We would also respectfully request that prior to the commencement of the 32 an offer of proof in reference to Mamed D. Mohammed because we haven't been provided with any information whatsoever in reference to this person. We want to be able to effectively cross-examine him and be prepared for his testimony.

The IO replied, "Okay. Anything else?" But in the end, the IO ruled that Colonel Steele would not testify. Moments later, Mr. Bergrin asked for Mr. Hussein's statement because the defense attorneys had been given no information about him. Mohammed and Hussein were two of the Iraqi soldiers on this mission. The prosecutor interjected:

> CPT FISCHBACH: Sir, both Hussein and Sergeant Mohammed have given a verbal interview with CID. It is my understanding that they are not literate so they couldn't actually write down their own statements. CID did a summary of the transcript and that was provided in an e-mail, I think, as well as on the CDs provided to all the defense counsel and to yourself, sir. Sir, we will send that out again to make sure everyone has it. Defense attorneys raised the issue of interpreters for the Iraqi witnesses (who never testified):

> CPT SUDDETH: The interpreters what type — the interpreters are they going to be Army interpreters for us, or are they going to be local nationals that will be interpreting?

> CPT FISCHBACH: It's my understanding, Captain Suddeth, that they're all going to be US hired simply because the Iraqi interpreters are frankly too scared to participate because of the potential media exposure.

In fact, all the interpreters were Iraqis, and they were, indeed, all scared to help the Americans, as I will show later. The hearing recessed at 7:25 p.m. and reconvened at 7:55 p.m. The prosecutor addressed the IO immediately:

> CPT FISCHBACH: Sir, just while we're back on the record I just want to discuss what occurred during the recess. The accused, all of them who have no security clearance or have had their clearance suspended, were all given non disclosure agreements that they could view classified information. There has been reference to Mr. Bergrin that he has advised his client not to sign that agreement. I just want to confirm that that is the case on the record.

> MR. BERGRIN: It is absolutely the case.

> CPT FISCHBACH: I also want to put on the record, both yourself, Mr. Bergrin, and Captain Rutizer are aware of potential consequences if you disclose classified information received pursuant to this case to PFC Clagett.

This is not even a veiled threat, but a direct warning. Mr. Waddington told me that he was similarly warned. Presumably Mr. Bergrin did not want his client to sign the agreement because his client might have jeopardized his chances further by accidentally disclosing classified information if he had access to it. We see again the double-bind situation in which the defense found itself: they were damned if they had access to the classified information and damned if they did not have access.

TESTIMONY OF SPECIAL AGENT JEREMY MCCORMICK

Many pages of the transcript were taken up by the testimony of Special Agent Jeremy McCormick. His long and unimportant testimony was about a black 9 millimeter pistol and a worn brown leather holster that was found in Sergeant Girouard's room. It turned out that the pistol was a trophy[1] and had no relevance to the case whatsoever. Further testimony revealed that it was common for soldiers to steal weapons as trophies while on missions, in addition to stealing liquor, television sets, refrigerators, and other items. The prosecution went through many pages of transcript about this trophy, and it did result in an additional criminal charge against Girouard — but the weapon was not used and has no bearing on the case. Mr. Waddington used the cross-examination of McCormick as an opportunity to lay the groundwork for questions that would later be directed to another special agent, Nichole Battle:

> Q: Do you know Special Agent Nichole Battle?

> A: Yes I do, sir....

> Q: Do you know why she was removed from FOB Warrior?

---

1 Thorstein Veblen's sociological theory is the only one that deals with trophies in general and trophies during wartime in particular.

A: I do not, sir.

Q: Do you know where the orange knife was at — where it's at now, the knife that was used to stab Specialist Hunsaker?

A: No, sir, we have not located the knife.

Testimony of Special Agent Billy Higgason

The next prosecution witness was CID special agent Billy Higgason. The gist of his testimony was that during an interrogation that lasted 6 hours and 7 minutes, Specialist Graber confessed to him that he shot at one of the three prisoners after they had already been shot, as a kind of mercy killing. Graber's military defense counsel, Captain Suddeth, cross-examined Higgason to ensure that Graber was not coerced into making a confession. Captain Suddeth asked: "At any time did you indicate to Specialist Graber, 'Before you bury yourself in a hole any deeper I want you to tell me the truth,' or something to that effect?" "Yes, sir, I'm sure I used that terminology" Higgason replied. Captain Miller, defense counsel for Sergeant Girouard, continued the cross-examination of Higgason:

Q: Physical touching by CID agents, is that appropriate during an interview?

A: It could be sir, as long as it's not harmful physical touching....

Q: If you were, for example, interviewing a female suspect, would it ever be appropriate for you to touch her knee for example?

A: Probably not. I would personally not do that.

Q: How about vice versa. If it was a female agent interviewing a male, would that ever be appropriate for a female agent to touch a male's knee?

A: So, I'm not a female, I can't answer that....

Q: How about a female agent walking up to a male, putting her arms around him so her arms were interlocked behind his back?

IO: Are you going somewhere with this? I'm sorry.

CPT MILLER: Yes, sir.

IO: Okay.

In case the reader is also wondering where this line of questioning was going, the answer is that the defense attorneys had found evidence that CID used female special agent Battle to touch male soldiers inappropriately in order to elicit confessions from them. This "technique" is reminiscent of the documented use of female guards at both Abu Ghraib and Guantanamo to elicit information from prisoners. It is important to note that by using females in this way, the Army was implicitly putting US soldiers and suspected "enemy combatants" in the same reference group. Mr. Waddington continued this line of questioning in his cross-examination of Higgason:

> Q: Special Agent, can you please describe to us why Special Agent Nicole Battle was removed from her last FOB and sent down here?

> A: There are various reasons there, sir.... There were some complaints from an agent working with her there that they didn't get along....

> Q: There were statements taken on 11 May and then on 29 May and at that point you had no conspiracy that you could prove, did you?

> A: That's correct, sir.

> Q: You guys were getting kind of desperate?

> A: I wouldn't say "desperate," sir.

Waddington went on to question Higgason about something called the Reid Technique[1], which is a method of interrogation widely used by civilian as well as military law enforcement in the United States. I heard first-hand testimony about this technique during the court-martial of Sergeant Michael Leahy in February of 2009, and was surprised to learn that it involves agents lying to the accused in order to elicit a confession. I had assumed that police agents, whether military or civilian, were not allowed to lie or trick suspects into confessions — but apparently, this practice is tolerated. Judges do not admonish the agents for lying and do not disallow the confessions obtained through deceit. Here is another major instance of systemic double-bind techniques used in the Iron Triangle and other cases: the suspect is in trouble if he does not tell the interrogator what he or she wants to hear, and is in trouble if he or she succumbs and agrees with the interrogator about something that he or she does not fully believe. The issue at hand is whether there was a conspiracy among the accused prior to the Iron Triangle killings or a government conspiracy to scapegoat particular soldiers in order to cover up the use of the unlawful ROE:

> Q: When I say "Reid" I don't mean like read a book, I'm talking R-E-I-D.

> A: I'm very clear on what you're talking about, sir. That's correct.

> Q: The first thing you did was suggest a theory of conspiracy to these gentlemen, didn't you?

> A: Yes, sir. Actually I told them that we knew that there was a conspiracy in the room, that there were people in the room talking about doing this, that's correct.

Of course, the investigators did not know any such thing, as Higgason had previously admitted, but wanted the conspiracy to be true. Waddington got Higgason to admit that he lied to Graber: "Yes, sir, I said that

---

1 *www.reid.com*

there were witnesses who had come forward and said that there was a conspiracy."

Q: Did you tell him that — What techniques — What did you tell him to tell you his story to go along with your theory?

A: Sir, it kind of came out like a lightening bolt....

Q: My question is this, what did you tell him in order to get him to say, "Yeah, there was a conspiracy."

A: I just continued with that basic thing that we know that there was a discussion in the house prior to these detainees being shot....

Q: Whenever you and your agents are interviewing people do you ever use lies, trickery, or deceit.

A: Occasionally, sir.

Q: Do you use all three or just one of these three?

A: Depending on the situation, sir. If there is an occasion that we need to lie and say someone has confessed to something then, yes, sir, we will use that.

Notice that the special agent did not refer to the need to ascertain the truth, but to the government's need to have the accused confess to something that fits their theory — even if it requires lies, trickery, and deceit.

The hearing recessed at 8:58 p.m. and was reconvened at 9:10 p.m. Mr. Bergrin continued the cross-examination of Higgason:

Q: Do you know of any disciplinary action or misconduct against any of the agents that are working in your office presently....

A: Sir, there was a claim by a victim in a sexual assault case involving Agent Battle.

Q: What was the allegation?

A: Actually, sir, it was not by the victim it was by Special Agent Nurse who felt that Agent Battle coerced the victim into changing her statement.

Q: Where is that investigation right now?

A: There was not an investigation in that, sir.

Q: What happened as a result of those allegations?

A: Sir, it was provided to our command via the nursing channels. I'm not exactly sure how all that proceeded.

Q: Have you reviewed the disciplinary records of Agent Battle?

A: No, sir, that's not what I'm privy to.

Q: Well, you are the OIC [Office in Charge], correct?

A: Yes, sir, that's correct....

Q: Now when you began your interview on 15 June 2006, you just testi-fied that you interviewed Graber not as a suspect and you didn't suspect him of anything, but reference to knowledge that he may have pertaining to conversations, correct?

A: Yes, sir, that is correct....

Q: Based upon that isn't it a fact that you intentionally didn't read him his rights at the beginning of interviewing him on 15 June?

A: I did not advise him of his rights, that's correct, sir.

Children are taught in American schools, and other Americans watch on films and other popular culture outlets, that suspects must be read their Miranda rights as soon as possible as a Constitutional right. "Read them their rights" is a common and average American understanding of what law enforcement officials are supposed to do with suspects. In practice, I have witnessed court proceedings in which agents admit routinely that they did not read the suspects their rights based upon the hair-splitting technicality that they were not suspects until the moment that they con-fessed. Judges pass over such language games in silence. Bergrin turned his attention to another charge made by Graber, that the co-accused soldiers had threatened him.

Q: Did you ask Graber if he was in fear for his life?

A: Sir, I'm pretty certain that he clarified that in there. I don't think he stated he was in fear for his life.

Q: As a matter of fact he stated that he was not in fear of his life, correct?

A: Yes, sir....

Q: Sir, isn't it a fact that at the time that you began your interview of Specialist Graber on 15 June, as you testified, you never read him his rights, correct? We've established that fact.

A: Yes, sir, that's correct. When I initially began interviewing him I did not advise him....

Q: So approximately six and a half hours [of interrogation]?

A: Approximately, yes, sir.

Q: To take a 10 page statement, sir?

A: I'm a very slow writer, sir....

Q: So it took approximately 6 and a half hours to go through 10 pages, and you're telling me it's because you're a slow writer?....

A: Actually, sir, it was not six and a half hours....

Q: Six hours, correct?

A: Yes, sir.

Q: To go through 10 pages?

A: I think it's 11 pages, sir.

Q: Doesn't the 11th page consist of three sentences?

A: I'm not sure, sir. I would have to see the 11th page.

Q: And you're telling us that you didn't review any of these statements before coming to testify in an Article 32 investigation for a murder?

A: No, sir, I didn't....

Q: As you sit here today isn't it a fact that there is no physical, forensic, or scientific evidence that proves your conspiracy theory?

A: Testimonial evidence, sir.

I have observed a common pattern in military court proceedings: They tend to rely upon the medieval proof of the confession more than verification from physical, forensic, or scientific evidence. In the Iron Triangle case, the bodies "disappeared," no ballistics tests were run, and no physical evidence of any sort was found to support the government's theory of what happened. I have observed defense attorneys becoming very agitated over this situation. Bergrin drove this point home: "And you have no evidence whatsoever based upon either scientific evidence, medical evidence, or any witnesses to establish that fact? Isn't that a fact?" Higgason replied: "Not that I'm aware of, sir." But ultimately, none of Bergrin's rational and scientific points mattered because courts uphold the doublespeak claim that a confession is the strongest type of evidence available. At the same time, judges and investigative officers do not seem to be concerned that the confessions were obtained through various coercive and deceitful "techniques." And they pay lip service to the claim that as officers of the law, they are always truthful. The legal profession's doublespeak often begets double-bind situations, which in turn promote paranoia and perjury, for those who become enmeshed in legal matters. If the suspect confesses, he or she has handed the government evidence — even if it is not entirely true — that the government regards as superior to physical evidence. If the suspect resists during interrogation, he or she is openly threatened with serious crimes even if the suspect was not directly involved in any crime. This is because the legal definition of "conspiracy" is so broad that mere proximity to a meeting of any sort prior to an alleged crime makes the "conspirator" as guilty as the perpetrators of the same crime. These legal definitions and tactics are far removed from commonsense.

Mr. Bergrin turned to the details of Graber's confession of the alleged mercy killing of one of the prisoners.

Q: Did Graber tell you what kind of shot, what kind of gun, excuse me, or weapon he was allegedly using?

A: Sir, I believe it was an M4. I believe he told me he missed one time and hit the dir beside the guy's head then had to actually site to shoot him the second time.

Q: And did he tell you approximately how far the rifle was from the object?

A: Sir, from standing position leaning down over him ... within a couple of feet....

Q: Based upon all your experience and training and all those courses you told us about that you took, what kind of burn pattern would an individual have on their face if they were shot with an M4 from approximately 2 feet away?....

A: I could give you some assumptions on my part and some based on my experience, however, I'm not forensically trained in that area....

Q: And you don't remember ever seeing powder on the skin [from the photographs], correct?

A: No, sir, I don't recall that...

Q: And you're about as sure of that testimony as you are about all of the testimony here today.

A: I'm not looking at the photo at this point. It was a fresher view at the time.

[MR. BERGRIN]: I've got nothing further for this guy.

The M4 rifle is a particularly lethal weapon that delivers 850 bullets per minute. If a soldier squeezes the trigger for only one burst, the weapon will deliver 3 bullets in that one burst. Why would Graber allegedly use this highly deadly weapon, intended mostly for battles of approximately 100 yards, for a close-range execution? And how can a soldier "miss" with such a weapon at a range of two feet? Harking back to Marshall's classic finding that soldiers are extremely reluctant to kill, one may speculate that Graber was shaken because of what had already happened, and did not really want to execute the prisoner. And it is also possible that he never carried out this "mercy killing." Perhaps he confessed to the crime for a host of psychological reasons which compel people to confess to things they did not do. But Bergrin is correct that scientific evidence could have settled questions as to whether Graber's confession was truthful. To remind the reader: the bodies of the Iraqi prisoners mysteriously disappeared shortly after being taken to the army base, and were never recovered. No scientific tests were performed on the bodies and no forensic or other investigations were ever performed based upon the photographs. Bergrin's frustration is understandable from the cultural perspective that American society usually demands scientific evidence in legal cases of this sort, while the army chose to take the path of relying upon confession — even a coerced, improper confession.

TESTIMONY OF SPECIAL AGENT MORA

Special Agent Ramon Antonio de la Mora took the stand. He had interviewed Graber on May 29th, two weeks prior to Graber's subsequent confession. The prosecutor had Mora admit that at the time of the interview, he "had no knowledge of any prior statements."

Q: And what suspicions, if any, did you have about Specialist Graber committing criminal acts?

A: I didn't have any at that point, sir.

Perhaps the prosecutor was trying to make the fine point that the suspects were not read their rights because they were not really suspects. But in that case, why were non-suspects being interrogated (the prosecutor preferred the word, "interviewed")?

Q: How many people were you all interviewing pursuant to this investigation?

A: At that particular point, I believe we interviewed between eight and ten people, sir. I can't remember the exact number; it was the whole squad.

The entire squad was "interviewed" but supposedly no one in the squad was "suspected" in the repeated interrogations that occurred on May 11th and May 29th. Under cross-examination, Mora said that all the soldiers were interviewed simultaneously by different agents, and, "once we were done with an interview, we would get together and compare notes as to what the other witnesses were saying, sir." At this point, 9:54 p.m., the cross-examination fell apart due to simple human exhaustion. Mr. Bergrin asked the IO for permission to finish the cross-examination the following day. In reality, this special agent would not be recalled to the stand.

CAPTAIN FISCHBACH: I think it be better if everybody gets a good night's sleep. I know you gentlemen had a very long flight.

MR. BERGRIN: Thank you.

IO: And you seem to be hungry. Okay, we'll recess until 0800 tomorrow.

The Article 32 hearing resumed at 7:52 a.m. on August 2, 2006. Mr. Waddington immediately requested that the government skips "over some of the foundation requirements, authentication" and focus on essential issues. The prosecutor's response was another grim reminder that they were in a war zone — albeit, due to the government's choice of venue:

> CAPTAIN FISCHBACH: Mr. Waddington, our position on that is, as I indicated, while I would hate for it to happen, I can't guarantee that Special Agent Higgason is necessarily going to be alive when we get to trial, and this may be our only opportunity to capture his testimony, and I understand your position, and I ordinarily would agree with you. If we were back in garrison it would probably be unnecessary, but in an abundance of caution, the government is going ahead and establishing the foundation while it's on the record right now.

> IO: And I also want to say it's not necessary to stand. When we speak here, we'll just stay seated just for convenience. Okay, go ahead, Government. Do you want to call your next witness?

THE GOVERNMENT'S STAR WITNESS: PRIVATE FIRST CLASS BRADLEY MASON

Private First Class Bradley Mason took the stand, and would take up 215 pages of transcript with his testimony. He was the government's star witness, and the defense was intent on discrediting him and his testimony. The prosecutor began:

> Q: PFC Mason before we get started, is it your understanding you're testifying under a grant of immunity here today?

> A: Yes, sir...

> Q: And do you know who issued that immunity to you?

> A: United States Army.

> Q: General Turner sound familiar?

> A: Yes.

> Q: Okay, who's that?

> A: It's our general.

> Q: Okay, now he didn't tell you what to say?

> A: No.

> Q: What is your understanding of how the immunity works for you here?

> A: I can't be held to anything I'm saying.

> Q: Okay, you understand that anything you say that is false could be grounds for a charge of perjury or false official statement?

> A: Yes.

Mason's testimony was already off to a shaky start, given that he understood that he "can't be held to anything," whereas the correct answer is that he is supposed to tell the truth and not perjure himself. The prosecutor was already coaching him minutes into the testimony, and did not correct Mason for failing to address the captain as "sir." On other occasions, I have witnessed officers correct an enlisted soldier immediately for failing to show respect by saying "sir" in every sentence — even in the midst of a court proceeding. The prosecutor got into the trial record that Mason was twenty years old; that the tragic mission on May 9, 2006 began at 5 am; that his military unit was also known as the Rakkasans; that they flew on Blackhawk helicopters for the mission; and that their target was an artificial island called Objective Murray, near the Muthana Chemical Complex.

Q: Okay what was the general nature of the mission that day during Operation Iron Triangle?

A: *To kill all the hajjis* [emphasis added].

Q: Could you be more specific?

IO: Could you repeat that. I didn't hear that.

A: To catch all the bad guys.

One may surmise that the IO and everybody else did hear Mason refer to the Iraqis with the racist label, hajji. The IO probably did not want to hear it. The prosecutor tried to remedy the situation by asking for clarification, which only muddied the waters further, because "to catch all the bad guys" is *not* the same as "to kill all the hajjis." One has to wonder: how commonplace was the phrase "hajji" as a reference to Iraqis? Was the order really to kill all the hajjis, as opposed to kill all military-age males?

Q: All right, when you landed on your first objective there what happened?

A: Nothing. There was nobody at the house, so we wandered around a little bit.

Mr. Waddington explained to me later what went through his head during this moment in the testimony: "Colonel Steele had made it seem like the mission was going to be a D-day landing, and all they found was some women and children and chickens." The soldiers must have been bewildered. The prosecutor continued:

Q: After you found nothing there at your fist stop on Objective Murray, what happened next?

A: We went to the second house or *the second small objective of the big event* [emphasis added].

Q: All right, how did you get there?

A: Blackhawk.

Q: How many Blackhawks?

A: Two.

Q: And who went to this second sub-objective there?

A: 3rd Squad and 2nd Squad.

Q: And who does that include?

A: Myself, Sergeant Girouard, PFC Clagett, Hunsaker, Graber, Sergeant Lemus, and then 2nd Squad, and then the LT and Gun 6 which is Helton and Ryan, and then Kemp and Doc went with us.

Mr. Bergrin objected "to the leading nature of the questions on behalf of Corey Clagett," but was overruled by the IO. Mason's choice of words in describing the mission as "the big event" is noteworthy. How big or small was it? The army has never revealed publicly how many Iraqis were captured or killed during Operation Iron Triangle. The prosecutor then made a Freudian slip by referring to Mason as Clagett, captured in the trial record:

Q: Okay, PFC Clagett [sic], what time did you land on the second sub-objective? I'm sorry, PFC Mason, what time did you land on that second sub-objective?

A: Around 0730....

Q: And what happened when the UH-60s landed on that second sub-objective?

A: We got off the Blackhawk, ran up to the house on the back side of the house, *shot at a guy through the first window we came up to.* We continued around the house, went inside the house; half of us split to one room; half of us split to the other room [emphasis added].

Throughout all the testimony of all the witnesses and participants in this mission, the killing of the unarmed man in the window is described in a perfunctory manner. The killing of that man was never prosecuted or even considered as a crime. That particular kill was supposedly in accordance with the ROE. In the many pages of testimony that followed, the prosecutor ascertained that Mason searched the three male prisoners and found no weapons; that he did not search the women; that he has performed approximately one hundred similar searches while in Iraq; that the unit found one AK-47 in the house and that by Iraqi law, every family s allowed to own one AK-47 for protection. Mason also said that "Sergeant Girouard told us that PFC Clagett and Hunsaker were going to kill the three detainees from the fist house."

Q: After Sergeant Girouard announced that PFC Clagett and Specialist Hunsaker were going to murder these three detainees —

MR. BERGRIN: Objection to the question. That's not what he said. He said "kill" not murder.

IO: That's correct....

Q: Who else was at this meeting?

A: Myself, Graber, and Sergeant Lemus.

A philosopher might wonder about the meaning of the "language game" of distinguishing between "murder" versus "killing" in this context. The man in the window was killed but according to the army's narrative, was not murdered. The killing of the three prisoners would be socially constructed into "murder" throughout the trial process. But one could just as arbitrarily refer to all the deaths (the man in the window plus the three prisoners) as either killings or murder. The same unlawful ROE that was issued could transform all the killings into routine deaths from combat. Why was the army intent on transforming the latter three killings into the category of murder? This is not only a debate for philosophers and scholars. Apparently, the soldiers engaged in a similar, philosophical debate:

Q: While you're in this room with the women, you see the other individuals down by the landing zone, what happens next?

A: Sergeant Girouard comes down to the door where I'm at, and we start arguing about Clagett and Hunsaker killing the three guys.

Q: What's the nature of the argument?

A: I told him that I'm not down with it, that it's murder, and he told me that I just murdered — just helped murder somebody, referring to the guy in the room...

Q: Who shot that man?

A: I — we don't know.

The sworn statements depict the Iraqi who was killed as alternately being "in" in the window or "in" the room or "outside" the house. Where was he when he was killed? The photograph taken after the event shows the victim's body outside the house. But Mason had testified to the location of the victim as "in the room." Mason continued with his story of how Girouard left the room after allegedly ordering two of his soldiers to kill the prisoners.

Q: Any particular reason you didn't leave the room about the same time as Girouard?

A: I don't have anything to do with what is going on.

Q: All right, what did you think was going on when you heard shots ringing out?

A: They were killing the three detainees.

Q: So, after you heard the second volley of shots come out — do you know how many it was?

A: Two.

Q: And what made you leave the room that time?

A: I wanted to see what was going on then....

Q: All right, how comfortable did you feel leaving the women unsecured in that room while you went around and checked to see what was going on?

A: I really wasn't worried about them.... After that, Clagett and Hunsaker show the women that Hunsaker got cut by the three males. They offered them water.

Q: Who offered who water?

A: The women offered them water, and then they left.

Why would the women offer water to soldiers who had just killed men who were apparently living with them? Nobody ever asked or resolved this issue, although it is apparent that opposing attorneys had opposing interpretations. The prosecutor asked:

Q: After Hunsaker and Clagett went into the room, tried to elicit sympathy from the females, what happened next?

MR. BERGRIN: Objection to the framing of the question....

CAPTAIN FISCHBACH: I'm sorry, sir.

IO: I agree. Frame it different

Q: What happened after Hunsaker and Clagett entered the room and showed their wounds to the females?

A: They left, and they sort of stayed until we went to the LZ [landing zone]....

Q: So all in all how long did it take you guys to depart the objective after Hunsaker and Clagett showed the women their wounds?

A: Three hours.

The prosecutor did not ask about what happened during those three hours among the US soldiers, women, and Iraqi soldiers. Mason said that the next day, Girouard, Clagett, and Hunsaker warned him "that if I said anything they'd kill me." How seriously did Mason take the threats? "I took them pretty serious." The prosecutor asked: "To what degree, if any, did you think they were pulling your leg or joking around?" "None." The prosecutor continued:

Q: Did you ever hear Sergeant Girouard use the term "crazy papers?"

A: Yes.

Q: All right, please speak up PFC Mason.... In what contexts and when did he use the term "crazy papers?"

A: He said that if he ever gets arrested for killing anybody he'll use his crazy papers to get out of it.

Q: And did he ever elaborate what his crazy papers were?

A: His post-traumatic stress disorder.

Q: And how did this subject of post-traumatic stress disorder come up in the conversation?

A: We were just talking about it.

Even though PTSD is a serious issue that inflicts documented damage to a soldier's psyche and performance, it does not seem to be treated seriously by the army. The army and the legal system seem to be the last social institutions that still fail to recognize and account for the role of combat stress and mental illness in the commission of crimes. Every accused soldier with whom I have interacted had been diagnosed with PTSD. The official rates for PTSD released by the army show that soldiers in the current war suffer from more combat stress than soldiers in any previous war. Yet soldiers such as Girouard are sent back on missions, with diagnosed PTSD, in contradistinction to norms in World War II in which the army replaced stressed soldiers and units with fresh troops.[1] Stouffer's as well as more recent studies suggest that the average infantry soldier becomes "useless" to the army after approximately 100 days of combat. Is the army unaware of this documented finding, or is it deliberately ignoring it? All of the soldiers in this particular unit had been exposed to combat for at least a year, without any break, and many were on their second tours of duty. The hearing recessed at 9:02 a.m.

The hearing reconvened at 9:12 a.m. Mr. Waddington began to cross-examine Mason. He launched forcefully into the explosive issue of the ROE.

Q: I want to start off by talking about the rules of engagement that were mentioned. What were the rules?

A: Kill all male detainees on the — or kill all male military aged males on the island.

Q: Okay, who gave you — who gave you that ROE?

---

1 The parallels between the reality of the army's attitude toward sending soldiers with diagnosed PTSD into battle with Joseph Heller's fictional account of sending "crazy" airmen on missions are not exact but close enough to quote Heller: "There was only one catch and that was Catch-22, which specified that a concern for one's safety in the face of dangers that were real and immediate was the process of a rational mind. Orr was crazy and could be grounded. All he had to do was ask, and as soon as he did, he would no longer be crazy and would have to fly more missions. Orr would be crazy to fly more missions and sane if he didn't, but if he was sane he had to fly them. If he flew them he was crazy and didn't have to, but if he didn't want to he was sane and had to" (p. 52).

A: Lieutenant Wehrheim and then Colonel Steele.

Note that Mason corrected himself after making the Freudian slip in claiming that the ROE was to kill all the male detainees. Was the ROE understood by the soldiers as "kill all male military aged males, even if they are detainees?" Mason is not the only one who accidentally implies an affirmative answer to this question. A pattern of evidence suggests that soldiers believed the rule was, "Take no prisoners." Mr. Waddington continued:

Q: Were you present when these orders were given?

A: Yes.

Q: What specifically did Colonel Steele tell you before you went out on the mission?

A: Kill all of them.

Q: Kill all of them? Did he say who these "them" were?

A: Insurgents; terrorists....

Q: So were you guys hyped up before you left on this mission?

A: Yes....

Q: And you mentioned earlier when you were testifying with Captain Fischbach, something about killing all hajjis. Is that what you said?

A: Yes.

Q: What does that mean?

A: Hajji?

Q: Right.

A: Just another word for Iraqi.

If soldiers understood their orders were to kill all insurgents, terrorists, Iraqis, and military age males, it would have been difficult for them to distinguish between "good" versus "bad" Iraqis. This is the issue that Mr. Waddington explored with regard to relations between US and Iraqi soldiers on what was supposed to have been an ideal joint mission:

Q: I want to talk to you now about your — your unit's — your squad's involvement with the Iraqi Army. You guys work with Iraqi Army soldiers?

A: Yes.

Q: And on this particular mission, who — how many Iraqi soldiers were with you?

A: Well at first — first they weren't there, then all of a sudden they all just appeared out of nowhere, and they were just wandering around the O-B-J or the objective the whole time....

Q: Now were they just observing, or were they taking part in the raid?

A: They were going to take part in the raid, but we never liked them working with us.

Q: Why not?

A: They really don't know what they're doing.

Q: Are there any issues with trust between the Iraqi army and your squad?

A: Yes.

Q: What are they?

A: We don't trust them because we know that some of them are bad too. Some over here we know, *but most of them are also terrorists....*

Q: Was there talk of the Iraqi army being infiltrated by insurgents?

A: We always thought that there were insurgents in the Iraqi Army [emphasis added].

It would be important to conduct research to determine the percentage of US soldiers that are as suspicious as Mason about the Iraqi army. Is this alleged mistrust a pervasive issue between the two armies? Given that US soldiers are not familiar with Arabic culture or language, it seems obvious that the Americans might be likely to lump all Iraqis into the same "reference group" as the enemy or the potential enemy within, even if they are an ostensible ally. Furthermore, the Iraqi soldiers may have identified with the Iraqis who were killed, because of common language, culture and other factors that determine reference groups. And of course, it is possible that some of the Iraqi soldiers were sympathetic to the enemy. Mason went on to describe the Iraqi soldiers as becoming very agitated after the Iraqi man in the window was killed by the Americans.

Q: What happened?

A: They [Iraqi soldiers] were arguing in Arabic, and then one of them charged their weapon, and then I guess the commander of those guys sent one of them away.

Q: Do you have any idea what they were arguing about?

A: No....

Q: Do you recall the word "terrorist" or "insurgent" being used?

A: No.

Q: Who was all present during that?

A: The whole company.

Q: The whole company witnessed this?

A: Yes.

Mr. Waddington then turned his attention to the issues of kill contests and kill boards in the military unit.

Q: Is there any type of competition of stats kept on which squad had the most kills?

A: Yes....

Q: Where are the numbers posted?

A: On a white board....

Q: What did it say on the board?

A: "Let the bodies hit the floor."...

Q: Did your first sergeant ever encourage you guys to get a certain number of kills?

A: Yes ... three hundred kills.

Q: He wanted — First Sergeant [Geressy] wanted 300 kills?

A: Yes....

Q: Do you recall any Iraqis objecting to what the rules of engagement were?

A: I know after we got to the rest house, the Iraqis wouldn't work for us anymore.

Q: Why?

A: They didn't agree with it.

Q: Did you personally witness a disagreement about the rules of engagement between the Iraqis and the Americans?

A: They just nodded and would listen but they wouldn't do anything we told them to do....

Q: Did anyone tell you why this fourth guy wasn't killed?

A: No.

> Q: Considering your rules of engagement, you guys could have shot all four of these Iraqis or whatever they were without a problem when you hit the objective, correct?

> A: Yes.

Clearly, based upon Mason's statements as well as descriptions of relations between the two armies supplied by other soldiers — the Iraqi soldiers did not agree with the American ROE. Given that the US soldiers were encouraged to kill as many Iraqis as possible through kill contests, it seems reasonable that they would not perceive the killing of prisoners as a departure from the ROE as they understood them to be. It is a mystery, indeed, why one Iraqi prisoner's life was spared. Given the overall context, one may speculate that the Iraqi soldiers would not stand for killing him in the name of ROE.

Next, Mr. Waddington turned to Mason's earlier allegations that the other US soldiers had threatened to kill him if he ever disclosed what had happened. Through extensive cross-examination, Mason changed his story and said that Hunsaker "didn't say anything." He also said the soldiers would often joke about matters such as robbing banks, killing, and other gallows humor, so that the "threats" may have been an example of such "humor." Mr. Bergrin took over the cross-examination:

> Q: You talked about the rules of engagement and Colonel Steele having a meeting with you, correct?

> A: Yes ... I can't remember the exact words, but it was along the line of just kill all of them.

> Q: As a matter of fact he cursed and said, "Kill all of the sons of a bitches," correct?

> A: I don't remember exactly those words, but it was around that, yes....

> Q: And when Lieutenant Wehrheim spoke to you, he used the same expression, "Kill all the son of a bitches," correct? "Kill all of them."

> A: I don't remember that. He just said that the rules of engagement were *that we get to kill all the male detainees.*

> IO: Speak up.

> A: *That the rule of engagement were that we get to kill all the male detainees or all the male insurgents [emphasis added].*

Mason had already made this same Freudian slip once before in his testimony. But now he repeated the "mistake" that the soldiers were allowed to kill the prisoners! "We get to kill" is different from saying, "We were ordered to kill." And, killing "detainees" is different from killing "insurgents." But did the soldiers perceive these differences? After two Freudian slips in a row, one begins to wonder what exactly was said to the soldiers, and what they understood. A psychologist might find it significant that Mason repeated this claim in a voice so low that the IO told him to speak up. Mr. Bergrin was relentless in his questions about these issues:

Q: You just said kill all the male detainees. Isn't that what you just said?

A: Yes.

Q: And you're under oath, correct?

A: Yes. It was a mistake.

Q: So when you hit the island on the 9th of May, in your mind you believe that anybody that you saw of military age was going to be killed, correct?

A: Yes.

Q: Now did you speak to anybody in your platoon about the rules of engagement once you got them from Colonel Steele and Lieutenant Wehrheim?

A: No.

Q: Did you say that these sound different? Did you question them at all?

A: No.

Q: And you didn't question them because you are a private in the Army and your job is to obey orders, correct?

A: Yes.

Q: So as soon as you saw a military aged male, you were going to engage him and kill him, correct?

A: Yes.

Q: Now when you testified for Captain Fischbach, you said, "kill all the hajjis." That's the word you use, correct?

A: Yes.

Q: That's the expression that you used?

A: Yes.

Q: A hajji isn't a terrorist, correct?

A: It's just another word for Iraqi that we use.

Q: Any Iraqi, right?

A: Yes.

Q: It could be an Iraqi civilian.

A: Yes.

Q: It could be an Iraqi Army person working with your unit.

A: Yes.

Q: It could be an Iraqi interpreters working with your unit.

A: Yes, but — ʹ

Q: And under oath you testified that when you were at that island you were going to kill all the hajjis, correct?

A: Yes.

Q: And those were words that came out of your mouth?

A: Yes.

Q: Now you also testified that you didn't trust Iraqi army soldiers, correct?

A: No, I didn't trust them.

Q: And as a matter of fact, you testified that you believed most of them were terrorists?

A: Yes....

Q: What's a terrorist to you?

A: Anybody that's against me, against the Army.

One should try to imagine the impact of such explosive testimony on the news media and the globe had this testimony and cross-examination occurred during a court-martial. No doubt the prosecutor made this thought experiment, and probably decided to avoid courts-martial at all costs. Mason made it seem as if in his mind, any and all Iraqis were enemies to be killed, much like the "no gook rule" in the Vietnam War. No journalists were present to witness this exchange. This chilling exchange would never be repeated on any court record.

If it is true that most US soldiers regarded all Iraqis as potential or actual enemies — and this has to be ascertained by careful research — the flip-side may also be true. Namely, the Iraqi perception of US soldiers as cowboys who shoot first and ask questions later (if at all) would reinforce the image of all Americans as potential or actual enemies as well. Neither side would create the necessary mental space to conceive of a reference group for "good" Americans or Iraqis. To the extent that this dismal assessment turns out to be true, it explains some of the tragedy of the current "war on terror."

Mason said that he looked at the kill board "about five hundred times" during his stay in Iraq. The number "three hundred" was written on the board by First Sergeant Geressy, and indicated the number of Iraqis he wanted killed.

Q: Do you believe that that's what the first sergeant wanted from you, correct?

A: Yes.

Q: And there's no doubt in your mind about that, right?

A: Yes.

Bergrin then turned to the issue of "joking around" that Mr. Waddington had introduced earlier:

Q: Did you ever talk about having sex with children in Thailand.

A: That was a joke.

Q: That was a joke?

A: Between all of us...

Q: Isn't it a fact that words came out of your mouth to the effect of you going to Thailand ... and having sex with nine-year-old girls.

A: As a joke. It has nothing to do with this case....

Q: Now you were granted immunity to testify, right?

A: Yes.

Q: And before Captain Fischbach gave you questions, he asked you what immunity meant to you, correct?

A: Yes.

Q: And what it meant to you, what you testified, is that you can say essentially anything that you want and you won't be prosecuted, correct?

A: Yes.

Another contentious issue exposed by Mr. Bergrin was that CID planted in Mason's mind the idea that the two additional gunshots that he heard were the mercy kill by Graber — an event he did not witness.

Q: Do you know why those second shots occurred?

A: Not until I talked to CID, and I found out that they were mercy kills.

Q: Who told you that?

A: CID did the first time.

Apparently part of the Reid Technique used by CID agents is to plant ideas and theories in the mind of a witness — and this is allowed in military trials. Mr. Bergrin also got Mason to admit that he had perjured himself previously:

Q: And in those two statements of May the 11th and May the 29th, you deliberately, intentionally, and purposely lied while under oath, correct?

A: Yes.

Q: And you knew what the oath meant, correct?

A: Yes.

Mr. Bergrin also got Mason to admit that even though his comrades had allegedly threatened him, he was not afraid to go out on missions with them. Bergrin was relentless in impeaching Mason. "Have you ever used any expression such as 'Every man, woman, and child in Iraq should die?" "Yes," Mason answered. Bergrin also got Mason to admit that he lied about reporting a fire fight when he was on the radio, and he was punished for this act. "And Clagett used to always joke about having sex with your sister, going out with your sister, correct?" Mason replied: "Yeah, I told him he could go out with my sister."

Q: Now did you ever tell anybody you wanted an early release from the Army?

A: Yes....

Q: As a matter of fact you talked about claiming post-traumatic stress disorder, correct?

A: I've been going to — actually *I was told I had post-traumatic stress disorder*....

Q: Did you go to a doctor?

A: Yes, up here....

Q: Tell us what the symptoms that you're having are.

A: Nightmares, stressed out; just like wake up in the middle of the night, and things like that....

Q: And what kind of nightmares do you have about the last mission?

A: ...I've had stressed out nightmares like one, we went to a house, and there was dead bodies everywhere, and me and Sergeant Girouard went to the very back room, and we were the only ones towards the very back room, and through the door I could see red eyes looking at both of us, and I woke up from that one....

Q: What other nightmares have you had?

DEPARTMENT OF THE ARMY
A COMPANY, 501ˢᵀ SPECIAL TROOPS BATTALION
101st AIRBORNE DIVISION (AIR ASSAULT)
COB SPEICHER, APO AE 09393

REPLY TO
ATTENTION OF

AFZB-KC-A   31 August 2006

MEMORANDUM FOR LTC Nathaniel Johnson, Jr., Appointing Authority

SUBJECT: Article 32(b) Investigation Findings and Recommendations – U.S. v. SSG Raymond L. Girouard, SPC William B. Hunsaker, SPC Juston R. Graber, and PFC Corey R. Clagett

1. Defense counsel present for the hearing: CPT Theodore Miller representing SSG Girouard, CPT Kevin Hynes and Mr. Michael Waddington representing SPC Hunsaker, CPT Sasha Rutizer and Mr. Paul Bergrin representing PFC Clagett, and CPT William Suddeth representing SPC Graber.

2. Substance of testimony – see attached transcripts.

3. As the Investigating Officer in the case US v. SSG Raymond L. Girouard, I find sufficient evidence to recommend the following charges against SSG Girouard be referred to a General Court Martial:

    a. Charge I, Violation of the UCMJ, Art. 80. In that SSG Raymond L. Girouard, U.S. Army, did, at or near the Muthana Chemical Complex, Iraq, on or about 9 May 2006, attempt with premeditation, to murder a male detainee of apparent Middle-Eastern descent whose name is unknown by means of shooting him with a firearm.

    b. Charge II, Violation of the UCMJ, Art. 81. In that SSG Raymond L. Girouard, U.S. Army, did, at or near the Muthana Chemical Complex, Iraq, on or about 9 May 2006, conspire with Specialist William B. Hunsaker and Private First Class Corey R. Clagett to commit an offense under the Uniform Code of Military Justice, to wit: premeditated murder of three detainees of apparent Middle-Eastern descent whose names are unknown, and in order to effect the object of the conspiracy, the said Specialist William B. Hunsaker and Private First Class Corey R. Clagett did shoot at the aforementioned three male detainees whose names are unknown.

    c. Charge III, Violation of the UCMJ, Art. 118, Specification (1). In that SSG Raymond L. Girouard, U.S. Army, did, at or near the Muthana Chemical Complex, Iraq, on or about 9 May 2006, with premeditation, murder a male detainee of apparent Middle-Eastern descent whose name is unknown by means of shooting him with a firearm.

    d. Charge III, Violation of the UCMJ, Art. 118, Specification (2). In that SSG Raymond L. Girouard, U.S. Army, did, at or near the Muthana Chemical Complex, Iraq, on or about 9 May

A: I've had a little girl that was saved and a little boy; I had dreams that they screamed — of them screaming....

Q: And that's why you want to get out of the Army and get released, correct?

A: That and this whole case.

Q: This whole case.... Now you talked about nightmares with children. Did you ever have a confrontation with a male child in Iraq that was wearing pink slippers?

A: Yes.

Q: What did you say about that male child that was wearing pink slippers?

A: I told him he looked like a queer.

Q: And how old was that male child?

A: Probably twelve....

Q: And you walked up to him and told him he looks like a little faggot, isn't that a fact?

A: I didn't walk up to him. I was in the turret, and I yelled it to him. We were throwing him candy....

Q: And in a loud voice you called him a little faggot and said, "Nice slippers," correct?

A: Yes.

Q: And you laughed because you thought that was funny, correct?

A: All of us were laughing [emphasis added].

If it is true that Mason was diagnosed with PTSD, that fact could explain some of the strange behavior attributed to him. More importantly, it seems to be the case that all of the accused and some of the witnesses had PTSD. Several soldiers confessed to me that they had similar nightmares based upon all the body parts, brains, blood, and carnage they had witnessed. PTSD is a real and serious affliction, and Mason deserves some empathy, even if the defense counsel showed him none. Bergrin turned to the killing of the Iraqi man by the window, which was considered legitimate by the Army, and was never prosecuted.

Q: What kind of weapon did you have at that time?

A: A SAW.

Q: And what is a SAW?

A: It's an automatic weapon....

Q: And by one squeeze, do you know how many rounds were fired?

A: Six to nine rounds....

Q: Do you know if you hit the old man?

A: No, I don't know now.

Q: But you were shooting to kill him, correct?

A: Yes.

Q: And this old man never fired at you, right?

A: No.

Q: This old man never engaged you, correct?

A: No.

Q: Why were you firing to kill him then?

A: Because we were told to.

Q: Who were you told to by?

A: Were told to kill all the males — males on the island.

Q: But that old man never fired a shot at you, right?

A: No.

One of Bergrin's points seems to be that the killing of the unarmed Iraqi man, even if it was treated as lawful by the Army, was in fact unlawful because the man never showed hostile intent toward the Americans. Strictly speaking, and with regard to the laws of war, Bergrin is correct. Why, then, would the Army condone this killing yet prosecute soldiers for the other killings that occurred?

The hearing recessed at 10:24 a.m. and reconvened at 10:35 a.m. Bergrin continued his cross-examination. He asked Mason, regarding his interviews with CID agents: "You didn't tell anybody that the [your] prior statements were absolute lies, right?" "No," Mason answered. Whereas in some of his sworn statements Mason claimed that he feared his co-accused colleagues, he admitted in court that this was not true:

Q: As a matter of fact, didn't you tell her [CID agent] that you did not have any fears for your life?

A: Not from Clagett.

Later Mason admitted that he also did not really fear for his life from any of the other co-accused. Mason also admitted that there were no witnesses to the alleged threats by the other soldiers. Bergrin kept on demolishing Mason on most of his testimony made on behalf of the government. "You don't even know if any kind of plan was ever carried out, correct?" "No, I don't," Mason answered. This is important, because the layperson's word "plan," translates into the serious legal charge of "conspiracy."

Q: Were you asked to sketch the individuals at the time of the shooting?

A: Yes.

Q: Isn't it a fact that you weren't present during the time of the shooting?

A: I wasn't present at the time of the shooting.

Q: Yet you drew a sketch of where each individual was, correct?

A: They asked me to draw out where everybody was.

Which is more incredible — that CID coerced Mason into drawing a sketch concerning facts he did not witness or that Mason complied?

Q: You drew a sketch of Hunsaker being cut and stabbed, correct?

A: Yes.

Q: You didn't see Hunsaker get cut or stabbed?

A: No.

Bergrin then turned his attention to issues of morale and discipline in the units, which are central to military missions as well as discourse on the military.

Q: Did you talk about how the squad has gone from good to bad?

A: Yes....

Q: Isn't it a fact that you told Captain Rutizer that the morale of the platoon had gone down prior to the mission of 9 May?

A: Yes.

Q: And it had gone down when Clagett and Hunsaker joined the platoon, correct? Wasn't that the words that you used to Captain Rutizer?

A: Squad.

Q: Squad, excuse me.

A: And I said when Hunsaker joined, it went down a little bit, and then when Clagett joined, it went down more.

Q: So you blamed Clagett and you blamed Hunsaker for the morale of the squad going down. Isn't that a fact, sir?

A: I said it went down, when it started going down, I blamed the incident. That's what I blamed....

Q: And you were upset the squad was falling apart because of Clagett and Hunsaker prior to 9 May, correct?

A: I don't really think it was all because of them cause I hung out, I mean, I was in Clagett's room a lot of the time....

Q: Morale went down, correct?

A: Yes.

Q: Discipline went down, correct?

A: Yes.

Mason held his ground against Bergrin on the specific issue whether he blamed Clagett and Hunsaker for the problems with morale and discipline, and maintained consistently that these were problems in the unit that became even worse following the tragedy of May 9th. Clagett told me that May 9th was his first day on a mission with this particular squad. All the soldiers as well as squads, platoons, and companies had been re-shuffled over the course of several months prior to this mission. I heard testimony concerning similar re-shuffling of units in Michael Leahy's murder court-martial for the Baghdad canal killings in 2007. While these two cases do not constitute sufficient data to draw a firm conclusion, they do illustrate Stouffer's overall finding from World War II that cross-leveling and re-shuffling of units automatically damages unit morale and discipline. This is because soldiers form emotional attachments to each other more than they do to any ideology, cause, mission, or leader. If these emotional attachments within the reference group are disrupted, unit morale suffers. The more relevant question is: Does the army teach Stouffer or his findings to its officers, and if so, why do commanders ignore these significant findings?

CPT Miller, military defense counsel for Sergeant Girouard, took over the cross-examination. He ascertained that the alleged "conspiracy" meeting took place five minutes after LT Wehrheim had left the objective on a helicopter; that it took no more than five minutes, and that the killings took place "about ten minutes" after the conclusion of the meeting. If Mason's testimony is true, it contradicts LT Wehrheim's sworn statement and personal statement to me that the killings took place about five minutes after he left the objective. Mason's testimony suggests that the killings took place fifteen minutes or more after the lieutenant had left. Mason said that after the killings, he went back to the room where he guarded the females, where he waited for another thirty minutes, then waited an hour at the landing zone — where he and other soldiers slept — then returned to the room again.

Q: And what did you do while you were in that room?

A: Slept.

Q: You slept again?

A: Yes.

Taken out of context, it may seem strange that Mason and other soldiers could and did sleep during a mission, and especially after killings took place. But this fact is not strange when one considers that soldiers are chronically sleep-deprived, as I learned at courts-martial. They sleep for less than 4 hours per day on the average. Many soldiers have told me outside the courtroom that they sleep on and off during missions, and demand only that their drivers stay awake. *Studies have documented that chronic sleep deprivation is a systemic problem in the Army in the current war.* Chronic sleep deprivation leads to negative consequences in terms of judgment, accidents, and performance. Ruth Benedict found that in World War II, Japanese soldiers were chronically and systematically deprived of sleep in the mistaken belief that this policy would make them tougher warriors. The fact that the US defeated Japan helps show how mistaken this widespread policy was. We gain some insight into the army's reaction to this systemic problem from the testimony that follows. It seems that the army punishes its soldiers for sleeping on the job rather than creating conditions that would help them get the sleep their bodies need:

Q: Have you ever been recommended for an Article 15?

A: Yes.

Q: For what?

A: For sleeping...

Q: When was that?

A: It was some time in May.

Q: Before or after Iron Triangle?

A: After.

Q: Who else was with you?

A: It was me, Sergeant Acevedo ... Specialist Niger and ... Sergeant Kugler....

Q: Was an Article 15 ever read to you?

A: They started the process, but they never finished it.

An Article 15 refers to disciplinary punishment. Recall from the previous chapter that Acevedo and Kugler were among the soldiers who criticized and exposed the killings in LT Horne's platoon. Were the Article 15 charges against these whistleblowers a warning from the army to keep quiet? Perhaps CPT Miller's intent was to further impeach and discredit Mason as a witness by bringing out the Article 15 for sleeping on missions. But given what is known about chronic sleep deprivation as a systemic issue in the Army, perhaps one should empathize with Mason and other soldiers who sleep on the job out of exhaustion. Moreover, harking back to Benedict's "patterns of culture" approach, one should note that chronic sleep deprivation is a problem in civilian American culture as well, and affects airline pilots, truck drivers, physicians, and a host of other professions. Its cumulative effect is one of diminished performance and heightened accidents and problems on the job. How has American culture come to resemble Japanese patterns of culture regarding the basic need of sleep from the 1940s?

The prosecutor tried to rehabilitate the government's star witness:

Q: Why did you finally come forward on the 15th and discuss the agreement that took place in that room?

A: They were already arrested, and I wasn't worried about being threatened anymore.

Q: When you say "they," who do you mean?

A: Sergeant Girouard, Clagett, and Hunsaker.

Q: When you said words to the effect of, "Every man woman and child in Iraq should die," how serious were you?

A: Not that serious.

Q: What did you mean by that statement?

A: It means that like — I mean, no matter what we do, I mean, there's always going to be terrorists.

Q: How fair is it to say that you personally have feelings against the war here in Iraq?

A: I do.

Q: Mr. Bergrin mentioned a remark you made to an Iraqi boy wearing pink slippers. Who else was laughing when you made that remark?

A: Everybody that was there.

Q: Let's go back to that statement that you made on the 11th of May. You testified earlier that nobody ordered you to write anything in that particular statement. Is that correct?

A: Nobody ordered me. *They just told me that this is the story that we're going to go with....*

Q: You testified earlier that the women offered you water. How did they indicate they were offering water?

A: They were just like — hand signals.

Q: Did they ever speak English to you?

A: No.

Q: You testified earlier that you didn't have fear from PFC Clagett. At some point did you have fear?

A: Yes.

Q: When did that change?

A: When — well when I was here — actually I was — I mean, I've been thinking about the whole thing, and me with the relationship me and Clagett had, I mean, we were friends, and I just don't see Clagett as — I ended up not seeing Clagett as the type of person that would actually try to harm or [emphasis added].

The IO also had some questions for Mason:

IO: After this incident, PFC Mason, did you attend a squad meeting or perhaps a platoon meeting at the helipad?...

A: Yes.

Q: And did Sergeant Girouard say anything at that meeting to the squad or to you?

A: The meeting — we were just all talking about how the squad's falling apart, like I couldn't stand it, and how we could fix it and all that.

Mason repeatedly brings up the issue of poor unit morale, which holds great significance for explaining the tragedy that occurred to the social scientist, but is largely irrelevant to the law and trial process. According to procedural issues, the issue of poor unit morale can only be raised in the mitigation portion of a court-martial, after the soldier has been convicted. Recross-examination began with Mr. Waddington again asking questions:

Q: Is it safe to say that over half of the statements you've given under oath in this investigation have been deliberate lies?

A: Just those first two [May 15 and May 29]

Q: And how many have you given?

A: Five, six.

Q: So about a third of your statements so far have been utter falsities?

A: Yes....

Q: And the version of the truth that you're supposed to tell is the version from the 15 June statement, correct?

A: From my truth; what I know.

Q: But based on your discussions with Captain Fischbach, the truth is what is in the June 15 statement?

A: Yeah.

Q: So if you actually came forward and say, "You know what CID got me a little mixed up, what happened is what happened on the 29th statement," the immunity deal would be off, correct?

A: Yeah.

Mr. Waddington would later characterize the entire testimony as a "perjury-fest." It is certain that he got Mason to admit to committing perjury. Mason's admission of perjury did not matter to the government in pressing its case against the accused. The government had no case without Mason's accusations, and in the opinion of the defense attorneys, the government kept forcing Mason to give statements until he "got it right" from their perspective. The June 15th statement became his reference point for becoming the government's star witness, and any deviation from that statement would have put him in the reference group of convicted felons. Mr. Bergrin also had additional questions for Mason:

> Q: Isn't it a fact that when you gave your statement on 15 June, when you were supposedly coming clean, you never told them that you also lied about your experiment with the zip ties, correct?

> A: They knew I lied about this whole statement.

> Q: The whole statement is a lie? There's nothing in it that's the truth?

> A: No....

> Q: A lot of things that came out of your mouth you're not serious about?....

> A: No.

> Q: They didn't mean anything to you, correct?

> A: I was more worried about myself.

> Q: And you deliberately and intentionally lied on purpose even after being given the oath?

> A: Yeah.

> Q: So the oath meant absolutely nothing to you, right?

> A: I'm more worried about myself than about the case.

> Q: The oath meant nothing to you, correct?

> A: At the time, no, it didn't.

Commonsense can explain Mason's perjury as well as admission of perjury: he was trying to save himself, even if that meant betraying his comrades. But it is more difficult to comprehend why the government would make an admitted perjurer its star witness. The defense attorneys have already suggested a commonsense reply — the government was desperate, and had no other evidence. But the government is supposed to use the US Constitution, the rule of law, and legal norms which condemn perjury as its reference points. What reference points or reference group was the government using? It is difficult to tell.

Captain Miller had some questions for Mason that yielded devastating replies with regard to the image of the Army:

Q: Okay, how do you treat high value targets? Can they be shot on sight?

A: Yes....

Q: Okay, prior to deploying, did you ever hear Colonel Steele make any comments concerning what he would do to reward people for the kill of insurgents?

A: Give you a coin....

Q: All rights, what's the motto of the Rakkasans?

A: "We give the enemy the maximum opportunity to give their life for their country."

Q: What have you been told about warning shots by Colonel Steele?

A: We don't use warning shots.

Q: Do you ever fire warning shots — well, let me ask you another way. Were you ever told "We don't fire warning shots. The warning shot is us shooting the buddy next to — the guy next to him?"

A: Yeah.

Q: So that's — the brigade commander's definition of a warning shot?

A: Yes.

Q: And that's what you were told?

A: Yes.

The prosecutor stepped in to rehabilitate the witness (and the Army's image):

Q: Assume for the sake of argument you were told the ROE was to kill all military aged males on the objective, what authority does that give you or anybody else from your unit to kill detainees?

A: It doesn't.

Q: And why not?

A: Because detainees — that goes against the Geneva Conventions.

Q: Talked earlier about combat action. How many fire fights have you been in, in Iraq?

A: This one and one other one at the Reeds.

Q: And this one, nobody shot at you back? They shot at you back on the Reeds?

A: They — yes, they were shooting us.

Q: How many has Clagett been in?

A: None that I can remember.

The prosecutor's questions make sense, except for the obvious fact that the ROE stated that no prisoners were to be taken: every military aged male was to be killed. This glaring fact explains why First Sergeant Geressy was surprised and angry that any prisoners were taken.

PFC Mason's testimony takes up 215 pages of court transcript — more than the length for many entire courts-martial, from start to finish. He had not used the word "sir" once in any of his statements. It is remarkable that all of the commissioned officers in the room allowed him to get away with this behavior. I have seen officers interrupt testimony to admonish an enlisted soldier to address them as "Sir." Why was Mason getting special treatment?

> "It was almost no trick at all, he saw, to turn vice into virtue and slander into truth ... brutality into patriotism, and sadism into justice. Anybody can do it; it required no brains at all. It merely required no character."
> — Joseph Heller, *Catch 22*, p. 336

There was no recess between the testimony of PFC Mason and Special Agent Nichole Battle. She testified that she had been a CID agent since the year 2003 and had been in the army since 1988. The reader may recall that she had interrogated the snipers and other soldiers who had criticized and exposed the unlawful killings in LT Horne's platoon. No one asked her about those sworn statements that she had taken, and she did not volunteer any of that information. The prosecutor walked her through her interview with Graber. The prosecutor got Battle to state that she followed procedures in obtaining Graber's confession of the mercy killing. When he finished questioning her, Mr. Waddington asked the IO if someone would put on a pot of coffee because "some of us are nodding off to include myself." This is understandable given that the civilian defense attorneys were experiencing jet lag from their difficult journey. But there was no empathy from the IO, who told Waddington, "Well, you can stand." Mr. Waddington replied sarcastically: "Hooah."

Captain Miller began cross-examining Battle. He asked her to list the people she had interviewed, and she named Sergeant Girouard, Specialist Kemp, Lieutenant Wehrheim, Specialist Bivens, "and possibly others," though she said she could not remember. She did not mention anyone from LT Horne's platoon. He asked her about "the theory behind" her behavior in a typical interview, and she replied, "We're doing our job." She said that she writes the questions as well as the answers in an interview. Portions of interviews or entire interview that "we're not using, they go into the shred box," Battle said.

Q: Did you shred any statements in this case?

A: It's possible I have, sir....

Q: In other words, if somebody writes up a statement and they say they don't want to sign it, but that it was the interview was conducted about and that was the contents of the interview, that still is essentially a statement, correct?

A: If they provided a statement and said they didn't want to sign it.

Q: Correct. Would you hang on to it, or would you shred it?

A: I would shred it.

Battle said there were typically no witnesses to the interaction between the CID agent and the suspect, and she kept no records of any sort of which or how many statements were shredded. Obviously, this practice allows the CID agent enormous discretion in determining which sworn statement is "the truth" and which is not. It also allows CID agents to keep conducting the interviews as long as they see fit until they get the version of "the truth" that they want.

Q: During your training, are you ever instructed what is appropriate right and left limits on conducting interviews? In other words, what themes should not be used, what types of tactics should be avoided?

A: So far as, you know, you can't make promises...

Q: Would you ever make promises regarding someone's family? In other words, if you ever get to see your family again or think of your family?

A: No, sir.

Q: That wouldn't — okay. So, you personally would never ask, "Think about your family."

A: I probably would say think about your family....

Q: When did you ever mention anybody's family or use family *as a theme* to try to get a statement or a confession out of anybody?

A: I don't remember using anybody's family trying to get a statement or a confession. I remember talking to Sergeant Girouard about his family [emphasis added].

I have noticed that military interrogators are consistently evasive in their answers on the witness stand. Interrogating a trained interrogator hardly ever results in a direct answer to a direct question. However, Battle basically admitted throughout her testimony that she did use *highly emotionally charged themes* such as family and religion to elicit confessions even though she stated that she did not do this. Captain Miller and all the defense attorneys knew that the Reid Technique focuses on such themes as a manipulative tool to break a suspect's resistance.

Q: Okay, what did you talk about?

A: He talked about his — his son, and we talked about his wife. Specifics right now, I can't recall.

Q: Okay, did you use that any point later in the interview?

A: It's possible I did. I think I may have said something to the effect of, you know, "You got a wife and kids at home, and think about them, you know, when you're making a decision, and think about your Soldiers."

Q: Did you ever say things along the line as "Your son will never get to see his father ever again?"

A: I don't recall saying that, sir.

Q: You don't recall saying it, so it's possible you did say that?

A: It's possible; it's possible, but I don't think I said that.

Most Americans are used to the infamous *theme*, "I don't recall but it's possible I did that" from watching televised hearings of politicians such as Attorney General Alberto Gonzalez and numerous others. This theme is the butt of jokes on late night TV shows and comedies such as Jon Stewart's "The Daily Show." Battle said it was "possible" she similarly used the theme of religion against Girouard.

Q: What about physical contact with interviewees or subjects? Did you ever make physical contact?

A: Yes, I did.

Q: Okay, do you ever touch a male's knee?

A: Yes, I do.

Q: How about a male's hands — hold his hands?

A: Yes, I do.

Q: Offer hugs?

A: Possibly yes, sir.

Q: Have you ever hugged?

A: Yes.

Q: Did you ever hug Sergeant Girouard?

A: I think I did.

Q: Did you hug any other witnesses?

A: It's possible. I don't recall.

Q: And you were taught that that's appropriate behavior for a female agent to touch another male's knee during the course of an interview?

A: Yes. It's no more inappropriate than a male touching a male's knees.

Q: During an interview, do you think it would be permissible for a male agent to touch a female's knee?

A: Yes, sir.

It is a fact that in the United States, it is highly inappropriate for a male in a position of power to touch a female's knee during any professional interaction. In fact, such behavior constitutes sexual harassment, and is against the law. Moreover, Higgason had already testified that such touching is inappropriate. From a commonsense perspective, what is of interest is that the army is using female agents as gender tools during interrogation of its own soldiers, much like it used female soldiers, agents, and interrogators as weapons against inmates at Abu Ghraib and Guantanamo. The strategic use of female sexuality as an interrogation tactic against presumed enemies has been well-documented. But the use of this doubly degrading tactic — degrading to the female agent as well as the subject of the degradation — against US soldiers by their own comrades is not well-known. Given the machismo culture of the army, it is difficult to imagine ordering male interrogators to touch the knees of male army suspects, much less to hug them — homophobic fears in American culture preclude such physical touching between males in professional settings. But the use of females for sexual extortion of males fits into American "patterns of culture," to use Ruth Benedict's phrase again. Popular culture is filled with examples of women using sexuality as a weapon against men at the same time that sexual harassment by men of women is strictly prohibited. My point is that Battle most likely did not dream up this technique on her own, because it fits too neatly with similar patterns involving female sexuality as a weapon at Abu Ghraib, Guantanamo, as well as popular culture.

The defense attorney will try to impeach the witness as an individual, because attorneys see such tactics as part of their job. Nevertheless, the average person should be interested in the army's policy of using female soldiers as "torture devices."[1] Using female soldiers as weapons of war solely on the basis of their gender is part of the "logic of emasculation"[2] in a macho culture such as the army. Any and all emotions pertaining to attachment, family commitment, religious views and other non-aggressive emotions seem to be regarded by the army as "feminine" and are used against the male soldier. Stouffer emphasizes that "reticence about emotional or idealistic matters" is part of the army's "code of masculinity" (volume 2, p. 131). For example, I had an opportunity to view videotaped interrogations of suspects in the Michael Leahy murder court-martial. I observed that in male-on-male interrogations in the army, the

1 See Kelly Oliver, *Women as Weapons of War: Iraq, Sex, and the Media.* (New York: Columbia University Press, 2007.)
2 Timothy Kaufman-Osborn, "Gender Trouble at Abu Ghraib?" *Politics and Gender* 1(4):597-619, 2005.

male interrogator typically defers to a suspect with prestige and power, such as a first sergeant. However, if the suspect is of lower rank or standing relative to the male interrogator, the male interrogator does, indeed, resort to exploiting the suspect through emotional themes such as family and religion. In US culture, for men to admit emotional vulnerabilities in these areas makes them feel "like women," and the male interrogator uses this cultural vulnerability to literally bring male suspects to tears. In the US, men are socialized to take on the role of "instrumental" bread winner and women to take on "expressive" (emotional) roles.[1] It is a logical step for the wizards of interrogation techniques to use American culture as a weapon against US soldiers much as they have used treatises on Arab culture, such as *The Arab Mind*, as a weapon against Iraqi prisoners.

I have never witnessed a male interrogator touch a male suspect other than to shake hands. But it is entirely consistent with the logic of emasculation to train female interrogators to touch and hug male suspects — with obvious fake sincerity — as an interrogation technique. Captain Miller is not a sociologist, so he persisted in attacking Special Agent Battle personally in order to try to ruin her credibility:

> Q: Isn't it true you were removed from the Special Agent in Charge of Kirkuk for complaints of abusive and overly aggressive interrogation tactics?

> A: No, sir, that is not true....

> Q: So Special Agent Higgason, when he testified that there were [complaints], he was mistaken?

> A: There was no complaints to me made about anything....

> Q: That's just — Special Agent Higgason may have been mistaken when he testified about that?

> A: I don't know what Special Agent Higgason talked about.

One also learns that Battle interviewed Girouard for approximately six hours. She also admitted that CID agents sometimes "fill in" the gaps in a suspect's memory or field of knowledge. Again, I can verify that I have observed this in videotaped interrogations, and would characterize the process as planting false memories in the mind of the suspected soldier. Captain Suddeth, defense counsel for Specialist Graber, took over the cross-examination of Battle:

> Q: And in relation to an infantryman, a CID agent would be considered a pogue, is that correct?

> A: I don't understand what a pogue is, sir.

---

1 This is a well-known finding by the Harvard sociologist, Talcott Parsons. For an application of his theory toward understanding the use and misuse of gender by the army, see Ryan Ashley Caldwell and Stjepan G. Mestrovic, "The Role of Gender in Expressive Abuse at Abu Ghraib," *Cultural Sociology* 2(3): 275-99, 2008.

Q: Someone who's an office personnel; doesn't get out; not into battle, doesn't conduct missions?

A: It's possible that's what they think, sir.

Q: Okay, and you are aware that they are considered that, right?

A: If you tell me, sir.

Q: And also they really don't have too many females in the infantry, is that correct?

A: I don't know of any females in the infantry.

Q: So that kind of puts you at a disadvantage during an interview of an infantryman, doesn't it?

A: I don't think so, sir.

Q: So you think that they respect a pogue CID female coming in asking them questions?

[CAPTAIN FISCHBACH]: I'm going to object to that question as absolutely unnecessarily demeaning.

IO: I agree. Reword the question.

Captain Suddeth did not reword the question but turned to other topics. It would be important, indeed, to conduct a Stouffer-like study of male and female attitudes of US Army soldiers toward each other. Stouffer did find that World War II combat veterans regarded rear-echelon troops with disdain. Given that women are still not assigned to front-line, combat positions — as they were not in World War II — it could be that the disdainful attitude exhibited by male soldiers toward female soldiers is due to this attitude toward non-combat troops, and not necessarily toward female soldiers per se. Careful research is required to clarify this issue. The important points are these: most soldiers do make a distinction — often unstated — between those who have been in a combat zone and those who have not. And, it is not at all clear how the "code of masculinity" relates to the increased presence of women in the military since World War II.

Mr. Bergrin was next in line to cross-examine Special Agent Battle. He took the typical tack of civilian defense attorneys, namely, that the army did not collect any physical evidence of any sort in this case:

Q: When you went to the scene, did you find any physical evidence there?

A: There were some shell cases found there, sir, and I wasn't — I didn't collect anything, so saying exactly what was there, I can't speak on everything that was collected.

Q: As the lead case agent, did you pick up these shell casings?

A: No I did not....

Q: As the case agent in this case, the lead case agent, you didn't think it was important to go to the scene prior to two weeks ago and look for physical evidence at the scene?

A: It's — it was important, but we just can't go out to the scene. There's a lot of coordination to go out to the scene.

Q: Two and a half months to go out to the scene. That's how long it took you to plan?

A: I didn't plan it, sir....

Q: Did you take any DNA from Hunsaker?

A: I did not, sir...

Q: Do you know if any blood or DNA was taken from any of the detainees or the POWs that were killed?

A: Not by CID, sir....

Q: Where is the knife that was used in this case?

A: We don't know, sir....

Q: Do you know if any bullets or bullet fragments were recovered from the scene or from the bodies in this case?

A: No, sir, I do not know.

Q: As the lead case agent do you make any effort to find out?

A: No. We don't have the bodies, sir.

Mr. Bergrin is probably correct to imply that in civilian law, complete and total lack of any physical evidence would be viewed with suspicion by a civilian judge.. After all, one cannot really be certain that any crime occurred because the bodies of the victims were never found. Moreover, one will never know for certain what truly happened on May 9, 2006 at the scene of this alleged crime. But in the cases I have observed, I have noticed that the army does not make even a minimal effort to recover physical evidence, and relies on the most ancient method of proof — the confession. The problem with this approach, even if it is admissible under law, is that it invites coercive interrogation techniques, abuse of suspects, perjury by comrades who are themselves coerced or threatened into testifying against the accused, and a host of other negative consequences. An important question which should be pursued in further research is why the military criminal justice system uses the ancient methods of interrogation and confession as its reference points while the civilian justice system turns more to scientific analysis of physical evidence as its reference points.

At long last, Battle was dismissed and instructed not to speak with anybody about her testimony, and the IO called for a recess at 2:31 p.m.. The hearing was reconvened at 2:46 p.m. and Battle was recalled to the stand, apparently because she did speak about the testimony with her colleagues. She was accused of saying, "I guess they're calling me a CID pogue." But her defense was that she didn't say that, and "somebody else said that." She claimed that the prosecutor had said it, and word spread like wildfire through the group. As soon as it was revealed that the prosecutor was involved, it became a dead issue, and the IO ordered that everyone move on.

The IO brought up the issue of potential witnesses who had "invoked their rights" and chose not to testify, including: Colonel Steele, Captain Hart, First Sergeant Egresses, and Sergeant Lemus. The co-prosecutor, Captain Mackey concluded, "They will not testify." Mr. Waddington asked whether Captain Sienko or Lieutenant Wehrheim would testify and Captain Mackey replied that they would. Private First Class Jason Joseph was sworn in and took the witness stand. Captain Miller asked him:

Q: Okay, what were your ROEs that day?

A: On the island, our ROE was kill all military aged males that are not actively surrendering because they were confirmed terrorists.

Q: Okay, what does actively surrendering mean to you?

A: Hands up in the air, showing no hostile intent.

Q: What happens if their hands aren't in the air?

A: You can tell the basically you can try to detain them and they're resisting — I don't know.

Q: What do you mean you don't know?

A: Well —

Q: Does that mean you'd shoot them?

A: If — it all depends on the situation.

Q: Is it possible you could shoot them?

A: Possible depending on what they're doing. I don't know.

If PFC Joseph simply did not know what the ROE meant in specific situations, one suspects that other soldiers also were not certain. Under re-direct examination by Captain Mackey, Joseph made it clear that he remembered only what his squad leader said about the ROE (which may explain the extra phrase, "unless they are actively surrendering"). He testified that Captain Hart and Colonel Steele also spoke about the ROE, but he could not remember what they said.

Q: Okay were you ever given any sort of law of armed conflict classes or law of war classes before this mission even occurred?

A: Not really.

Q: Okay, were you ever taught about how to treat people if they were surrendering when you were out on a mission?

A: Not specifically. I haven't taken classes, no.

Q: Has anybody ever told you what to do?

A: A little bit. I can't remember anything specific, but, you know, there's a fine difference between right and wrong for some people though.

Even though the Army typically releases press statements to the effect that its soldiers are trained in the laws of armed conflict and how to treat prisoners, the fact is that Joseph's testimony resonates with my research. From Abu Ghraib to other sites of war crimes, soldiers have told me repeatedly that they had *not* been given classes on these topics. Soldiers have also told me that the army spends more time lecturing the troops about sexual harassment and alcohol and drug abuse than how to treat prisoners. In her recross-examination, Captain Rutizer got PFC Joseph to yield much insight into the mind of the infantryman concerning ROE:

Q: PFC Joseph, do you know what actively surrendering means?

A: Hands up in the air showing no hostile intent.

Q: What about hands down? Can you shoot them if their hands are down?

A: Like I said, it depends on what they're doing. If they're — their hands could be down running at you, you know, it could show hostile intent. Like I said, there's a lot you don't know when you're out there. They could have a bomb on them. They could have a hidden weapon if their hands are down and you don't know what they're going to do.

Q: Got it, so, fair to shoot them if their hands are down?

A: I guess, yes.

Q: Is it a common TTP [tactical training point] for Al-Qaida members and insurgents to hide behind women?

A: Yes. I actually saw a lot of that myself that day as we were hitting another objective. A lot of them were hiding behind their families.

Q: It is common for them to use little infants as shields.

A: Yes, I've heard of that before.

There is no easy solution to the dilemmas for the US soldier that Joseph exposed. His testimony is in sync with what other soldiers told me from other courts-martial and missions. Namely, soldiers come to believe that it is okay to shoot an Arab who has no obvious weapon and is not displaying any obvious hostile intent. Even an Arab who is running away from the US soldiers is sometimes construed by them as possibly exhibiting latent hostile intent. There is a disconnect between the Army's training about the meaning of "active surrender" based upon the experience of World War II, which involved formal armies in uniforms, versus guerrilla warfare in the current war on terror, which involves suspected terrorists who are indistinguishable from the general population. The Army compounds this double-bind for the soldiers — they fear they will err if they shoot and also err if they don't shoot, because of the latent danger to them — by teaching them that the enemy hides behind women and children. Perhaps it is true that terrorists hide behind women and children. But it is also possible that any male will hide behind women and children if he knows he will be killed for simply being a male, and that the shooter will not kill women and children. The more important yet unintended consequence of this training, however, is that the soldier might conclude that *anybody* who hides behind women and children is a terrorist.

Captain Miller, military counsel for Sergeant Girouard, asked Joseph about "a TV and a generator recovered from your room that had to be returned to an insurgent's house." Joseph denied any knowledge of this. The attorney's wording is somewhat strange: he asked about returning a stolen TV and generator to an *insurgent's* house, not a suspected insurgent's house. It is difficult to imagine how the army managed to recover and then return goods that were stolen from an enemy.

Testimony of Sergeant Brian D. Hensley

Sergeant Brian D. Hensley took the witness stand. He testified that he is the usual squad leader for second squad, but that he did not go out on the mission on 9 May "due to an injury I sustained from a pick-up game of basketball." Normally, Clagett was under the command of Sergeant Hensley in second squad. This means that third squad — the unit involved in the crimes that were prosecuted — went out that day with two new members (Clagett and Hunsaker) as well as a squad leader who was new to the soldiers (Girouard). Based upon Stouffer's research, one should have expected for something to go wrong with this squad on that day — their normal unit cohesion was disturbed. Hensley was defensive in describing a conversation with Clagett following the mission: "He [Clagett] told me that he had gotten his first kill, and that he was excited about it but at the same time disappointed that I couldn't be there, and I told him, 'Hey, I wasn't there. I don't want to hear about it.'"

Hensley also commented matter-of-factly that "the locals are referred to as 'Beebs'." Hensley reiterated his relationship to Clagett: "I was his team leader, sir." Mr. Bergrin cross-examined Sergeant Hensley, and wondered why he was allegedly "turned off to the conversation." Hensley admitted that part of the reason was that it was his duty to report any offense to CID if he had believed that Clagett had done something wrong. Apparently, Hensley's solution was to not pay close attention to what Clagett was saying. But Bergrin went further in his questioning of Henley's attitude:

Q: Are you suffering now from post-traumatic stress disorder?

A: Not now, sir, no.

Q: At the time this happened?

A: No, sir.

Q: Have you ever suffered from it, sir?

A: Yes, sir.

Q: And when was hat?

A: A year or two ago, sir.

Q: A year or two ago?

A: Yes, sir....

Q: When you have post-traumatic stress disorder, do you try to forget or not remember particular facts?

A: Yes, sir.

Q: In this particular case, you were trying not to remember what was said to you; you didn't want to hear what was said to you, correct?

A: I didn't want to hear it, sir.

PTSD does not disappear after a year or two years: it is a chronic condition or emotional scar that the affected soldier carries for the rest of his or her life. Bergrin is correct that victims of PTSD avoid confronting or remembering stressful events, for the obvious reason that these events, or even the memories of these events, cause them great distress. Why did the army force squad leader Hensley to act in a leadership position despite his PTSD? What percentage of the entire squad, platoon, and company were afflicted with PTSD? Again, recall from Stouffer and other studies on combat stress that the longer a soldier with any form of combat stress is exposed to combat, the less capable he or she is to cope with the PTSD. Hensley's testimony offers valuable insight and further corroboration of the damaged military unit that was involved in the crimes under discussion.

Under cross-examination by Mr. Waddington, Hensley characterized his reaction to the stories he heard about the mission as having a "deer in the headlights look." This particular phrase is frequently used in clinical literature to describe the reactions of individuals suffering from PTSD to any event that triggers the memory of the original trauma. One should wonder: What was the original trauma or series of traumas that Sergeant Hensley experienced which caused him to respond in this way to the events of May 9th? Under further cross-examination by Captain Miller, Hensley disclosed some interesting facts:

Q: Sergeant Hensley, how long have you been in the military?

A: Five years, sir.

Q: How long have you been a noncommissioned officer?

A: Not quite a year, sir....

Q: Okay, how old are you?

A: Twenty-six, sir.

Q: Okay, do you know how old Sergeant Girouard is?

A: He's twenty-four, sir.... He was another squad's squad leader. [3rd squad]....

Q: Okay, what squad were you in?

A: 2nd Squad, sir.

Q: And what's your current duty position?

A: Squad leader, sir....

Q: Okay, how did it make you feel that you weren't out there that day?

A: Like a piece of crap, sir.

Q: Why?

A: It's just how I am, sir.

Q: What do you mean that's how you are.

A: I wanted to be with my guys, sir.

Q: Okay, why did you want to be with your guys?

A: Because that's my place of duty.

Apparently Hensley was out of action for a month due to his knee injury. When his knee had healed, he volunteered to return to the squad and assume his former position as squad leader. Individuals with PTSD often feel what clinician's call "survivor's guilt" if their comrades are exposed to dangerous situations which they finally escaped. The double-bind for a person with PTSD is that when he or she is safe, they suffer from guilt, and when they expose themselves to danger, they suffer from extraordinary anxiety.

A: I came back because there had been several IEDs out in our area, and one of my friends in another platoon happen to — he got hit by one, and both of his guys were seriously injured, and I spent 24 hours with him talking to him. It just made me realize that if something happened to one of my guys without me out there that it would just tear me up.

Q: And you went to Lieutenant Wehrheim and I'm assuming asked the First Sergeant?

A: I went to the First Sergeant, sir....

Q: Sergeant Hensley, you've been in a fire fight with PFC Clagett, right?

A: Yes.

Q: On MSR Tampa?

A: Yes, ma'am.

Q: Right there was — Blackwater security was getting attacked from both sides, right?

A: Yes, ma'am.

Q: He was operating the 240?

A: Yes, ma'am.

Q: He engaged the enemy?

A: Yes, ma'am.

Q: All the way, right?

A: Yes, ma'am.

In the re-direct examination, the prosecutor tried to get Sergeant Hensley to confirm that Clagett confessed to him about the killings and conspiracy on May 9th, but Hensley did not agree with the prosecutor. The gist of the long, back-and-forth exchanges with the prosecutor and defense attorneys was that Hensley was correct in his mind not to report anything to CID because he did not pay attention and did not want to hear what Clagett was telling him. Mr. Bergrin got to the point with this question: "You only remember bits and pieces of the conversation, correct?" "Yes, sir," Hensley replied. It is difficult not to feel empathy for Hensley and his double-bind situation. Both Sergeant Hensley and Sergeant Girouard (who also both suffer from PTSD) exhibit the typical behavior of the noncommissioned officer caught in the double-bind of two reference groups in the army, that of commissioned officers above them and the low-ranking enlisted soldiers below them in hierarchy. In line with Stouffer's findings, these and presumably other NCOs do their best to appease the "by the book" officers above them and protect as well as identify with the enlisted soldiers below them. Hensley's neutral testimony, not helpful to the prosecution or the defense, is easy to comprehend in the context of Stouffer's findings. The hearing recessed at 4 p.m.

Testimony by Specialist Lopez

At 4:13 p.m., the hearing reconvened, and Specialist Miguel Angel Lopez took the witness stand. It is of immediate interest that Lopez was assigned to 3rd squad (the same one as the accused soldiers), but in reality went on the Operation Iron Triangle mission with 1st squad. This is yet another intriguing instance of re-shuffling soldiers as if they were interchangeable machine parts, and goes directly against the advice and findings by Stouffer to keep soldiers in the same units in order to maintain morale. Lopez also said, "I was recovering from an injury, an IED attack." The prosecutor did not go into any more details about the soldier's injury or its effects on him. He wanted Lopez to discuss what his friends said to him about what happened during the mission. Mr. Bergrin objected on the grounds that "Lopez will be testifying to what they call 'double hearsay,' allegedly a statement made to him by Graber as to what Graber was allegedly told by somebody else." The prosecutor responded that eventually Lopez would testify directly about Graber's actions on the objective. The IO agreed with the prosecutor. In his very brief testimony — which really was hearsay, and involved no direct knowledge by Lopez about what happened — the witness said that Graber told him that "he was told by Sergeant Girouard to put the guy out of his misery, and he shot him ... close range; shot him once, missed, and shot him again in the head.".

Captain Suddeth, military counsel for Specialist Graber, cross-examined Lopez. He got Lopez to admit that he suffered from a head injury which caused memory as well as hearing loss.

Q: And as a result of the IED and having potential hearing loss, it's also difficult for you to actually hear what people are telling you?

A: Yes.... As a result because I was kind of being forced to kind of force everything out that I knew, but I'd heard so many stories already by that time that I wasn't sure what was true and what was not.

Q: Okay, so when you say "force" who was forcing you to say all of this stuff?

A: One of the CID agents. He just wanted to get everything out, and I was trying to help him out as much as I could....

Q: So it wasn't anything that you actually knew personally. Is that correct?

A: Correct.

Q: And you weren't there at the objective on that particular day. Is that right?

A: That's correct.

Q: Now when you made your statement, you made this statement approximately forty days afterwards, is that correct?

A: Sure.

Q: Do you recall making the sworn statement on 16 June 2006?

A: No....

Q: Okay, so you actually are suffering right now from memory loss of what happened in June. Is that correct?

A: Yes. Actually if you check my documentation and all my medical work ... my doctor had told me until I can regain full — full power of my memory, there were some times I don't remember stuff....

Q: Now the conversations that you had with Specialist Graber on this particular day, you indicate that there was never any talk of conspiracy. Is that correct?

A: Conspiracy to what?

Q: To do anything with the detainees.... I withdraw that question. Now as a result of being hit by an IED, that kind of upset you. Is that correct?

A: Yes.

Q: And as a result of being upset that — you were out on a mission one time. Is that correct?

A: Yes.

Q: And as a result of this mission, you were told that there was going to be some insurgents there?

A: Yes.

Q: And there wasn't? Is that correct?

A: Yes.

Q: Except a — one Iraqi male. Is that true?....

A: Yes.

Q: And as a result of coming in contact with that lone Iraqi male, you ended up roughing that Iraqi up. Is that correct?

A: Yes....

Q: Okay, and you were so aggressive that someone had to intervene and tell you to stop and say that this was actually an interpreter?

A: Yes somebody climbed in the turret and heard me yelling.

Only someone with a heart of stone would fail to feel compassion for Specialist Lopez's injuries and predicament. One also has to feel empathy for the Iraqi who was roughed up by a disoriented, injured, and stressed soldier. But why in the world would the army send a soldier with such extensive injuries on a mission? And why would the prosecution put Lopez on the witness stand, given his documented injuries, memory loss, and disorientation? Captain Miller asked about the TV and generator that was brought up in earlier testimony by Specialist Joseph. Lopez said "We took it back to our living quarters."

Q: Who's we?

A: The — our 1st Squad.

Q: Okay, did Specialist Joseph know about this?

A: Yes....

Q: Who told you to take it back, or what's your understanding of who told you to take it back?

A: My squad leader told me to take it back.

Mr. Waddington pursued the issue of CID "forcing" Lopez to testify about events he had never witnessed:

Q: They [CID] were asking you for factual knowledge of these alleged crimes, correct?

A: Yes.

Q: And you told them you weren't there so you didn't know, correct?

A: Yes.

Q: And they wouldn't take no for an answer.

A: Not really. They just wanted to know — I had told them I heard a lot of rumors and stories and all the stories that were going around ...

Q: So they told you to then write down rumors?

A: Yes.

A long series of cross-examinations and re-directs ensued by defense and prosecution. The prosecution tried but could not rehabilitate the witness because he couldn't remember which version of what he was told was which. Mr. Bergrin had Lopez admit, with surprise, that Graber was not present at the killings so he, too, was spreading what amounted to a rumor. Captain Suddeth exposed the absurdity of the prosecution forcing Lopez to testify:

Q: You had testified earlier that your memory is bad. Is that correct?

A: Yes.

Q: And a lot of this stuff came from rumors?

A: Yes.

Q: And because you weren't present?

A: Yes....

Q: Okay, and nowhere in your sworn statement did you talk about who may have been present if there was even a conspiracy. Specialist Graber never spoke about that. Is that correct?

A: That's probably true cause I'm not sure who was in — I don't even remember who was actually there at the time.

Q: Because you just don't know, is that correct?

A: No.

Q: And actually your conversation that you had with Specialist Graber, you just don't remember much, do you?

A: It's very sketchy, yes....

Q: And supposedly he spoke with you just a day or two after the incident on May 9th or the 9th of May. Is that correct?

A: Yes. I had just come back from the hospital, I think, May the 4th or the 5th...

Q: And your memory was still bad?

A: I was pretty much walking like I was brain dead, yes.

Q: Brain dead.

[CAPTAIN SUDDETH]: No further questions.

The IO jumped in with more questions. Lopez said that he was hit by the IED on April 30th at 9:45 p.m.. But he could not remember if anyone else was present for the alleged conversation with Graber. The prosecutor could not resist making an already bad situation worse, and asked: "Were you wearing your ear plugs during the conversation with Specialist Graber?" "I don't remember," Lopez said. He had already testified that a doctor had required him to wear ear plugs after his injury. One is at a loss to find a rational reason as to why Lopez was ordered to testify. Badly injured, diagnosed with memory loss, unable to remember the conversation with Graber, forced by CID to testify to things he never witnessed and could not recall, and obviously confused on the witness stand — finally, Lopez was permanently excused. The hearing recessed at 4:45 p.m.

Testimony by Lieutenant Wehrheim

The hearing reconvened at 4:52 p.m. Third Platoon Leader, First Lieutenant Justin Wehrheim, took the witness stand. It is remarkable that he did not invoke his rights against self-incrimination, given that all his superiors refused to testify. Co-prosecutor, Captain Mackey, began with June 15th, when Wehrheim was ordered to "apprehend" Sergeant Girouard. All the questions were about a trophy weapon in Girouard's room that had no relation to the case whatsoever. What was the point of this testimony for the prosecution?

In their long cross-examinations, the various defense attorneys wasted no time in getting to the heart of the matter: the unlawful ROE. Captain Miller began:

Q: What was your mission on 9 May 2006?

A: Mission, sir, was that we had positively identified an Al Qaida in Iraq stronghold. That was objective Murray. It was to go and positively identify any members of Al Qaida in Iraq; kill the — all members of Al Qaida in Iraq, Objective Murray.

Q: Okay, so that — what was your ROE?

A: ROE on that mission, sir, was anybody on that island identified as a military aged male was confirmed by intelligence to be a member of Al Qaida in Iraq —

Q: Okay, I'm going to play semantics with you here a bit, but your ROE was that you could engage them, but the actual mission was to kill — was to kill the Al Qaida on the island?

A: Yes, sir.

The eight-year-long history of faulty "intelligence" about Iraq as well as Al Qaida should make any thoughtful person suspicious of this word. No evidence was ever presented to show that, in fact, there were Al Qaida terrorists on Objective Murray. Moreover, the bodies of the killed Arabs were never found after they disappeared mysteriously from the forward operating base. It is entirely possible that the so-called intelligence was faulty.

Q: And your understanding was everybody on that island was Al Qaida?

A: We were told by Captain Hart through Colonel Steele that everybody on the island identified as a military aged male was, in fact, a confirmed member of Al Qaida in Iraq by high level intelligence.

Q: Did you hear Colonel Steele give any words of encouragement to the unit before you moved out on this mission?

A: Roger ... Colonel Steele addressed the company, a hundred plus....

Q: What'd he say?

A: He said ... we're going to hit the ground shooting, and kill all the Al Qaida Iraq members only.

Q: Did you hear it very similar to "Kill all the sons of bitches?"

A: Something of that nature, sir.

Q: Something a little more colorful?

A: Something a little more colorful, roger, sir....

Q: All right, describe to me when the helicopters landed.

A: The helicopters landed, sir. We left there, confirmed the ROE was still the same.... I noticed one military aged male identified in the window. I engaged the military male. At that point, Specialist Kemp had fallen out of the helicopter....

Q: You said he fell out of the helicopter?

A: Roger, sir. He had fallen out of the helicopter, spilled his stuff everywhere, so it's kind of centrally located at this point in the middle of this field.... I sent up a radio report: three detainees, one KIA at the first house on the objective we were pushed to.

Q: What happened then?

A: Upon making a call, *I received a call back from First Sergeant Geressy to the effect of "Why do I have three f___ing detainees that should have been killed?"*

Q: Okay.

A: I said, "Hey roger, First Sergeant. I'm not sure what thing happened," and then he said, "Okay. Make sure you get the stuff done and get bring it back here [emphasis added]."

If First Sergeant Geressy thought that the prisoners should have been killed, it is reasonable to suppose that the lieutenant as well as the enlisted soldiers under his command thought the same thing. What "stuff" was the lieutenant supposed to get done? It is common for a lieutenant to act in a deferential manner toward a first sergeant, even though he technically outranks him. The lieutenant said they moved to the second house, where "one man exited the house holding a baby pretty much over his thoracic cavity."

Q: Again, was that a known TTP for Al Qaida Iraq insurgents?

A: Yes. We had been briefed. That is a known TTP for Al Qaida Iraq.

Q: What's a TTP stand for?

A: Tactical training point.

Q: Okay, and was that man or the child shot?

A: No he was not.... Once the man came out with the baby, they did not engage. They removed the baby from his arms, and detained that one individual.

Note that rather than going by "intelligence" or any objective factors to determine whether the men were terrorists, the soldiers went by the "tactical training point" they had learned. Specifically, if a military-aged male hides behind a woman or a child, then, the soldier is trained to conclude, he must be an Al Qaida terrorist. Strictly speaking, this is a completely illogical conclusion. Even if Al Qaida terrorists do use women and children as shields, it is also possible that non-terrorists would use women and children under these circumstances. The more significant point is that if the soldiers believed what they learned in their briefings, they would have been convinced that the men they arrested were terrorists precisely because they hid behind women and children. In fact, all of the accused soldiers held to this belief throughout the subsequent court-martial proceedings.

Q: Okay, and what happened after that?

A: After that, we went and cleared the rest of the house itself. Not a whole lot to do. A lot of women and kids in the house. The house was very cluttered ... and it was a relatively small house ... then after that we interviewed with the "terp," Harry was his name, interviewed him on the side — I had him interview the women and children on the side of the house. Found out that they were farmers from the south of Baghdad that apparently worked for the guy in the house to the south....

Q: And what did you think of Harry?

A: Harry's been, especially during this mission, he was very sympathetic to the local populace, especially the Iraqi Army.

Basically, the lieutenant had just contradicted the alleged "intelligence" reports about the mission. Instead of finding terrorists, the soldiers found women, children, and farmers. But like all the other soldiers and officers in this drama, the lieutenant was suspicious of all Iraqis, including his own interpreter. One wonders if this was the same interpreter whom Lopez had mistakenly "roughed up" following his injury from an IED.

In a crucial part of the testimony, the lieutenant said that it was "approximately three to five minutes after" he left the objective in a helicopter that Girouard radioed him with the news that three prisoners had been killed. This short period of time completely contradicts Graber's and Mason's testimony that the prisoners were killed more than fifteen minutes after the lieutenant had left. The lieutenant said that he was taking the one dead body to the "drop-off" point, and that he got into an argument with colleagues as to whether he was supposed to deposit the body at a company or a brigade facility. He said he "stopped at the brigade facility, dropped off the body; after that we left and went back to the — what would have been the first objective."

One also learns that the mission began at 3 a.m.: one has to wonder at what time the soldiers went to sleep prior to the mission, and whether they were sleep deprived during the mission. Privately, soldiers told me they simply did not sleep prior to the mission. The issue of sleep deprivation came up again, regarding Sergeant Acevedo and Private Mason:

Q: Okay, now he [Acevedo] was also brought up or at some point after this investigation, he was being considered for an Article 15 for sleeping on duty, correct?

A: Right, another Field Grade Article 15.

Q: And that was along with Private Mason as well.

A: Private Mason, yes, sir.

Q: What happened with those two?

A: They were brought up for an Article 15. First Sergeant Egresses decided Private Mason would not be accused — not brought up on Article 15 charges. Sergeant Acevedo was Field Grade, and then he also got thrown, sir....

Q: Okay, and mysteriously Private Mason's Article 15 for that disappearing, that was during the course of this investigation?

A: Roger, sir.

Q: And today he's never received an Article 15 for that?

A: No, sir. He was moved from the company....

Q: And Sergeant Acevedo never got one either?

A: No, sir.

Q: That too mysteriously got nixed?

A: Roger, sir. We — we ended up presenting it in front of the colonel. I just — there were a lot of extraneous factors on that, *just leadership failures all around*, sir, certain things like that, so [emphasis added].

One wishes that the lieutenant had explained the "leadership failures" that led to his soldiers sleeping on duty at a combat outpost. The defense attorney is clearly implying that the "mystery" of charges being dropped against these soldiers *during the course of the investigation into the Iron Triangle killings* can be resolved easily. Mason and Acevedo would be motivated to testify against their comrades in exchange for charges being dropped for sleeping on duty. They would also be convinced by this "deal" to drop their criticisms of First Sergeant Geressy and the other killings that occurred during this mission (in LT Horne's platoon). Had these cases gone to trial by military panels, there can be no doubt that the defense attorneys would have hammered this point home. The solution to this vexing problem for the government was fairly straightforward — the prosecutors would do all they could to ensure that there would be no trials. Plea-bargains would ensure that information damaging to the government would not be explored. This portion of Wehrheim's testimony would never be repeated or used again. Captain Miller turned to the other explosive issue, the use of Special Agent Battle as a sexual weapon by CID, this time against the lieutenant:

Q: And who were the agents that interviewed you?

A: Sir, Agent McCormick, Agent Battle.

Q: Let's talk about Special Agent Battle.

A: All right.

Q: During the course of the interview — let's back up. All the CID agents, how were you treated?

A: Pretty — pretty rudely a lot of times, sir.

Q: What do you mean rudely?

A: All of threatening tone, holding, you know, murder charges and things like that....

Q: So from the 29th of May on, they — well, they were threatening you with murder?

A: Yes, sir.

It is important to interject here that all of the witnesses — officers and soldiers alike — with whom I spoke in all the courts-martial with which I was involved have told me that they were threatened by the government with the exact same crimes of those who were formally charged. It seems that fear and intimidation are the default methods used by army CID investigators. In other words, CID behaves as if all the soldiers in the military unit are guilty as a technique to ferret out who is not guilty. But this means that the subsequent hearings and trials are perfunctory, because CID creates the "theory" which in their view best fits the facts, and their theory and facts are used in later proceedings.

Q: And you talked to Special Agent Battle.

A: Yes, sir.

Q: And what was the interview with her like?

A: It was kind of strange, sir.

Q: What do you mean strange?....

A: It was kind of weird in action, sir.

Q: Okay, did she ever touch you?

A: Yes, sir.

Q: Where did she touch you?

A: On the arm and on the leg, sir.

Q: Okay, did she — where on the leg?

A: The outside of the thigh, sir.

Q: Did it make you feel uncomfortable?

A: Not a whole lot, sir.... She got up and spoke to 2nd Platoon and held the hands of one of the members of 2nd Platoon while giving a speech. I know that she had given hugs to Sergeant Girouard.

Q: Now did she ever mention God or religion in any of this?

A: Roger, sir. I was interviewed at a later date again, and she got into religious or asked me if I believed in God.... She told me that, you know, if I'm not guilty of these things, God will sort it all out, and things of that nature, sir.

Q: Did that seem appropriate at the time?

A: Not really, sir. That did make me a little uncomfortable.

Contemporary American culture is used to accusations of males harassing females by touching them without their permission. But it is strange to come across repeated accounts of a female in a position of authority — in this case, an army CID agent — sexually harassing a male officer. "Harassment" does not seem to be the right word to describe this phenomenon. It is more like the female CID agent is using her sexuality as a weapon to exploit powerful emotions (including those pertaining to religion) with the goal of obtaining or even creating desired information. Given the sexual codes in the United States, the lieutenant probably felt uncomfortable on the witness stand to have to answer whether Battle's actions made him feel uncomfortable! It is very "unmanly" in American culture to admit to being emasculated, and to make this admission for the record.

In response to a question, the lieutenant disclosed that "First Sergeant Geressy kept a machine gun type thing." Captain Miller continued: "So, having essentially captured weapons or war trophy, that wasn't uncommon?" "No, sir. It was pretty open." Soldiers have also told me privately that stealing war trophies was common. Yet the prosecution was trying to make it seem sinister that Sergeant Girouard also had a war trophy in his room, while it had no problem with First Geressy's war trophies. Captain Miller asked the lieutenant about Sergeant Girouard, and he answered: "He's a very good NCO, sir..., my best squad leader." Finally, Captain Miller asked whether Private Mason had ever come to him to say that he had been threatened by anybody. "No, he did not, sir" the lieutenant replied.

Captain Rutizer took over the cross-examination. She began by asking the lieutenant about his seizing cell phones from soldiers in the Iraqi army prior to the mission on May 9th.

A: Yes, ma'am. They — especially cell phones and things of that nature we're not supposed to have on patrols and things like that, but we constantly find them on them [Iraqi soldiers].

Q: To your knowledge, had any IEDs been activated by cell phones?

A: Yes, ma'am....

Q: Walk us through their reactions after the shooting of the first man.

A: Roger, ma'am. When we hit the first house, I went around to the side, saw the IA there. They were pretty abrasive toward me at that point. I brought the "terp" over to ask them what they were saying. They were saying, you know, saying, you know, "They want — they wanted to know why you shot him. Why you shot him. Why you shot," and I told them, I said, "Hey, you got to tell them that I briefed them on this mission, briefed them on the ROE and that's what the ROE was, and they were already privy to that knowledge." He said, "Okay, I'll tell them" and they got more hostile. They said, "Next time we'll go in and we'll detain. We'll detain." You know, very adamant on them going in the house first and detaining....

Q: And you got in your mind that they didn't agree with the ROE obviously?

A: Roger, ma'am. We didn't have a problem with them. When we briefed it to them, they didn't have any problem with it, but after — after that, especially the first guy, they had a big issue with it.

Q: So after the — the first man was shot, they became visibly agitated?

A: Yes, ma'am.

Q: Disappointed?

A: Yes, ma'am.

Q: Upset?

A: Roger, ma'am, and they were — they were — they became pretty — pretty hostile with what we were doing.

Q: At that point, were they any use to you?

A: No, ma'am.

The lieutenant told me much later, and over the telephone, that some of the Iraqi soldiers were crying because the first man had been killed. Given that the ROE was unlawful in relation to the LOAC and the Geneva Conventions, one can give credit to the Iraqi army soldiers for being the only reference group on the mission to object to the unlawful ROE. Instead, the lieutenant and the other soldiers came to regard the Iraqi soldiers as the enemy within. Captain Rutizer continued with the theme of mistrust of and among the Iraqi soldiers:

Q: Was there an incident that occurred at the rest house between two IA guys?

A: The rest house, oh roger, ma'am. One guy — we had a re-supply issue. They didn't have any food or water. They asked us for food or water. I eventually got it for them, but he's from the higher level of NCO officer. I had an issue with them asking us for stuff. He slapped one guy in the back of the head. The other guy turned around and locked and loaded his AK-47 on him.

Q: Did that strike you as odd?

A: It did, ma'am, yes it did.

Q: It is apparent that they didn't trust each other?

A: Yes, ma'am.

Q: How do you know that?

A: Just the way they interacted with each other. They were very — very stand offish, especially towards us, but then they have like, I guess cliques within themselves as well.

Q: Have you ever known any of the IA to be Iraqi sympathizers or Al Qaida sympathizers?

A: Not — could never confirm that, ma'am.

It's actually to be expected that some of the Iraqi soldiers would sympathize with Iraqis, or others in their cultural reference group. Suppose that a foreign army occupied the United States, and some American soldiers cooperated with the foreign invader. One would expect that in this unlikely but parallel scenario, some American soldiers would sympathize with fellow Americans in their reference group. The really significant question is why the US Army was involved in joint operations with Iraqi soldiers against Iraqis. The sociology of reference groups predicts that the outcome would be unsatisfactory. It was Mr. Bergrin's turn to cross-examine the lieutenant.

Q: You talked about the rules of engagement.

A: Yes, sir.

Q: The original rules of engagement were given to you by Colonel Steele?

A: Yes, sir.

Q: And again, what was that rule of engagement?....

A: That we were to kill — positively identify and kill any military aged male on the island because there was confirmed Al Qaida Iraq by a high level intelligence operative.

Q: And at any time did you give that order to Sergeant Girouard?

A: Yes, I did....

Q: How many times did you confirm that order?

A: Countless times, sir. I couldn't tell you.

Q: Is it fair to say that rule of engagement was given to you, reinforced, given to you again, and reinforced again?

A: Yes, several times, sir.

Bergrin's questions and the lieutenant's answers seem to rule out the possibility that the soldiers dreamed up the idea of killing the Iraqis in question on their own. Mr. Bergrin returned to the issue of the upset Iraqi soldiers, and the lieutenant reaffirmed "they were pretty visibly upset." He added that they "verbally argued with me" and were "hostile."

Captain Suddeth asked the lieutenant to recite the brigade motto, and he replied: "We give the enemy the maximum opportunity to die for his country." (The obvious logical fallacy in this motto is that the enemy is Al-Qaida, which is not a country.) Captain Suddeth also had the lieutenant agree that CID was "flirty" and "touchy" when they interrogated him. He also said that he had been "shouted at" by CID, and they yelled things such as "This doesn't make any sense." Suddeth asked: "Would they stand up for no reason, acting like they were mad?" "Yes," the lieutenant said. The IO had several questions for the lieutenant about the relationship between the US and Iraqi soldiers:

Q: And you had this Iraqi element? Was this a squad, platoon, company?

A: A platoon, sir.

Q: Iraqi platoon? Was he subordinate to you? Was this platoon subordinate?

A: Not to my knowledge, sir.

Q: So who was this platoon subordinate to?

A: Captain Hart, sir....

Q: How many soldiers were in the platoon?

A: I couldn't tell you, sir.

Q: Was it 20?

A: Twenty plus probably, sir.

Q: So there were 20 Iraqi soldiers that moved on to Objective Murray with you?

A: Roger — they got delayed, sir. I never saw anymore than those three....

Q: So, you had three soldiers with you, or you had a platoon of Iraqi soldiers with you?

A: It was split up, sir. We had the different chalks.

Q: Okay... So by the time the second lift came in, you had twenty Iraqi soldiers?

A: Yes, sir.

Q: Okay.

A: I believe there was a forty-five minute to an hour delay, sir.....

Q: So what was their mission?

A: They were to supplement our squads, sir, and work hand in hand with our squads as we went and assaulted the objective, sir.

Q: Hand in hand with your squad, so they were subordinate to your squad leaders?

A: Sir, we never really got into the issue of who's subordinate to who.

Q: So was the tactical relationship between you and the Iraqi soldiers confusing?

A: Yes, sir.

Q: Did your company commander tell you how you were supposed to use them?

A: Not particularly, sir. Usually it was, you know, usually use them as you see fit.

Q: Did you ask them what are these guys supposed to do?

A: Roger, sir....

Q: So, would it be correct to say that when you landed on Objective Murray, you weren't sure what you were supposed to do with Iraqi soldiers?

A: Yes, sir....

Q: Okay, were you supposed to provide this platoon supplies, food, water?

A: I was not briefed on that, sir. They did not bring supplies or water....

Q: And you said some — some bad things were happening in that [US Army] platoon. How did you know about that?

A: Soldiers told me, sir.

Q: So it's generally hearsay or rumors or —

A: Mostly hearsay, sir. I only know that charges had been brought forward....

Q: So you never actually saw any drug problems?

We learn from the lieutenant that his platoon and company had problems with drug use, sleeping on duty, and numerous IED injuries; that everyone was confused about the tactical relationship between the US and Iraqi soldiers and no one was certain who was subordinate to whom; that the Iraqi soldiers went on the mission without food or water; that CID tried to flirt with as well as intimidate and threaten him with murder charges; and that the unlawful ROE were reinforced numerous times. Privately, soldiers validated all of the lieutenant's observations to me, especially the drug use, sleep deprivation and confusion. He painted a picture of a military unit that is the opposite of what Stouffer describes in his book as an effective, integrated military unit with high morale and effectiveness.

It was the prosecutor's turn to try to rehabilitate the witness.

Q: How fair is it to say that CID isn't the most welcome down at Brassfield-Mora?

A: It's pretty fair to say, sir.

Q: Okay, you have a pretty good idea of, I guess, the feel of the Soldiers in our platoon?

A: Yes, sir.

Q: And you talk to other Soldiers in other platoons and other companies?

A: Yes, sir...

Q: About CID?

A: Not really, sir. It's pretty hands off, sir....

Q: Is it fair to say that the general consensus is people don't like CID down at Brassfield-Mora?

A: Yes, sir....

Q: So you're saying that they [CID] were going to charge you with murder?

A: Roger, well that and they had suspected me, sir.

Q: That you had been suspected?

A: Yes, sir.

Q: So you talked about Agent Battle and how she was coercing you into writing statements you didn't believe.

A: Yeah, *we were coerced, sir* [emphasis added].

Captain Rutizer asked the IO for a 3-minute bathroom break, and the IO refused! The prosecutor went on with his questioning, and did not get the lieutenant to change his version of events. The prosecutor did not want to let stand, for the record, the lieutenant's charge that he *and* his soldiers (he said "we") were coerced by CID into making false statements. The lieutenant stood his ground, and his statement will stay permanently on the historical as well as the court record. It is no accident that the defense counsel asked for a bathroom break at this crucial time — perhaps she really had to go the bathroom, but she almost certainly wanted to give the lieutenant a break from the prosecutor's questions. And it is no accident that the IO denied her the bathroom break, because he realized the importance of this testimony and how important it was for the government to break the lieutenant on this crucial point of coerced testimony. The government failed, and finally, the IO called for a recess at 6:16 p.m. The hearing was reconvened at 6:30 p.m. and Captain Rutizer started the recross-examination of the lieutenant.

Q: Okay, do you think these guys committed murder?

A: Not — not from previous experience and after ten months of working with all of them. It seems highly unlikely though.

Q: Do you think they did it?

[CAPTAIN DUGGAN]: All right, objection. A. It's asked and answered; B. there's always been previous objections about his opinion of whether they actually even occurred sustained by the investigating officer.

IO: I agree with the objection.

Q: Based on your observations, did you observe anything to make you indicate that these guys committed murder?

A: No, ma'am.

[CAPTAIN RUTIZER]: Thanks. I have nothing else.

Intrigue explodes from this short exchange. It seems that the prosecutor was already aware that the lieutenant did not believe his soldiers committed murder, and had already warned the participants not to open this door. Captain Rutizer opened the door slightly by rephrasing her question. Some of the defense attorneys believe that the lieutenant was in on the cover-up, because he took one dead body with him on the helicopter and left three live prisoners with his soldiers, right after First Sergeant Geressy expressed outrage that anyone was left alive. Were the lieutenant's actions a "green light" to his soldiers? Were his actions truly "his" or merely an extension of the wishes of the First Sergeant, who, in turn, was speaking for the command? It is almost certain that these and related questions will never be answered in a satisfactory way.

Captain Miller asked the lieutenant about ROE on other missions, and the prosecutor objected and the IO became involved. Apparently, there was an order to the defense attorneys that they were not to discuss other missions with similar ROE. All of the information that was disclosed to the reader in chapter 2 about similar killings was forbidden to be put on the court record! After some back and forth between the attorneys and the IO, the IO allowed general questioning in this area. The lieutenant was finally allowed to answer as follows: "Each platoon was tasked out a specific target. Once the targets were positively identified, they were to be killed, sir." Thus, one is able to confirm that the mission and supposedly strange ROE on Iron Triangle were not unique. The lieutenant was dismissed.

TESTIMONY OF CAPTAIN JASON SIENKO

Captain Jason Sienko took the stand. His position is that of executive officer in Charlie Company. He testified that First Sergeant Geressy said the following over the radio when he learned that prisoners were taken on the mission: "I don't know why you had detainees, but since you have them go ahead and package them up, get them to the helicopters, to the LZ, and bring them back for questioning." "Did he say anything else?" the prosecutor asked. "I believe he said, 'I don't know why you have all these f-ing detainees,' or something along those lines," Captain Sienko replied. When asked about the ROE, Sienko replied: "The rules of engagement for Operation Iron Triangle were that the — since the island was declared a hostile threat, the entire island, you were to kill or engage any — any males on the island that were military aged."

Cross-examination revealed that it was Captain Sienko who "preferred charges in this case." Captain Mackey turned to the issue of the kill board:

Q: There was also a board with a number of Iraqis killed, correct?

A: Yes....

Q: *Were there any women and children included on that board?*

A: *I believe there was at one time, and they were taken off because it was in bad taste, so they were taken off the board, taken off the kill count, and retabulated.*

Q: And at one point wasn't there a kill count that included at least one pregnant woman that was killed in a suburban one or two clicks outside Brassfield-Mora?

A: I don't remember if that woman was included or not [emphasis added]

Q: Okay, and that was — those were individuals killed by Charlie team?

A: Yes.

Charlie team is the unit of the accused in this case. It was more than "bad taste" that dead women and children were listed on the same kill board that listed alleged terrorists. Soldiers confirmed to me privately that the dead pregnant woman was, indeed, listed on the kill board. The captain used the classic evasive line with regard to this incident: "I don't remember." These egregious facts show a shocking problem in leadership and suggest a poisoned social climate in the unit. Sienko explained the situation with the dead pregnant woman and the suburban as follows:

> The situation in the suburban was that they were stopped at a — they stopped at a possible IED. They had four vehicles in a row, you know ... traffic was stopped ... and a suburban moved from the pack of cars that accumulated in the opposite lane approximately a hundred meters ahead.... At that point, I don't know who's in the lead vehicle, but they made a decision to engage based on hostile intent and hostile threat.... The vehicle moved out to the side of the road approximately fifty meters, and burst into flames.

The prosecutor objected that this incident was irrelevant to the charges, and the objection was sustained by the IO. Nevertheless, this brief testimony gives us a glimpse of this unit's "logic." Killing of non-terrorist civilians was justified on the basis that the soldiers thought the driver showed "hostile intent and hostile threat." The army's traditional ROE was invoked — albeit without questioning whether the hostile intent was real. No charges were leveled at soldiers for killing civilians in this incident. Soldiers confirmed to me privately that no weapons were found in this vehicle and all the occupants were undoubtedly innocent victims. In their words, they were ordered to "light up" the vehicle. Yet when soldiers followed an unlawful ROE and killed prisoners in the pursuit of that same unlawful ROE, some (but not all) of them were charged with murder. These contradictions make no logical sense. The hearing recessed for the day at 7:20 p.m.

TESTIMONY OF THE REMAINING US SOLDIERS

The next day, at 8:18 am, the hearing began with the prosecutor seeking an additional charge against Clagett for showing disrespect to his guards. Mr. Bergrin objected vehemently on the grounds that the prosecutor was merely trying to further prejudice the case against Clagett. Mr. Bergrin continued:

> Sir, I also think that you should consider — I know if I make one more argument, in fact on the record that essentially since the arrest in this particular case on approximately 15 June, Private Clagett has been almost caged like an animal in a 7 by 7 cage, 24 hours a day, segregated, isolated. He's gotten approximately one meal a day. He doesn't take showers, okay, he's treated like an animal when he's presumed innocent. These ministerial charges are the result of numerous calls and contacts that Captain Rutizer's had with individuals such as the one making the allegation here, and that's Damage Controlman First Class Mark O. King. There's been complaint after complaint made against him by Captain Rutizer through his superiors in the way he's treating Clagett, not letting him eat; making him sleep shackled. Can you imagine that sir, making an individual sleep shackled, his hands and his feet shackled to each other in a 7 by 7 cell for almost a month at this particular time in complete isolation when he's presumed innocent until proven guilty? So, these ministerial type charges, to be laid upon us at this time at the eve of trial have absolutely no place whatsoever to be considered by you.

The IO replied: "I understand your position, and I'll consider it." At the end of the hearing, the IO allowed these additional charges of disrespect toward his tormentor to stand. Later in the book, I will show that Hunsaker was abused in a similar way: shackled, isolated, and caged — even though by law he was presumed to be innocent until proven guilty.

More drama followed in that fourteen witnesses who were brought to the hearing for that day would not testify. The hearing recessed at 8:28 a.m. At 8:41 a.m. the IO said: "Let me explain what I'd like to do. It's been indicated that both defense and government don't intend to call anymore witnesses." The reasons for this decision were never made public. Presumably, the prosecution realized that it was losing its case with the previous day's witnesses; the defense saw no need to expose its witnesses to cross-examination because the burden of proof was on the government; and many witnesses decided to invoke their rights rather than testify. The IO decided to invoke his authority "to call the following witnesses: Acevedo, Bivens, Helton, Neuman, and Ryan."

Sergeant Armando Acevedo took the stand. Acevedo's testimony was brief and guarded: He said he never heard anything about what happened on the mission (even though he was on it) and never heard threats by the accused. The only substantive testimony he gave was to reiterate the First Sergeant's radio transmission, in his own words: "We're bringing back the detainees when they should be dead, but put them on the bird so that they can get questioned." Recall that Acevedo was facing an Article 15 for sleeping on duty. His testimony did not help the prosecution or the defense.

Specialist Micah Bivens was sworn in. He was the platoon medic. The IO stepped in immediately and said to Bivens: "I was also informed that you have been accused of another offense, so I'm required to read you your rights before you answer any questions." Bivens was told that anything he said or did could be used against him at a criminal trial. Nevertheless, he agreed to testify. I do not know what the charges were against Bivens, whether they were dropped, or what happened to him. Bivens answered that he did *not* hear a discussion of a plan to kill the prisoners. "You never heard anyone discuss this?" the IO asked. "No, sir," Bivens replied. The IO continued: "Did you ever hear Sergeant Girouard tell anyone to put the third detainee out of his misery?" "No, sir."

Under cross-examination by Mr. Bergrin, Bivens gave a slightly different interpretation of the tactical training point that terrorists hide behind babies: "It is a human shield or showing it saying he didn't have anything other than a baby, you know." Bivens also validated the many other witnesses who testified that CID mistreated them and accused them of crimes:

> Q: Did he [CID agent] try to treat you like you were a criminal, like you did something wrong?

> A: Yes, sir.

> Q: He tried to accuse you of wrongdoing?

> A: Yes, sir, and he tried to accuse everybody there.

> Q: And you felt intimidated based upon the fact that it was CID, correct?

A: I didn't enjoy his presence, no.... I'd tell him what I thought had happened what I knew at the time, and he'd tell me, "No, that's not what had happened."....

Q: Isn't it a fact that he tried to put words into your mouth?

A: I believe that after about six hours of somebody and anytime you say something and he says, "No, that's not what happened," and wouldn't take what you said, "No, I think you're lying to me. I think this is what happened," and then he told me what he thought happened, and he's just go running through scenarios again and again and again.

Q: Essentially he wore you down?

A: Pretty much.

Finally, Mr. Bergrin asked Bivens what happened immediately after the killing of the prisoners. Bivens replied: "I'm not sure anymore." Captain Miller took over the cross-examination for the defense. He asked Bivens about yet another incident in which US soldiers in the unit shot at civilians. The driver was killed but a little girl and boy were wounded seriously. "So these Soldiers, Sergeant Girouard, Clagett, Hunsaker, and Graber, they helped — they tried to administer aid to these local Iraqis?" "Yes, sir," Bivens replied. In response to Mr. Waddington's questions about what happened on the mission on May 9th, Bivens replied: "I'm not sure what I know anymore after being run through all these scenarios with CID. I'm not sure."

One wonders whether the soldiers who thought they were sure about what happened were also brainwashed by the scenarios that CID ran them through during long interrogations. What is certain is that all of the accounts by the soldiers contradict each other so radically — in sworn, written statements as well as sworn testimony — that we will never know for certain what happened on this mission on May 9th. It is ironic that the latest scientific innovations in interrogation techniques yield uncertainty and confusion. The postmodernists refer to this as the "implosion of truth."

In his re-cross examination of Bivens, the prosecutor tried to make it seem as if the Iraqis who were killed were *not* insurgents, even though testimony up to then had revealed that the soldiers were briefed into believing the Iraqis were insurgents.

Q: And isn't it true that based on what you say there today, there was nothing indicating to you that these were insurgents?

A: We didn't find any IED making materials or anything, no, sir....

Q: You found one AK-47 per house ... which is permitted under Iraqi law?

A: Yes, sir.

Q: You found three guys without shoes in the first house?

A: I'm not sure if they were wearing shoes or not, but we found three guys, yes.

Q: You found some sheep, right?

A: Yes, sir.

In his recross-examination, Mr. Bergrin took the opposite tack, and asked: "As you sit there today, even though based upon what you observed on 9 May of 2006, you can't offer any evidence whatsoever that these detainees, any of them, were not terrorists or insurgents, correct?" "That's right," Bivens replied. So who or what were the Iraqis who were killed on that mission, terrorists or shepherds and farmers? One will probably never know. And what were the soldiers thinking as they landed and started shooting at the Iraqis they were told were al-Qaida terrorists, even though they found no evidence for this expectation? We have seen that after being interrogated by CID, the soldiers were not even certain about what they remembered, thought, or felt about this surprise on the mission. Finally, even their testimony at the Article 32 was precarious, because they all knew that if they said the wrong thing, any of them could be charged with murder or conspiracy or both. This is not normal trial procedure relative to the average image Americans are socialized to have of trials, the rule of law, and police investigations.

Corporal Helton's testimony ran into a problem when he was asked a question by Mr. Bergrin that the prosecutor said was under a protective order. The IO agreed with the prosecutor. Mr. Bergrin rephrased his questions. However, Helton's testimony offered nothing new, despite the prosecutor's objections: he merely re-stated that the soldiers expected to find terrorists on the mission but found Iraqi men cowering behind women and children. Mr. Waddington got Helton to agree that Mason was a "storyteller" who "embellishes facts to make himself look good." Captain Miller obtained some new information from Helton. Helton testified that the processing of the three prisoners was rushed (the soldiers were given fifteen minutes to photograph them and fill out the required paperwork) so that they could leave with Lieutenant Wehrheim on the helicopter. Apparently, Sergeant Girouard personally escorted the fourth prisoner (who was not killed) to the helicopter.

Q: Okay, and then Sergeant Girouard started to go back toward the house?

A: Roger.

Q: And it was soon after that you heard gun shots?

A: Roger.

Helton also testified that he heard gun shots approximately four to six minutes after Girouard escorted the one prisoner who lived. He also said that he saw the three prisoners running at full speed away from the house and saw them get shot.

Q: Now at some point you also heard Sergeant Girouard say "We'd better get some pictures of this," correct?

A: Roger.

Q: And is it at that point Sergeant Lemus took photographs at the crime scene or of the scene?

A: Roger.

Q: Took pictures of the bodies?

A: Roger.

The amount of photographic documentation on this mission seems extraordinary compared to previous wars. Yet all the photographs pertaining to Operation Iron Triangle were confiscated by the government. If the photographs were ever revealed, they could show whether the engineering tape ("blind folds") on the heads of the prisoners were cut at the make-shift morgue. Captain Miller also got Corporal Helton to describe pressure by CID for Helton and Ryan to change their accounts so that they would be consistent:

A: So they asked you two to converse and say what you knew or they asked you to — to combine information, correct?

A: Roger.

Q: And come up with collective stories essentially, correct?

A: Roger.

Q: Rather than based on solely on what you remember?

A: Roger. Basically what they said whenever I went in there, they brought me and Ryan in there and they looked at me and was like "Your story's good. It matches up with everybody else's" and they looked at Sergeant Ryan and he's like "Your story is just full of shit," and so he's like, "I want you two to sit together and see if you can help him remember anything." Because — and all that his story didn't say that mine said was that Sergeant Ryan didn't hear no shots.

Q: And that is what they were concerned about?

A: Yeah.

Q: And that's why they used the word "full of shit."

A: Yeah.

Q: Is that what was said?

A: That was what was said.

Q: And this was during a formal CID interview?

A: Roger.

Clearly, forcing witnesses to collaborate in changing their accounts is non-normative in relation to American standards of criminal investigations and legal procedure. Corporal Helton's account of unlawful CID tactics is consistent with testimony by all other soldiers concerning CID. The IO said nothing in response to this testimony.

Captain Suddeth obtained still further inconsistent testimony from Corporal Helton relative to other soldiers. Helton testified that he did *not* see or hear Graber commit the infamous "mercy killing" of one of the prisoners to which Graber confessed.

Q: And you also didn't see any smoke coming out of the muzzle?

A: Nope.

Q: And you didn't see any dirt being kicked up off the ground?

A: Negative.

Q: And you didn't see shoulders move any way?

A: He was just standing there staring at the dead bodies?

Q: Like a statue? Is that correct?

A: Roger.

Captain Duggan, one of the government prosecutors, had his work cut out for him in the recross-examination of Corporal Helton. Duggan had Helton repeat the key points in the sequence of events: Helton was at the landing zone waiting for the helicopters, when he heard shots fired. He and Ryan ran to the house, which was about 200 meters away. He saw Sergeant Girouard run "counterclockwise around the house." Helton and Ryan positioned themselves as gunners outside the house in anticipation of further gunfire, because their first thought was that they had come under attack. Helton ran inside the house to check whether everyone was ok, and then went back outside. Surprisingly, Captain Duggan simply stopped asking questions at this point. In the social world of lawyers, this means that the prosecution lost points by Helton's testimony, and realized it would lose further if it persisted with questioning. The IO called for a recess at 10:40 a.m. on the 3rd of August 2006.

The hearing resumed at 10:54 a.m. Things immediately got messy. The IO announced that the next witness, Sergeant Neuman, was suspected of making a false official statement, so that he would have to be read his rights on the witness stand. The prosecutor added intrigue to the investigation:

[CAPTAIN FISCHBACH]: Can I just make a brief notation on the record. I just want to inform all counsel, your clients are still subject to the no contact order that was originally given by the battalion commander shortly before they went into pretrial confinement.

[CAPTAIN RUTIZER]: By who?

[CAPTAIN FISCHBACH]: I'm sorry, it was given by Captain Sienko. I apologize.

[CAPTAIN RUTIZER]: Right, and the content of that is don't talk about the case, right?

[CAPTAIN FISCHBACH]: I believe it was a straight no contact order.

[CAPTAIN RUTIZER]: Well, not the one you provided us. The one provided us says no talking about the case, so if you got a different one, I'm happy to look at it.

[CAPTAIN FISCHBACH]: I just want to make sure everybody understands that it still applies.

[MR. BERGRIN]: Do you have any evidence that they talked about the case? If you do, then we should know about that because that would be in violation of the no contact order.

[CAPTAIN FISCHBACH}: Actually I do have such evidence, but we can go into that here or later. It's up to you.

IO: Let's go into it after this witness.

But the IO and the attorneys never returned to this issue for the record. Was it something they discussed behind closed doors? The IO read Sergeant David Andrew Neuman his rights. Despite being threatened that anything he said could and would be used against him, Neuman decided to testify. The IO began the questioning. He ascertained that Neuman was on the mission in his role as a team leader in Charlie Company. He told the IO that Graber did tell him that he had shot someone, but not as a "mercy killing." Neuman testified that Graber told him "he shot a local national while clearing the objective." The prosecutor took over the questioning. The prosecutor referred to the written sworn statement that Neuman had made to CID in which he described what Graber had told him. Mr. Bergrin objected to the written statement being admitted into testimony on the grounds that it contained hearsay. The prosecutor responded that "the rules of evidence are relaxed." Captain Miller cited the Rules of Court Martial 405 which "says no statement can be admitted over the objection of the defense counsel." The IO ruled, "That's correct, so I won't admit it." Captain Suddeth asked "And during your conversation with Graber, never once did he ever say it was a mercy type killing, is that correct?" "Yes, sir" Neuman replied. The witness was dismissed. On the surface, it seems that Neuman was being charged with making a false statement simply because his testimony did not correspond with Graber's confession to CID that he committed a "mercy killing." But reading between the lines, and given the very short testimony by Neuman, a careful observer will conclude that both the prosecution and the defense regarded Neuman as dangerous to their respective positions. Neuman was a team leader and no doubt had plenty of stories to tell about other missions and incidents. There is intrigue in the very fact that nobody tried to ask him about other incidents, even if such questions were largely forbidden.

The IO addressed Sergeant Ryan: "Before we start any questions, I've been informed that you're also under investigation for false official statement in a separate situation, so before I ask you questions about this investigation, I'm required to read you your rights and ensure you understand them." The IO read Ryan his rights, and asked, "Do you understand your rights?"

WIT: I have a question, sir.

IO: Go ahead.

WIT: You said it has nothing to do with this incident. I have not been told what it has to do with, what I've been —

IO: This investigation here present is not an investigation of you.

WIT: What I'm being charged with, does that have to do with this investigation, sir?

IO: I believe it has something to do with something you did separately.

WIT: Okay, I guess I would like to speak with a lawyer then, sir.

IO: So you invoke your right not to testify?

WIT: Yes, sir.

IO: Okay, then you're dismissed.

Like a scene out of Franz Kafka's novel, *The Trial*, it appears that Ryan was being charged with a crime without knowing the charge. When he asked the IO what he was being charged with, the IO did not give him a direct answer. By American cultural standards, Ryan had every right to know who was charging him with what specific crime, and the IO had an obligation to tell him. Clearly, the average American does not expect to feel like he is in a fictional novel written by an Eastern European genius about life in an oppressive society.

The hearing recessed at 11:18 a.m.

CHAPTER 6. LOST IN TRANSLATION: TESTIMONY BY THE IRAQI SOLDIERS, AND
CLOSING ARGUMENTS

"The double-bind leads to the conclusion of despair."
— Gregory Bateson, p. 335

The hearing resumed at 11:33 a.m. The only witnesses left to testify were two Iraqi Army soldiers. A discussion ensued as to whether they would be available immediately, later in the day, or the following day. Everyone agreed that they would be available the following day at 9 a.m. The hearing recessed at 11:43 a.m. on the 3rd of August.

The hearing resumed at 10:10 a.m. on 4 August 2006. This was much later than the scheduled 9 a.m. time, and the Iraqi soldiers did not testify immediately as planned. Instead, the prosecutor immediately asked to proffer additional charges against Clagett for crimes of "disrespect." Mr. Bergrin objected: "We made an objection yesterday, sir, and we'll make the same objection today. It's almost getting comical. I mean, every day that we walk in here on the eve of essentially the end of the investigation, the eve of testimony, and we're handed new charges, new specifications that have absolutely not a scintilla to do with the original incident of 9 May."

The additional charge concerned alleged disrespect Clagett showed toward his guards on 21 and 22 July of 2006. The argument became heated. Clagett's military defense attorney, Captain Rutizer, said that the prosecution had placed the additional charges on her desk at 5 am, and she did not have time to study them. Mr. Bergrin complained that the government made no effort to bring officers to testify, such as Lieutenant Commander Karamidov, who was Chief of Mental Health. He also said that Clagett had not been read his rights. Mr. Bergrin also accused the prosecution of "muddying the waters" and of orchestrating "a trial by ambush — an investigation by ambush." He was referring to the fact that "we were served with these charge sheets this day the last of this proceeding." The prosecutor responded:

[CAPTAIN FISCHBACH]: I saw it [charge sheet] in my inbox at approximately 2220 last night. I contemplated going over and serving a copy of those charges with — on PFC Clagett right then and there, and the only reason I did not do it was because I did not want to interfere with his sleep.

[MR. BERGRIN]: With all due respect to you, sir, we — he knew exactly where we were staying. He knew exactly where Captain Rutizer sleeps, and you don't — you don't do those kinds of things with allegations of double murder against an individual.

IO: Okay, I understand. Even if he had done it last night, it still wouldn't have provided you enough time to get your witnesses here for today anyway, either side. What I want to do is take a ten-minute recess and discuss this with my advisor and come back, okay.

The hearing recessed at 10:24 a.m. The prosecutor's explanation that he was being considerate of Clagett's sleep is amazingly duplicitous, because he could have served Clagett's attorneys, who were undoubtedly working late into the night. The hearing resumed at 10:37 a.m. The IO began: "Okay, I just came out of a discussion with Captain Rutizer, Captain Rohrbach, Captain Fischbach, and Captain Duggan in the back room here to discuss the situation with the new charges." This was one of those famous back room discussions that Mr. Waddington told me about, in which all sorts of threats, decisions, and compromises are made that never go on the court record. The IO ruled that he would not allow written statements to be included with the additional charges, but he would allow the additional charges to be leveled at Clagett: "So the charges will stand alone. Okay, now I believe we were going to call the Iraqi witnesses."

The prosecution raised the point that both the interpreters and the Iraqi soldiers feared for their lives by testifying (they were afraid of retribution by other Iraqis) so that only their first names should be used on record. The IO proposed that all of the Iraqi soldiers who would give testimony or be mentioned in testimony would be referred to as "Mohammed," and their real names would be sealed in a special envelope. This becomes a little bit confusing, because the witness, Mr. Mohammed, will refer to the Iraqi squad leader, also a Mr. Mohammed. Furthermore, the interpreters as well as the Iraqi soldiers would be examined on the witness stand. Finally, Captain Fischbach and Captain Rutizer went on record stating that they played volleyball with or otherwise interacted with the interpreters on the US army base. Perhaps this was their way of vouching that the interpreters probably were not secret terrorists.

The overall theme of the testimony and cross-examination of the Iraqi soldiers was that they were potentially the enemy within. At one point, the prosecutor asked an Iraqi soldier on the witness stand, "Are you a terrorist?" Closely related, the Iraqi soldiers made it clear that they were risking their lives by testifying and fighting on the side of the Americans in general. Thus, the Iraqi soldiers were regarded as the potential "enemy within" by both American and Iraqi reference groups. Using Gregory Bateson's concept of the double-bind situation, it is not word play to suggest that the Iraqi soldiers on this mission were in a double-double-bind situation: they were damned for participating or quitting these missions by both the Americans and their fellow Iraqis. The Americans saw them as potential terrorists and the Iraqis saw them as traitors. The testimony by Iraqi soldiers contradicted the US soldiers' testimonies that the prisoners who were killed hid "behind" women. CID again emerged from the testimony seeming as if it coerced or fabricated this and other evidence. Overall, a picture of paranoid, suspicious, and hostile relationships among US soldiers, Iraqi soldiers, and Iraqi citizens emerged in the testimony. All this is in line with Bateson's theory more than he could have imagined.

The first interpreter, whom I will not name, stated that he was a Category 1 interpreter, which means that he was cleared for top secret testimony. He said he was proficient in Kurdish Arabic, as well as Mosul dialect, Baghdad Arabic dialect and Basra dialect. He learned to speak English in the US and was a US citizen.

TESTIMONY BY THE FIRST IRAQI SOLDIER

The first Iraqi soldier was called to testify, and cultural differences between the US and Iraq appeared immediately. The Iraqi soldier refused to put his hand on the Koran to swear on it, as requested by the IO, because, in his own words: "Before we swear, we put our hand on the Koran, we should be clean, you know, like take shower and our body would be totally clean to our hand on the Koran." Apparently, the act of a Westerner putting one's hand on the Bible is not the same as the act of a Muslim putting one's hand on the Koran — the cultural rules as to what is clean versus unclean, and sacred versus profane, are different in the two reference groups. The IO was willing to let the Iraqi soldier testify without placing his hand on the Koran, but Captain Suddeth objected, saying that he could not be sure if the soldier would be telling the truth without putting his hand on the Koran. The IO finally asked the interpreter for his opinion as to what should be done to resolve this problem. The interpreter said: "I think if — can we give him, like, five minutes? He can go, like, wash his body?" The IO agreed, and the hearing was recessed at 10:52 a.m. so that the Iraqi soldier could take a shower in order to take an oath on the Koran. Mr. Waddington later confirmed that this is exactly what the Iraqi soldier did.

The hearing resumed at 11:02 a.m. The court transcriber wrote into the record: "The witness held the Koran in his hand while taking the oath and continued to hold the Koran throughout his testimony." The ensuing testimony illustrates the importance of understanding cultural differences but eventually became a circus. There were a total of four different Iraqi interpreters in the room, and they began to disagree with each other — on the court record — as to the translation of what the witness was saying. The first witness eventually became confused and was dismissed. Ironically, the prosecution tried to get the Iraqi soldiers to depict the victims as ordinary farmers, while the defense tried to get them to depict the victims as terrorists and insurgents. The irony stems from the fact that the US soldiers were led to believe that everyone on the island on May 9th was a terrorist or terrorist sympathizer.

Q: Sergeant Mohamed, were you involved in Operation Iron Triangle?

A: Yes....

Q: Can you explain for us how you got on the objective and what happened?

A: First when we get out of the aircraft, we and American Soldiers — the American Soldiers, they shoot at the house.

Q: And what were they shooting at?

A: Just to the house; toward the house.

If this testimony is true, it contradicts the American soldiers' testimonies that some soldiers shot specifically at the "man in the window," whom they killed. Recall that no one was certain who fired, how many shots were fired, and who actually killed the "man in the window" (who was not in the window, but outside the house). The Iraqi soldier suggests that the US soldiers were firing at the house, which is believable given that many US soldiers testified about shooting at "hostile houses." (Privately, soldiers told me they "lit up" whatever they were told to destroy, from cars to homes, tractors, buildings, and so on.) According to US army society, a house can be declared "hostile" every bit as much as an individual can be declared hostile, and therefore subject to fire.

Q: When you got to the front door of the house, was there anyone at the front door?

A: There was a female outside. She was standing outside, the door, the female.

Q: How many females?

A: One of them she was standing outside, and one of them — one of them, she was inside the house....

Q: When you went in the house, did you find anyone else?

A: When I went inside the room, I saw three individuals.

Q: Were they hiding behind the women?

A: The lady, the female, she was standing outside. This individual, they were inside and they were kind of scared or they just was hiding inside. They was inside the room. They was hiding in the room.

Again, the US soldiers testified consistently that the Iraqis were hiding "behind" the women, but this is not what the Iraqi soldier said. Later in the testimony, it was revealed that the female inside the house was actually 12-years-old, which means obviously that she was a child. The Iraqi soldiers surmised that the "lady" outside the house was the wife of the man who was killed, the child was his daughter, and the men were his nephews or otherwise related to him. In sum, the soldiers came upon an Iraqi family, not a den of terrorists, as they expected. Note that the Americans referred to all the females as "women," even the child, whereas the Iraqis referred to them as "ladies."

Q: And when you got into the room, did they resist you or fight you at all?

A: No, no they did not. I take them outside, three of them.

Q: Was anyone with you when you took them outside?

A: They were — there was a body. There was a dead person outside. Me and my friend, when I take — when I took this people, these three individuals outside, the American Soldiers, they ask me for help to carry — me and my friend to carry this dead body and me and my friend and two American Soldiers, we carry that body.

Note that the Iraqi soldier refers to his Iraqi Army comrades as "friends." Consistently, the Iraqi soldier described the colleagues in his reference group as "friends" and the US soldiers as American Soldiers. Clearly, the Iraqi and US soldiers did not regard each other as friends.

Q: Once the detainees were taken outside, how were they situated?

A: They was very quiet, and we told them just don't talk, and they was very quiet....

Q: What did you do next?

A: They put the body in the plastic bag. They took the body then they came back, they pick up us.

Q: When you say "they," who?

A: The helicopter. The aircraft came, pick up the body, took us somewhere, and came back, pick up us, and we took — went to different place.

This is consistent with the testimony by Lieutenant Wehrheim.

The Iraqi soldier gave new information about the rest of Operation Iron Triangle. Apparently, they went to another house and found another man whom they detained, who was living with "many kids" and "most of them was kids around seven or eight." The Iraqi and US soldiers took about fifteen prisoners on that mission.

As the questioning continued, another interpreter suddenly interrupted the proceeding: "Sir, no, just I want to make clear what he's saying.... I have no idea what exactly happened. I think that Mohammed — Mr. Mohammed and some American Soldiers, they look inside the fourth house ... He said, 'I don't know exactly what happened to the last house or the last detainee.'"

This was not what the official interpreter had said, and confusion ensued in the courtroom. Which house and which mission were they talking about? The prosecutor changed tack. "Did you ever see any of your soldiers — any of the Iraqi soldiers make — make physical contact or converse with the detainees?" The Iraqi soldier answered: "Chief Mohammed and the Iraqi soldiers, they was talking nicely with them." Recall that the US soldiers were suspicious of what the Iraqi soldiers were saying to the prisoners, but the consistent testimony by the two Iraqi soldiers was that they were trying to reassure the prisoners. The prosecutor then launched directly into the "enemy within" theme:

> Q: In your time in the unit, how many of your soldiers have been — the soldiers you work with been fired, imprisoned for being involved with insurgent activity?

> A: None. If someone wants to quit, they just going to quit.

It may or may not be true that an Iraqi soldier can "just quit" being a soldier if he decides to become an insurgent or for any other reason. It is certain that a US soldier cannot "just quit" being a US soldier for any reason, but must go through a long and meticulous discharge process. "How many of the Soldiers who were on that objective that day, to your knowledge were involved in insurgent activity?" "Just four," the Iraqi soldier replied. But the interpreter, IO and prosecutor were not sure that he understood the question or the meaning of the word "insurgent." The question was repeated numerous times. Mr. Bergrin objected: "Objection. That answer has been asked and answered, and as a matter of fact, Mr. Mohammed answered that four were involved in insurgent activity. Let that reflect that loud and clear." The official interpreter disagreed: "He don't understand the question. It's not clear." Another interpreter in the room piped in: "I can help. He say what — he say what kind of insurgent activity?" Mr. Bergrin objected again: "I have to object. That's the second time the question's been asked and answered." The prosecutor replied:

> [CAPTAIN FISCHBACH]: Sir, I respectfully ask that we clear this up. It's clear that, I mean, you've got interpreters from the defense chiming in even though they are not supposed to be asking questions right now. Things get lost in translation....

> [MR. BERGRIN]: I think the question was loud, clear, was asked twice. He answered twice the exact way consistently. I mean, I think we should move on.... He didn't state that he didn't understand the question. Four insurgents, four Iraqi soldiers. Let's move on, sir....

> IO: Well, I do believe that the witness is confused, and I will allow one more attempt at that question. Let's ask it one more time. Are you rewording the question?

> [CAPTAIN FISCHBACH]: We're trying to clear it up.

The prosecutor asked the Iraqi soldier whether every other Iraqi soldier on the mission was a terrorist. "Is Chief Mohammed a terrorist?" "No. He's very good soldier. He's very good." Finally, the prosecutor asked the witness: "Are you a terrorist?" The Iraqi soldier answered: "If I'm a terrorist, I would go home. I wouldn't stay here between you. They American Soldiers outside, they know how many missions we've done together." The Iraqi soldier's testimony did nothing to quell the doubts. If his rule was that Iraqi soldiers who are sleeper terrorists simply quit and "go home," one has to explain — from the American point of view — why half the Iraqi platoon from that mission quit and went home the day after the mission. Perhaps Mr. Mohammed intended some other interpretation of this mass mutiny which makes sense from an Iraqi point of view. As the testimony continued, everyone became more confused and increasingly suspicious.

Mr. Bergrin cross-examined Mr. Mohammed. Bergrin wanted the Iraqi soldier to admit that he told CID that he said — regarding a knife that was found on the scene but was never recovered — "This knife the Mujahedeen use it to kill Iraqi and Americans." The Iraqi soldier denied saying that to the CID agent. "So I guess Agent Jones is a liar also?" Bergrin quipped. The prosecutor objected. The Iraqi soldier said: "I have my hand on the Koran, and I'm telling everything true."

Q: Your father fought with Saddam Hussein in the Iraqi Army, correct?

A: Yes.

Q: And your father was a dedicated soldier to Saddam Hussein, correct?

A: No, it wasn't like that. During the Iran war he got wounded on his leg and he was — he told us, you know, to — to come to the Army now and he was like a poor guy after he got wounded and he got nothing to do with the Army.

Q: But he served with Saddam Hussein, correct?

A: He was a soldier. He — he have to serve.

Cultural differences between the US and Iraq are important to note here. Serving in Saddam Hussein's army as a conscript is not the same as serving in George Bush's army as a volunteer soldier. Mr. Bergrin asked about cell phones and Mr. Mohammed said "Yes, yes, I have, and all of us, we have cell phones." He added, "If someone carry cell phone by secret, I don't know."

Q: Now, you had no idea about the backgrounds of the other soldiers in your platoon, correct?

A: That's correct. I don't know nothing about his background. If he go to his family when we — when he's with me — we work together. When he go to his family, I don't know what he's doing.

Q: As a matter of fact you told us that some of the members of your platoon could have been Al Qaida, Taliban, or have insurgent affiliation.

A: I don't know — I don't know nothing bout him again — about the background. They may be a terrorist, they may be not....

Q: Isn't it a fact that when the American Soldiers shot the old man his members of his [Chief Mohammed's] platoon became very upset and threatened to quit?

A: That's right....

Q: There was a lot of anger, they were upset, and there was a lot of arguments with the American Soldiers? Isn't that a fact?

A: Yes. Chief Mohammed, he talked to one of the American officer and he — he told the American officer, "We going to go raid and you guys secure or protect or secure us."

Mr. Bergrin returned to the issue of the cell phones and how the US soldiers searched the Iraqi soldiers repeatedly to find them. Mr. Mohammed's response was: "Why? We are soldier they are Soldier. Why they — they do that to us. We're doing same job." Changing topics, Mr. Bergrin asked: "So the men, the detainees, according to your testimony were not hiding behind the women." The Iraqi soldier kept to his position: "No, they wasn't hiding behind the women." He elaborated that one of the women "was standing in the door and they inside the room." And the other female, "the girl was just twelve years old" and "I don't think they are going to hide behind the girl." Mr. Bergrin again changed topics:

Q: Now you have no idea what the background of these detainees were?

A: No, I don't know that. Until this moment, I don't know even know the name of area we went to that operation.

Q: But he does know that that's a known terrorist area?

A: I do not — I never heard about that area, never.... Maybe yes, maybe no. They may be insurgents maybe not.... I know very well my hand is on the Koran. How — I can't tell — how I know if they — they are insurgents or not. When we — when we are with them or when we capture them, we give to American Soldier then we flew to different objective for we didn't know what happened after that.

It seems incredible that the Iraqi soldiers did not know the location of the area in Iraq where the mission was conducted, and did not believe it was a "known" terrorist area. If it is true that the Iraqi army could not distinguish between Iraqi "terrorists" and civilians, how could the US army be more certain? Clearly, US "intelligence" concerning alleged terrorists in this area was out of sync with apparent reality (the inhabitants were farmers and their families) as well as Iraqi soldiers' knowledge of the situation. Mr. Mohammed repeated that the Iraqi soldiers tried to reassure the Iraqi prisoners and told them "don't worry," and "if you guys are innocent you will get released." He also disclosed that all the Iraqi soldiers on the mission wore scarves around their heads and faces "to make the people don't recognize them." It seems that helping US soldiers was a dangerous undertaking for Iraqis. The hearing recessed at 12:25 p.m.

At 12:38 p.m., the hearing reconvened. The prosecutor asked Mr. Mohammed "what was the demeanor of the females?" Mr. Mohammed replied: "They was scared when we — when we went inside ... they were crying then they calm down; they were quiet." Mr. Mohammed's description of the females (that they were scared and crying) seems much more believable than the version of the US soldiers (that the women were caring toward the Americans). Who wouldn't be scared or crying under these circumstances? "What eventually happened to the women?" Mr. Bergrin asked. "We told them, 'Don't worry and everything is okay,' then the Americans came and they took them." Were the women also imprisoned? Nobody asked.

Q: And to your knowledge were these women related to this older man [who had been killed]?

A: I know one of them was his daughter. I don't know the other one. She was his daughter or his wife.

Q: When you were in the house, did the women tell you why the three men were in their house?

Mr. Bergrin objected at this point on the grounds of hearsay. The IO overruled him. Mr. Mohammed replied: "She didn't say nothing about these three men that was inside the house. Okay, one of them was the nephew of the old guy." Captain Miller objected and was overruled. The prosecutor asked about the professions of the three Iraqis who were killed, and Captain Miller objected again: "Hearsay. That's gross hearsay." The defense did not want information on the record that the victims may *not* have been terrorists. Mr. Mohammed was able to say, over the many objections, that Chief Mohammed told him "that two of the detainees was from same family and one of them was a nephew of that old guy." The fact remains that neither the government nor the defense ever established the identities or professions of the three Iraqis who were killed, and never established whether or not they were terrorists. The prosecutor continued:

Q: Why were you upset about the shooting of the old man?

A: *You guys know the situation.* This incident makes the people, the citizens hate us [emphasis added].

Q: Why?

A: All the insurgents and Mujahedeen they came after us and they hate us because we support United States and because all of this raid, so in case, like this incidents, you know, they make them hate us more.

Q: What is it about the killing of the old man that makes people hate the Iraqi Army?

[MR. BERGRIN]: Asked and answered....

[CAPTAIN DUGGAN]: He didn't answer specifically what about the killing of the old man.

IO: I'm not sure he understood. Ask it one more time.

Q: Why did he feel the killing of the old man was wrong?

A: This — this kind of incidence is effect all, you know, Iraqi Army reputation.

Q: Were the three detainees farmers?

[CAPTAIN MILLER]: Objection; calls for speculation.

IO: I'll go with it.

A: They look like farmers.

Q: Why do you think that?

[MR. BERGRIN]: Objection. That calls for clear speculation and conjecture....

IO: Okay, hold on.

A: When I get back home I'm a farmer.

Mr. Mohammed's explanation for why ordinary Iraqis would come to hate both Americans and the Iraqi army because of incidents of this sort seems obvious: there was no proof that the men were terrorists, and there were suggestions that they were ordinary farmers living with their families. He also referred to other, similar incidents, in which civilians had been killed. Who wouldn't be angry at systemic, wrongful deaths based on faulty "intelligence?" "You guys know the situation," Mr. Mohammed said, as if the reasons were obvious from a commonsense point of view. However, it is clear that the situation was not obvious to the Americans in the courtroom, or the Americans pretended that they did not understand. A serious reply is that persons outside the reference group of Iraqi families will not feel angry or even perceive a serious problem in killing people who are not the enemy. Americans feel outrage if a foreign enemy kills innocent Americans (as in 9/11), but do not necessarily empathize with foreigners who see themselves as innocents being killed by Americans. It is unrealistic to expect any people to feel empathy for others outside their reference group. The US attorneys were trapped in their respective reference groups and legal strategies, so that they did not seem to hear Mr. Mohammed's answer — even though he repeated it. Extrapolating from this one event and moment of testimony, it seems that US policymakers in general do not seem to comprehend that they have lost the "hearts and minds" of the Iraqi people, from their commonsense point of view, due to such incidents.

The prosecutor asked Mr. Mohammed for evidence that the men were farmers, and Mr. Mohammed pointed out the obvious: He found a tractor, sheep, and farm equipment. The IO dismissed the witness, and instructed him not to discuss anything he saw or heard at the hearing. "God willing," was Mr. Mohammed's response.

TESTIMONY BY THE SECOND IRAQI SOLDIER

The second Iraqi soldier was sworn in, and he was given the name Sergeant Hussein for his testimony. Immediately, the prosecutor asked:

Q: Are you a terrorist?

A: No.

Q: Is anyone in your battalion a terrorist?

A: No.

The prosecutor sat down, and Mr. Bergrin began his cross-examination of Mr. Hussein.

Q: Isn't it a fact that you served under Saddam Hussein?

A: Yes.

Q: And you were a soldier for Saddam Hussein for over two years.

A: Yes, that's right.

Q: So you're telling us that Saddam Hussein didn't train his soldiers to fight American Soldiers? Is that what you're telling us with your hand on the Koran?

A: No.

Bergrin was apparently trying to depict both Iraqi soldiers as suspicious because they had served previously in the Iraqi army during Saddam Hussein's regime. But the fact remains that Saddam Hussein's image changed from America's ally during the Reagan Administration to America's enemy during the first Bush Administration. Following the defeat of Hussein by the second Bush Administration, Iraqi soldiers became America's allies against a new enemy, "insurgents." This rapid change of reference groups as to who is friend or foe does not change the fact that Iraqi soldiers will follow orders no matter who is in power and who is depicted as the enemy. Nevertheless, Mr. Bergrin has a point: It must have been strange for Iraqi soldiers to switch from hating and fighting American soldiers to being their allies. This is an extraordinarily unusual set of historical circumstances.

Q: Isn't it a fact that the Americans killed your nine-year-old niece?

A: Yes. It was [my] uncle's daughter, my cousin.

Q: And you didn't hold any feelings about — against the Americans based upon that?

A: It wasn't on purpose. It was a accident. It was the same day Udie and Kusai they got killed and in the area there was shooting everywhere, so she got killed by accident.

Q: And it didn't bother you?

A: No, it was very normal....

Q: And we talked to you about your witnessing and seeing the Americans kill a lot of Muslims, correct?

IO: Okay, hold on a second. You're walking a thin line, so I hope you — you're going to tie this to this investigation.

[MR. BERGRIN]: I am. I'm going to establish credibility and bias.

IO: Okay.

Q: Didn't you tell us that whenever an American kills a Muslim it angers and upsets you?

A: He's try to explain if this Muslim, if he don't do something wrong, why the Americans will kill him.

Q: Didn't he tell us this morning that all the Muslims are his brothers and whenever a Muslim dies, he gets upset especially at the Americans for killing them? Isn't that exactly what he said this morning when we questioned?

A: Of course. There is a right way and there's a wrong way.

Presumably the "right way" to kill anybody is if the enemy is showing hostile intent, as specified in traditional ROE. It seems to make commonsense, based upon traditional thinking, that if the presumed enemy is not doing something wrong, he should not be killed. The social chasm exposed here is that the new ROE used at Operation Iron Triangle authorized the killing of people who were pre-designated as enemies, whether or not they showed hostile intent. Again, the irony is that the defense is taking the position that the new ROE justified the killing of the three men whereas the government — which authorized the unlawful, new ROE — is taking the position that the Iraqis should not have been killed. The opposing attorneys are taking these positions in order to win their cases. However, in the process of switching allegiance to reference groups, the government's position in the hearing comes closest to those of the Iraqi soldiers.

Q: Isn't it a fact that half of your soldiers in your unit quit?

A: Yes.

Q: About fifteen soldiers quit and left the army after May the 9th, correct?

A: Yes.

Notice the double-bind for the Iraqi soldiers. The fact that some of them quit the mission right after the killings is seen by the Americans as proof that they were terrorists, but the Americans also considered them as potential terrorists even when they fought alongside US soldiers. The Iraqi soldiers were truly in Bateson's double-bind, or a lose–lose situation. Captain Duggan asked questions on behalf of the government in the redirect examination:

Q: Sergeant, how long have you worked with American Soldiers?

A: Two years, four months.

Q: How do you feel — how does that make you feel working with American Soldiers?

A: I'm doing my job. There's many people they hate us because we work with the Coalition Forces, but I think I'm serving my country.

Q: What are the names of the fifteen soldiers who quit?

A: There are too many.

Q: All right. Chief Mohamed, did he quit?

A: We have many Mohameds, which one?

Q: I withdraw the question.

In a more ideal situation, such as World War II, Americans were regarded as liberators in Europe and resistance fighters against the Nazis who fought with the Americans were also liked by the general population. In the current war in Iraq, the situation is much more complicated. Iraqi resistance fighters (insurgents) are fighting the Americans and the Iraqi army, which was formerly Saddam Hussein's army, so that the sympathies of the general population are torn among several different reference groups. This problem seems intractable. Mr. Hussein was dismissed and instructed not to tell anyone about his testimony. His last words to the court were: "Even in my battalion, where they going to ask me, I don't tell them I'm coming here for testimony or testify." Mr. Hussein's testimony ended on a note of fear. The hearing recessed at 1:22 p.m.

CLOSING ARGUMENT BY THE PROSECUTION

The hearing reconvened at 1:36 p.m. on the 4th of August 2006. Captain Mackey delivered the closing argument for the government. He began with the sentence: "Sir, on 9 May 2006, Staff Sergeant Girouard, Specialist Hunsaker, and PFC Clagett planned a murder of three detainees." Given all the testimony in over 800 pages of the Article 32 transcript up to this point, it is difficult to relate to the word "plan." Most of the testimony exposed chaos, not anything like a rational plan by anyone. He continued:

> Sir, you've heard talk over the past few days as well as rules of engagement, about pressure to kill the enemy, but all this is basically a smoke screen, it's a distracter.... It didn't matter who they were before. It didn't matter if they were terrorists. It didn't matter if they were farmers. It simply didn't matter. When these Soldiers killed those detainees, they committed murder.

On the one hand, the prosecutor is appealing to the powerful, universal archetype that killing a person who has been disarmed and is no longer a threat cannot be justified. However, this case does not fit this ideal archetype. In fact, it matters very much that the ROE were unlawful, because these strange ROE desensitized the soldiers over a long period of time by normalizing and authorizing the killing of disarmed persons who showed no hostility toward US soldiers. The prosecutor tried to have his cake and eat it too, as the saying goes: dismiss the unlawful ROE yet condemn as murder the killings that took place in the name of that unlawful ROE. Moreover, the pressure to kill anybody pre-designated as the enemy (without ascertaining whether in fact they were the enemy or had hostile intent toward the US) was enormous and abnormal. It is not commonplace to issue an order to kill defenseless persons who do not show hostility, and then punish soldiers for carrying out such an abnormal order. To the US soldiers, it mattered very much whether the "detainees" (but not prisoners of war) were terrorists or farmers. They were instructed to kill terrorists on sight, or more precisely, persons pre-designated as terrorists on sight. The prosecutor continued:

> Now over the last few days, there hasn't been any testimony that said Staff Sergeant Girouard was the one who actually pulled the trigger. The legal concept of the principle says that if anyone sides, abets, counsels, or commands a crime and shares in that criminal intent, they have the same guilt, and they can be punished just the same. Here Staff Sergeant Girouard was the mastermind. He was naturally the leader, he was their squad leader.

Here the prosecutor was invoking the problematic legal understanding of "conspiracy." It is beyond the scope of this study to delve into the historical evolution of the meaning of conspiracy in civilian common law from the times of King Edward I in England to the present. Two important points need to be made from the vantage point of commonsense and the average person. First, Girouard was not "naturally" (essentially, by virtue of his personal charisma) the leader. He was assigned the social role of leader through the army, and army social life requires the soldiers whom he outranks to obey him. This is a special set of circumstances that is different from civilian life, in which the leader of an alleged conspiracy would have to personally persuade followers instead of relying on social structure. In sum, civilian conspiracy may not be the same as "conspiracy" in military units because by definition, every military mission involves a "conspiracy" of sorts. Every military mission involves the "conspiracy" to "lawfully" kill an enemy. Moreover, every combat military mission involves, in a sense, pre-meditation to kill. Second, more traditional understandings of conspiracy involved commonsense proof that the co-conspirators plotted, reflected upon, and planned a crime over a long period of time. But more recent conspiracy laws set no time limit or any other objective factors for determining whether or not a conspiracy existed. In other words, commonsense dictates that any commitment to any agreement is binding only if it is entered freely. But charging someone with conspiracy for merely associating or existing next to someone or a group of people who are committing a crime flies against commonsense. In sum, under contemporary, *civilian* conspiracy laws that are used in *military* contexts, any soldier who was a member of a platoon in which a crime was committed is potentially guilty of conspiracy simply for being part of that platoon. Much is "lost in translation" in this switching of reference groups (military versus civilian) for judging the meaning of killing, conspiracy, pre-meditation, aiding, and other legal terms It is not at all clear that a killing in civilian society has the same meaning as a killing on a military combat mission, even if both killings result in the legal charge of murder..

The prosecutor emphasized that the government's star witness, PFC Mason, "was under the threat for his life." But we have seen that Mason recanted this charge against his comrades, and that no conclusive proof was offered to the effect that he was threatened. The prosecutor charged that "it's uncontested that Specialist Hunsaker and PFC Clagett shot those detainees. The only thing that's contested is they seem to say it's in self-defense and it's not premeditated." It is usually precarious to state that any factor is the "only thing" that is important in understanding any phenomenon. The defense attorneys laid out many other factors, namely, kill contests, an aggressive commander, and an unlawful ROE.

It is not clear how it helped the government's case for the prosecution to claim that "these guys knew they were going into a hot LZ." And, "they knew this was going to be one of the most important missions they were going on." He continued: "These guys knew what they were doing. Beyond that, they said how they didn't trust the IA, so you're going to a hot LZ where they suspected terrorists, they didn't trust the IA." But it turned out to be a *cold* LZ, the soldiers encountered no hostility, they found some farmers and women with children, and the IA was helping them reassure the victims.

The prosecutor cited and defined each charge from the UCMJ. For example, under article 92, "that the failure to obey the lawful general order. That's for the weapon that he [Girouard] found and he took ... from the objective." But we have seen that several soldiers, including the First Sergeant, took war trophies and some even stole a refrigerator and television set from the Iraqis. Why was it necessary for the government to add what seems to be a trivial charge in relation to the capital offenses of premeditated murder and conspiracy?

"You also heard some kind of confusing testimony from Sergeant Neuman." Indeed, Neuman denied that Graber told him he had shot anyone. But the prosecutor concluded that "Specialist Graber had confessed." The prosecutor noted: "You've heard talk about the CID agents and about how their unruly strong-arm tactics had made everybody lie throughout this whole investigation." Indeed. The prosecutor's resolution of this incredible problem — that CID coerced false confessions and created perjury — does not seem adequate:

> While it's true CID does accuse people. They accuse people of crimes, and they question people. They make them feel uncomfortable, but that's how CID gets to the truth. That's how they catch criminals.

The prosecutor is making an "end justifies the means" argument regarding CID tactics. It is a short move from the prosecutor's rationalization to defending outright torture. Commonsense dictates that accusing everyone in a platoon of some crime does not lead to truth, but leads to perjury, false memories, and chaos. In this case, three separate sets of sworn statements were taken each on May 11, May 29, and June 15 — and they are all vastly different versions of what happened. Moreover, it is not true that the role of CID is to "accuse people of crimes." That is the role of the prosecutor, and CID must assume that everyone is innocent until proven guilty to be in line with American cultural values. The fact that the prosecutor could make this egregiously false statement, which flies against the principles of the US Constitution, and not be challenged by anyone in the courtroom shows how very far this particular reference group in this case had lost sight of the most basic principles of American culture.

The prosecutor was equally glib about the ROE: "So you've heard about the ROE, you've heard about pressure to kill. It's simply irrelevant." In fact, the unlawful ROE are extremely relevant, because their existence helps to explain why ordinarily good and well-trained soldiers did what they did on the mission. The prosecutor further muddied the conceptual waters of commonsense by adding that "US Soldiers must follow the law of war. It's what makes us better that the terrorists." Most Americans will probably agree with these claims. But it's also true that soldiers must be trained in the laws of war — and testimony indicated that in this unit, they were not. It is also true that the officers in charge must issue orders in line with the law of war, and that US soldiers are trained to obey their commanding officers. In his conclusion, the prosecutor said:

> Now, sir, you've got all the opportunity and we've all had an opportunity to scrutinize this evidence very closely. As you can see, no one small piece of evidence is perfect without its small flaws. That's why you have to look at the whole picture, and the whole picture on this case tells you there is more than enough evidence to show that all four accused committed these crimes, that these Soldiers murdered these detainees, and for this they're not war heroes. *They're war criminals*, and justice demands that they face trial by general court-martial [emphasis added].

It is safe to assert that the flaws in the evidence were egregious, not "small." There was no physical evidence of any sort; all the soldiers' accounts differed from each other; CID created perjury; and above all, the commanders issued an unlawful ROE.

It is precisely because of the unlawful ROE that this case does, indeed, involve war crimes and not just ordinary crimes of murder. But in international law, war crime charges are typically leveled at military and civilian commanders who laid the groundwork for others to commit the war crimes — not at the low-ranking soldiers who actually committed the war crimes.

One reason that the American public is not aware of this is that the US military handles war crimes through military courts-martial instead of international tribunals which prosecute war crimes. The phrase "war criminals" is buried in the prosecution's closing statement, and was never picked up by the news media.

It is very important to note that the prosecutor referred to the accused as "war criminals." As I stated at the outset, the notion of a "war crime" automatically presupposes government involvement. Most of the time, "war criminals" have been and continue to be high-ranking civilian and military officials. There is nothing typical, average, or common in the prosecutor's depiction of the accused and of this case. It is also important to note that Stouffer found that an overwhelming majority of World War II soldiers felt that Japanese and German *leaders*, not ordinary soldiers, should be punished for war crimes (volume 2, p. 158).

CLOSING STATEMENTS BY THE DEFENSE

Mr. Bergrin began the closing statements by the defense attorneys. He said: "This case is about one individual and that's essentially PFC Mason because the case rises and the case falls on his integrity and on his character." Recall that Mason testified that he had perjured himself and did not care about making false statements under oath. Bergrin took the position that the soldiers followed their ROE:

> In this particular case, what's been established is that on 9 May of 2006, these Soldiers put on their uniforms, put on their equipment, and they were ready to fight and die for their country.... They were briefed, re-briefed, they were prepared, and they were highly trained, and every single one of them, every single one of them followed their mission and their rules of engagement. When they came upon the first house, they saw a military aged male. He peered through the window, they took him out, and they captured the three detainees inside the house.... In this particular case, they could have shot them, they could have killed them. They would have been right up in their rules of engagement, but they didn't.

Bergrin is correct that had the soldiers killed every male on the island, they would have been following their unlawful rules of engagement, and would never have been charged with any crime. And this is an incredible conclusion, because it exposes how abnormal the situation was. After all, no charges were ever leveled at anyone for killing the man by the window (and we are not certain that he peered through the window, but may have been outside his house). Ironically, by not following the unlawful ROE when it came to the remaining males on the island — they spared their lives and took them prisoner — the soldiers were put into a double-bind. By not killing the three men, they violated the unlawful ROE. By killing the three men, they violated the traditional ROE, which was not the one that applied on the mission. Commonsense dictates that their military leaders should not have put them in this lose–lose situation. Turning to the issue of the Iraqi soldiers, Bergrin said:

> They were upset with the Americans. As a matter of fact, half of a platoon left and quit as a result of that. They're individuals who saw that old man get killed. They didn't believe the Americans had the right to do that. They didn't believe that the Americans would have given them food, water, taking care of them properly.

In fact, if one uses international laws of armed conflict as the reference point, the Iraqi soldiers were correct to conclude that the Americans had no right to kill the old man. They were right to expect their allies to share food and water with them. The Iraqi perceptions are also supported by commonsense: it is wrong to kill defenseless persons who showed no hostility, and allies should share supplies. Why is it that the Iraqi soldiers were able to orient themselves in relation to international standards of warfare as well as commonsense and quit in large numbers in protest while no one in the American platoon quit in protest? One should not overlook the obvious fact that US soldiers may not simply quit their jobs in protest or for any other reason.

Mr. Bergrin continued:

> If you look at the timeline, the *commonsense evidence* in this case, there is no physical, there's no forensic, there's no scientific evidence whatsoever that's been admitted to where you could say this proves that they did something wrong in this particular case [emphasis added].

I have heard other lawyers make a similar assessment. He was particularly critical of the contamination of the evidence by CID:

> You had an opportunity to sit there, listen to the witnesses, listen to how rules were overblown, how statements were taken, six, seven, eight, up to ten hours of interviews, interrogation, pressure, sexual touching. Even the strongest Soldier, the will would be overborne and that's what happened in this case. That's why statements were changed. That's why statements were given that were not proper. That's why you have individuals that were set together and get their stories straight. That's why you have reports that were shredded. That's why you have statements that were thrown out. That's why you have individuals that were called back to CID up to five different times because they failed to say exactly what the CID wanted them to say.

Mr. Bergrin attacked the credibility of the government's star witness, PFC Mason:

> You heard about the statements that he's made about the killing of every single Iraqi man, woman, and children. You heard about how he planned to commit robberies. You heard about when they threw candy to a young Iraqi boy. He called him a "faggot." You heard about incident after incident that attacks the morale — morality fiber of even the most decent human being. You heard about how he deliberately and intentionally lied over and over and over again, that the oath meant nothing to him. You don't know how to separate fact from fiction with PFC Mason.

Regarding the testimony of another government witness, Specialist Graber, who allegedly committed the "mercy killing" of one of the Iraqis, Bergrin had this to say:

> You have an individual that testified that he shot him in the face. There would have been loads of gun powder, tattooing, stippling, and half of his face would have been opened up as a result of the powder burns, but there was none. There was none. Graber was an individual also whose will was overborne. We didn't have the chance to cross-examine. We didn't have the chance to confront him, and there's essentially no corroboration for his testimony, no corroboration whatsoever.

Mr. Bergrin was relentless: "You heard Sergeant Hensley testify that not only was he suffering from post-traumatic stress syndrome, but he didn't want to hear anything." "You heard the lieutenant, a man that knows [Girouard], knows him intrinsically, has worked with him, trusts him. He does not have the type of character to orchestrate this, and he wouldn't do that." Similarly, "Hunsaker is an excellent Soldier; nothing but accolades; nothing but a good record." Finally, "PFC Clagett is a kid. He's a 22-year-old immature boy. You can hear about how he was affected from the witnesses, how it hurt him that he took a life."

The other defense attorneys added their closing statements. The gist of Mr. Waddington's speech was, "Sir, you cannot guess a man into prison."

Captain Miller asked the IO to "stand up and say enough is enough," and added that "this isn't a rubber stamp, this isn't a charade, this is a meaningful process."

Captain Suddeth added to the attacks on PFC Mason's character:

The one point that I find disturbing was the fact that he would talk about having sex with nine-year-old girls in Thailand. That is disturbing and warped, but the government is going to rely on that type of mentality. Mason brought nothing to this hearing in terms of physical evidence. He saw nothing.

And he especially attacked the female CID agent in charge of the investigation:

She has to have some type character to muscle her way in to getting these guys to do or succumb to her will, so how does she do that? She's abrasive. She's aggressive. If that doesn't work, she'll touch their knee and become sexual. If that doesn't work, she may attempt to do a hug, and then if that doesn't work, then to really get to the core of the issue, she invokes the name of God and says, "Oh, if you're telling the truth, God will work everything out," so this CID agent has run the whole gamut and time after time every witness that stood in here or sat here and told you, looked you in the eye, sir. They said that they were accused of things. They told you they were going to be charged with things. There was even cross-contamination when Helton indicated that Ryan — he had to go in and help correct Ryan's — Sergeant Ryan's testimony because they did not believe him.

Finally, Captain Suddeth pointed out that most of the soldiers who testified had been "titled," which apparently means that they had been charged with something and the IO had read them their rights. He asked the IO to "untitle" the individuals who would not be prosecuted because "if they don't like you, they title you and that will affect the lives of these Soldiers and their families" for up to "fifty years." I do not know if the IO addressed Captain Suddeth's pleas on behalf of the many soldiers who had been intimidated into giving testimony.

When the defense attorneys were finished with their closing statements, the government asked the IO to admit a sworn statement by Sergeant Lemus, even though he did not testify and was not cross-examined. Mr. Bergrin objected vehemently "that you should not admit this statement." The IO's response was: "Okay, your objection's recorded for the record, I'll admit the statement." According to the transcript, the "investigation closed at 1443, 4 August 2006." Ordinarily, one would have concluded that the Article 32 had come to an official end, and the IO would issue his decision about which charges would go to trial. But this atypical hearing would be re-opened five days after the closing arguments.

Chapter 7. The Inquiry is Reopened: Kicking the Soldiers While They're Down

> "I'll tell you what justice is. Justice is a knee in the gut from the floor on the chin at night sneaky with a knife brought up down on the magazine of a battleship sandbagged underhanded in the dark without a word of warning. Garroting. That's what justice is."
> — Joseph Heller, *Catch-22, p. 83*

At 8:42 a.m. on the 9th of August, 2006, the Article 32 "reopened." Not merely "reconvened," but re-opened. The reason for this unusual move was to consider two additional charges against PFC Clagett. Both were charges of "disrespect" as specified in the UCMJ. On the one hand, it seems extraordinary that the government would go to such great lengths to add these two charges to existing murder charges that could have resulted in a death penalty. On the other hand, there is something profoundly ironic in the fact that Clagett was expected to show perfect respect to his guards while he was in pre-trial confinement but was also expected to disrespect his superiors when it came to obeying the unlawful ROE. Harking back to Stouffer's study, Clagett's expectation that he should be treated with respect even in confinement is entirely in line with Stouffer's finding that combat veterans expected to be treated with respect by support troops who never experienced combat.

The first witness was Damage Controlman First Class Marco L. King of the US Navy, who gave testimony over the telephone. Petty Officer King is a guard at a US Naval prison facility in Kuwait. King testified that on 21 July 2006, the following incident occurred:

> A: During the course of the day, PFC Clagett was overlooked for the 1130 chow. One of my guards came to me, and told me he was outside his tent wondering why he hadn't been fed..... I went and saw the Doc, Commander Karamidov. She explained to me that she had switched him off

of that schedule that she originally put him on because of *some type of sleep disorder*. I said "Okay," then I had one of my guards try to get him chow.... I was in there explaining to him that he — in order to get respect he had to give respect and he needed to watch the attitude. He explained that — he started yelling that he wasn't going to respect anybody here or me *because we don't respect him*. I asked him what was his pay grade. He said "E-4." I asked him "What is my pay grade." He said, "I don't give a 'F', and —

Q: When you said I don't give a 'F' what do you — what did he actually say?

A: He said, "I don't give a f___" (emphasis added).

Clagett had not been fed and was suffering from a sleep disorder. Recall from previous testimony that several soldiers had sleeping problems, and it is well known that sleep deprivation is detrimental. At the very least, it can make a person grumpy. Shackled and imprisoned (even though Clagett was presumed to be innocent until proven guilty), not fed properly, and deprived of sleep, Clagett was still expected to show proper military respect to his tormentors. The guard could have shown some empathy and let the incident go under the circumstances. Saying "I don't give a f___" is not exactly an earth-shattering incident of disrespect, and it is understandable under these circumstances. Instead, Petty Officer King and the government leveled charges of disrespect against Clagett on top of his other serious charges.

There is something petty about the government leveling this additional charge in this context. And despite his immature way of handling the situation, Clagett was right to expose the hypocrisy of Petty Officer King's lecture to him: the army was not respecting him as a soldier and a citizen who is presumed to be innocent until proven guilty, so why expect respect from Clagett when he was not being respected? It is true that the army demands respect from a soldier to his or her superior under any circumstances. But to pretend that the typical, commonsense norm of "give respect to get respect" operated in these unusual and degrading circumstances is enough to trigger anger in any reasonable person.

Petty Officer King testified that his state of mind was that he was concerned he would look bad that Clagett was not fed. He added: "I paid for lunch for him. I picked out one of them — actually I went to Burger King and picked him up something." CPT Rutizer cross-examined Petty Officer King:

Q: Okay we had a conversation last night, didn't we?

A: Yes we did.

Q: Do you remember that conversation when you told me that you thought the proper disposition of this was a D and A board?

A: Yes it was.

Q: Do you remember telling me that, in your opinion, you were shocked that this had gone forward beyond the disciplinary board?

A: Yes I was....

Q: And in order for him to get a guard's attention, he must leave his tent. Is that correct?

A: That's correct.

Q: He has to stand inside the barbed wire area and essentially shout until he gets a guard's attention. Is that correct?

A: That's correct....

Q: Does PFC Clagett have any control over when he showers?

A: No he doesn't.

Q: Does he have any control over when his clothing gets laundered?

A: No that's scheduled....

Q: If I were to tell you that in the 36 days they've never changed his sheets, would that be accurate?

A: I would say that would be impossible, but anything is possible.

Essentially, and like Hunsaker, Clagett was kept in solitary confinement during the entire time that he was waiting for his trial. Nothing changed for Clagett at Leavenworth — over the course of the past three years he has been and continues to be in solitary confinement. Captain Rutizer's questions suggest that Clagett was treated worse than an animal, even to the point of not having his bed sheets changed for over a month. The IO had some questions for Petty Officer King:

Q: What's the purpose of pre-trial schedule?

A: To keep the pre-trial away from the post-trial inmates. We're not allowed to let them intermingle....

Q: Okay and tell me — please explain what happened with the lunch for PFC Clagett. Why didn't it get there?

A: That was an oversight on my part.

Captain Rutizer asked some more questions, and determined that there were other occasions on which Clagett was not fed. She also got Petty Officer King to admit that he was at least six days tardy in determining which schedule applied to Clagett as determined by the military psychiatrist. Petty Officer King was dismissed.

According to the transcript, "Master at Arms Second Class Michelle Behl, US Navy, was called as witness by the government counsel, Captain Mackey, was sworn, and testified telephonically as follows:"

I was inside the white house or the operational trailer and I heard somebody yell out, and I walked outside and I saw Clagett, and he usually does that when he needs something, so I walked over, asked him what he needed, and he needed his pencil sharpened, and at that time he had asked me about where I was stationed, and I told him I'm an activated Reservist from Utah. Then I said — when I came back with the pencil, I told him "Clagett I don't normally give out personal information about myself."

It is not apparent how Clagett's question about where she was stationed qualifies as "personal information." It is a routine question that soldiers ask each other. There is something disturbing about the image of Clagett being forced to yell to get attention or help from his isolated tent, behind barbed wire. Captain Rutizer's cross-examination makes one wonder how anyone in the army could have interpreted this incident as an example of disrespect at all much less one that was punishable under UCMJ:

Q: You didn't take what PFC Clagett said as disrespect, did you?

A: No, ma'am.

Q: In fact, he's never disrespectful to you?

A: That's correct....

Q: You and he were having a cordial conversation, isn't that correct?

A: Yes, ma'am.

Q: And he asked you a personal question, where you are from?

A: Yes.

Q: Besides me, *the guards are pretty much his only source of communication with humans.* Is that about accurate? [Emphasis added.]

A: Yes, ma'am.

Q: And so you, for whatever reason you chose, decided to respond to that question?

A: Yes, ma'am....

Q: Do you remember telling me that you were surprised to hear that this had gone anywhere above your incident report?

A: Yes, ma'am, I was surprised.

Q: You don't have any reason to believe that PFC Clagett was being rude to you?

A: No.

Q: That he was being disrespectful to your rank?

A: No.

Q: That he was having contempt for your position?

A: No.

Petty Officer Behl was dismissed. Before Master Chief James R. Donaldson of the US Navy could be sworn, the IO and Captain Rutizer argued about whether his unsworn statement could be admitted into evidence. Captain Rutizer tried to explain to the IO that the witness wasn't read his rights and that unsworn statements may not be entered over the objection of the defense. The IO overruled her and the testimony began via telephone. Master Chief Donaldson explained that his rank is "basically the equivalent of a command sergeant major" in the army, and he was in charge of the naval brig in Kuwait. He said that a disciplinary board hearing was scheduled for July 25, 2006, four days following Clagett's crimes of "disrespect." Donaldson said that on the day of the hearing, Clagett handed him a statement he had written by hand. Before he could recall what the statement said, Captain Rutizer objected on the grounds that it was hearsay. The IO overruled her. According to Donaldson, the statement read: "Yeah I said this to Petty Officer King. Yeah, I told Petty Officer King my lawyer would F__ you up." The Master Chief seemed not to realize how petty he sounded: "The whole thing started because he said he missed his lunch, and I agree with that." An offense against the Uniform Code of Military Justice because of some words over a lunch that was denied to Clagett! The Master Chief testified that he said to Clagett: "Hey, this is what the board can do to you ... it's like chain gang and the rank, and ... if you thought Petty Officer King maltreated you or mistreated you, then you needed to file the appropriate charges against Petty Officer King." Try to imagine the Master Chief threatening Clagett with being assigned to a chain gang and losing his rank because of an argument over lunch.

In the remainder of his testimony for the prosecution, the Master Chief said that as soon as an inmate is brought to the naval brig, "We try to explain the Navy rank structure to them, but it's — learning Navy/Army, Army/Navy is kind of difficult, so we don't expect them to get it all." In addition to being an argument over the fact that Clagett was not fed, this is an issue of Clagett not being adequately aware that a Petty Officer in the Naval rank structure was superior to him by one rank. Had Clagett said "I don't give a f__" to someone of equal or lesser rank, none of this would have been an issue. Captain Rutizer began her cross-examination:

Q: Do you remember telling me last night that you never read him his rights?

A: That's correct. I never did read him his rights....

Q: Okay, and to date you refused to give me that document [Manual for Guidance to Inmates]?

A: That's not my — that's not my call....

Q: Master Chief, do you recall having a conversation with PFC Clagett where he was staring at your rank?

A: ....He started to say Chief, and I said, "Hey, I'm Master Chief," and I explained to the Army form.

Q: Isn't it true that he couldn't even identify what your rank was?

A: I couldn't tell you that or not.

Much later in the hearing, CPT Rutizer stated for the record that she and the prosecuting attorneys also cannot identify navy ranks. Yet the government seemed to expect Clagett to learn an entirely different rank system while he was depressed, underfed, stressed, and maltreated. The Master Chief's obsession with his rank and his reference group (the Navy) seems excessive, given that all the soldiers have one reference group in common: They are part of the US military.

CPT Rutizer determined that the Master Chief never took the testimony of Petty Officer King and never read Clagett his rights. "You're a law enforcement officer," CPT Rutizer said to him, and added: "You know that if you suspect someone of a crime and they are going to incriminate themselves, you have to read them their rights." The Master Chief replied that Clagett "volunteered the statement." We see that the military guards are as lax about enforcing the Miranda rule as the CID agents are in this case — and the IO nevertheless accepted the evidence that was obtained unlawfully. "Do you know what the defense of divestiture is?" she asked him. "No." This term refers to the possibility that Petty Officer King was himself acting unprofessionally toward Clagett and thereby lost the privilege accorded to his rank.

The IO had some questions, and determined that the discipline board "was just me," according to the Master Chief, who added, "It was a one person board." Like a scene out of the book and film *Catch-22*, the military resorted to a one-person "board" to indict a soldier with a crime punishable under the code of military justice for a dispute over lunch. The IO asked "Why were you chosen for this board?" The Master Chief replied: "I don't know. The executive officer makes the decision." The Master Chief was dismissed and the investigation recessed at 9:41 a.m. on the 9th of August 2006.

TESTIMONY OF THE MEDICAL OFFICER

The hearing resumed at 9:45 a.m. and Lieutenant Commander Karen A. Karamidov, a physician at the military base in Kuwait, was sworn. Her navy rank is equivalent to that of a major in the army. She said that when Clagett "first came in ... he was extremely depressed and we're having a hard time figuring out what medication would be best for him." On the 15th of July she changed him to a schedule that would be suitable to his new medications, and she said it was tricky to match the feeding schedule with the particular medications, which incidentally had the side-effect of making the patient extremely hungry. The gist of her testimony was that she posted the correct schedule on the "big white board" at the brig, and that the guards made an error in not following her orders. She said that on the 21st of July,

> Well, I was in the medical hut at about, I think it was around one o'clock, and I was seeing a patient with my corpsman, and he [Petty Officer King] came in abruptly and started speaking to me about what kind of schedule Clagett was on and why is he asking for food, and he was very upset. He was huffing, I, and I told him that there should be no problem with the schedule, and it's posted on the board ... and I think he wanted to argue with me, and he ... [was] huffing like, "Was he on medication when he came here to begin with" [emphasized in a stern voice], and I told him that

it was not his business and that it was confidential and, you know, he's on a schedule and the schedule was to go as ordered.

Captain Rutizer asked LCDR Karamidov what was "Petty Officer King's tone to you during this entire conversation?"

A: Adversarial....

Q: Did you speak to anybody else about this?

A: Yes, I went to my executive officer, and told her that I wasn't comfortable considering the circumstances.... I didn't know what happened between them, but definitely, the order should have been followed, and he [Clagett] may have been more agitated because he was hungry. He was adjusting to medication....

Q: Ma'am, who is your executive officer?

A: Lieutenant Commander Patricia Melsen....

Q: Did she seem to listen to what you had to say?

A: I would hope so, yeah.... Then, when I heard that they were writing it up, I was really not happy with it..... As a provider of care, and you know, I have to advocate for my patients.....

Q: If you saw PFC Clagett commit a crime, you wouldn't do anything to cover it up, would you?

A: Absolutely not.

LCDR Karamidov seems to have experienced the role strain of trying to fulfill her roles in two distinct reference groups: as a physician, she was obligate to advocate for Clagett as a patient, and as a member of the military, she was expected to side with colleagues who came down hard on Clagett for his "disrespect." She resolved the situation by complaining to the executive officer, who basically ignored her concerns. But all the actors in this drama experienced similar reference group strain, even if they resolved it in different ways. For example, the guards are law enforcement officers, and according to the civilian norms of their professional groups, are expected to enforce Miranda rights and other rights of inmates — even soldier–prisoners. However, the guards generally ignored their civilian counterpart professional obligations and behaved in accordance with ancient military traditions that demand unequivocal respect from subordinates in all circumstances. CID agents and military lawyers, judges, physicians, and other professionals all must wrestle with this dilemma of treating their clients from a reference group in which rank structure does not matter versus treating their subordinates in a reference group that is authoritarian in its structure.

In his cross-examination, the prosecutor, CPT Mackey, shifted his tone toward the female officer who outranked him: He downplayed her medical obligations to her patient, and he notably did not call her "ma'am."

"You didn't hear him [Clagett] say that he didn't give a f___ about rank?" he asked. "No," the doctor replied.

Q: Okay, but you just felt you didn't — you weren't comfortable with what was going down afterwards. Is that correct?

A: Exactly. I didn't feel comfortable that something happened that was related to an order that I had written and it wasn't followed for my patient, and I was feeling like something happened because their procedures were not followed.

Note that the military doctor invoked both of her roles simultaneously: her order and military procedures were not followed in accordance with respect for her rank, and she was concerned as a medical doctor for Clagett as her patient. The subordinate captain did not have much room to maneuver, and sat down.

TESTIMONY BY THE EXECUTIVE OFFICER

Navy Lieutenant Commander Patricia L. Melsen was sworn. She was the executive officer for Theater Field Detention Facility in Camp Arifjan, Kuwait. She is the same military rank as the medical doctor who had just testified, and outranked everyone in the courtroom except the IO. I have learned that in questioning or cross-examining a superior officer, the subordinate officer must show deference and respect. Captain Rutizer began the questioning:

Q: Ma'am, do you recall me asking you for a copy of the MGI [Military Guidelines for Inmates]?

A: Yes.

Q: Do you recall refusing to give it to me?

A: Yes. I told you that my clear instruction was that we did not release that. After I got off the phone, I consulted with ASG. That's a judge advocate and they are researching it.

Q: Ma'am, who's ASG?

A: Area Support Group.

Q: Do you know the JAG that you spoke to?

A: I would have to look it up. I don't remember how he spells it.

Why would a military lawyer stand in the way of another military lawyer's legitimate request to examine a manual in order to defend her client? The obvious answer is that the executive officer did not want her authority challenged. Here again, we see the conflict between the professional obligations of attorneys versus the authoritarian structure of the army.

Q: Do you recall telling me last night that the interactions with Petty Officer Behl were not worthy of a D and A board?

A: That was just an observation report. We do not go to a D and A board based only on a observation report. It has to be a disciplinary report.

Q: Ma'am, do you recall having conversations with Lieutenant Commander Karamidov about the incident with PFC Clagett and Petty Officer King?

A: Yes, I talked to Lieutenant Commander Karamidov.

Q: Ma'am, what did she tell you?

A: .... She said it [order] was on the logs. He didn't initially believe her. He was angry about the subject matter, and that started a discussion between the two of them. He finally went inside, read the fact it was on the pass down, left the building, and then went and bought a hamburger.

Q: Ma'am, to date, what actions has your facility taken against Petty Officer King for his interaction with PFC Clagett?

A: We have had no — nothing against Petty Officer King. We have not taken any action against him.

Why not? In addition, why was no disciplinary action taken against the guard for his insubordination toward the medical doctor, who was his superior in rank? One can see in this mini-drama about the hamburger and the arguments over food and respect a microcosm of the larger drama of the Operation Iron Triangle investigation. In both the macro and micro dramas, military rank is the most salient factor. The battalion commander was ultimately responsible for the fiasco that was this mission, but the authoritarian structure of the army punished the lowest-ranking soldiers and did not question the commander's errors in leadership at all. Similarly, the executive officer on the witness stand was ultimately responsible for her guards mistreating and not feeing Clagett, but she made sure that all the responsibility was shifted onto Clagett. She did this by not releasing the guidelines, not sanctioning her guards, allowing a one-person board to punish Clagett, and being evasive about her own responsibility. The micro and macro dramas of the investigations of the hamburger incident and the killings on the mission are connected via the authoritarian structure of the army. Rank has its privileges, and apparently one of those privileges is the ability to evade accountability and shift blame toward subordinates. As a soldier said to me, "in the army, [bad stuff] flows downhill."

The IO confirmed that the executive officer "had never talked to Petty Officer King about the incident."

Q: Okay, a couple more questions. I see in the DD Form 2714 that you concurred with the recommendations of 14 days extra duty, and suspension of phone privileges for 14 days. Is that correct?

A: Yes.

Q: And you made that determination based on what?

A: That's based on his disrespect — his disrespectful attitude and be-havior. He needed some kind of discipline.

Essentially, Clagett was convicted of disrespect without due process and in a Kafkaesque manner. The definitions of his crime were deliberately withheld from his military attorney, CPT Rutizer. She was not given an opportunity to defend him, and the government then used his conviction of disrespect in the brig as an offense pun-ishable under the UCMJ in the general court-martial.

TESTIMONY BY CHIEF MASTER OF ARMS NACE

Chief Master of Arms Joseph Nace, also from the US Navy and the brig in Kuwait, testified briefly. He said that Clagett never gave him any problems and he had never heard "of any other guards who had problems with PFC Clagett." CPT Rutizer asked him: "So there's been no investigation to determine if Petty Officer King acted inap-propriately?" "Not that I know of, ma'am," he answered.

The prosecutor determined that no complaints had been made against the guards who interacted with Clagett. The IO determined that Chief Master Nace never spoke with Clagett and never investigated the charges against him. "Why did you not speak with PFC Clagett?" Chief Master Nace replied: "Sir, I don't handle that part of — any part of conversations with Clagett or investigations because I work inside the wire, and it would be like a conflict of interest."

TESTIMONY BY COMMANDER CHARLES CAVAIANI

Another naval officer testified, Commander Cavaiani, who was the officer in charge of the brig in Kuwait. His rank is equal to that of a lieutenant colonel in the army, so that he was equal in rank with the IO. I have observed that in such situations, the judge or IO and the equally-ranked witness do not refer to each other as "sir." The meticulous awareness among military soldiers and officers concerning their position in the military's authoritarian structure must be emphasized. CPT Rutizer asked:

Q: Sir, do you recall receiving an email from me on 22 July 2006?

A: Would you please tell me the subject?

Q: Yes, sir. I asked that PFC Clagett be fed three times a day.

A: Yes, I remember that email.

Q: Sir, do you remember in that memorandum, I informed you that Petty Officer King and PFC Clagett had an altercation?

A: I understand they had a — they had a conversation.

Q: Sir, do you recall me asking you to take a look into the conduct of Petty Officer King?

A: I remember the letter requesting, I guess....

Q: Sir, to date have you had any conversation with Petty Officer First Class King about the confrontation?

A: Not with Petty Officer King. I talked with his supervisor.

This interaction illustrates the role of power in the authoritarian structure of the army. As Clagett's attorney, CPT Rutizer humbly asked for the commander of the brig to look into the matter of Clagett not being fed three meals a day, and the commander — simply refused. He acknowledged receiving the emails and not acting upon them. The fact that a military officer had to request that the military feeds one of its soldier–prisoners three meals a day is incredible by civilian standards of treatment of prisoners. Commander Cavaiani did not express any surprise or embarrassment.

The IO got the commander to admit, "I did not ever talk to PFC Clagett." "Is it normal procedure not to talk to the accused about the offenses when you administer this punishment?" the IO asked. The commander replied: "There's nothing there in the case that I need to see — deal with the inmates directly on these such issues." The commander also said that he never spoke with Petty Officer King. The commander was dismissed.

The prosecutor immediately asked to admit into evidence "Prosecution Exhibit 44 which is PFC Clagett's unsworn statement that he submitted to the board." Captain Rutizer objected: "Sir, the defense objects in accordance with R.C.M. [Rules of Court Martial] 405." The prosecutor said that "Clagett wasn't give a formal oath, but a formal oath isn't required to swear to a statement." Only a lawyer or a judge would know whether the prosecution's assertion is true, and in this case, the opposing attorneys disagreed. The IO ruled: "Okay, I note your objection, but we'll admit it." The IO asked the attorneys to give their closing arguments.

CLOSING ARGUMENT BY THE PROSECUTION

Captain Mackey delivered the closing argument for the prosecution on this seemingly irrelevant charge of disrespect which would nevertheless hold serious consequences for Clagett:

> Sir, what you've heard today is the charges are relatively simple and the evidence that was presented today is relatively simple. He's being charged with two separate counts of specifications of disrespect and contempt towards two separate petty officers. In order to meet the Article 91, it's the simple elements that he's an enlisted member, that he either committed acts or used language toward or in sight of the petty officers, he knew it was his superior petty officer, the petty officer was in the execution of the office, and the language or act was either contemptful or disrespectful.

The prosecutor dismissed LCDR Karamidov's testimony because "her job, as she sees it, is to advocate for her client," but "she wasn't there to see what happened." Of course, the prosecutor overlooked her description of the petty officer's disrespect toward her, for which she was present. Regarding evidence, the prosecutor pointed out that "PFC Clagett voluntarily gave his statement that day and voluntarily [did] admit that he did commit those offenses." The prosecutor asked the IO to refer these additional charges to general court-martial.

CLOSING ARGUMENT BY THE DEFENSE

CPT Rutizer made a passionate closing argument:

Sir, I can't help but notice a pattern here. The government charges offense before they even investigate it. We've seen that with the allegations that Clagett made to Mason, and clearly that didn't happen, and we've seen it here today. You heard from Petty Officer Behl and Petty Officer King that they were shocked and surprised that this went any further than a simple D and A board or simple Inmate Observation Report. According to Petty Officer King, that action was settled in-house, and it should have stayed there.

I concur that there is a pattern here, and have already added that this micro-drama over the hamburger is a microcosm of the larger drama concerning the mission. CPT Rutizer agreed that there are six elements to the charge of disrespect under article 91 of the UCMJ, but Clagett's behavior met only three of these criteria: He is an enlisted soldier, he used language with the word "f__" in it, and this occurred within sight of a petty officer. (If using the "f__" word is a crime, probably most of the army is guilty of this crime.) But "PFC Clagett had no idea about the ranks of the Navy," so that he did not know that he was using this language in front of his superiors. She confessed that the prosecutor admitted to her, "We're all Army here, we don't the rank of Navy." In that case, she added, "How can we expect PFC Clagett to know it?" She also questioned the fifth criterion, that his superiors acted in accordance with their office. Finally, she pointed out that Behl testified "that he showed absolutely no disrespect for her, in fact to the contrary, she said that they were having a casual conversation." "Sir, at least two of the six elements are not met." She continued:

Sir, PFC Clagett is locked down 23 out of 24 hours a day. You heard from Petty Officer King that PFC Clagett is dependent upon the guards for almost everything. *The guards are essentially his umbilical cord to life.* They determine when his sheets get changed. They determine when he takes a shower. They determine if and when he does eat. Imagine not being able to be fed twice in one week. Imagine the frustration. Compound that with the medication that he's on which has completely altered whatever his psyche was, and you heard from Lieutenant Commander Karamidov that he was only four days into that particular schedule.... This board was completely flawed ... How can — this is not Shanghai. This is not trial by surprise here.... Master Chief Donaldson ... never once read PFC Clagett his rights. He's been a law enforcement officer for, I think he said, 19 years. He doesn't know that if you suspect somebody of a crime to read him his rights? That hearing was laughable. In fact, it was almost Machiavellian in nature to consider his statement without even advising him of his rights [emphasis added].

It is true that the army and navy do not recognize each other's ranks easily — even Master Chief Donaldson admitted this under oath. A one-man board is an oxymoron. American culture, going back to the US Constitution, expects that the accused know their accusers and the nature of the accusation. It is amazing that disrespect is treated as a "crime" in the US military. Civilians show disrespect to each other every day, from "flipping a bird" to drivers to foul language, but such behavior is considered offensive — not criminal. Above all, CPT Rutizer was appealing to commonsense: the victims of Clagett's alleged "crime" were not offended and were shocked that these incidents would go to court-martial. After all, Clagett asked a female guard for a pencil and where she was from, and said "I don't give a f___" to another guard. There does seem to be something Machiavellian in the government's efforts to characterize these petty offenses as crimes and tack them onto the charges of murder. A neutral observer cannot avoid suspecting that the prosecutors had become emotionally involved in this case — which is a violation of ethical rules of the legal profession. And one suspects that the prosecutors had become malicious. As Mr. Bergrin had put it earlier in the hearing, adding these charges of disrespect was akin to "kicking a person when he's down."

One of the co-prosecutors, CPT Duggan, gave a brief rebuttal:

> All right, sir. Captain Rutizer is almost like a broken record. She says the government sounds the same. I would say that her and — her and Phil Bergrin sound the same from a few days ago. PFC Clagett, as the master chief stated, was briefed ... of the Navy rank structure..... As far as not being read his rights, the Soldier has just an inherent right as any human being to voluntarily submit a statement. That statement is dated 24 July, the day before the hearing. He voluntarily gave it up.

For the record, Mr. Bergrin's first name is Paul, not Phil. The Article 32 hearing finally closed at 10:41 a.m. on the 9th of August 2006. The IO referred the charges of disrespect to court-martial.

Conclusions

Why did Clagett ask for a pencil? Nobody at the hearing bothered to ask. I followed up on this question and discovered that Clagett is an artist, and needed a pencil to draw. Others have observed, and I concur, that some of his drawings are excellent. The machine-like prosecutors focused on the word "f___" to prove that Clagett committed the crime of disrespect. But they overlooked completely Clagett's very human and correct charge against his guards and the system that they were treating him with disrespect.

Doesn't any US soldier deserve minimal respect during pre-trial confinement? Cultural standards ranging from the US Constitution to Stouffer's classic study on army morale suggest that he or she does. Why didn't the brig commander, executive officer, IO or other high-ranking officer notice that there is something terribly wrong with the situation in which a US soldier who is presumed innocent until proven guilty, or in general, is put into solitary confinement in a remote tent behind barbed wire as a matter of policy? This is a form of torture, not fundamentally different from how presumed enemies of the US are treated at Abu Ghraib and Guantanamo. Clagett had no choice but to yell and act "agitated" in order to draw the attention of his guards. The guards then used this double-bind situation against him: He was deemed disrespectful for gaining their attention through his agitation, but he would have degenerated into a vegetative state had he not had the spark for living that made him shout and act agitated in order to get their attention. He lost either way. CPT Rutizer used a powerful metaphor that resonates with Jung's and other studies of cultural archetypes, namely: the guards were Clagett's umbilical chord to life. The army was his mother, symbolically speaking, with regard to his biological needs and physical as well as mental health. How did the guards, prosecutors, and IO lose sight of this fundamental truth, which resonates in all the classical, biological models of society as a kind of living organism found in the works of Parsons, Durkheim, and other structuralists? The answer is painfully obvious: They had dehumanized Clagett and treated him as if he were a machine. Again, this is not only a personal problem particular to these guards and officers but is part of the general trend in modern society toward the mechanization of social life.

Two individuals, CPT Rutizer and LCDR Karamidov, were able to keep a balanced perspective on this situation. Both acted in accordance with their professional standards as advocates for their client, and both were able to keep a commonsense perspective. CPT Rutizer pointed out the obvious: Clagett simply asked for a pencil, and he was hungry. Karamidov politely pointed out that the guard was at fault for Clagett's predicament, and that Clagett was at the mercy of her medical orders and of the guards complying with those orders. Moreover, she testified that the guard was insubordinate toward her — but he was not punished. In this entire drama, one never encounters a situation in which any guard, CID agent, or other law enforcement official was punished, despite obvious transgressions by them. CID agents are allowed to lie, but Clagett was not allowed to ask for a pencil or food. None of this obvious reality was evident to the prosecutors and IO, who mocked both of these female officers.

CHAPTER 8. ADDITIONAL HEARINGS AND EMPTY RITUALS

"[This is] one of the most destructive forms of double bind, namely, the attack upon spontaneity or sincerity."
— Gregory Bateson, p. 136

Both civilian trials and military court-martial processes involve many long and detailed rituals. Following the Article 32 hearing, there were several additional and separate hearings for each of the co-accused. In the remainder of this book, I will focus only on Hunsaker's additional pre-trial hearings. On October 20, 2006, a military judge held the arraignment. He ascertained that all the participants, from the trial recorder to the various attorneys, were acting in accordance with the UCMJ. There is a quasi-religious quality to the proceedings. In a sense, the trial recorder is like an apostle who bears witness and records the "passion" of the accused, much like the apostles bore witness and recorded the passion of Jesus.[1] Much like weddings, funerals, and other civilian rituals are focused less on the individuals who are the object of the ritual, and more on the family and society, so courts-martial are more an exercise in American Civil Religion (as it is called by Robert N. Bellah[2]) than about the crimes of the accused. The military judge devotes much time to issues that have little if anything to do with the accused or the case. *The ultimate purpose of the rituals is to demonstrate to posterity that the accused was afforded all the rights that are guaranteed to him by virtue of being an American.* In order to promote social integration and solidarity, rituals are

---

1 This connection between a public trial and religion may come as a shock to some readers, but is a standard part of the sociological perspective. See Emile Durkheim, *The Elementary Forms of the Religious Life* (New York: Free Press, [1912] 1965). Durkheim wrote that religious distinctions between what is labeled as "sacred" versus "profane" permeate all of society, and are not restricted to religion. He invented the concept of "civil religion," which is celebrated in the national and political realms.

2 Robert N. Bellah (1967), "Civil religion in America," *Daedalus* 96:1-21.

---

supposed to be sincere, spontaneous and emotionally connected to collective beliefs. But in the case of Hunsaker, the rituals come across as empty and devoid of emotion. Bateson alerts us that a child will eventually become mentally ill if he or she is exposed to expressions of emotions such as saying "I love you" coupled with a mother's scowl, or any behavior which is out of sync with the emotions. Similarly, Durkheim insists that society's rituals must exhibit spontaneous "collective effervescence," or that particular society (large or small) becomes dysfunctional. I shall be focusing on the dysfunctional disconnections in the behavior versus the words expressed by the judges toward Hunsaker.

In the case of Hunsaker, the judge devoted about five pages of the ROT (record of trial) to the issue whether Major General Thomas R. Turner, who was the original commander of Ft. Campbell and of the 101st Airborne Division, and the convening authority for setting Hunsaker's trial into motion, could be succeeded in this authority by Major General Jeffrey J. Schloesser, who would become the new commander. This portion of the trial is captured by the following exchanges between the military judge (MJ) and trial counsel (TC) or military prosecutor:

> MJ: So, on 9 November or thereafter, is Major General Schloesser going to select new court-martial members?

> TC: Your Honor, it is my understanding the new Commanding General will adopt this convening authority — this convening order, and he'll appoint new members that won't apply to this case.

> MJ: He is going to adopt all of the members and all of the replacement members that Major General Turner has selected?

> TC: Yes, your Honor.

The fact that the jury pool of military members would remain the same even though commanders have changed was not a surprise to anyone. Other parts of the ritual may appear to be more surprising. The MJ in this portion of the trial process, Lieutenant Colonel Richard J. Anderson, stated that his involvement in this case would end as soon as this particular pre-trial hearing (or Article 39a, as it is called in the military) ended, and the case would be turned over to another MJ, Colonel Theodore Dixon. The MJ then informed Hunsaker of a series of possible traps:

> MJ: If we have another session of this court and the government demonstrates to Colonel Dixon that you are voluntarily absent, then the trial can just continue in your absence. Do you understand that?

> ACC: Yes, Your Honor.

> MJ: So, you haven't entered a plea, and that takes you to a default position, which is an entry of not guilty, and you haven't elected a forum, and so that take you to the default position of a panel of officers. So if you are not here and we have a trial without you, then it would be a contested trial in front of a panel of officers. Do you understand?

> ACC: Yes, Your Honor.

MJ: I tell you this for two reasons, one, because you need to know; and second, so that you would keep in touch with your chain of command and with your counsel about where you are supposed to be when, because sometimes dates on a docket have a way of changing. Do you understand?

ACC: Yes, Your Honor.

This exchange reminds me of numerous other trials when I have watched the accused dutifully state that he understands, whereas I myself and some attorneys confided afterwards to each other that we did not understand fully. Why does the government have the right to try the accused in absentia? More importantly, the accused could be tried in absentia simply because of a bureaucratic mix-up in the schedule. Finally, defense attorneys frequently complain that they do not have adequate access to confer with their clients, so that the possibility of such a mix-up is real, and terrifying.

This is a trap for the individual that is embedded in the ritual of the trial process, another instance of the ritual being more important than the right of the accused to be present at his trial.

In any and all social rituals, the words, gestures, symbols, and actions taken by the actors must be said and performed in exactly the prescribed manner. If even one tiny mistake is made in the ritual, the meaning of the ceremony can be nullified. For example, most of the world watched Chief Justice Roberts make a mistake in administering the oath of office to President-elect Obama. In order to avoid any questions about his act of taking office as President of the United States, Obama had Roberts re-do the ritual.

The precision of the ritual takes on overwhelming importance in weddings, funerals, baptisms, and many other ceremonies up to and including courts-martial. One consequence of this social fact is that in criminal trials, the facts concerning an accused person's case seem to take on secondary importance. I have observed judges read the words that are required to be said by them without much emotional involvement or as much concern for the facts as for the rituals. They seem to be comforted by the belief that if they made a mistake regarding the facts, it will be corrected later by an appeals court. Obviously, the accused finds little comfort in this belief.

ANOTHER HEARING

On 13 November 2006, a different military judge, Colonel Theodore Dixon, presided over yet another pre-trial hearing or Article 39a. This MJ also went through certain rituals, including the question whether anyone challenged his authority as a judge in Hunsaker's case (nobody challenged it). In this hearing, Hunsaker formally requested the rough equivalent of a civilian trial by jury, namely, "Specialist Hunsaker requests a panel consisting no less than one-third enlisted members." Significantly, despite this move, Hunsaker did *not* finally end up with a trial by jury but with a plea-bargain before this same military judge, Colonel Dixon.

The first witness called in this hearing was the court reporter for the Article 32 (or preliminary hearing), Staff Sergeant April Cogdill. The gist of her testimony is that the Article 32 began on August 1 and ended on August 9, 2006, and that she did not begin transcribing it until the 11th of August.

> Q: And why was there a delay in your transcribing?

> A: There was a delay, sir, because at the — the end of the month of June/early July, we had a trial term. We had roughly ten courts-martial that happened during that time....

> Q: And you started typing the 32 on the 11th. When did you finish typing?

> A: The last day that I finished was, I believe, right around the 26th of August, sir.

Sergeant Cogdill also revealed that the IO, Colonel Daniel, "made it very clear to me, sir, that he wanted the entire transcript." She testified that the transcript of the Article 32 hearing came to 954 pages in length, 43 prosecution exhibits that were attached to it, and defense exhibits marked Alpha through Romeo. In the cross-examination, the defense attorney got her to agree that "the fact of the matter is that much of the testimony that took place during this investigation related to charges unrelated to those faced by Specialist Hunsaker."

The second witness to take the stand was Major Russell Lance Miller, who identified himself as the Chief of Military Justice at Ft. Campbell, Kentucky. He testified that for various bureaucratic reasons, he did not receive the transcript of the Article 32 investigation and its attachments until September 21, 2006. "When did the Article 32 Investigation and the pre-trial advice get to Major General Turner?" Major Miller replied that it was sent to the Commanding General on September 28th. The Major then revealed that the CG traveled a lot after receiving the transcript, "but he didn't want to take the transcript with him ... and the reason for that is he sticks it in his luggage and his luggage gets misplaced, gets lost, and it falls into the wrong hands, it could be prejudicial to both sides and just a mess, and so it was some, if you want to call them, security concerns about the sanctity of the 32 and that he and he only look at it." This explanation is interesting in depicting the transcript of the Article 32 as "sacred" as well as a security risk, given that this document is presumed to be a public record (which does not detract from its "sanctity"). If it had been lost, it could have been replaced easily.

Cross-examination of Major Miller by defense counsel revealed that General Turner referred the cases over for trial on October 16, 2006. The MJ asked questions as well, and ascertained that the General referred the Operation Iron Triangle case along with another, unnamed case (for which the transcript ran over 1200 pages) on the same day, October 16. The Major added: "I remember that day because that's the day Vice President Cheney visited Fort Campbell." In the re-direct examination by the prosecutor, the following was revealed:

> Q: And the concurrent referral on the 16th was that by design or ...?

> A: Well there were some considerations about the 16th, and that was like, *the media frenzy that was ongoing*, owing to the Vice President's visit [emphasis added].

No one asked the Major to clarify his answer. Why would Vice President Cheney's visit to Ft. Campbell motivate the CG to refer two complicated cases to trial prior to this visit?

The defense attorney, Mr. Waddington, then argued at length that the government took too long ("an entire period of over 80 days") to process the decision to put Hunsaker on trial, which resulted in unnecessary pre-trial confinement for him. The defense argued that this period of time "is unreasonable considering the fact that Specialist Hunsaker has been in pre-trial confinement since the 15th of June at that point." He concluded that "this 86 day period from 1st of August to the 16th of October, did violate Specialist Hunsaker's right to a speedy trial."

The prosecutor responded, "Your Honor, this is a case of the defense wanting it both ways." Specifically, the prosecutor summarized the defense position as, "We want the Convening Authority to carefully review the charges and specifications, and carefully formulate his decision, but at the same time, you guys really need to move a lot faster." He argued that the prosecution had moved with diligence: "The law doesn't require constant motion, but the evidence before this court is that there has been constant motion by the government."

The MJ asked the defense to refer to a specific period of time in which he believed the government was not acting reasonably. Captain Maloney replied: "The second period, the one that we mentioned from the 22nd of September through the 16th of October, that period clearly, in the defense's position or from the defense's perspective I should say, Your Honor, is violative. The period preceding it, from the 1st of August to the 21st of September, taken as a whole, the defense believes it is violative."

> MJ: Government, when did the accused redeploy?

> ATC1: He redeployed — he left on or about.... My memory, Your Honor, is that he left, it was either at the very end of August or the very beginning of September.

Through a series of pointed questions by the MJ, one learns that on September 8, 2006, Hunsaker was sent back from Iraq to a brig in Charleston, South Carolina, where he arrived on September 11, 2006, after allegedly spending several days in Ireland due to mechanical difficulties with the military airplane that was transporting him. (Hunsaker told me later that he did not recall being in Ireland at all.)

> MJ: Has he been continuously confined in Charleston since that date?

> CDC: Yes, sir.

> MJ: When did he return to Fort Campbell?

> CDC: For this hearing, sir?

> MJ: After his tour in Iraq, when did he return to Fort Campbell?

CDC: He never did, sir. He went from Iraq to confinement. He came here for the motions hearing today and then he came here for the arraignment.

MJ: Okay. So his first return to Fort Campbell was for the arraignment?

CDC: Yes, Your Honor.

Following a recess, the defense called the accused to the witness stand. Mr. Waddington questioned Hunsaker about his mistreatment in both Kuwait and Charleston during his pre-trial hearing. His mistreatment in Kuwait is detailed in Chapter 1. Turning to Charleston, Mr. Waddington asked:

Q: Since you have been at the Charleston Naval Brig, what kind of access or what kind of ease of access have you had with respect to contacting detailed military counsel or your civilian defense counsel?

A: I have to put in a request chit and everything goes through paperwork. If I want to make a phone call to any lawyer, it has to be, put in a request and sometimes they will request it that same day and some days it may take 3 or 4 days, and in the beginning, I kind of had problems trying to contact my previous lawyer and in that aspect, he wasn't getting my messages and apparently, from what I heard, he was trying to contact the brig, but they weren't giving me any of his so, we had no contact.

Q: Would it be fair to say that you have had difficulty in making contact?

A: Extreme difficulty.

THE CROSS-EXAMINATION PERTAINING TO MALTREATMENT OF HUNSAKER

There are two sides to every story. The prosecutor attempted to justify this heinous behavior toward the accused by claiming that Hunsaker was angry and that they needed to keep him away from the media. It is always a warning sign for any legal team when the judge interrupts with the infamous question, "Where is all this going, counsel?" And that is precisely what happened in this case.

The prosecutor asked the accused whether he had told the psychiatrist (who, incidentally, was the same LCDR Karamidov who also treated Clagett) who had examined him "that you weren't sure if you could control your anger, is that correct?" "No, sir," the accused replied, and continued:

What I said was, and I have even read the same report that you have read obviously that she has written, and what I said is, "Yes, I am angry, because I am here," because I believed that I didn't belong there. And I didn't want to be put with the other rest of the inmates that are just, to me, were scum, and I wasn't. There was also plenty of other things in the same report that you probably read and which is probably where you are getting your answers from, sir, where she has messed up what I told her. She completely turned my words around.

Q: You told her that you weren't sure you were able to control your anger, is that correct?

A: No, sir. I confronted her about that also, later, when we had another session, because I read what she had to say.

Q: Well you told her that you weren't sure if you were able to keep yourself from hurting other confines, is that correct?

A: No, sir. I did not say that. I said that I was angry at the time, when I got there, and like I said before, I read her report. I came back and I told her, I said, "Ma'am, the first time we had an encounter, you messed a lot of things up of what I was saying. You misinterpreted what I was trying to say." She said, "Okay, I will try to fix that."

The prosecutor changed tack and asked,

Q: You are aware that PFC Clagett had actually conducted an interview with ABC Nightline News from the confinement facility there?

A: Yeah, I understand he did that, sir. [The prosecutor is referring to one of the co-accused in this case, Corey Clagett, who, in the presence of his attorney, Paul Bergrin, was interviewed by ABC Nightline prior to the Article 32 hearing. What is the relevance of this fact for the way that Hunsaker had been mistreated?]

Q: So you are aware that there is considerable media interest in these cases, is that correct?

A: Yes, maybe for him, sir, but not me....

Q: Are you aware that AR 190-47 actually requires that you wear shackles on your feet and hands when you are outside of any confinement facility?

A: I am not aware that you are supposed to sleep in them either, sir. No one showed me any kind of regulations or anything of the sort when I was kept in shackles. I just did what I was told.

I am not aware of the regulation cited by the prosecutor. However, I can vouch from observation that in all the other court-martial cases with which I have been involved, soldiers were not confined and were not shackled in any way prior to the court-martial.

Regarding the prosecutor's reference to the ABC television broadcast of Clagett, I can state that the general pattern seems to be that the military is very hostile toward the information media. I have learned that the army forbids its military lawyers, both defense and prosecution, from speaking with the media about any case. Military judges typically admonish all participants in a court-martial to avoid all contact with the media. Moreover, accused soldiers who do talk with the media are routinely punished afterwards. But the US Constitution guarantees the right of free speech to all citizens, including soldiers. Moreover, if the military were to allow the media to broadcast its "war crime" courts-martial to the world, much like the International Tribunal at the Hague does routinely for all its war crimes trials, the public would become better informed.

Turning to the accused's stay in the Charleston Brig, the prosecutor asked:

Q: You are allowed to go to recreational facilities?

A: No, sir.

Q: To go and lift weights?

A: No, sir.

Q: You are allowed to go to church services, right?

A: I'm allowed to go. Sir, I am allowed to go to services, sir, but only if a certain unit goes. If they don't go, I can't go, and they have only went once.

Q: You had actually — in talking about your treatment in Charleston, you had actually told the cadre down there that you feel like you are being treated very well, isn't that right?

A: Well, the cadre do treat me very well, sir. I have never said that I have been mistreated down there. I'm just saying that the area that I am in, I am not allowed to talk to anybody. I have not done anything wrong since I have been confined that would constitute me to be put in more or less solitary confinement. I am not allowed to talk to anybody. I am pretty much not allowed to do anything. I spend almost 10 or 11 hours of my day just sitting there staring at concrete walls because there is just nothing for me to do.

Q: But you told us that you are segregated from the convicted prisoners, is that right?

A: I'm segregated from everybody, sir.

Q: So you had said that the people who had actually been convicted and know that they did something wrong, you are not allowed to talk to them, right?

A: I am not allowed to talk to anybody, sir. Whoever comes in on that side, whether they are convicted or they are a detainee that has acted up in their unit and they put them in D-Seg, either way, I am not allowed to talk to them period.

TC: One moment, please, Your Honor. [Trial counsel confer at counsel table.]

From my experience in observing courts-martial, attorneys confer with each other during questioning when they are losing their battle. Up to this point, the prosecutor had not only failed to justify the way that Hunsaker had been mistreated, but he unwittingly uncovered further dimensions to that mistreatment. In addition to his solitary confinement, Hunsaker had been "silenced." One can be put into solitary confinement and still be allowed to speak with another human being when the rare occasion for social interaction arises. But Hunsaker was not allowed to speak with anyone for any reason. "Silencing" is an informal and unofficial method of punishment used in military academies and other military institutions whereby the victim's colleagues treat him as if he were invisible, even when they are forced to interact with him. Following the conference between the two military prosecutors, Hunsaker was asked about a photograph of him in shackles that had been leaked to the media.

Q: And you were smiling, weren't you?

A: Yes, sir, because I thought it was stupid.

Q: And you are aware that the Theatre Field Detention Facility in Kuwait was not allowed — you are not allowed to possess any photographs when you enter that facility, is that right?

A: I didn't know that, sir.

Q: But you were found in possession of these photographs when you entered the Theatre Detention Facility in Kuwait, isn't that correct?

A: Yes. I had some photographs. I never seen them. They were given to me in an envelope and the guard, when he was going through my stuff, he pulled it out, pulled out the pictures, he looks at them, lays them face down.... He said, "Well there are some photographs in there that are some pretty bad stuff." I was like, "Okay. I never seen them personally." He was like, "Okay, you are going to sign this document saying that we have them." I signed it and I left Kuwait and I left the pictures there....

Q: And the pictures did eventually go out in the press, correct?

At long last, the military judge interrupted: "Where are you going with this?" Indeed, one is at a loss to see how possessing a photograph Hunsaker did not know he possessed of him being shackled justifies the way that the Army mistreated him. Hunsaker could not control the media, and the fact that some journalist managed to photograph his predicament is sanctioned under the First Amendment.

MJ: What is significant about the pictures finding their way to the media?

TC: It is significant to show that: one, they were — his posing for the pictures shows that they were actually together, breaking the no contact order; that they violated the rules of the confinement facility down in Kuwait; and that there was a significant interest in preventing the media from turning his transport back to the United States into a circus. It shows why the short gag order was given and not to contact the media and his family, and so forth.

MJ: Is it the government's belief that Specialist Hunsaker is the one that released these photographs to the media?

TC: No, Your Honor.

MJ: Then what is the significance of your line of questioning?

TC: The significance is that it shows that the government had reason to believe that the transport of these three accused, all three of them at the very same time, could be released to the media and therefore, future pictures of him in his shackles could be taken, could be distributed, therefore constituting humiliation to Specialist Hunsaker. So, it was to prevent the media from finding out when they were coming back. The line of questioning about the pictures shows that there was a legitimate concern by the government that the media had interest in this, that they had received pictures in the past, and that if the media found out about the —

MJ: You are not attempting to argue that the government has a significant interest in keeping information from the media as it relates to this particular case?

TC: No, Your Honor.

MJ: Then what is the significance of your line of questioning?

TC: The significance was preventing Specialist Hunsaker from being photographed further in his shackles.

MJ: And the government has some legitimate government interest in preventing photographs of the accused?

TC: Preventing any kind of photographs that may appear to be derogatory or degrading or in any way humiliating to the accused....

MJ: Then I go back to my original question. Are you attempting to infer that the government has a legitimate government interest in preventing the media access to whatever facts are associated with this case?

TC: No, Your Honor.

MJ: Including photographs of the accused?

TC: No, Your Honor.

MJ: Then the objection is sustained.

TC: No further questions, Your Honor.

MJ: Redirect?

DC: No, Your Honor.

The judge upheld the First Amendment of the US Constitution in theory and in the courtroom. But nothing had been resolved about the issues that have been revealed. The judge did not rule that using solitary confinement to prevent the media from gaining access to Hunsaker had to stop. The government's strongest attempted justification for mistreating Hunsaker is that it was attempting to protect him from "humiliation" by the media. This is a clearly duplicitous and insincere argument. It is the government, not the media, which humiliated and abused Hunsaker by caging, shackling, isolating, and silencing him even though he was presumed to be innocent until proven guilty and had no history of violence or any behavior that could have possibly justified such treatment. The MJ examined the accused soldier:

> Q: While in Charleston Naval Brig, you are in some sort of segregated status?

> A: Yes, Your Honor. I am.

> Q: As part of that segregated status, you have been ordered not to communicate with anyone?

> A: Roger, Your Honor.

> Q: Anyone that would otherwise be a confinee of some sort?

> A: Yes, Your Honor. How the Naval Con Brig works is, detainees and prisoners stay in different areas. Because of the uniqueness of my case, I stay in special quarters. They have other prisoners come down there, because they acted up or have done something stupid, and they lock them up for their punishment and they stay in there. We also have — right now, I have just one max, and they bring them in and they throw them right in there. It is usually — they take a vote on whether or not they decide to bring this guy out of max confinement, because of his behavior.

> Q: And you are not allowed to communicate with anyone who happens to be in that area that would be a prisoner or a confinee of any sort?

> A: Negative, Your Honor. I can't talk to anybody.

Note that the MJ as well as the accused do not refer to prisoners in a straightforward manner, but to prisoners versus detainees versus "confinees" of various sorts. It is as if there are prisons within prisons in the US military penitentiary system. The terms "detainees" and "confinees" are dark allusions to designations for foreign fighters (again, of various sorts) imprisoned at Abu Ghraib, Gitmo, and other US-run military prisons. Thus, Hunsaker's status as a US soldier in a military prison does not seem to be fundamentally different from the status of a foreign "detainee." Note also that military prison officials vote on when and whether a US military prisoner will be released from "max confinement," which seems to be a euphemism for solitary confinement. None of these descriptions of prison life fit ideal descriptions of what it means to be a US citizen and soldier in prison — the norms governing such confinement come across as more whimsical than rational–legal requirements for a prisoner's rights or punishment.

> Q: And although if I understand you correctly, the area which you are allowed to move around in isn't very large, but it is not your cell, would that be accurate?

> A: That is accurate, Your Honor.

Q: You describe it as a day area, is that right?

A: That is what they call it, Your Honor.

Q: Is there a television in there and things of that nature?

A: There is a schedule for that, Your Honor. They wake you up in the morning. You can have the news on from 6 to 0715, which is a new thing that they just started in the past couple of weeks. Before then, you couldn't have anything until after 10, which you are allowed to read the newspaper or read a book. But until then, between 0500 and 1530, you can't do anything else other than that, unless it is work related, but for me, being special quarters, you know, *plus not being a prisoner*, I can't take certain courses or do a job [emphasis added].

If Hunsaker was not a prisoner, what, exactly was his social status? Was he in a legal no-man's land as a "confinee" or "detainee?"

Q: What is the gag order that you referenced?

A: That is just what the guards that were taking us back from Kuwait to the States, that is what they called it. They just said that, "You are not to have any contact with anybody due to the fact that the media might be there waiting on us." They told us that they "wanted to attract as little attention as possible."

Hunsaker was supposedly "innocent until proven guilty" during this time frame, and definitely should have been protected by 1st Amendment rights enshrined in the US Constitution, which includes speaking to the media. At least from his perspective, there was no formal "gag order" in the sense of a rational–legal document that forbade him to speak to the media. Rather, he perceived the situation as one of his military guards forbidding him "to have any contact with anybody." The MJ had no comment on Hunsaker's remarks. He asked whether the defense or government attorneys had any questions, and they said they did not. If Hunsaker was waiting for validation from the judge as to his Constitutional rights, he certainly did not receive any.

In the more formal language of sociology, Hunsaker was telling the judge that the already convicted co-prisoners in his various prisons were *not* his reference group. He was still perceiving himself as "innocent until proven guilty." His self-perception was apparently ignored by the MJ. Let us suppose that Hunsaker had already been convicted and had been treated in prison as he described his mistreatment. The MJ still had the option to demand that Hunsaker be treated with dignity and respect befitting the prestige of the reference group of US soldiers. For example, the convicted Abu Ghraib soldier, Specialist Jeremy Sivits, recounted to me that his guards would not allow him to smoke a cigarette while waiting on the tarmac to board a plane back to the US and prison. The MJ who had sentenced Sivits, Colonel William Pohl, allegedly castigated the guards for failing to treat Sivits with the dignity and respect due to a US soldier, and ordered them to allow him to smoke a cigarette. Colonel Pohl exhibited behavior commensurate with the belief that even though Sivits was a low-ranking soldier, both he and Sivits were in the same reference group, namely, the US

Army, and this membership demands certain degrees of respect. The reader should not conclude that as a colonel in the US Army, the MJ in Hunsaker's case did not have options to remedy Hunsaker's abusive situation.

THE GOVERNMENT'S MOTION FOR CONTINUANCE

Seeking to avoid legal jargon, I will note that the government's motion for continuance in Hunsaker's case amounted to a request to delay his court-martial so that he would be tried after Clagett and before Girouard. The motion was necessary because by normative standards in the US derived from the Constitution, the accused has a right to a speedy trial. There is no point in reviewing the legal literature on normative or typical reasons for delaying someone's trial. In this sociological study, I am more interested in how the government's arguments come across to the layperson with regard to "commonsense." To be sure, the government attorneys used legal jargon and arguments that only specialists in the law will comprehend fully. But the Constitution was written for the common person. From a commonsense and sociological point of view, it is clear that the government sought this particular order of trying the cases — namely, Graber, Clagett, Hunsaker, Girouard — in order to force lower-ranking soldiers to "roll-over" on the non-commissioned officer (sergeant) Girouard. I have witnessed military prosecutors follow this technique of trying the senior-ranking enlisted soldier last in the Abu Ghraib trials as well as the canal killings that involved Leahy, Mayo, and Hatley. This is an observable, empirically verifiable fact that is obvious to any objective observer of the aforementioned sequences of trials. Yet the government argued that even though Hunsaker's defense team was ready for trial, it was the fault of the other defense attorneys for the co-accused that the trial would have to be delayed and proceed in a specific order.

The prosecutor's first sentence in the argument was: "Your Honor, military jurisprudence has a very long history of courts granting to the government the maximum deference when it comes to choosing the order in which it requests to try cases." He continued:

> There are many things under the control of the government in this case, when charges are preferred, when hearings are held, when an accused are arraigned, the one thing the government cannot control is the availability of defense counsel. When the government first submitted Part A of its Docketing Request, I believe the first trial date requested was 8 December. Appreciating that we would go into the Christmas break after that, and panel members and witnesses would be unavailable, and starting up again with Clagett and followed by Hunsaker and Girouard. Various defense counsel shot back, all of the defense counsel, except for the counsel for Specialist Hunsaker, said, "Whoa, whoa, whoa, we can't be available until much, much later next year." Specialist Hunsaker, for the first time, demanded speedy trial.... If they really wanted a speedy trial, they could have been demanding it from Day 1. Instead they were requesting, and admittedly, they were receiving delays as well as encouraging due deliberation by the general court martial convening authority. Putting that aside, the various defense teams should not be permitted to scuttle the government's requested order, by some of them putting their availability dates

out in times such as April and May, and March. I can't control when they are going to be available, Your Honor.

The prosecutor admitted that Hunsaker's defense team did not ask for a delay and did request a speedy trial. The prosecutor also made it clear that he was seeking that the accused be tried in a particular sequence. It is up to legal scholars to debate the merits of the prosecutor's arguments within the narrow and specialized reference group of the lawyers. More important, the prosecutor did not hide his intentions to try the cases in a specific order: "We are asking for a reasonable amount of time, in this case, to process the cases of two co-accuseds, that is, Specialist Graber and PFC Clagett, before getting to *US versus Hunsaker*." The prosecutor cited a precedent:

> The *McCollough* case also comments on how it was reasonable, in that particular case, for the government to choose the appellant to try last. They said that it was reasonable because the appellant was most culpable. That is essentially what the government is doing here, Your Honor.

Thus, the government had pre-determined that Sergeant Girouard was the most culpable, Specialist Graber was the least culpable, and the culpability of Clagett and Hunsaker fell somewhere in the middle. What is the point of the cultural value enshrined by the phrase, "innocent until proven guilty," if the government has already determined who is more guilty, and will therefore use the least guilty to testify against the most culpable defendants? Even if this is a well-established technique in the legal profession, it is out of sync with American cultural values. In fact, and contrary to the prosecutor's pre-judgments, Sergeant Girouard (who was presumed to be the most culpable) received the lightest prison sentence of nine years. The prosecutor was blunt concerning his strategy:

> Many have described this case of Graber in the media as a mercy killing. So, it probably does not represent the same level of culpability as that of Girouard, Hunsaker, and Clagett, who in contrast, conspired to commit a much more traitorous, a much more perfidious premeditated murder. So, that is why Graber should go first, because he is essentially between the four, the least culpable.... So, the proposed order of cases here by the government is particularly reasonable.

The prosecutor concluded his argument by repeating his opening statement, albeit in an extraordinarily long sentence: "In summation, Your Honor, we just ask that this court recognize the traditional deference afforded the government when it comes to the order in which to try cases and not let that order be disrupted by an 11th hour demand for speedy trial by the defense, particularly when the government's reasons for its proposed order are reasonable and the government intends to move with due diligence in all cases in moving them to trial." Was the prosecutor's position "reasonable" from the commonsense point of view? It is clear to the average person that the prosecutor assumed that the government is more privileged than the accused. But this assumption is not commonly understood to be part of American culture, which tends to privilege the individual over the government. The allusion to the accused's 11th hour demand for speedy trial is jarring in the sense that the US Constitution did not specify that the accused must demand a speedy trial in the 1st hour or at any particular point — only that the accused has a Constitutional right to a speedy trial.

THE RESPONSE BY THE DEFENSE

Captain Maloney, the military defense counsel for Hunsaker, gave the counter-argument::

> Essentially the government does have, and the defense concedes, the government has a legitimate interest in wanting to try cases in a particular order, no question about that. However, the question is not whether they have a legitimate interest in doing that, but whether that interest takes precedence over the accused's interests in having a speedy trial, particularly where, as in Specialist Hunsaker's case, he has spent to date, 152 days in pretrial confinement, under circumstances which are particularly rigorous, as the court is now aware from the testimony that we received prior to hearing argument on this motion.

An objective observer might concede that the government has a logistical interest in trying the cases in a particular sequence (namely, to maximize the number of convictions), but not necessarily a "legitimate" interest. The accused's pre-trial confinement was not only "rigorous," but abusive. And the defense counsel was so respectful of his superiors that he did not voice the obvious fact that Hunsaker was presumed to be innocent until proven guilty, even though he had been treated as if he were already guilty. Stouffer's observations in *The American Soldier* are helpful in understanding the military defense counsel's deference: the MJ and the prosecutor are the defense counsel's reference group, and he dare not offend them. Yet his designated role is to defend the accused vigorously. He cannot fulfill his role completely while cognizant of the fact that the MJ is his military superior and the prosecutor is his supervisor. A military defense attorney is automatically in a double-bind by virtue of the army's authoritarian structure. By contrast, a civilian defense attorney typically does not regard the judge or prosecutor as his reference group. The defense counsel continued:

> What the government would like is to have the cases tried according to their timeframe, to achieve the results that they want, without any consideration whatsoever of the effect that they have created by placing all these co-accuseds in pretrial confinement, under these types of conditions, for such a lengthy period of time.

But what if the government did consider the effects of the lengthy and abusive pre-trial confinement? Again harking back to Stouffer's classic study, one may conclude that over the course of several months of solitary confinement for the accused soldiers, the government was slowly but surely creating a new reference group in the minds of the accused — namely, the reference group of guilty soldiers. Being treated as if one were convicted and guilty, even if one is supposedly innocent until proven guilty, will eventually force the accused soldier to define himself in sync with his treatment. In these cases, the accused would be more likely to confess to guilt and accept plea-bargains than if they had not been confined prior to trial. For example, in the canal killings cases, Sergeants Leahy and Hatley were also charged with premeditated murder, but were not confined prior to trial, and both pleaded not guilty in their trials. By contrast, in the Operation Iron Triangle cases, Graber, Clagett, and Hunsaker were also subjected to pre-trial confinement, and all pleaded guilty in plea-bargains in lieu of trials by military juries.

What followed was a complicated discussion in which the judge tried to determine how many of the 154 days that Hunsaker spent in pre-trial confinement were the fault of the government versus the defense. He deferred a ruling on this issue. The MJ was clearly aware that once Graber's trial began, "then the domino effect starts." He did not rule on but also did not object to the domino-theory approach to convicting soldiers. Turning to the prosecutor, the MJ asked:

> My question to you is, would you propose that this court rearrange the docket every time a legitimate good cause request for continuance is presented to the court in one of the particular four cases? At some point in time, we have got to lock this down. It is locked down currently, but circumstances may change. So, what is the government's position?

Surprisingly, the prosecution replied to the MJ by again invoking its fear of the news media, rather than replying in legal jargon:

> Now, the government is cognizant of the fact that it could immunize certain accused, use them as witnesses, establish a Chinese wall, and kick those cases over to other trial teams ... but I believe that this case has garnered significant media attention. It is one thing to wall off a trial team when it is your standard drug case, for example. I mean, McCollough is a great example of this. It involved a lot of people, methamphetamines, drug rings, not the kind of thing that is going to generate, *as in the case of PFC Clagett, a primetime interview on ABC Nightline. So, even if, assuming for the sake of argument, we could catalog our evidence, freeze it in place, dictate different trial teams to handle different accused, on different dates, it may very well be impossible for anybody that pays attention to the news, who looks at the Internet to get their news, to not in some way be contaminated by that.* We request that the court consider that, the extraordinary public interest generated by this case, rather all four of these cases, and the likelihood that it could compromise other prosecutions if we had to try them out of the requested order, grant immunity, throw up Chinese walls, and establish different trial teams [emphasis added].

> MJ: Well, Captain Fischbach, you have raised, both in your argument and I might as well as address this at this time, as well as in this argument, factors that are not appropriate for the court to consider. I note for the record that everyone in the gallery is in uniform. I don't see the media interest that you are addressing. Even if I did, it would not be a factor that I should consider of whether the media has a particular interest in one or all of these cases.

The prosecutor's allusions to "Chinese walls" are not self-explanatory. Presumably the government's position was that it could grant immunity in exchange for testimony to certain accused soldiers and not be constrained by the proposed sequence of trials — but it did not want to do this. I had already suggested in previous chapters that the government was seeking to avoid trials by military jury based upon the fiasco that was the Article 32 hearing and the damaging evidence against the government that was uncovered. Most likely, the prosecutor was going through the motions of pretending to want trials by military jury, while wanting his particular sequence in order to secure plea-bargains and avoid trials altogether. From the perspective of American cultural values, which ideally put a premium on free speech and information, the prosecutor's comments on the media come across as un-American. The MJ seemed uncomfortable with the prosecutor's speech, yet he did not explain why he believed that he should not consider the prosecutor's anti-media sentiments. Was it because the MJ wished to uphold the 1st Amendment to the Constitution? Or was the MJ embarrassed that a military prosecutor would come across as un-American in his attitudes toward free speech, given that the MJ had already signaled the prosecutor that he was prepared to go along with the "domino effect" of sequencing the trials in a particular order? It is impossible to tell. Nevertheless, the prosecutor's argument suggests that he wished to avoid at all costs the airing of all the details of the Operation Iron Triangle killings in the media, presumably including Colonel Steele's role. In summary, the MJ's question and the prosecutor's reply seem disconnected to the average person as well as to the MJ. Furthermore, the prosecutor's reference group does *not* seem to include civilian American culture, with its guarantee of free speech. Rather, the prosecutor consistently behaves and speaks as if the US Army were a reference group set apart and even against US culture as a whole.

The MJ also discounted the prosecutor's argument that it wished to move against the accused in order of presumed culpability:

> In your original argument, you wanted the court to consider the relative culpability of these individuals. The court is not going to consider relative culpability at this stage of this trial. I understand your argument. But it is not going to be the court's position to try to determine who is more culpable than another and allow the government to then prosecute the least culpable, in the court's mind, first. It is not a factor to be considered. It may be a factor in your request, but it is not a factor that the court is going to try to ascertain or consider.

The MJ did not explain why he tried to close the door to the prosecutor's reasons for his strategy, which he clearly supported. Did the MJ realize that essentially, the prosecutor was willing to pre-judge that certain soldiers were guilty prior to trial, and some more guilty than others, despite the Constitutional presumption of innocence? One will never know the answer to this question. The MJ was diplomatic in expressing his discomfort: "So, it concerns the court that you are making arguments that may otherwise be misinterpreted at some future point in time." The MJ continued:

> The court's concern with your request is weighing the prejudice to the accused, the length of the delay against the government's interest in having that delay, and whether it is reasonable or not. Now, I am paraphrasing the test. But that is all the court is going to consider. Any arguments that would otherwise be beyond that are not properly before the court.

Perhaps it would have been helpful for future trials had the MJ explained why the prosecutor's reasons seemed improper. What are the normative parameters and standards for determining proper versus improper treatment of US soldiers who have been accused of crimes and how they should be treated before and after their courts-martial? The MJ sidestepped these crucial issues. The engaged reader may wonder: What is the MJ's reference group that prevented him from identifying with the accused soldier's reference group as a US citizen with allegedly inalienable Constitutional rights? Was the MJ identifying with the other colonels and generals in his reference group, including Colonel Steele? The MJ continued:

> The overall concern of the court in granting the government's request to prosecute thee individuals in a particular order, can be thwarted at any point in time by any of the accused, and it would be remiss on the part of the defense counsel not to attempt to disrupt the government's desired procedure. Given any good cause, the court will grant continuances in those other cases or this case, for that matter. And to whatever extent the government believes one accused can be used against a follow-on accused, I suspect that is within your consideration of which case should be tried at what time. Again, the court is not going to attempt to assess whether Private Graber can be used against Specialist Hunsaker. That is for the government to do. I am simply trying to weigh the government's request and whether it is reasonable against any prejudice to the accused. So, I am making this statement to you, and I am looking at you, simply because you are making the arguments, but I am making it for purposes of the record, that there are certain things that you have argued before the court, that the court is not even going to consider.

The MJ considered the issues of the media and sequencing the cases important enough to enter into the record — repeatedly. But he clearly regarded the technique of using one accused soldier as a tool to convict a fellow soldier as routine. Indeed, I have witnessed this technique in every single sequence of military trials with which I have been involved. But the obvious "prejudice" against all the accused soldiers, is obviously as follows: the Army invests enormous resources in promoting social integration, cohesion, and loyalty among soldiers, and then switches to the opposing strategy of forcing the "band of brothers" to "rat" on each other through various techniques that involve fear, intimidation, and abuse. The obvious drawback here with regard to "prejudice" and the search for truth in a trial is that soldiers will be motivated to lie or at least distort the truth in order to save themselves at the expense of their fellow soldiers. This technique is well-known in the civilian trial system as well, and is a derivative of "Prisoner's Dilemma" paradigms that have been worked out by psychologists and economists. The Prisoner's Dilemma comes down to an individual weighing the costs versus benefits of self-interest versus loyalty to a co-accused individual. Its effects are entirely predictable, namely, that most individuals will betray their friends in order to save themselves, but the legal profession has not seriously addressed the consequences of this technique for the meaning of the original, American, cultural understanding of a trial as a search for truth that balances a government's powers with inalienable rights of the individual. To summarize: American culture seems to value the Constitutional premise that an individual is innocent until proven guilty at the same time that it seems to value cost-efficient techniques of presuming which accused individuals are more guilty than others prior to trial, and using them to streamline the process of proving guilt, not innocence.

The prosecutor tried to placate the MJ, reaffirming his request to try the cases in order of presumed guilt at the same time claiming that he was not asking the judge to join him in this presumption of guilt prior to trial:

> TC: I apologize if I failed to properly convey my argument. The government is not requesting the court to make any judgments whatsoever on relative culpability of the accused. The government is simply proffering as to why its decision is at least reasonable.... I was simply trying to show the government's thought-making process. I am by no means requesting this court to make any judgment whatsoever that any accused is even guilty in any of these cases, let alone, least culpable or more culpable. We are simply demonstrating our own calculus and how we orchestrated the proposed order.

> MJ: And that may have been better stated than the court's concerns addressed, as it relates to your argument. I understand your argument to be of that nature. Thank you.

The judge then ordered a ten-minute recess, followed by arguments that were made by the civilian defense attorney, Mr. Waddington.

The Civilian Defense Attorney Speaks

Mr. Waddington's civilian defense attorney's reference group is unlike that of any of the other uniformed military personnel in the courtroom. He was the lone civilian in the courtroom. He was not comparing his values and beliefs with officers, the US Army, or the military system in general. However, this assessment must be qualified in at least one important respect. Mr. Waddington, like every other civilian defense attorney I have observed in military courts-martial, is a former military officer. I am not aware of statistical studies on what percentage of civilian lawyers who argue in military courts are former military officers. From personal experience, I do know that there is a small handful of civilian attorneys (including Paul Bergrin, Frank Spinner, and Michael Waddington) who represent most of the convicted "war criminals" in the current war on terror. By virtue of their military histories, the new reference group that emerges in describing them is that of the "inside-dopester." They have one foot in the civilian world and did have one foot in the military social world, so that they possess an insider's knowledge of both social worlds, yet do not belong entirely in either reference group. The consequences of this insight, as I have witnessed the process, is that civilian attorneys in the military courtroom are much more forceful and willing to push the envelope of "disrespecting" the MJ that their military defense counterparts do not dare approach. In every coupling of a civilian and military defense attorney that I have witnessed, the civilian defense attorney scored more points against the government than a coupling of overly-respectful military defense attorneys. One must keep in mind that a military attorney is always subservient to the judge by virtue of being outranked by the judge in the military system in addition to the usual deference shown to judges. Mr. Waddington's behavior and arguments illustrate this important point pertaining to the role of reference groups in the military courtroom.

To get to the point: Mr. Waddington asserted that the government had not produced the bodies of the dead Iraqis and had not provided any forensic, ballistic, or other specialized tests that are routine in civilian murder trials. He requested that an expert witness in these matters be allowed to testify, and of course, the government objected. According to Mr. Waddington: "There is a question about what range they [Iraqis] were shot, were they shot at close range, were they shot farther down closer to a berm." And he added: "Those are relevant factors in determining what actually happened out there." The discussion moved into the issue of needing an expert's opinion as to whether the allegedly self-inflicted wounds on Hunsaker were truly inflicted by him on his self or by another individual or group of individuals. This point seems logical. The government's response suggests a postmodern implosion of meaning with regard to the term, "self-inflicted," such that he argued that self-inflicted wounds were inflicted by others. The prosecutor argued:

> Your Honor, "self-inflicted," for the purpose of this motion would mean that the wounds were, on the government's theory, inflicted by Staff Sergeant Girouard, and/or potentially PFC Clagett. I am unaware of any evidence indicating that Specialist Hunsaker, himself, made those wounds, but the government's contention certainly is that the detainees who were shot did not make those wounds.

By commonsense standards of logic, this argument is absurd: A "self-inflicted" wound, by definition, cannot be inflicted by someone else. This is another illustration of the chasm between lawspeak and ordinary speech. The MJ did not respond directly to the prosecutor, and instead addressed the defense attorney: "Okay, you may proceed, Mr. Waddington. You may proceed with the argument. What else is it that Dr. Wecht [the expert witness] might assist the defense with?" Mr. Waddington's long reply includes the following issues: whether the wounds on Hunsaker are consistent with the government's theory versus the facts, "spoliation of evidence," whether "a proper homicide investigation was conducted," "what an autopsy would have revealed," and "help the jury in understanding the overall picture." The MJ asked the prosecutor for his opinion on allowing an expert witness in forensics to testify, and he prosecutor replied that he did not think that any "forensic pathologist would render any helpful information." This is an extreme statement: commonsense suggests that an expert could render at least *some* useful information. The MJ ruled: "The government will produce Dr. Wecht to assist the defense." It is worth noting here that in the military judicial system, the defense must request the court's permission to have an expert testify for the defense, and if the request is granted, the costs are borne by the government, not the defense. Finally, it is ironic that even though this expert was approved — much as I was approved as an expert in Clagett's case — in the end, no expert testified in Hunsaker's defense, just as I was not allowed to testify in Clagett's defense. These sorts of linguistic tricks and traps of the legal profession seem incomprehensible to the layperson. Situations of this sort, wherein a judge makes a ruling that is never enforced, are more familiar by comparing them to numerous scenes in *Catch-22*.

CREDIT FOR HUNSAKER'S CONFINEMENT

The MJ then turned to the issue of crediting the days that Hunsaker was already confined — prior to trial — toward any sentence that he would eventually receive. Mr. Waddington sought credit from June 15th, when Hunsaker was first arrested, to July 31, 2006. But Waddington was not making a purely quantitative analysis of number of days. He reminded the MJ of the abusive quality of Hunsaker's pre-trial confinement:

> Specialist Hunsaker testified that there was approximately a 3-day period, after he was ordered into pretrial confinement, where he was confined in what he described as an abandoned house or abandoned building without provision being made by the command to his knowledge, for food or water, sleeping conditions.... [he was kept] in a 7 foot by 7 foot metal cage, and that he was kept in this situation for approximately 23 hours a day. Certainly, this is above and beyond the kinds of circumstances that one would expect a pretrial prisoner in the United States Army to face, in both terms of the amount of time spent in confinement per day, as well as the living space available to the confinee. Paragraph 9-6 (a) (1) (B) states that, "when confinement exceeds 10 hours a day, there must be at least 80 square feet of total space per occupant." And that clearly isn't possible in a 7 by 7 foot cell.

Turning to the issue of Hunsaker being silenced while confined, Mr. Waddington said: "Clearly, again, this is the kind of circumstances which are unduly harsh in relation to what a pretrial prisoner might expect to face in the Army system consistent with AR 190-47." Note that Waddington was using the "Army soldier" as the reference group for evaluating Hunsaker's suffering, in addition to citing an Army manual for treatment of its own prisoners. It is also worth noting that even when Senator John McCain was a prisoner in solitary confinement in Vietnam, he was afforded a cell by the Vietnamese army that was 15 by 15 feet[1]. Thus, combining the cultural with the quantitative and legal perspectives, one may conclude that enemies of the US who tortured Senator McCain gave him more humane living space than the US Army gave Hunsaker. The response by the MJ comes across as indifferent to the cultural argument as well as the legal argument Waddington made:

> MJ: Well now, unless you are asking the court to take judicial notice of AR 190-47, the contents of AR 190-47 are not before the court.

> DC: Understood, Your Honor.

> MJ: You may proceed.

> DC: Without referencing 190-47, those conditions are however, particularly stringent, in light of the fact that other co-accused were not facing similar circumstances, but were charged with similar offenses.

There does not seem to be any good, commonsense reason why the MJ would not order the contents of AR 190-47 to appear on his desk if he desired to see them. More-

---

1 *http://www.newyorker.com/reporting/2009/03/30/090330fa_fact_gawande*

over, I have witnessed military judges in similar circumstances state that they had no reason to doubt an attorney's claims, or ask the opposing attorney whether reasons existed to doubt an attorney's claims. This MJ simply did not pursue the issue of Hunsaker's abuse while in confinement.

Mr. Waddington brought up other issues pertaining to the abuse, "including [Hunsaker] being required to sleep in these restraints," and that these are "unusually rigorous circumstances for a pretrial confinee." Again, what in the world could justify forcing a US soldier in confinement at a military base (which is already secure) to sleep in chains? If a foreign government treated a US soldier in this manner, one would rightly label such mistreatment as torture. Waddington reminded the MJ of "difficulties that he [Hunsaker] experienced in contacting his attorney." "Anything else?" the MJ asked. "No, Your Honor" Waddington replied.

The prosecutor argued that the circumstances of Hunsaker's confinement "don't rise to the amount of unduly harsh, especially when you look at the circumstances and legitimate government interests, which the government was pursuing at the time — throughout his confinement."

First, the government argued that when Hunsaker was confined in an abandoned building, and not given food or water, "the guards stepped up and gave that to him on their own accord. The guards basically are the government, so the defense has conceded that he was provided that food and that water." Of course, the guards are not the government, in the sense of the entity that embarked on the process of depriving Hunsaker of his liberties. The guards are Hunsaker's reference group, namely, fellow-soldiers who most likely felt pity for him at the same time that they were compelled to follow their orders. Commonsense suggests that precisely because the government failed to provide Hunsaker with food and water, his guards made an effort to take care of him. It is nothing short of incredible that a discussion of this sort took place: that the prosecutor tried to rationalize instead of apologizing for the fact that the US government deprived one of its soldiers (still presumed innocent until proven guilty) of food and water. What would one think of a foreign government which similarly deprived one of its soldiers, and especially a US soldier, of food and water while in confinement? The prosecutor continued his rationalizations:

> Second of all, the government asks that Your Honor keep in mind that all of this occurred while in Iraq, so although no ideal of situations, it certainly isn't as luxurious as other places throughout the world, hence that is why he was kept in a tent during the time of the Article 32, and why he stayed in what he described as an abandoned building before he went down to Kuwait. I am going to talk briefly about the shackles that the accused was placed in at COB Speicher. Again, the accused ... was housed in a tent. He wasn't in a place where there was a lock and key in any way confining him other than the tent itself, and the person who was placed in there with him. There was certainly a legitimate government interest in keeping the accused confined. At that point, he had already been charged with premeditated murder, with conspiracy to commit murder, obstruction of justice, and communicating a threat. The accused did present a threat, and for that reason he remained in shackles and in leg irons and hand irons.

For the sake of accuracy, let us note that the tent was behind a barbed wire fence. Other soldiers have been charged with premeditated murder in Iraq and have not been mistreated like Hunsaker. I have worked on the cases of soldiers who were accused of committing premeditated murder in Iraq who were not confined or restrained in any manner prior to trial. Hunsaker was charged, but by American cultural as well as legal norms he was presumed to be innocent until proven guilty. Finally, there is something profoundly degrading about chaining a US soldier in the manner described above. Insurgents and suspected terrorists who are arrested by US soldiers are not put into leg and hand irons, but are restrained with plastic cuffs. Even animals are not shackled to the extent that Hunsaker was — shackles, leg irons, and hand irons. There is no way to escape the conclusion that the mistreatment of Hunsaker constitutes what the sociologist Erving Goffman called a "degradation ceremony." Its purpose was not to confine but to humiliate. From a cultural point of view, the government's treatment of Hunsaker comes across as positively medieval.

The MJ did not comment on these arguments and did not issue an immediate ruling. He called for a recess at 2:16 p.m. and called the court back to order at 3:02 p.m.

DETERMINING WHO WOULD BE ON THE WITNESS LIST

The next item on the agenda was approval of who would be approved by the MJ to be called to testify as a witness. The tight choreography of the typical trial makes one wonder if it leaves any room at all for spontaneity and genuine dialogue. Everyone knows ahead of time what will be said and by whom. The real legal battles occur in back rooms (literally) and are never recorded. Secret decisions are made as to who will be allowed to participate as an "actor" in the rehearsed drama of the trial. Nevertheless, this portion of the hearing is particularly interesting because Hunsaker never had a real trial, so that one is able to learn what witnesses would have said had they been allowed to testify.

Defense counsel began by stating that regarding Colonel Steele, "We are no longer going to call him as a witness." The MJ responded, "Very well," and nothing more was said on this matter. Given that the Clagett defense team won approval from the MJ to have Colonel Steele testify at his trial (which was also cancelled), one has to wonder why Mr. Waddington rescinded his request to have the Brigade Commander testify. I asked Mr. Waddington this question. He replied that "the prosecutor threatened us moments before we went into Hunsaker's guilty plea that if we attempted to reopen the Steele/ROE incident and try to muddy the name the of the 101ˢᵗ in the media, then they would pull out of his deal, which would make him face life in prison with no parole."[1] I was somewhat shocked at the idea that threats and deals are made in back rooms while the court record captures a ritual of a supposedly open and free trial. But Waddington seemed to be resigned about the reality of how courts-martial are run. The next witness for consideration was Sergeant Lemus. Defense counsel spoke:

---

1 From a telephone interview with Mr. Waddington. He added: "At this point, Steele was off our witness list. I did not call Steele because it was irrelevant to our defense, i.e., that the previously identified hostile targets were trying to flee and therefore, they became active targets and could be shot on sight."

Sir, Sergeant Lemus, as it states in our request, not only is he a first-hand witness, he was on the objective, he was supposedly involved in this alleged conspiracy that happened, he heard the gunshots first, he went to the scene shortly thereafter.... His first hand testimony will disprove the government's theory about the conspiracy. He will also be used to impeach PFC Mason. PFC Mason speaks of a 5-minute conspiracy meeting. Sergeant Lemus completely contradicts that, and says there was no 5-minute conspiracy meting, as well as other information that completely refutes government testimony on the merits, sir.

MJ: Government, Sergeant Lemus is on your witness list, is he not?

ATC2: Yes, Your Honor.

MJ: So, you believe he is relevant and necessary for purposes of the government's case?

ATC2: Yes, Your Honor.

MJ: Why are you objecting to the defense requesting the same witness?

ATC2: Your Honor, the government believes that the defense has failed to meet its burden under R.C.M. 703 by giving a detailed narrative of what he is going to testify to.... Several people heard gunshots on that objective, and then there is some testimony in here that is completely irrelevant. That PFC Mason never argued with Staff Sergeant Girouard. *Finally, the last part of this synopsis goes into CID's coercion or interrogation of Sergeant Lemus, which is wholly irrelevant* unless we are going to attempt to impeach Sergeant Lemus with his own statement[emphasis added]....

MJ: Is it the government's position that none of the information that this witness would testify to is relevant and necessary for the purpose of the defense?

ATC2: No, Your Honor. The government sticks by the fact that we believe that their synopsis of testimony was inadequate under R.C.M. 703.

MJ: Government will produce Sergeant Lemus.

ATC2: Yes, Your Honor.

Translated into plain English and commonsense terms, this strange exchange may be summarized as follows: Lemus is helpful to both the prosecution and the defense, but he is much more helpful to the defense. This is because he would testify that CID coerced his confession at a time when he was also a suspect. For this reason, the prosecution would rather lose him as a witness than risk a military jury learning about deceitful and coercive techniques that the government used to obtain testimony. The MJ apparently saw through the government's transparent cloud of legal jargon and ruled without comment that Lemus would testify. But of course, Lemus never did testify.

DC: The next witnesses are Number 5, 6, and 8, Sergeant Hartman, Specialist Powell, and Staff Sergeant Jake Jurden. Those are going to all be — they are going to provide Good Soldier testimony about Specialist Hunsaker....

MJ: Government?

ATC2: Your Honor, the government again thinks that these are both cumulative witnesses.... I mean, it looks like they cut and pasted basically the exact same narrative just switching out years and experience in the Army for all of these witnesses.... Additionally, Your Honor, if I might, if you look at the Soldiers we have agreed to produce, Lieutenant Wehrheim, the accused's platoon leader; Lieutenant Horne, another platoon leader within the company; Sergeant First Class William Christy, the accused's Platoon Sergeant while in combat.... These soldiers, we believe, have more probative, I mean, their testimony is more probative value of the Soldier's reputation and character than the Soldiers we're refusing to produce at this time.

It is fascinating to note that (1) the government seemed willing to produce LT Horne and other witnesses who would have been extremely damaging to the government's case and (2) none of these witnesses were ever produced. Note also that the court recorder capitalizes the letter "s" in the word Soldier. In general, Army documents consistently refer to Soldiers with a capital "S," and almost never as soldiers. In other words, American culture's respect for the self-sacrifice of soldiers is expressed through this norm in using language with regard to soldiers. Similarly, the Good Soldier Defense (again, capitalized) is an emotionally charged and meaningful term within the reference group of enlisted soldiers. I have personally observed soldiers give such a defense about a fellow-soldier, and it has never been a perfunctory, mechanical exercise. Soldiers will testify about a fellow soldier as a Good Soldier only if they "mean it." Without a doubt, the prosecutor was well aware of this empirical observation, and therefore launched into a vigorous effort to prevent the Good Soldier testimony from taking place. From the prosecution's vantage point, the Good Soldier Defense is just another defense strategy, but the defense team knows the genuine emotions that will be elicited by the enlisted soldiers who have agreed to give such testimony. The usually reticent MJ also engaged in this discussion vigorously.

MJ: Captain Maloney, what's unique about these three witnesses that would not otherwise be able to be testified to by the witnesses the government has agreed to produce?

DC: Your Honor ... they can offer different perspectives on the nature and quality of his service in the United States Army, his conduct, his character as a Soldier.... Which may be different considerably from the perspectives of the senior leader like the platoon leader or the platoon sergeant.

MJ: Well now's not the time that maybe, possibly, could be. What is the difference between these individuals and what they will testify to compared to the individuals that the government has already agreed to produce?

> DC: Your Honor ... they simply out rank him and the context of their relationships which are different because they are not in leadership positions ... that's the primary difference, Your Honor, that they know him more as peers than as supervisors.

In sociological vocabulary, the soldiers who would offer the Good Soldier testimony are in the same reference group as the accused, whereas the officers who were promised by the government are in a different and superior reference group. The defense attorney captures this insight well with the simple observation that the proposed witnesses are the accused soldier's peers. It is not true that reality is self-evident, because it always differs based upon one's social vantage point. Moreover, everyone in the room probably knew that the commissioned officers who were supposed to testify against Hunsaker would have done so under promises of immunity, which would have lessened the chances that their testimony would have been overly damaging to the government. The judge sided with the government:

> MJ: Well, Captain Maloney, it is impossible and certainly not incumbent upon the court to try to decipher what it is that is unique about the individual's testimony that's not otherwise going to be provided by other witnesses...

> DC: Understood, Your Honor. Again, the primary difference is the nature of the relationship being different from that of a supervisor like a platoon sergeant or a platoon leader...

> MJ: The motion to produce Staff Sergeant Harman, Specialist Powell, and Specialist Shellman is denied.

Mr. Waddington attempted to have yet another soldier testify on Hunsaker's behalf, and the MJ denied his request. Mr. Waddington then turned to requests to produce witnesses who would speak on Hunsaker's behalf during the sentencing phase of the proposed trial. Military courts-martial differ significantly in this regard from civilian trials. The same military panel that convicts a soldier in the "findings" phase then sits in judgment and delivers a sentence in the "sentencing" phase. Based upon my experience, military judges typically allow family relatives as well as fellow-soldiers and even expert witnesses to testify in the sentencing phase. But this military judge comes across as less lenient than other military judges in his reference group:

> CDC: Sir, to the last four witnesses here, the sentencing witnesses, these are four family members of Specialist Hunsaker. The first two are his aunt and uncle. The third one there is his grandmother, and the last one there is his stepfather.... We argue that the jury is entitled to a couple of different perspectives on him as a boy, him growing up, what type of young man he is....

> MJ: What makes their personal appearances required under the rules?

> CDC: What makes it required, sir?

> MJ: As opposed to alternate forms of presenting that information?

CDC: There's nothing that per se requires every single witness to testify. Some of these witnesses will come either way to watch the court-martial, sir, and if they are denied or they do become cumulative, then we do intend to offer the testimony.

MJ: Well the question before the court is, is the court going to order the government to produce them at government expense?.... The question that I have for you is, what about their testimony requires their physical presence?

CDC: Your Honor ... there's nothing like having live testimony of someone's grandmother talking about their grandson live and in person explaining in detail the relationship with him, what it's been like since he was a young boy growing up.

MJ: Let's stop on the *grandma* for a second. *Government, you want to address grandma?*

ATC2: Yes, Your Honor. For — we think that the grandmother falls under the factors of R.C.M. 1001 (echo) 2.

MJ: She's a grandmother.

ATC2: Yes, Your Honor, I understand... The grandmother is going to give testimony, at least purportedly, about how he was a good grandson which I don't see is a matter of substantial significance to determination of appropriate sentence....

MJ: Government will produce the grandma [emphasis added].

The MJ allowed the grandmother as a witness because her role is prescribed in "the book" (namely, *Rules of Court-Martial*). But the MJ's thinly veiled contempt shows through his questions and his calling her "the grandma." He is not concerned with her name, and does not even refer to her as the grandmother — but with the mocking phrase, "the grandma." The prosecutor and the MJ clearly share similar values based upon their reference group. But a deep and wide chasm of cultural values separates them from the reference group on the other side, that of an extended family and their opinions which most likely would have resonated with jurors as they contemplated their grandmothers and their extended families. I have witnessed a military juror cry during a sentencing phase after listening to family members, especially mothers and grandmothers, who also cried on the witness stand. The important point is that one should not be seduced by the MJ's and prosecutor's perspectives into believing that only their points of view are legitimate, since they represent the government. In fact, both reference groups are equally legitimate. The MJ's "by the book" approach is as valid as the grandmother's "we the people" approach, and to the Army's credit, the book in question, *Rules of Court Martial*, allows for both sides of American culture to be expressed in a court-martial. "The book" does not require, yet does provide, for the values of grandmothers to enter into the legal discourse of military judicial proceedings.

However, the MJ refused to allow any of the other family members or other witnesses requested by the defense to testify. Based upon my first-hand experiences and research in courts-martial, this judge's rulings regarding family members as witnesses are not typical. He summarized his position, which includes a sheepish admission of his disrespect toward the grandmother, as follows:

> The court ordered the production of Sergeant Lemus and the court meant no disrespect to Marcella Ponder, but in referring to grandma, that's who we were referring to, and those are the only two witnesses the government, excuse me, the court has ordered the government produce at government expense.

I met Hunsaker's grandmother in Warrenburg, Missouri, in June of 2009. It is worth informing the reader that she is outspoken, knowledgeable about the case, reasonable, and impressive in her demeanor. Had she been able to testify, there is no doubt in my mind that she would have made an excellent witness and would have been a formidable opponent for the government.

MOTIONS ON WHAT MAY OR MAY NOT BE ADMITTED INTO TESTIMONY, INCLUDING THE "GOOD SOLDIER" DEFENSE

The MJ next turned his attention to a number of motions filed by both sides. The MJ turned to the prosecutor and asked:

> MJ: Government, did you mark the government's motion *in limine* as it relates to the reprimand that was supposedly given to Colonel Steele?

> ATC1: We did not, Your Honor. As you pointed out, the defense has not requested it pursuant to discovery, and so essentially the issue has not ripened at this time.

The MJ ordered the prosecutor to mark and submit this motion formally. "*In limine*" means that during the proposed trial, nobody in the courtroom would ever be allowed to refer to the reprimand that Colonel Steele, did, in fact, receive. The MJ said that the reprimand was "supposedly" given, but in fact, there is no doubt about the existence of the reprimand. It has been reported by the media, and several defense attorneys have told me that they have examined the reprimand, although none was allowed to photocopy it. The existence of the reprimand against Colonel Steele is undeniable, but its contents remain classified or "classifiable." Mr. Waddington knew ahead of time that this would be the MJ's ruling based on the "back room" meetings. Military trials routinely prohibit certain things from being said in the courtroom, and unless one is privy to the pre-trial hearings, no one will ever know what was prohibited. This is a systemic, secret component of purportedly "open" trials.

There then ensued a long discussion as to whether or not to admit a sentence supposedly overheard by a soldier: that Sergeant Girouard allegedly said, "this is going to test our brotherhood" at some point in the alleged conspiracy. The prosecutor wished to admit the statement, and the defense wished to exclude it on the grounds that the witness was not present at the meeting and was not aware of the context for the remark. He simply heard the phrase about testing the brotherhood of soldiers as a random remark. Following a long debate, the MJ ruled: "The court will not permit Sergeant Acevedo to testify as to that statement."

The MJ then turned to the multiple issues surrounding Private Mason as the government's star witness. Again, the Good Soldier template is introduced into the discussion as a legal technique for one side to pursue and the other side to tear down:

> MJ: You qualified your response as it relates to any statements made by Private First Class Mason that might refer to a trip to Thailand as well as any other criminal activity Private Mason may have referred to. Am I right?

> CDC: That's correct, Your Honor.

> MJ: Why do you believe that's relevant?

> CDC: Your Honor, as we laid out there, unless the gov — we can't bring that testimony in unless the government somehow during the trial opens the door. For example, they start unloading a lot of Good Soldier character evidence on, which we cold object to but we may not on Mason. If they try to show that he's a Good Soldier. He's a brave man that came forward, just an all-around good citizen, then we think that may possibly open the door to impeach his general good character or his Good Soldier character.

> MJ: Well what would make his Good Soldier character relevant in the first place?

> CDC: We could not make that relevant, Your Honor. They could ask questions to him. For example, the Article 32, and he's been sort of portrayed by a lot of people as this brave young man that came forward, you know, he had the courage to come forward. He's a Good Soldier. He's the type of Soldier this Army needs. On the other hand, and that testimony came out once he was impeached with constant criminal lying, but if the government somehow opens the door to his Good Soldier character, if they bring in evidence that he's a Good Soldier and we don't object to it, then it may open the door, Your Honor. I know it's a stretch.

> MJ: Government, do you intend to elicit evidence that Private First Class Mason is a Good Soldier?

> ATC2: No, Your Honor. We're not going to bolster the credibility of our witness unless it's attacked and we have to rebut it, but we're not going to talk about his character for being a Good Soldier. We're going to talk about — we're going to ask him questions that are relevant.

Several aspects of this exchange are worth analyzing. First, the issue is not whether Mason was a good soldier in the everyday sense of asking whether one is a good football player or a good student in the civilian world. Rather, Good Soldier refers to an archetype or symbol in Army culture that carries enormous meaning at the same time that it is used by both the prosecution and the defense as one of many techniques in the legal arsenal at their disposal. The strictly legal debates about the Good

Soldier defense[1] are of less concern here than the cultural import of this defense. In the civilian social world, it does not matter culturally or legally whether one is a good or bad person with regard to guilt or innocence. American civilian culture focuses on the act, not the character of the accused. However, American military culture allows for the Soldier's character to play a role in determining the relative degree of guilt or innocence, albeit, at the discretion of the judge, and subject to cross-examination by the opposing side. Second, the cultural question is not whether Mason *or* Hunsaker were the Good Soldier. Rather, it seems that both Mason *and* Hunsaker were the Good Soldier, depending upon one's reference group or point of view. From the prosecution's perspective, Mason was the Good Soldier for reporting the killings, but if the prosecution admits this, then the defense will try to destroy the image of Mason as the Good Soldier. For this reason, the prosecutor said that he would not try to portray Mason as the Good Soldier initially. From the perspective of the defense, Mason ratted out his friends, and more importantly, was coerced and intimidated by the Army into making false statements. For these reasons, from their perspective, he was not the Good Soldier. On the other hand, from the perspective of the defense, Hunsaker was the Good Soldier for carrying out the ROE on the infamous mission at issue. However, the prosecution cannot admit this characterization, so that it had to try to destroy Hunsaker's symbol as a Good Soldier and turn it into that of the bad soldier who committed murder. The reader may wonder: Which one of them, in fact, was a good soldier? Is one of these good soldiers better than the other? There is no way to answer these and related questions objectively. Everything depends on the reference group one chooses as one's reference point in conceptualizing the issue.

> MJ: If you have evidence that would demonstrate Private First Class Mason has a motive to fabricate his testimony be it that he himself was under investigation for something or some other motive to fabricate, then you would be permitted to elicit that evidence, but it is difficult for the court to understand how the evidence of Good Soldier qualities of Private First Class Mason would be admissible at all; therefore, Government, you won't elicit such testimony, such evidence.

> ATC2: Correct, Your Honor.

> MJ: And then you won't have the need to rebut it with additional inadmissible evidence.

> CDC: Yes, Your Honor.

> MJ: However, that doesn't necessarily impact the defense's ability to otherwise bring out admissible evidence that may go to Private First Class Mason's credibility or any motive to fabricate.... But simply trying to rebut otherwise inadmissible testimony with additional inadmissible testimony will not be permitted.

---

1   For example, see Eugene R. Fidell and Dwight Hall Sullivan, *Evolving Military Justice* (Annapolis: U.S. Naval Institute Press, 2002) and Elizabeth Lutes Hillman, "The good soldier defense: character evidence and military rank at court-martial," *Yale Law Journal*, Volume 108, 1999.

In plain English, the judge seems to be stating simply that the Army's cultural archetype of the Good Soldier may not be invoked with regard to Mason by either the prosecution or the defense, and that the usual rules of evidence and cross-examination will apply. I leave it up to legal scholars to argue the merits or consequences of the judge's decision. But from the point of view of the sociologist, the immediate consequence is that a military jury — had there been one in Hunsaker's trial — would have been allowed by the judge to entertain the thought, "the accused is a Good Soldier, and for that reason he may not be as guilty as the prosecution claims," but would *not* have been allowed to entertain the thought, "the primary accuser, Mason, is a Good Soldier, and for this reason his motives in betraying the accused are noble."

LEGAL CHARGES AND THEORIES

The MJ then asked the prosecutor: "Government, I understand what has been alleged on the charge sheets. Is it the — does the government believe there is any theory of criminal culpability other than that alleged on the charge sheet?" The judge's reference to "theory" constitutes more lawspeak that is incomprehensible to the layperson. Mr. Waddington explained to me:

> The judge made us present our theories to determine if the witnesses were in fact relevant based on our theory. The prosecution said that it was either 1st degree murder or nothing. They called their boss and had a discussion. The boss told them to agree that the men could have shot if they tried to escape and to agree that they were declared hostile. By agreeing that the men were declared hostile/al-Qaida, they made many of the witnesses irrelevant. This was different from the Article 32 where they claimed that the men were innocent farmers. The problem here is that they could double cross us at trial and we would be without our witnesses.[1]

From a commonsense perspective, it seems that the opposing attorneys are playing a game of chess with the accused's future at stake. Clearly, the prosecutor's moves and counter-moves had more to do with winning the case than with the reality of what happened in Samarra on May 9th. Translated into the jargon of the social sciences, the legal system seems to demand "deductive thinking" (testing pre-conceived hypotheses) rather than "inductive thinking" (coming to a conclusion based upon all the facts).

For our present purposes, and in layperson's terms, the issue comes down to the following: popular culture portrays American court trials on television and in films as primarily inductive. Supposedly, the jury absorbs a massive amount of seemingly unrelated facts, and comes to a decision in the name of "the people." Supposedly, all the witnesses tell "the truth, the whole truth, and nothing but the truth." What popular culture omits is that the judge and opposing attorneys are working from the opposing, deductive model of reality. They filter which "truths" and facts the jury will be allowed to hear, and they never know about the "truths" and facts which the judge excluded from their consideration. In practice, juries are never exposed to the "whole truth," but to two opposing, deductive "theories" of the truth. The sobering reality is

---

1 From a phone interview with Mr. Waddington.

that "truths" which may set a client free also may not be permissible in court. For example, we have seen that the MJ closed the door to the possibility of reading Colonel Steele's reprimand in court. No doubt, the average person will wonder, "What is in that reprimand, why did the government go through such great pains to cover it up, and what would have been its impact on Hunsaker's case?" One will never know.

The prosecutor asked for a long recess to reply to the judge's question on theory. The court session recessed at 3:59 p.m. and was called back to order at 5:47 p.m. According to Mr. Waddington, most of the time, the prosecutor was on the phone with his boss discussing how to proceed. When court resumed, the MJ pronounced without explanation that the government "did not intend to pursue any other theory of criminal culpability other than which is charged." The MJ then reviewed a large number of exhibits for the proposed trial which were numbered in Roman script, as in, "Exhibit LXXXIII." Why wouldn't the Army use English numbers? The sociologist Thorstein Veblen noted long ago that the use of archaic scripts denotes prestige.[1] In general, people attribute high status and respect to things and matters that are difficult for them to comprehend, and regard as low status or vulgar things and matters that the average person can comprehend. Veblen's uncanny insight suggests that trials and court proceedings such as this one are treated with respect in proportion as they are mysterious. The MJ asked whether there were any other matters of any sort that should be entered into the record, including e-mails. After both sides answered in the negative, the MJ announced that "the government is asking for 5 February 2007" as the trial date. Mr. Waddington indicated that he was free on that date. The MJ recessed at 6:10 p.m. and called the session back to order at 6:43 p.m.

The MJ then issued a series of rulings: "The defense Motion to Dismiss for Lack of Speedy Trial under Article 10 of the Uniform Code of Military Justice is denied." Next, the MJ ruled that "the government's Motion to Continue ... marked as Appellate Exhibit XCVI is granted." The MJ continued:

> The defense Motion for Appropriate Relief under R.C.M. 305 (k) is granted in part. The court will award the accused the appropriate Allen credit. The court will award the accused 1 day for every day of pretrial confinement up to 5 December 2006. The court will award the accuse 2 days for every day the accused continues administrative segregation at the Charleston Naval Brig, or at any other pretrial confinement facility, until the date of trial, not including the day of trial.

Note that the MJ did not order that Hunsaker be taken out of solitary confinement (renamed "administrative segregation"), only that he be given 2 days credit toward his eventual sentence for every 1 day the government continued the harsh treatment against him. The MJ did not criticize the government's treatment of Hunsaker in any way. The court "awarded" the accused with "credit" for his suffering, but did not condemn it or order it ceased. The choice of terminology suggests that the Army is always right. Finally, the MJ asked Mr. Waddington to enter a plea to all charges and specifications on behalf of the accused. "Not guilty," Mr. Waddington replied. At 6:52 p.m. on 13 November 2006, the MJ's last words were, "Court is in recess until

---

1 Thorstein Veblen, *The Theory of the Leisure Class* (New York: Penguin, [1899] 1965).

0900, 5 February 2007." However, he actually called the court back to order at 9:59 a.m. on 11 January 2007.

A lot of behind-the-scenes drama occurred between November 13, 2006 and January 11, 2007. According to Mr. Waddington, the prosecutor sought to resolve all the cases through plea-bargains rather than trials by military juries. To this end, he offered the defense team a deal that they could not refuse: the guaranteed sentence of eighteen years with possibility of parole and a promise to drop the possibility of a death penalty in exchange for Hunsaker accepting a plea-bargain and dropping his demand for a trial by military jury. Other conditions would be attached as well, including the promise by the defense team not to mention Colonel Steele or the ROE in the plea bargain hearing. Apparently, Hunsaker was delighted to take the "deal," and escape the threat of the death penalty. The majority of cases in American civil and criminal cases are "settled" prior to going to trial. In this sense, the ending of this atypical case was typical. However, the average American does not seem to know this cynical fact about the settlement of cases.

For example, Hunsaker's family, like all the other families of the accused that I have come to know, believed that if a jury were to know all the facts of the case, they would find their sons innocent or at least guilty of far-lesser crimes. In fact, the average views of average families in this regard are accurate. Juries, too, tend to view "war crimes" from a more average point of view than judges. A military defense attorney did a research study on sentencing in such cases and found that soldiers who plead guilty to premeditated murder involving an Iraqi prisoner were sentenced to an average of 8.27 years by a judge. But soldiers who contested their charges and whose cases went before military juries were sentenced to an average of 3.79 years. Attorneys for both the defense and the prosecution are well-aware of this trend. For this reason, the average trial process becomes a cynical contest or sport of sorts between opposing attorneys: prosecutors seek to avoid trials by jury and defense attorneys do all they can to get a speedy trial by jury. We have seen this tendency illustrated in the arguments between Captain Fischbach and Mr. Waddington.

CHAPTER 8. THE PLEA-BARGAIN HEARING AS A DEGRADATION CEREMONY

"The case against Clevinger was open and shut. The only thing missing was
something to charge him with."
— Joseph Heller, p. 75

It was 9:59 a.m. on the 11th of January 2007. The court session began for what the
military calls an Article 39 hearing. The accused answered "Yes, sir" to a long series
of questions by the MJ: Did the accused remember from previous court hearings that
he has a right to counsel? Did he still want to be represented by Captain Maloney
and Mr. Waddington? Did he remember his rights? Did he previously state that he
wished to be tried by a military jury? Did he change his mind? Did he recall the difference "between trial before members and trial before military judge alone?" Did he sign
Appellate Exhibit CIX indicating that he wished to be tried by military judge alone?
At the time he signed this document, did he know that this particular MJ would be
the military judge in his case? Was the accused soldier's request voluntary? The questions went on and on, with the manifest purpose of demonstrating forever that the
government respected all of the rights of the accused.

MJ: If I approve your request for trial by me alone, you give up your right to be
tried by a court composed of members. Do you understand that?

ACC: Yes, sir.

MJ: Your request is approved. The court is assembled. [The Article 39(a) session
terminated and the court-martial began at 1001, 11 January 2007]

It took three minutes for Hunsaker to give up his right to a trial by military jury.
What followed is referred to typically as a "court-martial." However, in some ways it
was a simulacrum court-martial. This is because the MJ would not really determine
Hunsaker's guilt or innocence — the accused had already worked out all the details
with the Convening Authority down to the 18-year sentence that he would receive
in exchange for pleading guilty to certain charges. Possible surprises included the

chances that the MJ might sentence the accused to a sentence lower than eighteen years, but not greater. This possibility was remote. Another potential surprise would have been the accused changing his mind at any point in the ritual and claiming that he was not guilty. I know that he was warned by his attorneys not to do this. If he did, the MJ had the right to disavow the plea-bargain, continue the court-martial and sentence the accused as he pleased. An additional trap is that the MJ had to state on the record that he was convinced that the accused was making this plea-bargain "voluntarily," and that the accused was "really" pleading guilty. If the MJ was not convinced of Hunsaker's "sincerity" in the ritual, he again had the option to invalidate the plea-bargain and convert the hearing into a real court-martial. In summary, this court session was not a real court-martial and not a simulacra court-martial either, because it could convert from simulacra to real court-martial at any moment. Every person in the courtroom surely knew that Hunsaker was making the plea-bargain out of fear and intimidation, wishing to avoid the possibility of a life sentence without parole or worse, the death penalty. Yet he had to engage in "fake sincerity" throughout the ritual in order to avoid the real and fearful possibility of this severe sentence.

"Specialist William B. Hunsaker, how do you plead?" the MJ asked, and added, "Mr. Waddington will speak for you." Indeed, this was a dangerous juncture, and an accused might lose his composure or stumble through the lengthy and confusing list of "specifications" and "charges," which would destroy the ritual. Mr. Waddington kept his composure and read all the specifications and charges, and pleaded guilty to all of them except that he pleaded "not guilty" to "the Specifications 1 and 2 of Charge IV and Charge IV" and "to the Specifications 1 and 2 of Additional Charge II and Additional Charge II." I have sat through such rituals on other occasions, and always found them confusing for the simple reason that the charges and specifications are never actually stated. It really does not matter, because this entire exchange had been rehearsed ahead of time. The layperson and the public are excluded from purportedly "public" trials by the rituals and legalese language. It is much like signing a hundred page plus contract to buy a house. Who really understands everything to which their signature attests they approved? The MJ then read a statement to the accused that I have heard on other occasions. It is a standard, boiler-plate speech:

> Your plea of guilty will not be accepted unless you understand its meaning and effect. I am going to discuss your plea of guilty with you.... A plea of guilty is equivalent to a conviction, *and it's the strongest form of proof known to the law.* On your plea alone, and without receiving any evidence, this court can find you guilty of the offenses to which you have pled guilty. Your plea will not be accepted unless you realize that by your plea you admit every act or omission and element of the offenses to which you are pleading guilty, and that you are pleading guilty because you actually are, in fact, guilty. If you do not believe that you are guilty, then you should not for any reason plead guilty. Do you understand everything I just told you? [emphasis added]

Hunsaker replied, "Yes, Sir." It is a wonder that a plea of guilty is "the strongest form of proof known to the law" given the widespread knowledge among lawyers that most cases are settled by plea-bargains on the basis of cost-benefit analyses to the accused and the government, as well as fear and intimidation for the accused. The MJ was engaging in legal fiction, and everyone in the courtroom went along with it. The MJ went on to explain that by his plea of guilty, the accused gave up three important rights: first, the right against self-incrimination; second, the right to a trial of the facts by the court; and third, the right to be confronted by and to cross-examine any witnesses called against him. The MJ asked the accused whether he had any questions and whether he understood that he no longer had these rights. Hunsaker answered "no" to the first question and "yes" to the second. Then the MJ read to Hunsaker:

> MJ: If you continue with your guilty plea, you will be placed under oath, and I will question you to determine whether you are, in fact, guilty of the offenses to which you have pled guilty. Anything that you tell me may be used against you in the sentencing portion of this trial. Do you understand that?

> ACC: Yes, sir.

> MJ: If you tell me anything that is untrue, your statements can be used against you later for charges of perjury or making false statements. Do you understand that?

> ACC: Yes, sir.

It is as if the legal profession does not grasp the obvious contradiction that if a guilty plea is "the strongest form of proof known to the law," then there should be no need for a judge to determine whether the accused (who has pled guilty) is, "in fact, guilty." Clearly, one is in the realm of irrational ritual, not rational discourse, in this portion of the hearing. The system demands the appearance of sincerity from the accused who pleads guilty, yet any possibility of real sincerity is thwarted by the threats issued by the judge. Family members who watch the proceedings are typically confused by this portion of the ritual. On the one hand, I have heard mothers tell me that the judges seemed caring in wanting to make sure that their sons admitted they were "really" guilty, which brought up mixed emotions in the mothers toward their sons. On the other hand, they heard defense lawyers instruct their sons to agree with and not contradict anything the judges said, or there would be dire consequences. Indeed, the average layperson is bound to find this portion of the ritual to be very confusing.

The MJ wanted the accused to read through various prosecution exhibits, but the printer in the courtroom would not work properly, so there was some delay and confusion. When Mr. Waddington finally produced a printed copy, the MJ made a Freudian slip. He referred to Hunsaker as "Specialist Waddington — excuse me, Specialist Hunsaker, you have now seen Prosecution Exhibits 1 through 18." For those who take Freud seriously, a possible interpretation of this slip is that the MJ unconsciously regarded both the accused and his civilian defense counsel with contempt.[1] The MJ asked Hunsaker whether he was "voluntarily entering into this stipulation because you believe it is in your best interest to do so?" "Yes, sir," Hunsaker replied.

---

1 Sigmund Freud, *The Psychopathology of Everyday Life* (New York: W.W. Norton, [1902] 1965).

The contents of the stipulation were not revealed, but presumably they included the terms of the plea-bargain. Then the MJ issued another scary-sounding statement:

> Specialist Hunsaker, a stipulation of fact ordinarily cannot be contradicted. If this stipulation should be contradicted, after I have accepted your guilty plea, I am going to have to reopen this providence inquiry. You should, therefore, let me know if there is anything whatsoever you disagree with or feel is untrue.

Again, the layperson with commonsense will notice the double-bind: If the accused finds anything "whatsoever" objectionable in the plea-bargain, then severe consequences will follow. On the other hand, if the accused feels too intimidated to voice any objections to the stipulations, then other severe consequences may follow. The accused is in a lose–lose situation. The MJ asked the accused to read the stipulations silently. The two opposing attorneys conferred with each other and with their counterparts. The MJ said: "It appears, Mr. Waddington, that you would like to delete the names 'Specialist Graber' and 'Sergeant Lemus' from the second sentence of Paragraph 12, is that correct?" The government agreed with the change, and the accused was asked for his approval. This must have been a tense time for the defense, because the MJ had just warned that *any* changes to the stipulation would have dire consequences and that the stipulation could not be changed. Yet the stipulation had errors in it, because humans err. Luckily for the accused, the errors were changed, the government did not object, and the MJ proceeded with the ritual.

Once Hunsaker agreed that the corrected stipulation was true, the MJ said to him that he would ask him for each "element" in the charge sheet, "Is the element true and second, whether you wish to admit that it's true?" What is the difference between the two questions? Perhaps in the reference group of judges, one can agree that something is true yet not wish to admit that it is true. But for the average person, to admit that something is true is to believe that something is true. The reference group of lawyers and judges is remote from the reference group of the common person. The MJ also explained that "by elements, I mean those facts which the prosecution would have to prove beyond a reasonable doubt before you could be found guilty, if you had pled not guilty." It is difficult to comprehend this statement. The accused did not plead "not guilty." So the accused has to plead guilty to every element *as if* he had pled "not guilty" to it and been found guilty by a judge or a jury. But this hypothetical "as if" scenario omits the possibility that if the accused had challenged the charges, he might have been found not guilty or guilty of lesser charges.

The MJ read through every charge and specification before asking Hunsaker the two questions mentioned above, but he made mistakes in reading. For example, in the specifications of Charge III, the MJ referred to conspiracy against "the third military detainee." Could this have been another Freudian slip? The prosecutor said:

> ATC1: Your Honor, I don't mean to quibble, but it is actually "male detainee" which is contained in the specifications, not "military detainee." I am sure we're all clear. I just want to be certain on that.

> MJ: Did I confuse you in anyway, Specialist Hunsaker?

ACC: No, Your Honor.

MJ: I don't recall whether you answered my question. Do you wish me to repeat any of the elements of the specifications of Charge III?

ACC: No, Your Honor.

The MJ did not admit his mistake. He asked Hunsaker whether he had confused him, and of course, Hunsaker answered that he was not confused. Yet the prosecutor was confused! The average reader might be confused. Moreover, in this awkward moment, the MJ stated on the record that he did not hear Hunsaker's reply, when clearly the court recorder transcribed it. The situation is reminiscent of ministers who foul up the ritual words required to consecrate a wedding, or more memorably, the Supreme Court Justice misspeaking the oath of office at President Obama's inauguration. The MJ continued reading as if there had been no problem, and turned to the charge of conspiracy:

> The agreement and conspiracy does not have to be in any particular form or expressed in formal words. It is sufficient if the minds of the parties reach a common understanding to accomplish the object of the conspiracy, and this may be proved by the conduct of the parties. The agreement does not have to express the manner in which the conspiracy is to be carried out, or what part each conspirator is to play.... Now, based on the stipulation of fact, I also advise you that a member of a conspiracy is criminally responsible under the law for any offense which is committed by any member of the conspiracy in furtherance of that conspiracy.

I have often heard military judges read this same speech on conspiracy, and each time I find it perplexing. In plain English, and with regard to the reference group of "the people," the legal definition of conspiracy states that one does *not* have to conspire in the ordinary sense of the term (use words, have a plan, delegate responsibility, act in secret, and so on) in order to be guilty of conspiracy in the legal sense. Note that the conspiracy does not even "have to be in any particular form." Lawyers, judges, and to some extent juries supposedly determine what is in "the minds of the parties" who are accused of conspiracy, even if their overt behavior does not correspond to what is allegedly in their minds. I have heard exasperated defense attorneys state that conspiracy is whatever the government wants it to be. And government prosecutors frequently charge suspects with conspiracy in order to obtain more severe sentences and also to convict other alleged co-conspirators of more serious crimes. As the judge informed Hunsaker, a co-conspirator need not be convicted of the overt crime in question — being a co-conspirator automatically makes one guilty of what someone else did.

In truth, one will never know what was in the minds of the accused in the Operation Iron Triangle killings. What the accused and other witnesses said about the crime in question changed many times and was always filtered through various interrogation techniques, fear, intimidation, group loyalty, military protocol, and a host of other factors. The legal definition of conspiracy is out of sync with everyday, common understandings of conspiracy. Throughout this book, I have argued that according to the commonsense understanding of conspiracy, the government, Hunsaker's commanders, prosecutors, and CID agents conspired against Hunsaker and his comrades in order to cover up the unlawful ROE.

The MJ also read to Hunsaker that "the intent to kill does not have to exist for any measurable or particular length of time before your act constituted the attempt." Philosophers and psychologists have written seemingly countless volumes on how the intent to kill comes and goes even in the minds of people who do not kill; how the intent to kill is difficult to ascertain even by the individual who allegedly does the intending; and how difficult it is for outside observers to know what goes on in the mind of an individual.[1] Yet, for the reference group of lawyers and judges, these difficult issues do not pose a problem. The legal profession pretends that it has solved philosophical problems that continue to baffle scholars, and it can determine a person's intentions from an act. At the same time, the legal profession continues to ignore genuinely psychological and sociological factors which serve as mitigation (sleep deprivation, combat stress, unit morale, and so on).

On and on the judge read, as I have observed other judges read these same words. It almost comes as a relief to the reader that the prosecutor interrupted by noticing yet another mistake by the MJ:

> ATC1: Your Honor, once again, I don't mean to quibble, but you drew the accused's attention to Additional Charge III, but are providing instructions on conspiracy to obstruct justice. Additional Charge III is actual obstruction of justice. The conspiracy to obstruct justice is contained in Additional Charge I.

> MJ: Captain Fischback [sic], I was reading the elements as it relates to Additional Charge I and the Specification. Did I misstate and say I was reading elements as it related to The Specification of Additional Charge III?

> ATC1: You did, Your honor, you drew the accused to that particular specification.

> MJ: Specialist Hunsaker, did I confuse you in anyway as it related to The Specification to which I was referring? In other words, I was reading you the elements applicable to The Specification of Additional Charge I and Additional Charge I. Did you understand that?

> ACC: Yes, Your Honor.

The prosecutor did not understand what the MJ was saying. I recall attorneys being confused as to which charge or specification was which at various trials. Yet the accused answers meekly that he understands what was said. The MJ continued reading, and finally allowed the accused to speak in words that are easy to comprehend:

> MJ: All right. Specialist Hunsaker, at this time, I want you to tell me why you are guilty of The Specification of Charge II. *Just tell me* what happened.

---

1 The most salient authors on these topics are Sigmund Freud, Emile Durkheim, William James, and Arthur Schopenhauer.

ACC: Well, Your Honor, I realize that I illegally was breaking the law when I attempted to kill three of these individuals.... Sergeant Girouard told me and Clagett to go out and kill them, and that's what was done....

MJ *Just tell me* what happened, Specialist Hunsaker. *Just tell me what was going on at the time* [emphasis added].

Note that the MJ changed his tone and vocabulary after he stopped reading, and used the folksy expression, "just tell me." It is as if the MJ was doing his best to bridge the abyss between the language of the reference group of the legal profession and the language of the ordinary soldier. Hunsaker explained what happened in his own words:

ACC: Well, Your Honor, we had just done completed this objective. We had these four detainees in total, and we had them all four outside. Lieutenant Wehrheim was getting to ready to leave the objective with the 2nd squad.... I came inside and we were all standing around, and Sergeant Girouard was like, okay, this is what we are going to do. He said, "These guys, we are going to cut them loose and we are going to kill them."... He had me, Mason, and Clagett stay behind, and he gave us three the orders to kill these three individuals....

MJ: Do you believe that was an order by Sergeant Girouard?

ACC: It came from his mouth, Your Honor.

MJ: Well, how did you interpret it?

ACC: It was an order from him to me. It was him telling me what to do....

MJ; Do you understand that even though the order provided by Staff Sergeant Girouard was an unlawful order, your compliance with that order could be a defense under certain circumstances, understand that?

ACC: I understand, Your Honor.

MJ: For example, if you didn't know it was an unlawful order that may provide you a defense to the offenses to which you have pled guilty. Do you understand that?

ACC: Yes, Your Honor.

MJ: So, under certain circumstances, an unlawful order may be a defense if you didn't know it was unlawful *and if the order was one which a person of ordinary commonsense under the circumstances would have known to be unlawful.* Do you understand that?

ACC: Yes, Your Honor. (My emphasis.)

It is doubtful that the accused understood the MJ's legal lecture. Jurists and law professors constantly debate and disagree with each other concerning judges' interpretations. Who is this imaginary person of "ordinary commonsense under the circumstances," and what would he or she have "known" versus said in court versus truly believed? It is true that the MJ used the term "commonsense," which I have also been using throughout this book. It is also true that judges routinely instruct juries to make their verdicts based on "commonsense." But I have heard judges such as Colonel William Pohl argue that compliance with an unlawful order is *not* a permissible defense. Judges, jurists, and legal scholars do *not* agree on this issue.

What would a person of ordinary commonsense conclude about the unlawful ROE as it was passed down from Colonel Steele through many commissioned officers to Sergeant Girouard and finally to Hunsaker? It should be obvious to the reader that the unlawful order was treated as a lawful order from the Brigade Commander all the way through and down the chain of command to Sergeant Girouard. If all those commissioned as well as noncommissioned officers "knew" or acted as if the unlawful order was lawful, commonsense tells us that the MJ is putting an unreasonable burden on the accused to be the only one in the chain who should have figured out that it was an unlawful order. To the extent that the phrase "commonsense" has a meaning, commonsense dictates that the officers had the education, training, and obligation (enshrined in the doctrine of command responsibility) to disobey the unlawful order long before it reached the accused, who is the lowest-ranking "grunt" in the chain of command.

Why was the MJ pretending that "commonsense" puts all the responsibility onto the accused, and exonerates his superiors? I dare say that the average American knows that the grunt infantry soldier's job is to obey orders and expects elected leaders to make sure the orders are lawful and in the name of the people. Commonsense also suggests that the accused agrees with whatever the MJ says out of fear that he might get a life sentence or the death penalty.

"Tell me what happened to MD3," the MJ said to Hunsaker, referring to the third prisoner. The accused replied: "As far as to my knowledge, sir, was that I guess he didn't die all the way due to inaccurate shooting, and was later shot by Specialist Graber, but as far as me physically seeing it or knowing exactly what happened, I don't know." The accused's medically incorrect phrase "didn't die all the way" suggests the tacit understanding by the soldiers that every Iraqi male on the island was supposed to "die all the way," which is to say, that no prisoners were to be taken.

The accused then explained to the MJ that when Girouard discovered what had happened (even though he allegedly gave the order to shoot the prisoners), "he pulls out his pocket knife, his little Gerber pocket knife and flips it open, and makes the comment, 'It's got to look good'." And Girouard allegedly proceeded to slash Hunsaker on his arm and face to make it seem as if the accused had been attacked by the prisoners. If these allegations are true, it seems that the cover-up of the killings began almost immediately. However, one should also note that Girouard's alleged actions suggest that he was torn between two reference groups. The higher-ranking officers above him in the chain of command, such as First Sergeant Geressy, were clearly angry that any Iraqis were left alive, and he was complying with their orders. We have seen that Charlie Company had a history of covering up "mistakes" of this sort, so that the cover-up strategies were pre-established. In one sense, the tendency to cover up atrocities of this sort had already been established by the command. At the same time, Girouard was identifying with the enlisted soldiers as part of his reference group, and protecting them. And we have seen throughout this discussion that the entire military unit was involved in the cover-up from the top to the bottom of the chain of command. Because these points are crucial to the entire discussion, I would like to quote from Samuel Stouffer's scientific description of the conflict experienced by Sergeant Girouard as a non-commissioned officer:

> The writer became especially interested in the problem when considering the strains to which the non-commissioned officer in the Army was subjected. On the one hand, the non-com had the role of agent of the command and in the case the orders from above conflicted with what his men thought were right and necessary he was expected by his superiors to carry out the orders. But he also was an enlisted man, sharing enlisted men's attitudes, often hostile attitudes, toward the commissioned ranks. Consequently, the system of informal controls was such as to reward him for siding with the men in a conflict situation and punish him if he did not. There was some evidence that unless his men had confidence that he could see their point of view, he was an ineffective leader; on the other hand, open and flagrant disobedience by him of an order from above could not be tolerated by the command.[1]

It is amazing how accurately Stouffer's theoretical analysis from the year 1949 still fits the nuances, details, and facts that have been uncovered in this analysis concerning this incident. The MJ and the government would have one believe that Girouard and the co-accused were ordinary criminals. Stouffer's analysis of the American soldier reminds us that Girouard and his men were *soldiers* and as such experienced role conflicts that are unique to the army and their particular roles in the army. In plain language, Girouard and the others were not merely covering up a crime. Girouard was behaving as a non-com was expected to behave on a mission, even if the mission had gone sour. The judge continued with his questions:

> MJ: Did he [Girouard] explain what he was talking about?

> ACC: No, Your Honor, he didn't. All he said was, "Got to look good." And that's what we done. And I kind of — I started cursing at him because I didn't know what he was doing. And when he stopped, he left and that was when "Doc" came in to clean it.

If the accused did not know what Girouard was doing or why, commonsense suggests that the soldiers did *not* engage in a conspiracy prior to the killings. The MJ called for a recess at 11:18 a.m. When the court-martial was called back to order at 12:25 p.m., the MJ explained:

> During the recess, the court held what is called an R.C.M. 802 conference. Basically what that is, it is a meeting between the defense counsel, the trial counsel, and myself. At that time the government notified the court that they wished to amend two of the specifications. Do you want to identify your motion, Captain Fishback [sic]?

---

1 Samuel Stouffer (1949) "An analysis of conflicting social norms," *American Sociological Review* 14(06):707-17.

The prosecutor "identified" the "Specification of Additional Charge I and The Specification of Additional Charge III, essentially to omit any mention of Private First Class Clagett" — but no one other than the MJ and the attorneys knew what he was talking about. Nevertheless, Hunsaker dutifully answered "Yes, Your Honor" when the MJ asked him whether he still wanted to plead guilty to the amended charges and specifications. At long last, the MJ seemed satisfied that Hunsaker was "voluntarily" pleading guilty to all charges and specifications. The MJ turned to the prosecutor,

> MJ: Captain Fischbach, what do you calculate to be the maximum authorized punishment in this case, based solely upon the accused's guilty plea?
>
> ATC1: Reduction to the pay grade of E1; forfeiture of all pay and allowances; confinement for life without the possibility of parole; a dishonorable discharge; and a fine.
>
> MJ: Do you agree Mr. Waddington?
>
> CDC: Yes, Your Honor.
>
> MJ: Specialist Hunsaker ... based upon your guilty plea alone, this court could sentence you to the maximum punishment which I just stated. Do you understand that?
>
> ACC: Yes, Your Honor....
>
> MJ: Government, have you made arrangements for lunch for the accused?
>
> ATC1: Yes, Your Honor.
>
> MJ: Is this a good time to take that break?
>
> ATC1: It would be, Your Honor.
>
> MJ: How much time will be necessary?
>
> ATC1: I anticipate the accused's food will be here in about 10 minutes, Your Honor.
>
> MJ: So the food is not here yet?
>
> ATC1: It should be here in about 10 — yes sir.
>
> MJ: Then we will take a break in approximately 10 minutes.

There is something odd about the MJ threatening Hunsaker with the possibility of life imprisonment without the possibility of parole, then bringing up lunch, and then deciding to rush through the last stages of the proceeding prior to letting Hunsaker eat his lunch. The reference group of the legal profession seems to be out of sync with average American values. A more reasonable approach might have been to allow everyone to go to lunch and to finish the proceedings at a more leisurely pace following lunch. Perhaps the MJ and the government were fearful that the accused might change his mind about the plea-bargain during lunch. In any event, what followed — before the lunch break — was a seemingly endless, bureaucratic, and tedious reading of the plea-bargain. It is clear that the most important parts of the agreement, for the government, were that Hunsaker would be forced to testify against his comrades in exchange for a sentence of eighteen years instead of a life term without parole.

> MJ: Subparagraph 1c states that you are agreeing to cooperate fully with the United States Government in the following courts-martial: United States versus Clagett; United States versus Girouard; and United States versus Graber. Is that what you are agreeing to do?

> ACC: Yes, Your Honor.

> MJ: Now, "fully cooperate" is further defined in that particular paragraph. Have you discussed the expectations that the government has with you with your defense counsel?

> ACC: Yes, Your Honor....

> MJ: Now if you are called as a witness in any of those three cases, and either refuse to testify or testify falsely, do you understand that the Convening Authority is no longer going to be bound by your pre-trial agreement?

> ACC: Yes, Your Honor.

Worse than the consequences of a parole violation, the pre-trial agreement pressures the accused to say what is expected against his comrades, and if in the government's estimation he changed his testimony such that it is deemed "false," he may be sentenced to life without parole despite the agreement. Clearly, this is a contract that favors the government, not the accused. The MJ went through the other paragraphs and obtained the accused's agreement on the trial record. One subparagraph is particularly noteworthy:

> MJ: Subparagraph 1f states that you agree that the government will not be required to bring more than two witnesses located more than 50 miles outside of Fort Campbell, Kentucky. However, it goes on to state that you can present evidence in this court-martial in other ways, such as stipulations of expected testimony, letters, photographs, awards and certificates, and telephonic testimony. Is that your understanding?

> ACC: Yes, Your Honor.

According to the "commonsense" which the MJ invoked earlier in the proceeding, a soldier's life is in the balance, and the government is too cheap to bring more than two witnesses to testify on his behalf if they live more than 50 miles away. Subparagraph 4e seems particularly frightening:

> MJ: Subparagraph 4e states that if I refuse to accept your plea of guilty or I change your plea of guilty at any time during the trial that may also cause your pretrial agreement to be canceled. Now, I will tell you at this point in time that I intend to accept your plea of guilty, but there are cir-

cumstances that could occur before sentence is announced that would cause me to enter a plea of not guilty on your behalf to one or more of the specifications and charges. Do you understand that?

ACC: Yes, Your Honor.

MJ: Have you discussed that possibility with your defense counsel?

ACC: Yes, Your Honor.

Far from being a remote possibility, this is precisely what happened to Lynndie England, one of the so-called "rotten apples" in the Abu Ghraib courts-martial. For reasons no one in the court room could fathom, the MJ in that case, COL William Pohl, stopped her plea-bargain court proceeding and changed her plea to not guilty — against her objections and the objections of her defense attorneys. A new trial was ordered on her behalf, and she was given a much more severe sentence than the one in the plea-bargain. I have been told firsthand that defense attorneys are typically "sweating bullets" during the entire plea-bargain process because of the enormous power given to the MJ to accept or reject the accused's humble acceptance of all the charges and specifications. I have also learned that defense attorneys coach their clients to agree with the MJ on everything and disagree with nothing because of this fear of the judge's enormous power. The MJ's seemingly endless reading of similar threats continued relentlessly:

MJ: Now Paragraph 5 says that you understand that you may request to withdraw from your plea of guilty before I accept it — excuse me — after I have accepted it, but before sentence is announced, and if I grant that request, that that may cause your pretrial agreement to be canceled. Do you understand that?

ACC: Yes, Your Honor.

MJ: Now I am going to advise you, if for any reason or no reason whatsoever, you just simply change your mind prior to my acceptance of your plea of guilty and announcement of findings, that this pretrial agreement may be canceled, but you have the right to do that. Do you understand that?

ACC: Yes, Your Honor.

The MJ continued: "Paragraph 6 states that nothing in this agreement would prevent the United States Government from prosecuting you, should you provide false or untruthful information at any point." After several more pages of trial record, the MJ asked:

MJ: Now, Specialist Hunsaker, are you pleading guilty not only because you hope to receive a lighter sentence, but because you are convinced that you are, in fact, guilty of the offenses to which you have pled guilty?

ACC: I am pleading guilty, Your Honor, because I believe I am truly guilty of what I am accused of.

MJ: Do both counsel agree with the court's interpretation of the pretrial agreement?

ATC1: Yes, Your Honor.

CDC: Yes, Your Honor.

Commonsense dictates that were it not for the threats, enormous power of the MJ and the government, and fear of life imprisonment without parole, the accused would not agree to his guilt. After all, he had initially pled not guilty to all charges. Yet the ritual of the court-martial demands that the accused agree for the trial record to this and a series of related questions that followed. Did Hunsaker have enough time to discuss his case with his attorney? Did he consult fully with his attorneys? Was he satisfied with his attorneys? Was he satisfied with the advice given to him by his attorneys? Was he pleading guilty voluntarily and of his "own free will?" Hunsaker replied "Yes, Your Honor" to these and other questions. At long last, the MJ pronounced:

MJ: Specialist Hunsaker, I find that your plea of guilty is made voluntarily and with full knowledge of its meaning and effect... Specialist William B. Hunsaker, in accordance with your plea of guilty, this court finds you: Of all Charges and Their Specifications: Guilty. Please be seated. Government, have you received notice that the accused's lunch is available?

ATC1: It is here, Your Honor.

MJ: Court's in recess.

The court-martial recessed at 1:06 p.m., much past the ten minutes the MJ said he would fill. The MJ found Hunsaker guilty on page 246 of the typed court record. In other words, it took 245 pages of legal ritual to simply accept Hunsaker's plea-bargain. His reward for cooperating as he did was that he would be served lunch.

THE MITIGATION PHASE

Lunch was exactly one hour long, and the proceeding resumed at 2:06 p.m. on 11 January 2006. In my experience with courts-martial and lunch breaks, I have found that most military judges are obsessive about the lunch break being exactly sixty minutes long, not one minute more or less — as if they wait by the door with a stopwatch. It was quite different at the war crimes trials at the Hague, where one of the judges bicycled to meet his wife at a park for lunch, and was typically late in returning for trial. Cultural differences between the USA and Europe, the military and the civilian world, are very real when it comes to the meaning of the term "lunch break." Finally, I should add that on military bases, one hour is never enough for lunch, because the attorneys either order their food from civilian vendors on base or send assistants to go through a drive-through restaurant (usually a Burger King, which apparently won franchise rights with the US Army), while they work on the case. At best, lunch means wolfing down a less than healthy burger and fries while talking about legal issues and watching the clock nervously. The MJ said to the accused:

MJ: Court is called to order. All parties present prior to the recess are again present. Specialist Hunsaker, we now enter the sentencing phase of this trial. You have the right to present matters in extenuation and mitigation, that is, matters about the offenses and yourself that you want me to consider in deciding your sentence....

ACC: Yes, Your Honor.

The MJ decreed that Hunsaker would be given credit for 368 days toward his sentence, including 158 days "of extra credit for solitary or restricted confinement." The MJ did not elaborate or admonish the government for mistreating Hunsaker. He merely gave Hunsaker "extra credit" for his suffering — like getting "extra credit" on an examination taken by a student, in commonsense terms.

The first witness called by the defense to speak on behalf of Hunsaker's qualities as a good soldier was Sergeant First Class William Christy, "the platoon sergeant of the accused." As a Sergeant First Class and a noncommissioned officer over the course of seventeen years, Christy's position in the Army's hierarchy and the unit's chain of command is important. By virtue of his rank and position, he is not entitled to the formal respect and privileges of a commissioned officer (such as a captain), yet platoon sergeants typically elicit more common respect and trust from grunt soldiers than captains. The first sergeant as a platoon leader straddles two reference groups, the "by the book" commissioned officer and the common soldier. The defense attorney examined Christy on the witness stand:

Q: If you had to describe Specialist Hunsaker as a Soldier, what are the characteristics that stand out most in your mind?

A: Tactically and technically proficient, very well disciplined.

Q: Would you describe him as a professional?

A: Yes, sir.

Q: I assume that as a noncommissioned officer for 17 years, you've supervised a great many Soldiers of Specialist Hunsaker's age, experience, and grade.

A: Yes, sir.

Q: If you had to evaluate Specialist Hunsaker in comparison to these other Soldiers that you've supervised across your career, how does he fare in terms of that comparison?

A: One of the better Soldiers that I had, sir; always very well disciplined.

Q: In terms of Specialist Hunsaker as a duty performer, how would you describe him?

A: He always had a good work ethic; never had to go back and correct him or follow up and see if he did, you know, what he was asked to cause you always knew it was going to get done.

Could it be that Hunsaker's work ethic, as described by his platoon leader, was such that Hunsaker would make sure that the ROE — unlawful or lawful — was "going to get done?" The defense attorney continued with his questions:

Q: There's a term that we use in military law "Good Soldier" essentially describing someone as a Good Soldier which encompasses not on their duty performance, but also characteristics including their character, integrity, things of that nature. Knowing that this term encompasses not just his duty performance, but everything else about him, do you believe that Specialist Hunsaker is a Good Soldier?

A: Yes, sir.

Q: Sergeant First Class Christy, do you feel that you know Specialist Hunsaker well enough to form an opinion as to his rehabilitative potential, by which I mean his potential to be rehabilitated to a useful place in society?

A: Yes, sir.

Q: If I were to ask you to quantify that opinion on a scale of 1 to 10, 1 being the least potential and 10 being the greatest potential, where would Specialist Hunsaker's potential fall?

A: Between 9 and 10, sir.

Q: Sergeant First Class Christy, would you be willing to serve with Specialist Hunsaker again if that were possible?

A: Yes, sir.

The Army's "Good Soldier" archetype is the central motif of this book. Its meaning to the Army has been explained in the above exchange. One may extrapolate it and wonder whether all the soldiers on that infamous mission on that fateful day qualify as "Good Soldiers" in terms of Army culture, including Sergeant First Class Christy. The ROE was unlawful, but the soldiers were carrying out their duty as they saw it, and apparently believed in the positive character and integrity of their unit and cause. Samuel Stouffer illustrates this widespread belief about the duty of soldiers to obey with a rhyme: "Theirs not to make reply, theirs not to reason why, theirs but to do and die" (p. 65). Because commonsense would lead one to arrive at such a conclusion, the prosecutor engaged in a vigorous cross-examination of Christy on precisely the issue of the ROE in relation to duty and being a Good Soldier — even though this move contradicts the fact that the prosecutor forbade the defense from raising the issue of the ROE:

Q: You described the accused as a Good Soldier, correct?

A: Yes, sir.

Q: You described him as a professional, correct?

A: Yes, sir.

Q: And you said in the years of the Army service, he had received multiple briefings on the rules of engagement, and the law of war, correct?

A: Yes, sir.

Q: And it is unequivocally emphasized at all those briefings and all those classes that US soldiers do not murder or kill detainees, correct?

A: Yes, sir.

Q: Every Soldier under your supervision, underneath your command knows it is wrong to murder detainees, correct?

A: Yes, sir.

Q: We beat that into their heads, don't we?

A: Yes, sir.

Q: There's no question about it.

A: Yes, sir.

Q: You said you'd serve with the accused again.

A: Yes, sir.

What would be the commonsense appraisal of this exchange? It is that the Army has two sets of ROE which contradict each other. One set of ideal ROE prohibits the killing of prisoners, and the other ROE, which was issued for this mission, practically gave a green light to the killings. Commonsense suggests that one can empathize with the soldier's dilemma in dealing with this double-bind situation. Thus, the platoon sergeant rates Hunsaker highly as the Good Soldier and would serve with him again, at the same time that he agrees that the ideal ROE prohibit the crimes that were committed. The prosecutor does not push hard, most likely because he does not want this contradiction to be explored further on the record. The defense attorney simply wants the hearing to be over and for his client to receive the eighteen years in the plea bargain rather than life imprisonment, so he does not re-direct any questions to Christy.

Next, the accused's stepfather, Dan Hunsaker testified. The reader may recall that the stepfather was not approved to testify initially, but last-minute and additional pleadings by Mr. Waddington resulted in his being allowed to testify:

A: He is one of eight kids ... We done a lot of things together, pretty much with all my kids. We go camping, and fishing and stuff all the time together.... I adopted Billy when he was about nine years old, hi and his sister. He was real quiet and shy for the first year I'd say and then we just bonded good together, rode four-wheelers. He minded me good.... He was an excellent student; he never got in trouble in school. He graduated.

When he got out of high school, you know, I said, "Son, it's time to get a job." He went and got a job. He never missed his job, I mean, never missed a day. He went to work every day. Me and him lived together by ourselves for quite a while, and I mean, you know, he'd get off work, we'd clean house. I mean, we just done everything together.

Q: Is he — to your knowledge does he have any prior convictions, or has he ever gotten in any trouble with the law?

A: No, none.

Q: So this is the first run in with the law?

A: This is the first problem, yes, sir.

Q: Now were you involved in his decision to go ahead and join the Army?

A: Yes, sir. He had a recruiter to get him like a year early, and I told him, I said, "No, you have to wait till a certain age," and then I agreed with it, and so that's what he done.

Q: What was his attitude towards joining the Army? Why was he doing it?

A: That's what he wanted to do when he was about ten years old, and that's all I ever heard....

Q: And is it safe to say he's been a pretty patriotic young man?

A: Very.

Q: And even throughout this, and you've had lots of talks with him about what's going on and about his situation, has his attitude ever changed towards our country, or towards the military, towards the Army?

A: No way. He's 100 percent just like he was. He believes in his country. He believes in the Army, and it's just — it's just an unfortunate situation...

Q: Are you and your family going to be there to support him, and what support would you give him if he is given the chance to get out of prison earlier?

A: He'll have the same support as he always has. He'll have a loving family, and you know, wherever he's at we'll be with him 110 percent....

Q: You've sat here through this whole court-martial, right? You heard out of his mouth what had happened out there. Does that change anything, change the way you feel about your son?

A: Not at all.

Q: Why not?

> A: Because I love him. You love somebody, you love them from the heart, and it's always there, and he done what he felt he had to do at that point and time, and we all make mistakes, but we all should have a right to correct the mistakes and go on with our life.

The prosecutor had no questions, and the witness was excused. Perhaps the father's remarks in general and his concluding statement in particular best capture the ordinary American's "commonsense" views and values toward all the issues being examined in this war. It does seem to be the American credo that one should act sincerely in what one does and if one makes a mistake, one should have a chance to correct it. This set of core, cultural values can be found from President Obama's approach to the war in Iraq and the Wall Street meltdown that started in the year in 2008 to the soldiers and their families in the war in Iraq. In every court-martial case that I have witnessed, the soldiers had no prior criminal records. They were all patriotic and seemed to love the Army as if it were a substitute parent. I realize that this depiction of the soldiers and their families resembles Norman Rockwell paintings of American life, and in particular American military life. But that is the point: the cultural values in Rockwell's paintings could not have become iconic had they not resonated with the core cultural values of the US. The World War II generation is commonly referred to as "The Greatest Generation." On a more critically intellectual level, one should note that the prosecutor's depiction of Hunsaker and other soldiers in these incidents is out of sync with core American values. The prosecutor and the law try to force the accused into the reference group of the deviant who has a tendency to break the law. But, in fact, all the soldiers whose trials I have witnessed were typical "American kids" (including the fact that they came from broken homes, given that divorce is common in the US) who joined the Army and absorbed its values, and bonded emotionally to the institution as well as to their fellow-soldiers. The reference group of the "deviant" is simply out of sync with the reference group of the typical American kid.

The other component in the father's remarks that is typically American is his focus on love and social support despite his son's troubles. One should recall Ruth Benedict's contrary finding in *Chrysanthemum and the Sword* that, in World War II, Japanese families rejected their sons for becoming prisoners for any reason. Scores of other classic cross-cultural studies by Durkheim, Riesman and others have found that in general, tradition-directed societies reject the son who has been imprisoned or the daughter who has been raped, whether or not the "disgrace" was their fault or the fault of others. Shame and guilt pour out of the pages of ancient and traditional writings about the family. But the contemporary American cultural value system — which also pours out of recent films, stories, novels, and texts of all sorts — really does seem to be the "other-directed" nexus of values that was discovered by Riesman. Specifically, the other-directed, American type of response to "personal troubles" is that such troubles are never completely personal and always require social support.

Next, Hunsaker's mother, Frances Thexton, testified:

> Q: Could you please just give us an idea, and let the judge know what family members came out to support your son?

A: Sure. He has — he's the oldest of eight children. All of them are here. His oldest sister, Libby, is here. His grandmother, of course his dad, his step-dad, his uncle Willie, his Aunt Leslie; he even has his Catholic summer school teacher here, his brother Daniel, Clara. Mary is watching his niece and nephew in the hall. Did I miss anybody? There's a bunch of us.

Q: You all come from a big family?

A: Very. Very big, and we all support each other, especially Billy. We're very proud of him. This is an unfortunate mistake. Billy has always wanted to be a Soldier.... I kid you not, since he was five years old that's what he wanted to do. How he knows at five, I don't know, but he talked about it. I tried to talk him out of it a couple of times, but he had his heart set on it, and that was it.... He was never in trouble, ever. The worst trouble I remember him being in is when him and his youngest sister hid from his grandma in a creek out behind the house, *but he always did what he was told which may seem unusual for a boy, but that's the way he was*, and he was always afraid of getting in trouble. When I heard the news, first I thought there's no way; it couldn't be Bill, because he always tried to what was right; a very dedicated brother. I might be going into a little more than I should, but even at 12 and 13, how many boys at that age would come in, get their younger sisters up, get them ready for school, and then get his self ready. You know, 12 and 13, I mean just so that I could get a little extra sleep, you know. He just has a lot of character, a lot of integrity. A lot of times he would even tell on himself. I'm just really proud that he's telling the truth. That makes me very proud even when it's a bad situation. I'm just proud that he was able to stand up and say I did wrong, and Billy has always been goal oriented. Even when he went into the service, he had his goals set. He wanted to go to Ranger school... He was ready to make new goals, and he's not a vindictive person, he holds no grudges. He's ready to move on.

Q: And about that. I want to talk to you about that because, again, the judge is going to make a couple of decisions here. Since he decided to come forward and face the facts and accept responsibility, have you and he been discussing what his goals are for the future.

A: Yes.

Q: For example, this may seem odd, but wasn't he talking about what he wants to do in prison, what courses he wants to take, and how he wants to get this behind him so he can actually get into those courses?

A: Exactly, which I'm very proud of. I've always wanted all my kids to go to college. He wants to go to college and he has different options. He's a very intelligent individual, and very articulate, and he — so he has several options, I think.... He's an avid reader, and he just loves history so I'm trying to push him that way, but he wants to get his college degree while he's in there, get out.... I had a lot of concerns about what he wanted to do next because that's all he's wanted is to be a Soldier, and he wanted his career in the Army, but right away, he looked to what his other options were and I'm just really — I know this sounds really strange, but what's done is done. We want to move on, as a family, and I'm just excited that — I know — trying to use that word today is probably really kind of strange, but for Bill to get his college education and for him to start his family — to me it's exciting just to get past this and to see him move on with his future.

Q: Is there anything else you'd like to say to your son or the judge before you step down?

A: Bill, we love ya, and we're all very proud of you for what you've done, *and I want my son back.* He has so much more to offer. He really does, and he won't be making any mistakes, I promise you, and he does have a lot of integrity, and he does what he says he's going to do. That's all [emphasis added].

The prosecutor had no questions. Note that Hunsaker's mother said that the accused always did what he was told, and added that this may be unusual for a boy. Perhaps there is a connection between the boy and the soldier in that the accused did what he was told on the mission as well. From the descriptions of his family life by his parents, it does not seem that Hunsaker's reference group (his family) had any occasions to question the equivalent of an unlawful ROE in the family. One gets the impression that he did what he was told because he trusted his family as a reference group, and he kept that character trait in the Army. Despite legal and other scholarly treatises on the advisability of disobeying unlawful orders, the more powerful, sociological points are: first, the US Army still trains its soldiers to both trust and obey its command structure, much like the way the American family socializes its children, and second, Hunsaker and the typical soldier do not have a reference point or group in their pasts to imagine the equivalent of a trusted authority figure giving them an unlawful or immoral order. It would be the atypical, deviant individual who would be forced to learn the necessity of questioning immoral admonitions in a deviant family.

I note again, for the historical as well as sociological record, that Hunsaker's mother, like his father, exhibits the typical American values of optimism, can-do attitude, social support, and overcoming obstacles. She does not delve into negative emotions such as shame and guilt. The absence of these negative emotions may seem strange to someone examining this situation from a difference reference point. Perhaps further studies are in order to examine Iraqi versus American or other cultural perspectives on crime and punishment. For the present, I will repeat my finding that the attitudes and testimony of Hunsaker's parents are in line with testimony and perspectives of all the other family members of other soldiers whose courts-martial I have observed since the year 2005. All the prosecution teams typically try to depict the soldiers from Abu Ghraib to Iron Triangle as criminals who brought shame and disgrace to the Army. That is their consistent reference point. On the other hand, all the defense teams and families typically depict the soldiers as good soldiers and good Americans who did their duty, despite America's mistake in going to war with Iraq and other "mistakes" that were made in the war on terror. The families seem to want the same generosity they and other Americans offer to the US in forgiving its mistakes to be extended to their sons and daughters.

STATEMENT BY THE ACCUSED

Part of the court-martial ritual is that the accused is allowed, but not required, to make a statement to the court that is not subject to cross-examination. Hunsaker took this option, and the MJ allowed him to make his statement. The court transcript reads: "Specialist William Hunsaker, the accused, made the following unsworn statement while seated at counsel table:"

> Yes, Your Honor, I'd like to say my unsworn statement today, say my piece, and I'd just like everybody to understand that despite what happened, I don't — I made a bad choice that day. I know what I did was wrong, and there's no excuse for that. I accept full responsibility for that. Nobody forced me to pull the trigger that day. That was the choice that I made, but I chose a lesser evil for a greater good. I chose to take these men's lives and hoped that they would never have the chance to take American lives because I honestly believed these men were Al-Qaeda or foreign army there to hurt us, and to prevent any future occurrences, but they didn't do anything to any of us. I shouldn't have done it, and I took it on my own, but I did, and I'd just like to — I just want the court and everyone to know and understand that despite of what happens here today and any other time that the faith and love for my country and that I have for the Army will never falter. My whole life my family said I hold no grudges because no one forced me to do this. I'm totally at fault for what I've done, and I accept any punishment you give today, but I do, like everyone else, sir, that what amount of time that you give me won't take away the fact that I am a US Army Infantry Soldier. I serve the 101st, and I serve proudly, and still will serve proudly whether I'm in prison or not. That's just what I'll always be. A Soldier is not defined by a signature, or paperwork, or this uniform he wears. What defines us is our spirit and love for our country, and that, sir, no matter how much time you give me or whatever punishment you give me, that's something that will never be taken away.

Given the strained nature of most of the legalese material that was read by the MJ in a perfunctory manner throughout the proceeding, Hunsaker's statement comes across as genuine as well as eloquent. The MJ convicted him of murder, but Hunsaker spoke with conviction about his values and pride in being an American soldier. He admits that what he did was wrong, but he also explains that he thought the men he killed were his enemies. Of course, he was told repeatedly that they were his enemies and to kill them regardless of circumstances. Nevertheless, he bypasses this thorny philosophical and legal problem of causation and "choice" and admits the obvious and commonsense point that nobody forced him to pull the trigger. In addition, one should note that the accused continues to identify with the Army as his reference group even though the Army was preparing to expel him from this reference group through the degradation ceremony of the dishonorable discharge and sentencing. The Army would place him in the reference group of the convicted criminal.

Despite the Army's efforts at social expulsion, every soldier I have witnessed at this phase of trial continued to see himself or herself as a Soldier. The sincerity of such remarks is best illustrated by one such soldier, Javal Davis, who served his time for abuse at Abu Ghraib, and said at his first news conference upon being released from prison, "I am not a rotten apple." The reader would be missing an important component of the human drama that is a court-martial by failing to note this battle between reference groups. Subsequent reports have vindicated Davis and the other so-called "rotten apples" by demonstrating beyond any doubt that he and other soldiers were following authorized (albeit unlawful) techniques approved by the White House. It is an open question how many and which soldiers "break" under the pressure and submit to the self-definition of the Army's reference group, namely, convicted criminal who dishonored the Army.

The MJ had no comment. The prosecutor had no comment or rebuttal to Hunsaker's statement, and the MJ wasted no time at all in moving to the closing statements.

CLOSING STATEMENT BY THE PROSECUTOR

"Your Honor, the government requests that you sentence Specialist Hunsaker to be dishonorably discharged and to be confined for life with the eligibility for parole." Strictly speaking, the prosecutor was showing mercy by asking for eligibility for parole, which would occur after serving twenty years of a life sentence. The reference to a "dishonorable" discharge refers to a long-standing ritual in the Army which amounts to a degradation ceremony. In practical terms, it means that the accused would have little or no possibility of ever finding a meaningful job upon release from prison. The prosecutor continued:

> Specialist Hunsaker deployed to Iraq with ... US insignia above his heart. When he went to Iraq he didn't just represent the 3rd Brigade Rakkasans, not just the US Army. *He was a representative of the United States.* He stepped into foreign land somewhat as *an ambassador for this country.* He went there with opportunity, opportunity to make a difference, opportunity to improve the situation in Iraq, opportunity to leave a lasting impression of heroism, valor, and honor. Instead Specialist Hunsaker took this opportunity and he threw it away, with that, tainting the reputation of his unit and giving his comrades *the shame and dishonor of having one of their brethren commit a war crime,* to have one of their brethren conspire and murder with premeditation [emphasis added].

It is difficult for commonsense to accept the claim that a soldier is an ambassador of any sort. The role of the ambassador is to talk, negotiate, hold ceremonies, and other things that always fall short of any possibility of killing in the name of one's country. By contrast, the role of the soldier is to follow lawful orders and to kill in accordance with the "laws of armed conflict." These two roles are incompatible. Moreover, the war crime in question was not committed solely by Hunsaker, but was part of the unlawful ROE that was established at high levels in the chain of command. In a typical fashion, much like the prosecutor in the Abu Ghraib trials, the prosecutor evokes the negative emotion of shame. It is ironic that by emphasizing shame to the army, the prosecutor most resembles the Japanese army's point of view from World War II as depicted by Ruth Benedict. In reality, various politicians who were closer to being real ambassadors for the US (after all, all officers who reach the rank of colonel must have their promotions approved by the US Senate) established the policies that Hunsaker and other grunt soldiers carried out. The prosecutor continued:

> Specialist Hunsaker, early during providence, described to you how he went about killing these people. In doing so, he painted himself somewhat as a professional, compassionate Soldier in the way that he killed them. Told them how he deliberately took specific aim at their heads and at their hearts. He knew what he was doing was wrong, but in him telling you this, it doesn't show that he was the professional, compassionate Soldier. All that that does is emphasize the depth of the premeditation with which he acted. All it does is emphasize the fact *that he disregarded the Rules of Engagement, that he disregarded the law of war, that he disregarded the laws of humanity. He disregarded the very thing that separates US Soldiers from the enemy, the fact that US Soldiers follow the law of war, period* [emphasis added].

Which ROE was the prosecutor talking about? The Article 32 testimony showed conclusively that the ROE was to kill all the military-age Iraqi males on the mission — and this was precisely what Hunsaker did. But in this closing argument, the prosecutor invoked the traditional ROE which prohibits such killings, even though Hunsaker did not issue the unlawful ROE. The other noteworthy part of the prosecutor's statement is the cultural allusion to the widespread belief that the rule of law is what separates Americans from all enemies at all times. This was an important theme in World War II in the depiction of Nazi and fascist enemies, and can be traced back to the American War of Independence. Robert N. Bellah has enshrined this and similar beliefs in what he calls American Civil Religion. The prosecutor's statement speaks directly and powerfully to core emotions and values in the US. However, it is obvious that the prosecutor's observation can be applied also to the Brigade Commander and the entire US Army in its war in Iraq — the Army disregarded its own traditional ROE, which are believed to make America superior to its enemies.

But why put all the blame on Hunsaker? The prosecutor concluded his brief closing statement as follows:

> He [Hunsaker] talked about what defines US Soldiers, "That's what defines US soldiers. That's what makes us better than the enemy." Even today, Your Honor, even just a few minutes ago as Specialist Hunsaker was talking, he's telling you that he still felt that he did the right thing in killing these men, but in your sentence, Your Honor, send a message to the world that Specialist Hunsaker does not represent the 3rd Brigade Team Rakkasans. He does not represent the US Army in his views, and he does not represent the United States of America. Let the public know that the US will not stand by while one of its own violates *the most sacred values and morals that make our Soldiers and make this nation great,* and finally, send a message to all those Soldiers out there that any deviation from these rules, these values and our morals, will simply not be tolerated. Thank you [emphasis added].

The obvious logical flaw in the prosecutor's appeal to emotions is that, strictly speaking, Hunsaker's actions did represent his brigade's, the army's, and the nation's unlawful ROE at this phase of the war. He did not dream up the unlawful ROE which he followed. It was passed down to him by his chain of command.

CLOSING ARGUMENT BY THE DEFENSE

Mr. Waddington delivered the closing argument in defense of Hunsaker:

Why would a guy that has never been in trouble in his life, a guy that is a devout family member, obviously a devout patriot, devout Soldier, why would he make that decision at that last second to kill three men, and you heard him.... He would be lying if he got up there and said he just did it because someone told him to do it because he thought it would be cool. He did it because in his mind he thought these are three Al Qaeda operatives and they will kill no more US soldiers, they will kill no more Iraqi women and children. That's why he did it.... In his mind he believed it was a lesser evil for the greater good. That's three less terrorists trying to kill our people. Either way, it was wrong, but what you need to look at, Your Honor, is does this guy need to spend the rest of his life in prison? Is he such a bad guy that he needs to be locked away without the possibility of parole, and on top of that when he gets out of prison, are we going to make sure that he gets out in the worst possible situation he could ever be put in which is to be a federally convicted murderer and to give him a dishonorable discharge? Now his entire service has not been dishonorable. Some would debate as to whether these actions are disgraceful under the circumstances; however, his service to the country, his devotion to the country, to the Army, and his willingness to get up, join the military and go and serve and protect all of us should not be something that's just thrown in the trash. Given the limited options you have, Your Honor, we ask that you do not give him a dishonorable discharge.... Giving him another kick to the stomach while he's already down, and he is. I mean he's about to be carted off in handcuffs with a dishonorable or another punitive discharge serves really no purpose.... Your Honor, we ask that you follow the prosecution's recommendation that he is given the opportunity to get paroled out and also that you do not punitively discharge him, Your Honor. Thank you.

The unintended consequence of indoctrinating US soldiers with the belief that their enemy is almost monstrous in its disregard for law is that soldiers to come to believe that killing the enemy under any circumstance is a sort of service for the greater good. One need only recall Colonel Steele's pep talk to find the source for this widespread belief. Mr. Waddington disclosed to me later that the prosecutor was upset after the trial that Hunsaker showed no remorse. Mr. Waddington's explanation was straightforward: How could Hunsaker be expected to show remorse given the entire history and context of this tragedy?

The MJ called for a recess at 2:44 p.m. Court was re-convened at 3:25 p.m. and the MJ announced his verdict:

Accused and Defense Counsel, please rise. Specialist William B. Hunsaker, this court sentences you: To be reduced to the grade of Private E1; To forfeit all pay and allowances; To be confined for the length of your natural life with eligibility for parole; and To be dishonorably discharged from the service. Please be seated.

The MJ then referred to Exhibit CVIII which "states that the Convening Authority has agreed to disapprove any confinement in excess of 18 years." The MJ asked Hunsaker, "Do you have any questions about your post-trial and appellate rights?" "No, Your Honor," Hunsaker replied. MJ: "This court is adjourned."

CHAPTER 9. VISITS TO FT. LEAVENWORTH AND ALEXANDRIA

"Prisons are built with the stones of law and brothels with bricks of religion."
— Gregory Bateson, p. 131

The tiny city of Ft. Leavenworth appears immediately as one crosses a bridge across the Missouri River into Kansas. The name, "Ft. Leavenworth" is associated with three separate federal prisons, the town, the army base, and the war college that is the intellectual center of the army that is on the base. I entered the base through the main gate after making arrangements ahead of time to be admitted. Various lawyers who are assigned to each of the five prisoners I would visit in June of 2009 contacted Sergeant Illichman and authorized me to make the visits under their auspices. My car was searched and my driver's license was checked against the lists at the gate. The entry onto the base went smoothly each day that I made the visit.

The particular prison which I was visiting is officially called the United States Disciplinary Barracks, and is referred to as DB. It is the only Department of Defense maximum security prison in the United States. DB seems to be an odd name for a prison, but is in line with military culture which holds that the inmates are still members of the military during their incarceration. Officially, they are being "disciplined," not punished. DB is tucked away about five miles deep into the army base. The drive, at 30 mph maximum speed, took me past the War College (which looked like any modern American university), parks, fountains, the commissary area and the old and now abandoned DB, which was originally built in 1877. However, as I drove past the old DB, I noticed that it was under active re-construction and re-modeling. Rumor has it that the old DB was being prepared for Gitmo detainees in anticipation of the scheduled closing of the prison at Guantanamo, Cuba.

The road to DB becomes particularly beautiful the closer one approaches the prison. To the right, I could see the Missouri River. There was a forest on both sides of the road. I saw horses with the visible brand, "DoD" (Department of Defense). I passed an artillery range and an active airstrip. Finally, I approached warning signs about approaching a secure area, and warning that no photography was allowed. DB is a modern, high-tech, and scary looking prison with barbed wire and all that one would expect to see, looking at a prison.

I parked in the parking lot and walked to the front entrance. As I walked, I wondered to myself: Was "maximum" security really necessary in a military prison on a military base that was already secure? Where could the inmates possibly escape? DB holds approximately 500 inmates from all branches of the military, all males. Approximately 12 of them are "war criminals," and about 90% of the remaining 488 inmates are some sort of sexual offenders. The overwhelming majority are first-time offenders. I saw numerous guards everywhere I looked inside DB, and I asked one of the guards how many of them are there. The guard replied that there are 60 to 80 guards on a shift at any given time. That would make the ratio of guards to prisoners at DB 1 to 16. At Abu Ghraib, this ratio was 1 guard to 150 prisoners. Why would the army invest ten times more effort and cost to guard its own soldiers than it did to guard alleged terrorists at Abu Ghraib?

Because I had worked on some of the Abu Ghraib cases, I wondered why the army was over-competent in most ways regarding DB and so grossly under-competent in most ways regarding Abu Ghraib. The lobby inside DB is carpeted. The concrete floor at Abu Ghraib was filthy and unsanitary. I made my way through another set of security checkpoints and was escorted to Sergeant Illichman's office. In fact, he insisted that I use his office to interview the prisoners. He and his staff were courteous and respectful. A guard escorted William Hunsaker into the office. He was holding several books and many documents in his hands. We spoke privately for hours.

He told me that there was much more to Colonel Steele's speech than what is shown on You Tube. The speech was preceded by a video which showed the twin towers being destroyed on 9/11, terrorists cutting off people's heads, and explosions. These associations suggested to me that the army was deliberately creating in the minds of its soldiers a link between the war in Iraq and the tragedy of 9/11, even though no logical connection exists between them. The Bush Administration forced the same illogical connection onto the American people as a whole.

Mr. Hunsaker told me that Colonel Steele had also invited a guest speaker whom he introduced as his friend, Lieutenant Colonel Dave Grossman. "Have you read Grossman's book?" Mr. Hunsaker asked me. Surprised at having an intellectual discussion inside a prison, I answered affirmatively. Grossman published a book entitled *On Killing: The Psychological Cost of Learning to Kill in War and Society*. Mr. Hunsaker said that in his speech to the soldiers at Steele's pep rally, Grossman told them not to be scared to kill and that killing is a part of war. Mr. Hunsaker opened Grossman's book to page 108 and showed me a paragraph which he said encapsulated what both Steele and Grossman conveyed to the troops at that rally.

It is worthwhile to analyze the overall gist of Grossman's book, given his indirect link to Operation Iron Triangle. Grossman's message and the message of the army regarding killing are thereby connected to the tragic mission of May 9th. Much as I began my book with a reference to S.L.A. Marshall's classic study of World War II soldiers, *Men Against Fire*, Grossman begins his book with Marshall's central finding: American soldiers are extremely reluctant to kill, except in self-defense, such that only 20% of them will generally open fire on an average combat mission. Whereas I follow Marshall's conclusions from this overall finding, namely, that soldiers are not machines and that long-term killing wears them down and ultimately destroys an army through combat stress, Grossman pursues a different line of reasoning. Grossman's overall aim is to show that the reluctance to kill can be broken down by standard conditioning techniques: "With the proper conditioning and the proper circumstances, it appears that almost anyone can kill."[1] He turns to Stanley Milgram's famous study of obedience to authority and draws a conclusion that is completely different from the lessons drawn by a preponderance of professors who cite Milgram. The lesson drawn by college professors is that blind obedience to authority is a bad thing which can lead to atrocities. The lesson drawn by Grossman is: "Never underestimate the power of the need to obey." Grossman turns to Lieutenant Calley's role in the My Lai massacre to draw conclusions that are startling to the civilian: "The leader must also communicate a clear expectation of killing behavior" (p. 145). He illustrates this by pointing out that Calley was not obeyed the first time he ordered his soldiers to kill, but was obeyed when he showed them how to kill by personally firing some rounds into the victims.

The connections among the central message in Grossman's book, his role in Steele's pep rally, and the outcome on the tragic mission of May 9th are clear and disturbing. Grossman's book is about conditioning the soldier to kill because of the well-established fact that the American soldier is reluctant to kill. Grossman's participation in Steele's rally may explain the use of the kill board, coins, and other rewards used to "condition" soldiers in the brigade to kill. In his sworn statement Geressy referred to the kill board as a technique intended to "desensitize" soldiers toward killing. All this constitutes the application of behaviorism and operant conditioning toward the desired goal of increased killing. On the other hand, the disconnect between the intellectual reference group of the army and the intellectual reference group of civilian university professors could scarcely be greater. And which approach is more valid? Marshall and scores of academics have found that soldiers who go on missions for more than 100 days invariably develop symptoms that disable their performance as soldiers, from PTSD to suicide, alcoholism, accidents, and aggression. The more important point is that the army does not seem to pay attention to the reference group of civilian professors and researchers, and listens to its own reference group of intellectuals who try to transform the American soldier into a killing machine.

Mr. Hunsaker seemed to be aware of the costs of the army's approach. He asked me: "Did you know that Ft. Campbell was shut down for two days because of a spike of suicides by soldiers at the base?" I did know, but was surprised that he knew. He added that immediately following the shut-down of Ft. Campbell, the army held emergency suicide prevention seminars at DB as well. He said that he and all of the other "war criminals" at DB had PTSD, but he shrugged off his symptoms. I found that the other four soldiers I interviewed also discounted their suffering. All of them wake

---

1 Dave Grossman, *On Killing: The Psychological Cost of Learning to Kill in War and Society* (Boston: Back Bay Books, 2001), p. 4.

---

up with nightmares. None sleeps for a full eight hours, but sleep on "Iraq time" or, as they explained, they dose off for two hours at a time. Often they would wake up in DB and not know where they were, and search for their guns, uniforms, or equipment. Some of them scanned the office in which we spoke. I asked them what they were doing, and one of them told me, "I'm thinking of how to clear this room, Sir." There is little point in noting that they exhibited all the classic symptoms of PTSD, including hyper-vigilance. To the army, they are war criminals. In their minds, they made clear to me that they regarded themselves as "war criminals" in quotes. In Stouffer's vocabulary, they are psychiatric casualties of war, not war criminals.

Mr. Hunsaker filled me in on details of the many side-atrocities committed by Charlie Company. He said that everyone in the company knew that other platoons, in addition to his, executed prisoners on May 9th. The sworn statements taken on May 11th were all false and were dictated to the soldiers by the officers. "Our company had a reputation for destroying everything," he said. Mr. Hunsaker said that First Sergeant Geressy "was in a lot of trouble" after May 9th because four separate soldiers reported him to CID for four separate atrocities that occurred on or soon after their mission. All of the four whistleblowers were punished in some way, from receiving permanent KP duty to receiving Article 15s. He said their orders on May 9th were to "kill on sight," and they would have carried out their orders had it not been for the women and children who got in the way. "At the time, I believed, I bought into this," he said. Now he is not sure if the Iraqis on that mission were terrorists or not.

According to Mr. Hunsaker, two weeks after Operation Iron Triangle, 1st platoon of Charlie Company carried out a similar mission. They were told to find an Iraqi named Omar, and were given the code-word Rumpelstiltskin to kill him. Omar was found, unarmed; instead of taking him prisoner, four soldiers were given the code-word and "wasted" him. Mr. Hunsaker was not on that mission, but everyone talked about it. He confirmed that two weeks before Iron Triangle, he and members of headquarters platoon were ordered to pick up body parts of dead Iraqis, including severed heads. I asked him if he could name the other soldiers on that mission to validate his claims, and he said that he could if he were given an Alpha Roster of the members of that platoon.

Mr. Hunsaker confirmed the infamous tomato truck incident, which we have already analyzed. He added several details that are not found in the sworn statements. He said that the order was given to "light up" the truck after it tried to move past a check point, and that the US soldiers used armor-piercing rounds. Mr. Hunsaker said that he was the one who was ordered to drag the bodies of the two dead Iraqis out of the truck. They were unarmed. He described blood, brains, and body parts all over the passenger compartment as he struggled to clear the bodies. Afterwards, the platoon leader ordered that the soldiers shoot at their army HMMMV to make it seem as if the two Iraqis had opened fire on them. He said that the proof lies in the fact that the army vehicle was shot with armor-piercing rounds, and only the Americans had such bullets. Here is another logical reason for the demands by the civilian defense attorneys that experts in ballistics, forensics, and other scientific methodologies should have been used at the trials. Scientific data could confirm or disconfirm Mr. Hunsaker's claims and the claims of other soldiers who submitted sworn statements.

But we have seen that from the IO to CID and the military judges, the army's attitude has been to keep civilian science (including psychological and sociological facts and findings) out of its proceedings.

Mr. Hunsaker said that he slept for four days in the same uniform he wore on the day of the tomato truck incident. He couldn't escape the smell of blood and death. "I didn't have a uniform without blood," he added. From the perspective of the reference group of civilian scientific researchers, this incident alone was sufficient to cause Hunsaker to have PTSD, which, in turn, would have affected his judgment and performance on May 9th. But we have seen that throughout the trial process, the tomato truck incident was excluded from proceedings, and my testimony as an expert witness in such matters was excluded from consideration.

I asked Mr. Hunsaker about his sleeping patterns and those of his comrades while in Iraq. He said that they were on patrols for fifteen hours per day, and averaged four hours of broken sleep per night. (I have come across this same pattern in the Leahy, Mayo, Hatley case.) He said that everyone believed that "if you sleep, they will kill you." He said that his typical sleep cycle, in Iraq as well as DB, was "restless, you wake up, your body is used to getting two to four hours of sleep." "I'm still on Iraqi schedule," he said, into his third year at DB. To make matters worse, his work schedule at DB varies from week to week, so that sometimes he is on the night shift doing laundry for forty cents per hour. Like all the other soldiers with whom I spoke, he said he refuses to take medications for his sleeping problems. The standard refrain from all of them was: "I don't want to get addicted."

I asked Mr. Hunsaker to give me his best guess as to how many missions he thought that his brigade conducted which used the same unlawful ROE as the one on May 9th. He said "sixty percent." "Why?" I asked. "We were in the Sunni Triangle," he answered, and "It was the way that First Sergeant Geressy wanted things done." "We saw Steele and Geressy more than the battalion leader," he added. Their motto was, "Bring the fight to the enemy." We talked about the book *The Warrior King*, by Lieutenant Colonel Nathan Sassaman, who said that his soldiers were rough with the Iraqis in order to preserve law and order. Mr. Hunsaker agreed that Steele's brigade did the same. Soldiers knocked out headlights, kicked in cars, threw Iraqis off of trucks, and in general, "We terrorized the Iraqis." He said that "Innocent people got caught up but in the long run we saved lives." As proof, he said that "when we were taken off sector after the investigations began, the unit that replaced us had guys blown up daily." "If it were one of our guys getting blown up, somebody was going to die," he added. His depiction is entirely in line with Sassaman's assertions.

Mr. Hunsaker spoke about the soldiers being under a lot of stress in Iraq. "We needed beer, and we needed a morale platoon." By "morale platoon" he meant that soldiers went without sex. "They expected us to shave every day" in the desert. "I didn't get RR [rest and recreation leave] the whole time I was there." His assessment was that a lot of the sexual offenses committed in Iraq were due to the stress and lack of any breaks in combat missions. He confirmed what we have learned from the court transcripts, that soldiers stole TVs, VCRs, generators, and liquor from "the locals." Sometimes the soldiers would steal, and sometimes they would trade pornography for liquor. "What kind of liquor was it?" I asked. "Black Jack or something vodka-ish," he answered. The commission of these crimes for the sake of obtaining alcohol is a predictable consequence of the army's "no alcohol" rule in Iraq. By contrast, the army allowed German POWs during World War II to drink beer while in detention, with no negative consequences.

Mr. Hunsaker returned to the topic of suicides in the Army. "It's always bad news for the commander," he said. At DB, the inmates were shown a film titled "Shoulder to Shoulder." "What was the reaction of the inmates?" I asked. "We're pissed off. We're not allowed to leave DB to bury our family members, but we are forced to go to suicide prevention." It is true that the army forbids inmates at DB from attending the funerals of family members. What were the soldiers told about suicide prevention? "Use commonsense, go see a chaplain," Hunsaker said. However, he added that "if you tell anyone you're having any sort of problems, the army comes down hard on you." Hunsaker's proposed solution was that the army should let any inmate who volunteers to go back to Iraq and fight in return for reduced time at DB. He said that he would be the first to volunteer.

He told me that soldiers in his unit were routinely issued syringes filled with valium while on missions. He described incidents in which soldiers would inject themselves with valium and "sleep through" a mission. Some readers may find such assertions difficult to believe. But many soldiers have already written books about their experiences in Iraq which validate many of the claims made by Mr. Hunsaker. *Salon* has published a review of some of these books and has found that soldiers report that: Valium is widely used and available in Iraq; pornography is used to trade for liquor; Iraqis are routinely mistreated during raids; innocent civilians are frequently killed in Iraq at checkpoints; soldiers frequently steal from Iraqi civilians.[1] One such soldier–author, John Crawford, described similar experiences during a radio broadcast by National Public Radio.[2] Patterns of connections exist between Mr. Hunsaker's descriptions and descriptions by other soldiers in the public domain.

I turned to the topic of the tragic mission of May 9th. Hunsaker said: "If the ROE wasn't questioned when it was first issued, why would I question it at a later point?" He said that everyone in the platoon knew that "First Sergeant was pissed" that any Iraqis had been left alive. Mr. Hunsaker said that he was present when the lieutenant told Sergeant Girouard that First Sergeant Geressy was angry. I asked him why he thought that this particular incident went to court when there were so many similar incidents. He explained that it had to do with Sergeants Acevedo and Hensley trying to blackmail the first sergeant into withdrawing Article 15 proceedings against them for sleeping on duty. Acevedo and Hensley heard the radio transmission by First Sergeant Geressy, knew the outcome, and "would have gained by holding this over Geressy's head." According to Hunsaker, the first sergeant did not like Acevedo and made a phone call to brigade headquarters; "then we got arrested." The first sergeant "jumped his chain of command" to put all the focus on Hunsaker and his comrades and thereby deflect attention from charges made by Acevedo and others. "What happened to Acevedo?" I asked. "He got out of the army but kept his rank." Mr. Hunsaker's assertions are in line with what the trial record shows, namely, that great efforts

1 http://www.salon.com/opinion/feature/2007/11/06/thought_police/print.html
2 http://www.npr.org/templates/story/story.php?storyId=4783583

were made to keep Acevedo from testifying by charging him with crimes which were dropped after Hunsaker and his comrades went to prison. Furthermore, Hunsaker's story is believable to me because I have witnessed nearly the same dynamics in other military court cases.[1]

"How do you feel about the whole thing?" I asked him. "I feel betrayed," he said, and added: "The army took my patriotism, and took advantage of me and my squad." As I left Hunsaker and Ft. Leavenworth, I was reminded of a line by Samuel Stouffer: "The privates can see what the generals won't admit or do anything about" (Vol. 1, p. 68). Military physicians, too, see things that many generals willfully ignore.

Mr. Hunsaker and I spoke about many other things, including his daily routine at the DB, the point system within the prison, his interests, reading, and hopes. I also spoke with four other soldiers. It is beyond the scope of this study to report on the full extent of all these conversations. Suffice it to say that the most overwhelming impression on me was how closed off and isolated the prisoners are from the rest of society and each other.

In contrast to the "Lone Star Stalag" at Camp Hearne, Texas, which housed Nazi prisoners of war in the 1940s, US soldiers at DB do not give plays, play musical instruments, engage in art, drink beer, sleep well, correspond with the outside world, or eat well. American attitudes toward prisoners, including US soldier–prisoners, have changed dramatically since World War II. Most of this change has taken place in the last thirty years as a result of politicians "getting tough on crime." The economic and social costs of this ill-conceived policy are only now becoming slowly apparent. As a final illustration, I will cite this example. One of my daughters wrote a separate poem for each of the soldiers I would visit, and decorated the card with beads and stickers (she is fifteen years old). For Mr. Hunsaker, she wrote the following in her own hand:

> Thank you for protecting us. It takes a lot to build up the courage it takes to go out there and protect us all on a daily basis and be willing to risk your life for us, and that's what makes you a HERO. Never forget that.

I asked Sergeant Illichman for permission to give this card to Mr. Hunsaker. He took it from me and said he would check with the chief legal officer at the DB. When he returned, he announced that the decision was negative. Mr. Hunsaker could look at the card and poem, but could not keep it. The reasons were that the beads could be used as weapons, and correspondence was not allowed with any person who is not on an approved list, restricted to family and lawyers. My daughter was not on that list. (I do not know whether the sergeant's rationalizations are true or not.) I also asked permission to buy a Coke for the soldiers I visited, and that request was

---

1 Let me be specific and to the point. In the Baghdad canal killings, the government's star witness against Sergeant Michael Leahy was Sergeant Cunningham. Cunningham had been charged with an Article 15 prior to the incident, and he became the government's star witness. Nevertheless, the government went ahead and charged him with conspiracy to commit murder. After he testified against Leahy, the government dropped all charges against Cunningham. The pattern of government manipulation in both cases is clear.

granted. The mother of one of the soldiers wrote to me later that her son was so very grateful for the Coke, which he had not tasted in many months. In sharp contrast, I note that Nazi prisoners in Texas corresponded freely with whomever they pleased to keep up their morale, and in the process, spread the word about the good treatment they were receiving from their American captors.

APPEARANCE BEFORE THE CLEMENCY AND PAROLE BOARD IN ALEXANDRIA

On April Fool's Day, 2009, I traveled to Alexandria, Virginia. Corey Clagett's civilian appeals lawyer, Mr. Tim Litka, had arranged for Lieutenant Colonel Edward Horvath, now Colonel Horvath, and me to appear before the Army Clemency and Parole Board. We would be given ten minutes in total to speak on his behalf. The colonel and I each wrote formal letters to the clemency board ahead of time, stating our professional opinions as to mitigating factors. We would be given three and a half minutes to summarize our positions to the board in person. Colonel Horvath is a physician and Army Reserve officer, who has been an advocate and mentor for many soldiers, regardless of their circumstances. He first learned of Mr. Clagett from Corey's step-grandmother, who resides in the same small Ohio community as Dr. Horvath, and who transcribed his dictated notes from Iraq. She asked him to help her grandson and he agreed to do so. Dr. Horvath is an unusual person. A man of great compassion and courage, who evidently takes both his medical and military oaths seriously — so much so, that he was willing to risk incurring the ire of the army in advocating on behalf of an imprisoned soldier.

I arrived in Alexandria the night before the meeting, which was scheduled for 8 a.m. on April 1st. My hotel was five miles from the meeting place in downtown Alexandria. The instructions that were sent to me gave an address, and I thought that leaving forty minutes ahead of the meeting on the 1st would give me sufficient time to arrive promptly. I fully expected the GPS unit in the rental car to direct me to the address. My reasoning was that the location was obviously not on a military base, whereas on previous occasions, the GPS units were unable to locate addresses on military bases for me. So, I typed in the address, and the GPS unit responded that no such address existed. I drove to the location based upon the directions that were given, but could not find the street that was listed. I finally parked in a nearby parking garage and asked pedestrians for the location. Most had never heard of the address. Finally, one said, "Oh, you mean the secure area!" He pointed me in the right direction. Apparently, the street name used by the government is not an official street name in the city of Alexandria: when I found the street sign, I noticed that it was a different size and color from all the other street signs. The building looked like any other impersonal business building, surrounded by buildings that supposedly housed insurance companies, legal offices, financial offices, and so on. When I entered the correct building, I noticed that the directory simply did not list the floor or the office I was seeking. I asked people in the lobby for assistance. They said, "Oh, you want the secure area on the second floor." When I pushed the elevator button for the second floor, nothing happened. "Oh, you can't get to the second floor without a special key," another person told me. A janitor suddenly came out of nowhere and used her key to allow me to get to the second floor.

When the elevator doors opened, two federal security guards were waiting for me, searched me and allowed me into the secure area. I was late. All the other attorneys and advocates were in a conference room listening to the chair of the Clemency Board explain the procedure. He left, and we were left in the room to be called, one group at a time, to appear before the Board. I recognized Captain Jonathan Crisp, who had defended Lynndie England in one of the Abu Ghraib trials. He was out of the army now and working as a civilian attorney. We exchanged information and memories of the "good times" in the England case. In the far corner of the room, attorneys for Sergeant Girouard huddled together. Later this same year, Mr. Nathan (defense attorney for Hunsaker during the present clemency phase) would come to this location, again, to seek clemency for Mr. Hunsaker. His previous appeal for clemency had been denied.

At around 11 a.m., the three of us representing Mr. Clagett were called before the board. It consisted of five members. Three were army colonels, and two of these officers were female. One was Asian-American. There were two civilian members, one white and one African-American. It was clear immediately that the army was trying to present a multi-ethnic, inclusive, tolerant, image. The logo for the Board read: "Mercy, Compassion, Justice." I thought to myself, "Could it be that the army has a human face?" Mr. Litka and I spoke briefly, mainly about Colonel Steele's unlawful ROE and problems with the command climate in the brigade, including the "kill board" and rewards for killing Iraqis. The Board seemed to be paying attention, but the one male, white colonel seemed stiff and stern. Was he annoyed at me for exposing him to these facts — or at the facts themselves? I told them that since I was not allowed to speak at Mr. Clagett's court-martial, because it had been canceled, the information I was giving them had never been put on the trial record.

Colonel Horvath wore his dress uniform, stood the entire time he spoke to the Board, and addressed the Board respectfully. Instead of merely summarizing what he said, I will quote from his entire letter to the board, because of his extraordinary eloquence. In his impassioned concluding plea, Colonel Horvath paraphrased remarks made before the American Bar Association by Supreme Court Justice Anthony Kennedy:

> I'm writing to appeal for clemency for PFC Corey Clagett, 3rd Battalion, 187th Infantry Regiment, 101st Airborne Division, who is currently prisoner number 82477 at the Army Disciplinary Barracks at Ft. Leavenworth.

> I'm not an influential politician, media celebrity, or even a human rights activist. Rather, I'm a husband and a father, a physician and citizen-soldier — an Army Reserve officer, who's served two tours in Iraq. At age 59, I left home and family to care for the "neighbors' kids" — the young people in uniform who grew up during the same time as my own children. I did so in places with names like Abu Ghraib, Baghdad, Camp Bucca, and COB Speicher. I also treated Iraqis, including insurgents, providing them the same compassionate care given to our own soldiers. I experienced the horrors of war firsthand, witnessing things no human being should ever have to see, all the while in harm's way. I know what war — especially this war — is like, and how it can affect the actions

of otherwise good and decent people. It's a morally bruising, ethically confusing environment, where one's internal compass can inadvertently go awry.

The incident resulting in PFC Clagett's incarceration need not be detailed here. Suffice it to say, what actually happened on that day in May 2006 will never be known beyond a reasonable doubt. However, such incidents share characteristics which have become all too familiar. . . and all too disturbing: Overly aggressive and ever-changing Rules of Engagement; a chaotic combat environment with a brutal enemy; and young, battle-weary American soldiers uncertain exactly how to proceed under confusing circumstances.

Legal proceedings in such cases have also had many features in common: Inexperienced military defense counsel; prosecutors overcharging and threatening the accused soldiers with the death penalty; conflicting witness accounts; unsupportable forensic evidence; exculpatory evidence withheld; "unwarranted command influence"; and finally, coerced guilty pleas in exchange for testimony. "Convictions" obtained under these circumstances should give pause to every American citizen concerned about justice.

Those who have never experienced war, especially a counterinsurgency campaign against a brutal enemy — who hides in civilian clothes and behind innocent children — cannot possibly comprehend the dilemmas our soldiers face on a daily basis. Often suffering from sleep deprivation, they're thrust into confusing, chaotic situations where their own lives are at risk, held to a standard few others could ever achieve, and then convicted with evidence which would not be accepted as sufficient in a civilian court. One cynic has written that in military justice "someone has to pay — it doesn't matter whom". Others have suggested that lower ranking soldiers have been sacrificed to appease a hostile media, mollify domestic opponents of the war, protect senior officers, and placate Iraqi politicians. As with most exaggerations, these contain some elements of truth.

After his conviction, PFC Clagett was placed in solitary confinement at Ft. Leavenworth, and permitted to leave his small cell only one hour each day. After months of being subjected to such conditions, PFC Clagett, who had a prior history of mental health problems, developed a serious psychiatric illness. The possibility that this condition was precipitated or aggravated by the circumstances of his confinement, cannot be dismissed.

I have been in contact with PFC Clagett during most of his incarceration. Although repeatedly denied visiting privileges by the officials at Ft.

Leavenworth, I maintain a close relationship with him through letters and phone conversations, and have come to know him quite well. It is my professional and personal opinion that PFC Clagett has excellent potential for rehabilitation. This mirrors the initial assessment by a Navy psychologist, who, after conducting a pre-trial evaluation of PFC Clagett in 2006, described him as a "very sensitive" individual without any anti-social personality traits.

But PFC Clagett's potential for rehabilitation is inversely related to the length of his imprisonment. Simply stated, the longer he's incarcerated and separated from external support systems, the greater the risk for permanent mental harm, and the greater the difficulty he will experience during reintegration into society. I have promised to actively assist PFC Clagett in rebuilding his life as soon as he's released. I've done this for other young offenders over the years and have been witness to some remarkable success stories. For my efforts on behalf of incarcerated teenagers and young adults, the Army awarded me the Military Outstanding Volunteer Service Medal. I will do the same for PFC Corey Clagett; I give you my word as an Army officer.

Since returning home, I've been frequently asked to address various groups throughout the country about my experiences in Iraq. During these speaking engagements, more listeners have expressed anger about the manner in which our soldiers have been prosecuted, convicted, and imprisoned for actions taken during combat, *than for any other aspect of the Iraq war.* Disapproval and disbelief are most intense among combat veterans, the group usually most supportive of the military. These views have not gone unnoticed in Washington. As legislators from both parties become more involved in this issue, some form of Congressional or Presidential action seems increasingly likely.

But the military justice system need not await legislative or executive pressure, since it possesses the ability to address such concerns through its clemency process. And no one is more deserving of clemency than young soldiers like PFC Clagett, who left home and family to defend our Constitution, our country, and our freedoms. Many are now languishing in prison, deprived of their own freedom and separated from loved ones, not because of any deliberate intent to commit a crime, but rather due to negligence, carelessness, or errors in judgment made in the confusion of war.

The United States Army demonstrated courage, strength, and resolve in toppling a brutal regime and bringing freedom to Iraq. In so doing, it has earned the respect of allies and adversaries alike, and, more importantly, the genuine admiration the American people. Such an institution, rightfully confident in its mission and values, need not fear being merciful. Although PFC Clagett may not have served his full sentence, he has suffered enough. Give him what only you can give. Give him what he fought for on our behalf...give him his freedom.

Sincerely,

Edward P. Horvath, M.D., M.P.H.

Lieutenant Colonel, Medical Corps, U.S. Army Reserve

The board did not respond with any substantive questions at all. One of the female colonels thanked us for coming all this way to appear personally. She then asked Colonel Horvath how he had become involved in this case, and on hearing his reply, remarked how "fortunate" PFC Clagett was to have someone of his stature advocating on his behalf. She also thanked Dr. Horvath for apprising the board of PFC Clagett's mental health status, which strangely was not known by the board. The other female colonel noted that I was an Aggie (I teach at Texas A&M University) and said that her son will be a freshman at my university in the fall. The angry-looking male colonel said nothing. The three of us were dismissed; we regrouped in a hotel lobby for coffee and discussion with Clagett's family.

Again, I felt like I was part of an umbilical cord — to quote Captain Rutizer from the Article 32 hearing — linking the army and the soldier-prisoners with the outside world. The three of us tried to convey to Clagett's mother what we had said to the board, that they smiled and seemed friendly, even though they asked no questions about his case. A month later, their decision came down: no clemency, and no explanation.

Dr. Horvath was especially angry at the board's negative decision. He told me that he had come in good faith (and at his own expense) and given his word as an army officer that he would personally ensure Clagett's rehabilitation. Instead of acknowledging this incredible commitment, the board rebuffed it — a rejection Dr. Horvath took personally. "What harm would have been done by reducing his 18-year sentence by one year, or even six months," Dr. Horvath asked me. "Instead of providing Corey a glimmer of hope — and increasing his trust in me as an effective advocate — the board chose to do nothing." Indeed, it seems that the entire hearing had been a charade, or at the very least a mere formality. Dr. Horvath said that he thought the board had no intention of granting clemency. Dr. Horvath told me that Clagett's mental health had deteriorated from the many months of solitary confinement and he feared it would now get worse. But, ever hopeful, like Mr. Nathan in chapter 1, this compassionate and determined physician spoke of the need to bring the truth about these young soldiers to the attention of Congress and the American people.

Chapter 10. Conclusions: The Lonely Crowd Disconnected from the Lonely Army

> "All we ask is to be treated like Americans again."
> — an anonymous soldier quoted by Samuel Stouffer, *The American Soldier*, p. 371

An anonymous colonel approached me as I sat on a curb in front of the military court building at Ft. Hood, Texas. He sat down next to me. It was the year 2005, and I was taking a cigarette break from the court-martial of Lynndie England, one of the so-called rotten apples of Abu Ghraib. "The government must have clean hands," he said, as he shook his head. I knew instantly what he meant in the language of commonsense. It was evident from the trial back in 2005 that the real "rotten apples" — the politicians, lawyers, and commanders who dreamt up the torture policies — were in Washington, D.C., not on trial at Ft. Hood. The Levin–McCain report confirmed this fact in the year 2008. But this dramatic insight seems to have had no appreciable effect on how the war on terror continues to be waged. Several years from now, no doubt, a similar report will pinpoint the origins of the unlawful ROE to a particular cabal in the nation's capital. Meanwhile, the effects of the torture as well as the un-lawful ROE policies continue to exert extremely negative consequences for the United States, its image, soldiers, and objectives in the war on terror. Nowadays, it seems to be very difficult for people to make obvious and commonsense connections, and to see patterns. And for those who are able to make the leap in sociological imagination, it does not seem to matter. What can one do? What are the obstacles to making real, constructive change?

To begin with, some team of social scientists needs to replicate Samuel Stouffer's classic World War II study, *The American Soldier*, with regard to the American soldier in the current war on terror as well as contemporary American society. Why hasn't such a study been conducted already? Annual meetings of the American Sociological Association, the American Psychological Association, and the American Anthropological Association generally ignore issues pertaining to war crimes, abuse, and torture in the current war, and focus on issues pertaining to gender and race and ethnic relations. This focus in also reflected in course offerings in American universities, topics of government grants that are awarded, and publications in scholarly journals. There is a vacuum in understanding of the American soldier's attitudes, morale, problems, strengths, and performance in the current war on terror. Scores of eminent social scientists addressed the topics of World War II and the American soldier in relation to American society: Margaret Mead, Gregory Bateson, Talcott Parsons, Erik Erikson, David Riesman, and Ruth Benedict, among others. All of them were structuralists, which is to say, they assumed that society is an interconnected system. In the new millennium, post-structuralism has replaced structuralism, which is to say, the dominant assumption today by academics is that "grand narratives" and "grand theories" must be deconstructed and torn down. This general attitude of postmodernism — to de-construct — poses a serious obstacle toward any effort to re-construct the American can-do spirit from World War II.

Nevertheless, what conclusions may be drawn applying Stouffer's "grand theory" concerning the American soldier to Operation Iron Triangle and other similar missions? I shall put aside the postmodern attitude that Stouffer is quaint and irrelevant. The conclusions that follow are based upon a limited sample, but are informative nonetheless. Stouffer found that commissioned officers in World War II went "by the book" while enlisted soldiers were more "down-to-earth." Both officers and enlisted soldiers saw their roles in World War II as primarily defensive, not offensive: they felt that they had no choice but to fight Germany and Japan, but they did not like war. Combat stress was mitigated by high unit morale, which was maintained by keeping military units intact as far as possible. The mythology of the "Band of Brothers," which is the name given to the 101st Airborne Division, arose out of this policy: the same group of soldiers in the same unit fought until the job was done. Ironically, and half a century later, this same 101st Airborne Division was involved in the Operation Iron Triangle killings. Stouffer emphasized that the US soldier did not fight for mom, apple pie, ideology, or their leadership but that soldiers fought for each other. In other words, American soldiers fight for their country but die for their buddies. In contrast to his German and Japanese counter-part, the American soldier was much better fed, rested, and supplied. What aspects, if any, of Stouffer's portrait of the American soldier apply to the contemporary "Band of Brothers" who fought on May 9, 2006, during Operation Iron Triangle?

"Going by the book" is a commonsense expression. "The book" refers to the US Constitution, common norms in American culture, army manuals, regulations, and of course, rules of engagement. In the course of the present study, we have encountered numerous instances in which commissioned officers did *not* go "by the book." The ROE for Operation Iron Triangle were unlawful. Law enforcement agents lied to and tricked their own soldiers. Miranda rights were not read to suspects. The dimensions of the prison cells and cages violated the army's own minimal standards for confinement. Required autopsies on the bodies of dead Iraqis were not performed. Scientific and forensic tests were not performed. Some sworn statements were not passed up the chain of command. Other sworn statements were shredded. Information and reports were withheld from the Article 32 hearing. Perjured testimony was admitted. Fear and intimidation was used to coerce testimony. Witnesses were told to align their stories so that they would please what CID wanted to hear. Accused soldiers and lawyers were threatened not to mention certain leaders and policies. I leave it up to the reader to complete this list of "not by the book" practices that are documented in the trial records.

The command climate went completely against the grain of the defensive soldier portrayed by Stouffer. Steele's brigade encouraged kill contests, kill boards, and rewards for kills. Of course, pre-emptive strikes are justified in Stouffer's book against uniformed enemy soldiers. But the idea of a pre-emptive strike against targets who could be enemies or civilians is completely absent in Stouffer's study, and is documented in Steele's brigade. This attitude is also connected to the Bush Doctrine of the pre-emptive strike in general.

As for morale in Charlie Company, several soldiers testified that it was poor. Soldiers were frequently re-shuffled among units. Stouffer found that any change in membership or leadership in military units immediately resulted in increased symptoms of stress for soldiers. Stouffer's solution for the problem of combat stress was the old-fashioned one: soldiers relied upon each other and their feeling of belonging to a surrogate family to thwart the fear of death. In the absence of this tried and true technique, verified by mountains of sociological research, the soldiers developed PTSD, became aggressive toward Iraqis and each other, and abused drugs and alcohol. Suicides reached such a pitch in the 101st Airborne Division that Ft. Campbell was shut down for two days. In general, suicide and alcoholism rates in the army are at a 30-year high. We have seen that the court transcripts are full of examples of soldiers with PTSD, instances of stealing from local Iraqis, unnecessary harshness toward civilians, a general sense of hostility toward all Iraqis, sleeping while on missions, and instances of "snapping" in stressful conditions such that innocent Iraqis were killed. The findings in this study, in combination with existing reports and studies, suggest that Stouffer's recommendations are valid and should be followed: sleep is a logistical need for the army just like food and water; cross-leveling (re-shuffling soldiers among units) should be avoided; and unit morale is the most is the most important factor in warfare.

I shall touch briefly on the larger patterns of culture in American society which are connected to these findings concerning Charlie Company and the army as a whole. The idea of re-shuffling troops is connected to the widespread, corporate practice of re-shuffling "units" (employees) in the business and corporate world. Former Secretary of Defense Donald Rumsfeld moved from the corporate reference group into the military reference group, and the morale-destroying techniques from corporate American were transplanted into the army. In general, the proportion of Americans who suffer from chronic sleep disturbances, alcoholism, and drug abuse continues to grow. All these connections are documented and explained in Durkheim's seminal study, *Suicide*, in which he found that in any society, as "social integration" (stability, rootedness, predictability) decreases, suicide rates and other indicators of stress increase.[1] Humans are fundamentally social and sociable creatures: if their social connections and bonds are disturbed, they and their society — large or small — suffer. But who reads and takes Durkheim seriously any longer, even within academia? The important point is this: Stouffer's study and findings are rooted in fundamental sociological principles, and the army seems to be ignoring them.

From "Men Against Fire" to Conditioning Soldiers to Kill

Marshall's book *Men Against Fire* is an undisputed albeit controversial classic. Most commentators follow Grossman to focus on Marshall's finding that, in any given battle, 75% of the soldiers will *not* fire their weapons. Steele's brigade took this finding as a challenge to raise the proportion of soldiers who kill in battle through operant conditioning. It is an open question whether the army's intellectual elite shares this mistaken understanding of Marshall's findings and intentions. But there can be no doubt as to Marshall's message, which is entirely in line with Stouffer, Durkheim, and sociological classics.

Marshall writes that combat battles are not decided by resources, weapons, training, drill, or discipline. Rather, he writes: "On the field of fire it is the touch of human nature which gives men courage and enables them to make proper use of their weapons" (p. 41). He links the battlefield situation to similar drama concerning human nature in the civilian world of the office or workplace: there, too, only a small fraction of the group "opens fire," metaphorically speaking, in terms of doing things that will win the "battle." The rest are there for the ride. I can certainly testify that in a class of approximately a hundred freshmen, no more than twenty or so are curious and engaged. Over and over again in his book, Marshall asks, "But what of human nature?" (p. 52). He explains what makes a soldier fire and a unit win a battle in terms that are entirely understandable to the common person, and apply to all spheres of social life:

> I hold it to be one of the simplest truths of war that the thing which enables an infantry soldier to keep going with his weapons is the near presence or the presumed presence of a comrade. The warmth which derives from human companionship is as essential to his employment of the arms with which he fights as is the finger with which he pulls a trigger.... He is sustained by his fellows primarily and by his weapons secondarily. (p. 42)

Marshall's assessment resonates with Durkheim, Stouffer, and commonsense. People do things for others, in families, military units, on the job, and in general social settings. Elsewhere he adds: "Only when the human, rather than the material, aspects of operation are put uppermost can tactical bodies be conditioned to make the most of the potential units" (p. 38). Substitute any other profession for "infantry soldier" — such as teacher, student, janitor, banker, or doctor — and the commonsense and sociological connections in Marshall's findings become glaringly obvious. In sum, Marshall argued that the soldier is *not a machine*, whereas we have seen that throughout the Operation Iron Triangle tragedy, soldiers were treated as if they were machines.

---

1 Stjepan G. Mestrovic and Barry Glassner (1983) "A Durkheimian Hypothesis on Stress," *Social Science and Medicine* 17(18): 1315-27.

Marshall writes of emotions, passions, and the "touch of human nature" which inspires people. He gives the examples of a commander patting a soldier on the back, or giving a soldier chocolate. I was surprised that buying a Coke for a soldier in DB qualifies as an example of what Marshall was discussing. As I search my memory for such moments in all of the data I have gathered across numerous trials, one stands out: It is the instance when military judge Colonel Pohl ordered guards to let Jeremy Sivits smoke a cigarette, even though Pohl had just convicted and sent him to DB. Conversely, I invite the reader to join me in recalling numerous instances in the Operation Iron Triangle drama in which officers and soldiers missed opportunities to display the "touch of human nature:" The IO could have let CPT Rutizer have a bathroom break and Mr. Waddington have a cup of coffee. The prosecutor could have made pleasant and smooth accommodations for the defense attorneys who were flying to Iraq to defend US soldiers. The petty officers could have let Clagett have a pencil and understood his anger at being caged like an animal. SGT Illichman and his superior could have allowed Mr. Hunsaker to keep the poem my daughter wrote for him. Military judge Colonel Dixon could have stated forcefully that Mr. Hunsaker deserves better, as a US soldier in pre-trial confinement, than to be caged and shackled like an animal. The members of the clemency board could have engaged fellow military officer Colonel Horvath in substantive dialogue. The army could have scheduled essential R&R for Charlie Company. Soldiers with obvious brain injuries and PTSD should have been taken out of combat. And so on.

I anticipate that some readers will conclude that such "softness" is both unmanly and un-military. But those readers will have to contend, first, with the fact that such "touches of human nature" are precisely what Marshall intended. Second, that classical sociologists also write about human "sympathy" as being the metaphorical glue that holds together any and all societies, large and small, military and civilian. No social group can be held together for very long by negative emotions such as fear, intimidation, or hatred. Third, and most important, the overwhelmingly harsh, inhumane, dehumanizing, and *machine-like* attitudes and behaviors of most of the actors in the Operation Iron Triangle led to the tragedies of both the massacres and the unfair trials which scapegoated a few low-ranking soldiers for the errors of commanders.

Indeed, the overwhelming impression given by most actors in this drama is that they acted like machines, not like human persons animated by the "warmth" of human presence which Marshall describes. Marshall's findings do fit the facts as they emerge from the court records. Despite all the dehumanizing forces deliberately used on the soldiers, human nature prevented them from killing women and children, or unarmed men hiding behind women and children. It was the result of the kill boards, kill contests, and coin rewards that prompted them to act like machines and "finish the job" after their first sergeant yelled at them for not killing everybody. CID agents behaved in a mechanical manner to convict the soldiers who were chosen to go to prison, and admitted under oath that they lied, suppressed and destroyed information, and used techniques to obtain the desired outcome. From Marshall's perspective, those CID agents must have been fighting their human nature every step of the way to mistreat their comrades as they did. Special agent Battle allowed her female gender to be used as a sexual "weapon" or tool against male soldiers. She obviously knew the full extent of the massacres that occurred on this mission, and she withheld that information — going against human tendencies to be truthful. The prosecutors fought their own human nature with fury by resorting to threats, fear, and intimidation against the accused as well as the defense attorneys. All of these mechanical approaches can be rationalized as "doing one's job," but none can be characterized as doing one's job well, in a way that the average person would regard as inspirational or well-done. There is no way that the average person can conclude that the outcome of these courts-martial was real justice. It was not.

In summary, the import of Marshall's classic study is that soldiers should be treated as human beings, not machines, and they perform well when they are inspired by the human touch of their comrades and commanders. Conversely, when soldiers are cursed by poor unit morale and a failure of leadership, they lose the "moral and spiritual" battle, no matter how many of them did or did not pull the trigger. There is a link here between Marshall's overall findings and Bateson's theory of the double-bind. The double-bind goes against human nature, and leads to negative consequences for individuals as well as groups and societies. The double-bind situation is the rough equivalent of the "poisoned social climate." We have come across numerous examples of double-bind situations in this study that could have been prevented and avoided.

FROM RUTH BENEDICT'S STUDY TO THE PRESENT

Ruth Benedict's famous study *The Chrysanthemum and the Sword* attempted to answer a question that was on the minds of many people during World War II: Why were Japanese soldiers willing to die rather than be taken prisoner, and why did Japan keep fighting even though it was losing the war? The answer to this question was of vital national interest to the United States at the time. By analyzing Japanese cultural life across many dimensions, she found that "hundreds of details fall into over-all patterns." And Japanese versus American patterns of culture were extremely different. For example, "Americans thrill to all rescue, all aid to those pressed to the wall" while "Japanese valor repudiates such salvaging" (p. 36). Japanese culture regarded prisoners, the sick, and wounded as "damaged goods." On the other extreme, "preoccupation with mercy toward the damaged ... is especially high in the United States." She made the important connection that

> If this attitude of the Japanese toward damaged goods was fundamental in their treatment of their own countrymen, it was equally important in their treatment of American prisoners of war. According to our standards the Japanese were guilty of atrocities to their men as well as to their prisoners (p. 37).

To the American cultural mind, prisoners "are not disgraced either as soldiers or as citizens or in their own families" (p. 38). To the Japanese mind, "honor was bound up with fighting to the death," such that there was great shame in being taken prisoner as a Japanese soldier or being an American prisoner. "To the Japanese therefore Americans who had become prisoners of war were disgraced by the mere fact of surrender. They were damaged goods" (p. 39).

I have no interest here in validating Benedict's findings in relation to historical facts. Her findings have found wide acceptance. The more urgent issue is to explain why, to a lesser degree than the Japanese, but nevertheless somewhat like the Japanese from Word War II, it is the Americans in the new millennium who are showing a pattern of abuse toward foreign as well as American prisoners. This connection is bound to be disturbing to the average American, because most Americans think of themselves in the merciful and just manner that Benedict portrayed them in World War II. But one cannot ignore eight years of steady reports of abuse from Abu Ghraib, Gitmo, "black hole" detention sites, rendition sites, and other sites in Iraq and Afghanistan. And one cannot fail to make the connection to the manner in which US soldiers from Iron Triangle were abused during pre-trial confinement. What has changed since World War II in the American cultural attitude toward prisoners, and why?

We can safely rule out shame as the paramount emotion that is driving this new trend, which Benedict isolates as the explanation for Japanese attitudes toward prisoners. Like their predecessors, today's Americans see nothing shameful in being a prisoner, foreign or domestic. It is beyond the scope of this study to do an exhaustive study of American culture that would rival Benedict's study. However, we have uncovered "hundreds of details" in the court records that do form a pattern.

What is missing in Benedict's descriptions of Japanese as well as American prisoners, and is omnipresent in the present study, is the idea of *empty ritualism*. The means, habits, steps, and rituals that people use have to be connected to specific goals, aspirations, and ends in order to make sense to the average person. And in line with Marshall, Bateson, Stouffer, Durkheim and other classical theorists, as well as common-sense, the connection between goals and means has to be emotional as well as logical. Most of the rituals uncovered in this study, before, during, and after Operation Iron Triangle, make little or no sense in terms of goals and means used to achieve them. We have seen how precious little spontaneity emerged from the hundreds of pages of court records. The reasons are obvious. Soldiers were coached on what to write in sworn statements in the first place. CID agents were trained on how to use the Reid technique to make any person confess to a given theory. Lawyers were trained on how to spar with each other, score points against the other side, and "win" regardless of whether or not the accused is guilty or innocent. Judges were trained in techniques to use to exclude certain evidence and include other evidence, all the while appearing neutral. The only social spaces in which genuine emotions could emerge in such a mechanized social system were those in which an individual in one reference group was not aware of the other reference group's techniques. For example, Lieutenant Wehrheim seemed to be genuinely surprised that CID agents assumed he and his entire platoon were guilty of some crime. He is correct that it makes no sense that an entire platoon of soldiers were criminals. Hunsaker seemed shocked to be treated like a criminal during his pre-trial confinement. Colonel Dixon seemed annoyed that the prosecutor dared to point out to him that he was reading the wrong charges, and confusing the attorneys. And so on for the hundreds of other details that have emerged in this study. The actors in this drama most often behaved like zombies, as if they were on auto-pilot, but the final destination was unknown.

Widening the scope of the analysis to include Abu Ghraib and other Iraqi prisoners, a similar pattern emerges. The author of the Taguba report as well as most

Americans seemed genuinely surprised that 90% of the Iraqi prisoners had no information to give to the American interrogators, for the simple reason that they were innocent civilians. The vast majority of prisoners from Gitmo have been quietly released without a trial when it finally became apparent that they had been arrested by mistake. The distinctly American credo, "innocent until proven guilty," has been quietly but steadily replaced with the technique-driven assumptions that "If you are arrested or charged, you must be guilty of something." I have spoken with lawyers who are aware of this subtle shift in their profession. For example, a military defense lawyer I met had a sign on the wall in his office that he makes his clients memorize, and which reads: "If someone is reading you your rights, they are not your friend." A civilian attorney once disclosed to me that the advice he gives his clients is, "just stay out of the courtroom altogether." Lawyers are keenly aware that most cases, civil as well as criminal, are settled through plea-bargain, so that guilt or innocence is never resolved.

Empty ritualism can be found in the wider cultural patterns pertaining to the war on terror as well as contemporary American society. People and institutions go through the rituals of the means toward an end or goal, but the end or goal is the wrong one, or unclear. For example, Charlie Company was prepped to go into a "hot" zone, but landed in a "cold" zone — they found farmers, women, children, and goats. The entire war against Iraq was supposed to find weapons of mass destruction, and found none. The war in Iraq was justified to the American people by linking it to 9/11, but Iraq had no connection whatsoever to 9/11. No one seems to be clear as to the goals of the Bush Doctrine of the pre-emptive strike. What goal is it supposed to achieve, given that its results so far have been that most of the Muslim population hates the United States? Similarly, Wall Street executives and bankers went through the empty motions and rituals of their professions while trading and investing in "derivatives," which are basically simulacra assets that nobody can define. Increasingly, the health care system does not deliver health care for the American people as a whole, though it does deliver profits for pharmaceutical and other corporations. Schools and universities rely increasingly on multiple-choice tests as the means to produce graduates with credentials. But the complexities of real life cannot be reduced to a multiple-choice test. In general, I have referred elsewhere to this widespread disconnection between goals and means, emotions and behavior, as "postemotional society."[1]

Benedict seems to be correct about the behavior of the Japanese versus the Americans regarding prisoners in World War II. But Americans were not merciful and kind to their captured enemies out of some sort of mindless habit or empty ritual. For example, the book, *Lone Star Stalag*, documents in meticulous detail the treatment of German and Japanese prisoners of war in Camp Hearne, Texas. One learns that the inmates had a theater, library, education program, and orchestra. The food was plentiful, and of better quality than was available to the Texans outside the gates of the camp, who were rationing food. In the words of one soldier: "We had better food that we ever had before, either as civilians or military men in Germany" (p. 24). Prisoners put on plays for each other, learned to play musical instruments, and developed

---

1 Stjepan G. Mestrovic, *Postemotional Society*, (London: Sage, 1997).

personal libraries from reading donated books. The prisoners were even allowed to drink beer at Camp Hearne: "Schlitz and Budweiser brands were available, and they cost ten cents a bottle" (p. 45). The availability of beer is a particularly human touch, in stark contrast to the fact that American soldiers in Iraq as well as prisoners at DB are forbidden to drink beer. The inmates at Camp Hearne wrote to their families praising the Americans. Nobody wanted to escape. In contradistinction to the steady streams of reports of abuse and torture in contemporary prisons, there were no such reports from Camp Hearne: "Indeed, the American government adhered to a strict interpretation of the Geneva Convention, often exceeding the agreed upon requirements. Former POW Fritz Haus marveled about his good treatment at the hands of the Americans and asked his American friend, Chaplain Gustave Zoch, about it." Haus later wrote in his memoir:

> Right from the beginning, on my first day in the comfort and luxury of the Pullman car, the question had nagged me: Why are they treating us so well? Later I discussed this aspect of our prison life with my friend, the [American] Chaplain G.A. Zoch. He smiled and said he would give me three reasons which were obvious and entirely selfish: Firstly, well-fed prisoners were content and happy, and easier to control than hungry ones; they caused little trouble. The prison authorities were not keen to have constant riots and strikes on their hands. Secondly, they wanted to demonstrate that the American democratic way of life was superior to the dictatorships of Hitler and Mussolini. Americans were proud of their liberties and freedom of speech, thought, and religion, without having to fear arrest or punishment. Hopefully, we prisoners would, after the war, reject Hitler's tyrannical and oppressive rule by force and work for a new democratic, Germany, which will rise from the ashes. But thirdly, and most importantly, they were deeply afraid that many thousands of American prisoners in German hands might suffer retaliation and reprisals if America does violate the Geneva Convention on the treatment of prisoners of war. Atrocities and irregularities must not occur lest the Germans have an excuse to rough-handle American captives, as they do with Russian and Polish POWs (p. 19).

The former German POW concludes: "Now I understood their [American] motivation and purpose, and why we had such a good time in American custody" (p. 21). How many contemporary prisoners, American or foreign, have said that they had a good time in American custody? No doubt some readers will be skeptical, but space does not permit a full analysis of other POW camps run by the Americans. Evidence does exist that the American government as a whole had the goals that were voiced by the chaplain. The ultimate proof that the strategy worked is that Japan and Germany emerged as democracies and friends of the United States following their defeat.

The important conclusions that follow are these: In World War II, America had clear objectives for defeating the enemy it felt compelled to fight purely for purposes of self-defense, and for treating the enemy with mercy and kindness. The government's goals were in line with commonsense and with religious teachings ("do unto others as you would have them do unto you"), such that a chaplain could summarize government policy in a coherent manner that was acceptable to a German prisoner. But in the current war on terror, the American government's objectives for defeating the enemy and for treating enemy as well as its own prisoners are not clear or coherent. The Abu Ghraib fiasco in the year 2003 should have been a wake-up call to change goals and strategies, yet the abuse at Gitmo continued. The documented abuse at both Abu Ghraib and Gitmo should have led to dramatic changes in procedures for handling prisoners on the battlefield. We have seen from Operation Iron Triangle, which occurred in 2006, that no substantive changes in policy were made. Worse, the data from the court records shows clearly that the army mistreated its own prisoners, denied them some rights granted by the US Constitution, shackled them and put them into solitary confinement while they were still innocent until proven guilty, and intimidated them and the entire military unit. The German ex-POW, quoted above, wrote about the American way of life as one in which one did not have to fear arrest or punishment. But we have seen that all Iraqi males live in fear of arrest and punishment — or being killed on sight — simply for being Iraqi males. And all the soldiers in Charlie Company lived in a social climate of fear of arrest or punishment for carrying out missions based upon a dubious ROE. The ordinary Iraqi has become the enemy. The good soldier has increasingly become the enemy within, and this is social situation that requires immediate remedy.

It is true that statistical data does not exist on all the missions, captures, prisoners, and abuse in the current war that would lead to completely firm conclusions. But such complete data has never existed and will never exist. Benedict extrapolated a "pattern of culture" based upon hundreds of facts. Similarly, enough references have been made in the court record to similar brutalities and harsh treatment of civilians which, when coupled with accounts by journalists, other soldiers who have written books or given interviews, and human rights groups, give one reason for concern. As I have suggested, everything in society is connected to everything else. I traveled to the site of Camp Hearne which used to exist near Hearne, Texas. Nowadays, it is an abandoned field two miles west of downtown Hearne. I walked through the site, and easily found the foundations of the barracks and other relics that correspond to maps. And I found the sculpture of a castle and moat created by some unknown POW artists, which still stands, and corresponds to a photograph on page 224 of Lone Star Stalag. Here was the "human touch" that fascinated Marshall: American captors allowed their enemy captives, some of whom were Nazis, to engage in art. In fact, the caption that accompanies the photo in the book reads, "Note the small Nazi flag flying from the turret." The flag is gone, but the empirical proof of Benedict's assertions concerning American values of mercy and kindness remains. I thought of the irony that Claggett was not allowed to have a pencil to draw while in pre-trial confinement, and was charged with a UCMJ charge of disrespect because he asked for one. Similarly, one does not need massive statistical data to notice that each and every time a US soldier is convicted at a court-martial, he or she is led out of the courtroom in shackles and leg irons. It is not enough to dismiss this as protocol. The fact that Americans used to treat their Nazi prisoners with more dignity and respect than they do their own soldier–prisoners at the present time is disturbing.

LONELIER THAN THE LONELY CROWD

Who has failed to notice that the current war on terror engages the interest of the military and the families of combat troops, but fails to engage the interest of the general public in the US? The most seismic change since World War II concerning the army, soldiers, and American society has been the replacement of the draft by the all-volunteer army. The draft equalized all Americans and made American society the primary reference group for understanding and engaging emotionally in wars fought by the United States. Almost every American could relate to World War II as a topic that was held in common with other Americans. This sense of common purpose was reinforced by rationing and other direct sacrifice by ordinary Americans in support of the war effort. Millions of women joined the work force for the first time in order to augment the war effort as well as support their families, due to the absence of men, who were fighting and dying on various fronts. To some extent, this kind of common, shared experience was also present during the Vietnam War, even if the draft was weakened by exemptions which created a class system such that educated and privileged Americans could "dodge" the draft while lower-class Americans were sent to fight in Vietnam. But there was a sufficient mass of identification with the common "reference group" of Americans to ignite anti-war protests: most people worried that their children could die for a war that they did not think was worth the fight. One may refer to numerous studies of both the army and of American society between World War II and the present to validate this portrait of a by-gone era. These studies include once-popular books by Samuel Stouffer, Ruth Benedict, Gregory Bateson, David Riesman, and Margaret Mead, among others.

The current war on terror is being fought by an all-volunteer army. Americans do not make direct sacrifices in support of troops that are felt as keenly as rationing used to be felt. The war is largely funded by deficit spending and support is showed primarily by displaying stickers which state "Support Our Troops." The overall effect has been and continues to be that the *average* American today is not as emotionally engaged in the war on terror compared with the average American of a bygone era. The current war is perceived, in general, as something that affects "volunteers." The problems uncovered in this and other books are perceived — if they are noticed at all — as somebody else's problem. This assessment is not meant to cast aspersion on American society, but is an accurate depiction of the fact that Americans in general versus Americans who fight in the war on terror belong to two different reference groups. Recall that a reference group is "a social group that serves as a point of reference in making evaluations and decisions." Can Americans find common reference points with regard to the current war? The answer to this question is vital for resolving the many issues that have been raised in this book.

The gist of social scientific thinking and writing since World War II suggests a general trend toward narcissism and membership in quantitatively more yet ever-narrower reference groups. Writers such as Daniel Bell, Christopher Lasch, Anthony Giddens, Jean Baudrillard, Zygmunt Bauman, David Riesman, and the postmodernists in general illustrate this phenomenon in various ways. I shall take up Riesman's *Lonely Crowd* as a reference point. Riesman points out the obvious: the generation that grew up during World War II was raised by very limited and fixed authority figures that rarely went beyond one's parents, immediate family, and teachers. The advent of television was slow and took several decades to reach the point of offering color instead of black-and-white, and offering a selection of more than a few channels. In all arenas of social life, choice was generally limited to Ford versus Chevrolet, Tide versus Cheer, Coke versus Pepsi, and so on. Schoolchildren sat in assigned seats, and their assignments, drawings, and work was between themselves, their teachers, and their parents. In that simpler social world, it was easier to find common features in being American and things American. After all, differences between consumer goods were largely tiny differences in "marginal differentiation."

All that has changed in ways that Riesman predicted but could scarcely have imagined. Nowadays, television offers literally hundreds of choices in channels, programs, and networks, yet ordinary people still complain that "there's nothing on." Consumers have been trained by the culture industry to become connoisseurs of staggering choices in automobiles. Laundry detergents now comes in various scents, liquid or gel or powder, with or without certain bleaches, and other choices that make the task of washing one's clothes a time-consuming, anxiety-driven chore. Soft drinks come in a myriad of flavors, sweeteners, amounts of calories, and varieties — they also take up two sides of an entire aisle in an average grocery store. Grocery stores have expanded to the size of airplane hangars. Schoolchildren sit where they want, which exposes them to the anxiety of being liked or disliked or accepted by ever-changing peers. Nowadays, assignments, drawings and schoolwork are displayed in the classroom as well as the refrigerator at home, so that the child feels that he or she is being watched by the entire world. The introduction of the Internet, You Tube, karaoke, open mikes, twitter, cell phones, and other cultural phenomena only accentuates these tendencies toward the anxiety of being constantly judged by others. Riesman called this the "other-directed" society, where the quantity of reference groups and reference points explodes exponentially compared to the simpler societies of our ancestors.

The title of Riesman's book, "the lonely crowd," is a deliberate oxymoron. He sought to capture the irony that when the human person is confronted by unprecedented choices in reference groups and points, he or she becomes apathetic. At best, the contemporary person may develop a temporary brand loyalty to one network, genre, news outlet, product, or cultural phenomenon. But the loyalty to a particular reference group is always subject to change. People do not react in unison to what would have been stirring occurrences and crises in the past. The sheer number of different responses, and the self-consciousness of one's emotions and views relative to one's peers (who now include imaginary friends, as in Facebook), short circuits genuine, strong emotional responses. My students are well aware of their predicament. They tell me, for example, that they often find out that their boyfriend or girlfriend broke up with them on Facebook, long before they learn of the break-up in person from their partners. In general, people have become blasé, allergic to involvement, and disengaged from events and issues in the public domain even as they have become increasingly more "hooked into" their I-pods, computers, walkmans, and other electronic gadgets. This is the paradox of the "lonely crowd."

For verification, the skeptical reader needs only to ask his or her grandparents about their lives and limited choices. For contemporary validation, one needs only to visit a contemporary coffee shop or bar. One will find people "hooked into" their computers or video games or other electronic apparatus, but oblivious to the people around them. In fact, rowdy, boisterous behavior in most public places nowadays is immediately punished. People are similarly "hooked into" their brains via electronic gadgets yet disengaged from other people on airplanes, family outings in automobiles, and most other public gatherings. For example, hardly anyone remembers the contents of President Obama's first speech to Congress, but most people who watched the event will remember that a great many members of Congress were twittering or e-mailing during his speech, and not paying attention. Where can one find common ground, a common reference point, in the lonely crowd?

But the army, too, has taken on characteristics of the lonely crowd. The issues uncovered in this book are unknown to the general American public, and if they were known, would not necessarily move people to demand constructive changes. After all, the abuses from Abu Ghraib and Gitmo have continued in some form over the course of eight years. We have seen that US soldiers still throw Iraqis out of moving trucks. The Geneva Conventions are not rigorously enforced as they were during World War II. One might have thought that following Steele's secret reprimand, the army would have abandoned the unlawful ROE which amount to "shoot first, ask questions later." But these same unlawful ROE continue to be used in Afghanistan. American society and its military have become disengaged from each other and from anything that might be called "public policy." The present situation may be characterized as the "lonely army" as loosely connected to the "lonely crowd."

For example, the chief government prosecutor, Captain Fischbach, was "other-directed" in his hyper-vigilant efforts to keep the media out of the courtroom as well as away from the trial process. He was not merely doing his job, but was constantly worried about how his performance would be judged by the jury of *his* peers, the American public. Ironically, no one from the media showed up at any of the trial proceedings, as noted by the IO and MJ. But this is probably because the information media is also other-directed and concluded that the American public is not interested in war crimes in the US army.

By contrast, the Hague trials on the war crimes in Bosnia were broadcast on fifteen-minute delay over the Internet and via television so that anyone who was interested could be informed. Why wouldn't the US government make its war crimes trials available on television and the Internet in a similar fashion? The obvious answer is that various reference groups with vested interests for and against various aspects of the war would veto any such effort. Riesman was prophetic when he wrote in 1950: "Undoubtedly many currents of change in America escape the notice of the reporters of this best-reported nation on earth" (p. 307). For the past eight years, reporters have not noticed the unlawful ROE, the personal troubles of the soldiers who became ensnared in these ROE, and the public issues represented by these ROE.

My role in this drama as author of this book has been to record faithfully the hundreds of available facts that have been missed in this, the best-reported and most-wired and informed nation on earth, in the hope that others will grasp the patterns contained in the facts. Hopefully, some readers will be moved to action. It seems more likely that Americans will remain forlorn and disconnected from each other, despite or because the fact that increasingly more Americans are connected to all sorts of electronic gadgets. At the very least, I hope that my efforts will have prevented the tragic story of Operation Iron Triangle from imploding into the black hole of history.

Postscript: Mr. Hunsaker's Mother Meets Colonel Steele

Mr. Hunsaker's mother Fran personally met Colonel Steele at Ft. McPherson, Georgia, on August 5, 2009. I learned about this visit the following day. She had not told anyone about her proposed visit ahead of time because she did not want anyone to suggest to her what to say or not to say to him.

I had spoken to her earlier that week when she called me from Ft. Campbell, Kentucky, where she was trying to find an army official who would give her the list of names of soldiers who were with Mr. Hunsaker on the day that he was ordered to pick up the severed heads of Iraqis. As noted in Chapter 2, Mr. Nathan had been trying for a long time to verify this event. Some of the army officials told Fran that the roster was classified, but she found one who said she would do what she could to find the list and give it to Mr. Nathan. This was remarkable, but her ability to see Colonel Steele seemed even more extraordinary.

"How did you get on base?" I asked her. "I have a military ID card," she said. "It's incredible," I said, "that you got to speak with Colonel Steele when nobody else has been able to get to him, not even journalists." She replied: "I just went to the first building on Ft. McPherson and asked where I could find Colonel Steele, and they gave me the contact information." "How did you know he would be there?" I asked. "I Googled him," she said. She added that Colonel Steele asked her the same question, and did not seem happy with her answer. She continued with her story:

> I called him from the lobby of the Control Center, but he didn't know I was in the lobby. He said he was at a meeting and would I call him back in twenty minutes. I gave him forty minutes, and called him again. This time he said he was at lunch, so I called him again ten minutes later. When I got him on the phone, he asked me where I was, and I told him I was in the lobby. He said that I should have told him that right away and he would have seen me. He walked out into the lobby and we met.

I had spoken to his wife, Leah, about three years ago, right after Bill was arrested and [she] offered to help me, with lodging arrangements at Fort Campbell, and to see how Bill and the rest of us were doing. Leah was compassionate and reached out to me during a very difficult time. I could tell she wanted to do more, but we were all too scared, at what may happen next. She did call me again, about 7 months ago, to see how we doing, but I never returned her call.

"What was he like?" I asked. "Oh, he's a real person," she said, and added, "he has that look of pain and despair, like he might as well be in Ft. Leavenworth." "What did you say to him?" I asked. "Will you please help to get my son home, please... Please call Mr. Nathan. He's a lot like you. He's blunt, and he's a man of his word." "That certainly describes Mr. Nathan," I said. Fran continued: "Colonel Steele hugged me, and kept hugging me."

"What did he say?" "He asked how Bill was....I said 'he misses the Army.' I know it touched him. His face turned red like he wanted to cry, but I know he could control that."

"Did you cry?"

"Yes, I cried. Then, as he was hugging me, he said: 'If I could re-write time, I never would have let that happen to them [his soldiers].' I truly believe if he could, he would."

"Wow. What else did he say?"

"He said, 'I did not tell the men to shoot those guys.'"

"Did he say he would do anything to help Bill?"

"He said he would call Mr. Nathan the next day...."

"I just think this is incredible. Congratulations! You've done what all the lawyers and officials could not do.... Why do you suppose he wants to help now?"

"He said that he had quit the Army that same morning. He said 'quit,' not resign. He said that all this was affecting his family too much."

"I just wouldn't have expected such emotions from him. I would have expected him to be stand-offish, like the others."

"He was, at first, on the phone, but sometimes you just have to talk to a person face-to-face to know what they're really like. He said that when a child misbehaves, you don't just abandon them. He said he was sorry that he hadn't stepped in, but he was ordered not to, and he was told that it would have been inappropriate for him to get involved."

"I hope he comes through."

"Remember what I had said to you earlier? I think the Army will let Bill and the others out of Leavenworth only after Col. Steele resigns and Bush is given immunity."

"Yes, you did say that. But why? It's not logical. Bill and the other soldiers wouldn't know anything that Bush and high-ranking officers knew."

"Just call it mother's intuition. It may take a year, two years, even ten years, but the truth will eventually come out."

"Well, ten years is too long to wait. A year or two is reasonable. Still, I'm just amazed at what you've accomplished."

Our conversation ended for that day. Several thoughts ran through my mind. One was that the role of mothers in this war is under-estimated and under-appreciated by sociologists and by people in general. In the 1880s, Johan Bachofen wrote that matriarchy preceded and was a stronger social force than patriarchy. In the 1950s, Erich Fromm wrote much about the distinction between unconditional motherly versus conditional fatherly love. But hardly anybody teaches Bachofen and Fromm in contemporary universities. Contemporary feminists obsess about breaking the glass ceiling, which is important, but nevertheless it is tantamount to trying to join the "code of masculinity" or go along with society's instrumental and conditional values. As David Riesman once told me, "The girls want to be like the boys." This book documents many instrumental, machine-like, machismo behaviors by many people, including judges and officers, but sometimes a mother's unconditional love seems to be able to penetrate all that. Nevertheless, it is to Steele's credit that he responded in a human way to Fran's human touch. I dare say that his choice of words expressed a mixture of fatherly and motherly love. I also entertained — for a few moments — the idea of hope. Would Mr. Nathan and Colonel Horvath, the two primary idealists in this narrative, be vindicated in their hope for reform in the military justice system and justice in particular for these specific soldiers?

Finally, I thought about the ancient concept of "honor." This idea and its various derivatives, including "dishonorable," crops up in the writings of Thorstein Veblen and in the trial records. After all, the soldiers in question were given "dishonorable" discharges on top of their other punishments. I have scrupulously avoided, and will continue to avoid, making any omniscient inferences about Colonel Steele's motives, thoughts, and feelings. But this much is certain from an objective point of view which examines behaviors and patterns: Honor is one of the primary values in the US Army. The Army behaved dishonorably in the way that it prosecuted and mistreated these particular soldiers. Up to this point, the Army has only compounded the tragedy of Operation Iron Triangle through coercion, cover-up, and other non-honorable tactics. It is an open question whether Colonel Steele will restore honor to his legacy and to the Army by helping the soldiers who were under his command.

No one can go back and rewrite history or restore the lives that were taken and those that were ruined. But the story of these soldiers, and this war, is not yet finished. There is still time to admit mistakes, to ensure that individuals and the military as a whole learn from these tragedies and make changes to prevent this kind of thing from happening again ... to do what is right and honorable now.

ACKNOWLEDGEMENTS

I am grateful for and would like to acknowledge the support and assistance of many persons who made this study possible. I am grateful to William Hunsaker and his family for giving permission to disclose facts about and by him. This required courage on their part; I know from past experience that the army tends to punish insiders who disclose intimate knowledge of army life to the outside world. I can only hope that the army will not take retribution against him.

I am grateful to two attorneys in particular, Geoffrey Nathan and Michael Waddington, for sharing unclassified information with me, and for their generosity in giving me a lot of their time for discussions. I am also grateful to numerous military defense attorneys for the same reason, but will not give their names out of the same concern I have about the army's possible retribution toward them. I am grateful to the US Army for giving me access to certain documents as a routine part of my role as expert witness. These documents are understood to be public records. Although attorney Frank Spinner is not directly related to the Operation Iron Triangle cases, I am grateful to him for many helpful conversations and insights. I am especially grateful to Colonel and Doctor Ed Horvath for proofreading and discussing this work with me.

Special thanks go to my undergraduate research assistant, Rachel Lindsay Rhinehart, for her invaluable assistance with printing, collating, organizing, and photocopying data. The department secretary, Christi Ramirez, has always been helpful. I acknowledge and am grateful for a research grant from Texas A&M University to support this project. I appreciate the support of the Deans of Liberal Arts, Charles Johnson and Ben Crouch, and the Head of the Sociology Department, Mark Fossett, at Texas A&M University. Among colleagues, I would like to thank Ryan Ashley Caldwell, Keith Kerr, John McDermott, and David Rosen for discussing the ideas in this book with me. I would like to thank Rachel Romero, James Chinouard, Ronald Lorenzo, and my daughter, Ivy Mestrovic, for their insights.

Finally, out of a sense of courtesy as well as academic protocol, I would like to acknowledge that Raffi Khatchadourian's article on Operation Iron Triangle appeared in the July 6, 2009 issue of *The New Yorker* at about the same time that I completed this book. He does not acknowledge my earlier book on this subject, *Rules of Engagement?* However, I wish to make two things clear: First, for his article Khatchadourian contacted and used me as one of his several sources during the year 2008 and the spring of 2009, and I gave him leads. Second, I did not approach or use Khatchadourian as a source in any way for any of the documents, facts, or interpretations that are contained in my book. In my experience, it is typical for journalists to take information from their sources but not to give any information to their sources. He and I obtained our information — even if some of it overlaps — independently of each other. Our interpretations and conclusions are different in some significant ways.

INDEX